THE OFFICIAL PRICE GUIDE TO
ANTIQUES
& flea markets

BY
THE HOUSE OF COLLECTIBLES, INC.

We have compiled information herein through a *patented computerized process* which relies primarily on a nationwide sampling of information provided by noteworthy collectible experts, auction houses and specialized dealers. This unique retrieval system enables us to provide the reader with the most current and accurate information available.

EDITOR
THOMAS E. HUDGEONS III

S0-CFW-209

THIRD EDITION
THE HOUSE OF COLLECTIBLES, INC., ORLANDO, FLORIDA 32809

IMPORTANT NOTICE. The format of **THE OFFICIAL PRICE GUIDE SERIES,** published by **THE HOUSE OF COLLECTIBLES, INC.,** is based on the following proprietary features: **ALL FACTS AND PRICES ARE COMPILED THRU A COMPUTERIZED PROCESS** which relies on a nationwide sampling of information obtained from noteworthy experts, auction houses and specialized dealers. **DETAILED "INDEXED" FORMAT** enables quick retrieval of information for positive identification. **ENCAPSULATED HISTORIES** precede each category to acquaint the collector with the specific traits that are peculiar to that area of collecting. **VALUABLE COLLECTING INFORMATION** is provided for both the novice as well as the seasoned collector: How to begin a collection; How to buy, sell, and trade; Care and storage techniques; Tips on restoration; Grading guidelines; Lists of periodicals, clubs, museums, auction houses, dealers, etc. **AN AVERAGE PRICE RANGE** takes geographic location and condition into consideration when reporting collector value. **A SPECIAL THIRD PRICE COLUMN** enables the collector to compare the current market values with last year's average selling price indicating which items have increased in value. **INVENTORY CHECKLIST SYSTEM** is provided for cataloging a collection. **EACH TITLE IS ANNUALLY UPDATED** to provide the most accurate information available in the rapidly changing collector's marketplace.

All of the information, including valuations, in this book has been compiled from the most reliable sources, and every effort has been made to eliminate errors and questionable data. Nevertheless the possibility of error, in a work of such immense scope, always exists. The publisher will not be held responsible for losses which may occur in the purchase, sale, or other transaction of items because of information contained herein. Readers who feel they have discovered errors are invited to **WRITE** and inform us, so they may be corrected in subsequent editions. Those seeking further information on the topics covered in this book are advised to refer to the complete line of Official Price Guides published by The House of Collectibles.

Published by: The House of Collectibles, Inc.
                 Orlando Central Park
                 1904 Premier Row
                 Orlando, FL 32809
                 Phone: (305) 857-9095

Printed in the United States of America

Library of Congress Catalog Card Number: 83-081911

ISBN: 0-87637-473-9 / Paperback

TABLE OF CONTENTS

PHOTOGRAPHIC RECOGNITION

Cover Photograph: Photographer — Bernie Markell, Orlando, FL 32806; Location — Courtesy of Shirley's Antiques, Shirley Smith, Winter Garden, FL 32787.

NOTE TO READERS

All advertisements appearing in this book have been accepted in good faith, but the publisher assumes no responsibility in any transactions that occur between readers and advertisers.

INTRODUCTION

Flea markets are fourishing.

This big business grew by leaps and bounds in the last few years and should see continued growth with larger numbers of buyers and sellers.

Today flea markets come in all forms, from yard sales to antique shows — but large outdoor shows are doing the best business and drawing the largest crowds.

Part of the mass appeal of flea markets reflects the current yearning for nostalgia. Such popularity also reflects a trend toward bargain hunting and perhaps a return to the old market place bartering system.

Whatever the reason, flea markets are a solid part of our culture and a haven of treasures for the collector. The important thing is to know what you're looking for and be able to recognize and identify what you see.

With such knowledge who knows what fabulous finds you may uncover at the next flea market or garage sale that you attend. A browser at a recent neighborhood sale in Maryland spotted a tri-colored vase, with roses cut in relief, for $1. Upon inspection, he found that it was a marked piece of Gallé glass; he bought it and sold the exquisite piece at auction for $825. A lovely irridized vase, signed by Louis Comfort Tiffany, sold at a flea market for only $25. There are many such tales and most veteran collectors have found great treasures among inexpensive knick knacks.

But whether you spot that once in a lifetime find or not, flea markets afford the browser an opportunity to add to collections or begin new ones — usually at bargain prices.

This guide should aid novices new to flea markets as well as seasoned buyers who need to know current prices.

BUYING AND SELLING FLEA MARKETS

Arrive early! The best buys disappear during the first couple of hours on the first day of the event, so get there early, and move around. If you can take someone along to scout for you, you can split off in different directions and cover the ground in half the time. The object is to make a quick circuit around the entire grounds when you arrive, and to get a feel for the layout in case something fabulous is out in full view.

If you want to haggle, be careful how you do it. Part of the trick is in knowing the real value, of course. But even if something is already priced low, a deft haggler takes the position that it can be driven down much further. If he's going to make an offer he'll make a considerably lower one, representing maybe 50% of the asking price or even less, figuring that the end result is likely to be a compromise.

If you want to sell at a flea market, simply follow a few basic rules. Pick the flea market where you want to sell, make space arrangements and find out the rules and regulations. Specifically you'll want to know what the flea market manager provides for the cost.

Decide on what to take to the show and always take a variety of merchandise. If you take small or valuable items use a display box with glass top and lock. Always clean your items before taking them to a sale.

Clearly mark prices on your merchandise, and remember that you may want to put a higher price on items than what you're actually willing to sell them for. It's good customer relations to be able to lower the asking price some when a customer asks.

GARAGE SALES

Since you can examine the entire selection of most garage sales in 15 or 20 minutes, pre-plan an itinerary that takes you to many garage sales in the same general neighborhood. Use the classified listings in your daily newspaper to make up a schedule. Many garage sale ads provide a general description of some of the available articles whan an estimation of the price range ("Nothing over $50,"). Most of the desirable buys will disappear quickly, so it is important to arrive early.

Be organized at your own garage sale. Start your sale early in the morning, but be set up and ready even earlier than your posted time since dedicated garage sale customers often start their rounds early. In the first hours of the sale, when you are most likely to have the most browsers, have at least two people on hand to help — you may want more depending on the size of our sale. Keep money locked and in a safe place if possible, and try to have plenty of change on hand. Do not let strangers into your house unattended, and keep pets away from the sale and the customers. Have an extension cord outside so that you can demonstrate electrical appliances; provide paper for testing typewriters.

If you have collector's items for sale, mention them in your newspaper advertisement and on your posted signs. Feature them prominently, arrange them attractively, but display them so there is a minimum danger of breakage.

FLEA MARKET DIRECTORY

The following flea markets are listed in alphabetical order according to state. Within each state the listings are in alphabetical order according to city or town. If you would like to have your flea market listed free of charge in the next edition of this book, please send us your information using the format found below. We provide this directory as a service to our readers and would like to expand it to include as many flea markets as possible.

One word of caution — be sure to verify flea market dates and hours of operation before driving long distances to attend.

CALIFORNIA

GARDEN GROVE
Westminster Abbey
Antique Mall — 11751 Westminster Ave.
Daily 10:00-5:00, Friday 10:00-9:00 PM — Closed Tuesday.

FLORIDA

BRANDON
Joe & Jackie's Flea Market
3 miles north of Brandon between Parsons and
Kingsway on Hwy. 574
Daily — (305) 689-6318.

FT LAUDERDALE
Oakland Park Boulevard Flea Market
3161 W. Oakland Park Blvd.

HIALEAH *(Miami area)*
DAV Swap Meet
1000 E. 56th St. — (305) 685-1296.

HIALEAH GARDENS *(Miami area)*
Palmetto Flea Market
7705 NW 103rd St.
(305) 821-8901 — 822-4478 — 825-9605.

LAKELAND - AUBURNDALE
International Market World
Highway 92 East of Lakeland
Friday, Saturday and Sunday — (813) 665-0062

MIAMI
Flea Bazaar
14501 W. Dixie Hwy.
(305) 945-3553

MIAMI
Metro Flea Markets
701 SW 27th Ave.
(305) 541-3400.

MIAMI
Turnpike Drive In Theatre Flea Market
12850 WN 27th Ave.
Wednesday, Friday, Saturday, Sunday — (305) 681-7150.

MIAMI
119th St. Flea Market
1701 NW 119th Street
(305) 687-0521.

MIAMI BEACH
World's Largest Indoor Flea Market
1901 Convention Center Dr.
(305) 673-8071.

NORTH MIAMI
Seventh Avenue Flea Market Inc.
13995 NW 7th Ave.
(305) 688-3852.

NORTH MIAMI
North Miami Flea Market
14135 NW 7th Ave.
(305) 685-7721.

MT DORA
Florida Twin Markets, Jim Renninger — proprietor
Highway 441 in Mt. Dora, ½ mile north of Highway 46
Every Saturday and Sunday — 8 AM - 5 PM
(305) 886-8946.

ORLANDO
Bobbie's Flea Market
5620 W. Colonial Dr.
Daily — (305) 298-0386.

ORLANDO
House of Bargains
6021 E. Colonial Dr.
Thursday through Sunday — (305) 273-5555.

ORLANDO
Northgate Flea Market
1725 Lee Rd.
Weekends — (305) 293-3600.

ORLANDO
Orlando Flea Market
5022 S. Orange Blossom Trail
(305) 857-0048.

PALMETTO (Tampa area)
Country Fair
U.S. Highway 301 and 41
(813) 722-5633.

PLANT CITY (Tampa area)
Country Village Flea Market
One mile north of 1-4 Exit 13 on St. Rd. 39
Wednesday, Saturday and Sunday — (813) 752-4670

SANFORD *(Orlando area)*
Flea World
Hwy. 17-92 between Orlando and Sanford
Friday, Saturday, Sunday — 8 AM - 5 PM
(305) 645-1792.

SARASOTA
Trail Outdoor Flea Market
6801 Tamiami Tr N, across 41 from Sarasota airport
(813) 355-6329.

TAMPA
Bargain Barn Flea Market
2400 Gehman PL.
(813) 248-1208.

TAMPA
Buccaneer Flea Market Inc.
4260 Dale Mabry Highway S
(813) 831-4499.

TAMPA
Oldsmar Flea Market
180 Race Track Rd.
(813) 855-5306.

TAMPA
Seminole Flea Market
7407 Hillsborough Ave.
(813) 623-5662.

TAMPA
Top Value Flea Market
8120 Anderson Rd. corner of Anderson and Waters
Saturday and Sunday — (813) 884-7810.

THONOTOSSASA *(Tampa area)*
North 301 Flea World Inc.
11802 US Hwy. 301 N, one mile north of Fowler Ave.
Thursday, Friday, Saturday, Sunday — 8 AM - 5 PM
(813) 896-1344.

VENICE
Dome Flea Market
5115 St. Rd. 775, one mile off 41
(813) 493-2446.

WEST PALM BEACH
Farmer's Flea Market
1200 S. Congress Ave.
(305) 965-1500.

WEST PALM BEACH
West 45th Street Flea Market
3500 45th St.
(305) 684-8444

GEORGIA

ATLANTA
A Flea Market at Moreland Ave.
1400 Moreland Ave. SE
Every Friday and Saturday from 10 AM to 7 PM
Sunday from 12 AM to 6 PM — (404) 627-0831

ATLANTA
Arnold's Flea Market
2298 Cascade Rd. SW
Every day — (404) 752-9507

ATLANTA
Flea Market at Forest Square
4855 Jonesboro Rd. FPK. just outside 1-285
1½ miles south
Friday and Saturday 10 AM to 9 PM
Sunday 12 AM to 6 PM — (404) 361-1221.

ATLANTA
Flossie's Flea Market
636 Lindbergh Way NE, behind Victoria
Station at Piedmont
Monday through Saturday 11 AM to 6 PM
(404) 237-6273

ATLANTA
Funtown Flea Market
500 Northside Dr. SW
(404) 659-9806.

ATLANTA
Golden Key Flea Market
833 Cascade Rd. SW
(404) 758-8780.

ATLANTA
Scavenger Hunt on Peachtree
4090 Peachtree NE
Seven days a week 10 AM - 6 PM
(404) 237-9789.

ATLANTA
The Second Act Inc.
82 Peachtree St. SW, one block from Five Points
(404) 523-9490.

CHAMBLEE *(Atlanta area)*
North Perimeter Flea Market
5000 Buford Highway
(404) 451-2893.

CHAMBLEE *(Atlanta area)*
Atlanta Flea Market and Antique Center
5360 Peachtree Industrial Blvd. Cham.
(404) 458-0456.

DECATUR *(Atlanta area)*
Bailey's Flea Markets
3372 Memorial Drive
(404) 298-9726.

DECATUR *(Atlanta area)*
Decatur Flea Market
724 W. College Ave.
(404) 378-4784.

DECATUR *(Atlanta area)*
Kudzu Flea Market
2874 Ponce de Leon Blvd.
(404) 373-6498.

DECATUR *(Atlanta area)*
Let's Make a Deal Flea Market
205 E. Ponce De Leon at Church
(404) 377-8676.

DECATUR *(Atlanta area)*
Sims Flea Market
902 W. College Ave. between East Lake Marta Station
and Agnes Scott College
Monday through Saturday 9 AM - 6 PM — (404) 371-8032.

ILLINOIS

AMBOY
Antique Show and Flea Market
Route 30, 4-H Fairgrounds
Third Sunday in each month 8 AM - 4 PM.

BELLEVILLE
Belleville Flea Market
Route 13 and 159, just off 460, Belleclair Exposition Center
Third weekend of every month.

BELVIDERE
Boone County Flea Market
Boone County Fairgrounds
Check ahead of time; the dates vary.

BLOOMINGTON
McLean County Flea Market
McLean County Fairgrounds
Check ahead.

CHICAGO
A Mart Flea Market
1839 S. Pulaski Rd.
(312) 542-6619.

CHICAGO
Archer & Damen Flea Mart
3450 S. Archer
(312) 927-3556.

CHICAGO
Buyers Flea Market
1126 N. Kolmar
(312) 227-1889.

CHICAGO
The Christian Hope Enterprise
8357 S. Halstead
(312) 488-5025.

CHICAGO
First Chicago Flea Market
4840 N. Pulaski Rd.
(312) 545-3149.

CHICAGO
North Side Flea Market
5906 N. Clark
(312) 334-8982.

CHICAGO
Paris Flea Market
Sheridan Drive in Theatre, 7701 South Harlem Ave.
Every weekend — (312) 233-2551.

CHICAGO
Roseland Great American Flea Market
10131 S. Michigan Ave.
(312) 995-5503

CICERO *(Chicago area)*
Flap Jaws Flea Market
1823 Cicero
Every day — (312) 656-3616

ROCKFORD
Greater Rockford Indoor-Outdoor Antique Market
Highway 251 South, corner of 11th St.
and Sandy Hollow Road
Every weekend 9 AM - 5 PM — (815) 397-6683

ST CHARLES
Kane County Flea Market
Kane County Fairgrounds, Route 64
Check ahead.

INDIANA

CEDAR LAKE
The Barn & Field Flea Market
151 St. and Parrish, one mile east on Route 41
Every weekend — (219) 696-7368.

CENTERVILLE
Webb's Antique Mall
200 W. Union and 106 E. Main
Daily 9 AM to 6 PM

EATON
Robyn's Nest Flea Market and Antiques
103 W. Harris St.
Monday through Saturday 9:30 AM - 5 PM.

FRANKLIN
Antique Show and Flea Market
4-H Fairgrounds
Third weekend of every month — (317) 535-5084.

FT WAYNE
The Speedway Mall
across from 84 Lumber
Friday, Saturday and Sunday — (219) 484-1239.

INDIANAPOLIS
The Antique Mall
3444 N. Shadeland Ave.
Every day.

INDIANAPOLIS
Traylor's Flea Market
7159 E. 46th Street
Every weekend.

INDIANAPOLIS
West Washington Flea Market
6445 W. Washington St.
Every Friday, Saturday and Sunday — (317) 244-0941.

MUNCIE
Highway 28 Flea Market
State Road 28, east of Highway 3 North
Every weekend, 9 AM - 6 PM — (317) 282-5414

NEW WHITELAND
The New Whiteland Flea Market
1-465 on U.S. 31, 10 miles south of Indianapolis
Friday, Saturday, Sunday — (317) 535-5907.

RICHMOND
Yester Years Flea Market
The Old Melody Skating Rink 1505 S. 9th Street
Thursday 11-5 — Friday 11-7, Sat/Sund 9-5.

SOUTH BEND
Thieve's Market
2309 E. Edison at Ironwood
Every weekend.

KENTUCKY

LOUISVILLE
Louisville Antique Mall
900 Goss Avenue
Daily 10 AM - 6 PM Mon-Sat; 1-5 PM Sunday
(502) 635-2852

LOUISIANA

BATON ROUGE
Deep South
5350 Florida Blvd.
Friday, Saturday, Sunday — (504) 923-0142

LAFAYETTE
Deep South
3124 NE Evangeline Thorway
Friday, Saturday, Sunday — (318) 237-5529.

MASSACHUSETTS

NORTON
Norton Flea Market
Route 140, take exit 11 off Route 495
Every Sunday.

MICHIGAN

YPSILANTI
Giant Flea Market
214 East Michigan at Park
Every weekend — (313) 971-7676, 487-5890 (weekends).

MISSOURI

SPRINGFIELD
Olde Towne Antique Mall and Flea Market
Every day except Thursday — (417) 831-6665

SPRINGFIELD
Park Central Flea Market
429 Boonville
Every day — (417) 831-7516

SPRINGFIELD
Viking Flea Market
North Grant and Chase
Every day except Wednesday — (417) 869-4237

NEVADA

LAS VEGAS
Tanner's Flea Market
Nevada Convention Center
Call (702) 382-8355 for dates.

NEW YORK

BROOKLYN
Duffield Flea Market
223 Duffield Street between Fulton and Willoughby
Monday through Saturday 11 AM to 6 PM
(212) 625-7579.

DELKALB JUNCTION
Antiques Flea Market
Route 11
Every Friday 10 AM-4 PM, Saturday and Sunday 9 AM-5 PM
(315) 347-3393

DUANESBURG
Gordon Reid's Pine Grove Farm Antique Flea Market
Junction of U.S. Rte. 20, NY Route 7 and I-88
1985 Dates: May 3-4; July 5-6; Sept. 6-7
(518) 895-2300.

OHIO

AMHERST
Jamie's Flea Market
West of Route 58 on Route 113
Wednesday evenings, Saturday and Sunday
(216) 986-4402.

AURORA
Aurora Farms Flea Market
Route 43, one mile south of Route 82
Every Wednesday and Sunday — (216) 562-2000.

CINCINNATI
Ferguson Antiques Mall and Flea Market
3742 Kellog Ave.
Every Saturday and Sunday — (513) 321-7341.

CINCINNATI
Paris Flea Market
Ferguson Hills Drive in Theatre, 2310 Ferguson Road.
Every Saturday and Sunday
(513) 223-0222 weekdays; 451-1271 weekend.

CINCINNATI
Strickers Grove
Route 128, one mile south of Ross
Every Thursday, June through September
(513) 733-5885.

DAYTON
Paris Flea Market
Dixie Drive in Theatre, 6201 N. Dixie
Every Saturday and Sunday 7 AM - 4 PM
(513) 223-0222 weekdays; 890-5513 weekend.

FERNALD *(Cincinnati area)*
Web Flea Market
1-74, Exit 7, north 5 miles to New Haven Road
Every Saturday and Sunday — (513) 738-2678

MANSFIELD
Antique Show and Flea Market
Richland County Fairgrounds
Last weekend of the month, February through November.

MONTPELIER
Fairgrounds Flea Market
Williams County Fairgrounds
Every Thursday — (419) 636-6085 L & K Promotions
Rt 1, Montpelier, OH 43543.

SPRINGFIELD
Antique Show and Flea Market
Clark County Fairgrounds
Call for information: (513) 399-7351 or 399-2261.

TIFFIN
Tiffin Flea Market
Seneca County Fairgrounds
April through October
Call for information: (419) 983-5084.

WILMINGTON–WAYNESVILLE
Caesar Creek Flea Market
Intersection of 1-71 and State Route 73
Every Saturday and Sunday — (513) 382-1669.

PENNSYLVANIA

BEAVER FALLS
The Antique Emporium
818 7th Ave.
Everyday except Monday — (412) 847-1919

PUBLICATIONS

AMERICAN ART AND ANTIQUES
1515 Broadway, New York City, NY 10036

AMERICAN RIFLEMAN
National Rifle Association
1600 Rhode Island Avenue, N.W., Washington, D.C. 20036

ANTIQUE COLLECTING
P.O. Box 327, Ephrata, PA 17522

ANTIQUE COLLECTOR
Chestergate House, Vauxhall Bridge Road, London SW1V
1HF, England

ANTIQUE MONTHLY
P.O. Drawer 2, Tuscaloosa, AL 35401

ANTIQUE TOY WORLD
3941 Belle Plaine, Chicago, IL 60618

ANTIQUE TRADER
Dubuque, IA 52001

ANTIQUES (The Magazine Antiques)
551 Fifth Avenue, New York City, NY 10017

ANTIQUES AND THE ARTS WEEKLY
5 Church Hill Road, Newtown, CT 06470

ANTIQUES JOURNAL
P.O. Box 1046, Dubuque, IA 52001

ANTIQUES WORLD
P.O. Box 990, Farmingdale, L.I., NY 11737

ARMS GAZETTE
13222 Saticoy Street, North Hollywood, CA 91605
(firearms)

COINage
16001 Ventura Boulevard, Encino, CA 91316

COIN HOBBY NEWS
300 Booth Street, Anamosa, IA 52205

COINS MAGAZINE
Iola, WI 54945

COIN WORLD
P.O. Box 150, Sydney, OH 45367

COLLECTIBLES ILLUSTRATED
Dublin, NH 03444

COLLECTIBLES MONTHLY
P.O. Box 2023, York, PA 17405

COLLECTOR'S DREAM
P.O. Box 127, Station T, Toronto, Canada M6B 3Z9

COLLECTOR EDITIONS QUARTERLY
170 Fifth Avenue, New York City, NY 10010

COLLECTOR'S PARADISE
P.O. Box 3658, Cranston, RI 02910

COLLECTOR'S SHOWCASE
P.O. Box 6929, San Diego, CA 92106

COLLECTORS UNITED
P.O. Box 1160, Chatsworth, GA 30705 *(dolls)*

COLONIAL NEWSLETTER
P.O. Box 4411, Huntsville, AL 35802 *(colonial coins)*

COMIC TIMES
305 Broad, New York City, NY 10007

DEPRESSION GLASS DAZE
P.O. Box 57, Otisville, MI 48463

DOLL TIMES
1675, Orchid, Aurora, IL 60505

GOLDMINE
700 E. State Street, Iola, WI 54990 *(records)*

GRAPHIC TIMES
25 Cowles Street, Bridgeport, CT 06607

GUN REPORT
P.O. Box 111, Aledo, IL 61231

HOBBIES
1006 South Michigan Avenue, Chicago, IL 60605

INDIAN TRADER
P.O. Box 31235, Billings, MT 59107 *(indian relics)*

INSIGHT ON COLLECTABLES
P.O. Box 130, Durham, Ontario NOG 1RO

JOEL SATER'S ANTIQUE NEWS
P.O. Box B, Marietta, PA 17547

JOURNAL OF NUMISMATICS AND FINE ARTS
P.O. Box 777, Encino, CA 91316 *(ancient coins and classical antiquities)*

JUKEBOX TRADER
P.O. Box 1081, Des Moines, IA 50311

MAIN ANTIQUES DIGEST
P.O. Box 358, Waldoboro, ME 04572

MEMORY LANE
P.O. Box 1627, Lubbock, TX 79408

NATIONAL VALENTINE COLLECTORS ASSOC.
Box 1404, Santa Ana, CA 92702

NEW YORK/PENNSYLVANIA COLLECTOR
Wolfe Publications, 4 South Main Street, Pittsford, NY 14534

NUMISMATIC NEWS
Iola, WI 54945

NUMISMATIST, THE
P.O. Box 2366, Colorado Springs, CO 80901

OHIO ANTIQUE REVIEW
72 North Street, Worthington, OH 43085

OLD CARS WEEKLY
Iola, WI 54990

OLD TOY SOLDIER NEWSLETTER
209 North Lombard, Oak Park, IL 60302

OWL'S NEST
P.O. Box 5491, Fresno, CA 93755 *(owl-motif items)*

POLITICAL COLLECTOR
503 Madison Avenue, York, PA 17404

POSTCARD COLLECTOR
700 E. State Street, Iola, WI 54990

RECORD PROFILE MAGAZINE, INC.
24361 Greenfield, Suite 201, Southfield, MI 48075

THE DOLL AND TOY COLLECTOR
International Collectors Publications, Inc.
168 Seventh Street, Brooklyn, NY 11215

THE MILK ROUTE
4 Oxbow Road, Westport, CT 16880

THE SHAKER MESSENGER
P.O. Box 45, Holland, MI 49423

WHEELS OF TIME
American Truck Historical Society
Saunders Building, 201 Office Park Drive, Birmingham, AL 35223

HOW TO USE THIS BOOK

The editors of this book have included as many categories of items often found at flea markets as possible. The sections are alphabetised for easy reference, and each section includes information and price listings.

The prices shown for each item represent the current range, while the third price column shows last year's average value. Since prices change constantly, the values given should be used as a guide only.

A general overview of topics is represented here, so for more detailed information please consult *The Official 1985 Price Guide to Antiques and Other Collectibles*. A complete series of The *The Official Price Guides* is also available.

ADVERTISING COLLECTIBLES

TOPIC: Advertising collectibles are considered to be any items with a company's name or logo on them.

TYPES: Advertising collectibles can be found in any form. Common items used for advertising range from ashtrays to posters to yo-yos.

PERIOD: Advertising has been around almost since humanity became literate, but advertising collectibles of interest to the modern enthusiast began around 1800. Pre-1900 items are scarce and valuable.

MATERIALS: These items are usually made of ceramics, glass, paper or tin, although the material depends on the item.

COMMENTS: Many large companies (such as Coca-Cola) put much effort into producing promotional items that are now very collectible. Because of this, a collector may focus on procuring items that pertain to a particular company. Other enthusiasts, however, collect a certain item (mirrors, for example) regardless of the company or product that is advertised.

ADDITIONAL TIPS: The listings in this section are arranged in the following order: item, company or product advertised, title, description, what it was used for, material, shape, size and date manufactured. Other information was included where relevant.

	Current Price Range		Prior Year Average
☐ **Ashtray,** Armstrong Tire, clear, red decal, round, 5⅞″ diameter	9.00	12.00	10.50
☐ **Ashtray,** Bacardi Rum, white china, round, 4½″ diameter	3.50	7.00	5.00
☐ **Ashtray,** Budweiser, glass, round, 5″ diameter	3.00	5.00	4.00
☐ **Ashtray,** Camel Cigarettes, Camel logo in center, tin, round, 3½″ diameter	1.50	2.50	2.00
☐ **Ashtray,** Chivas Regal, Wade china, triangular with rounded sides, 11½″	5.00	9.00	7.00
☐ **Ashtray,** Firestone Tire, 1936 Texas Central Expo	13.00	18.00	15.00
☐ **Ashtray,** Goodrich, for Silvertown Heavy Duty Cord, round, 6⅜″ diameter	6.00	12.00	9.00
☐ **Ashtray,** Goodrich, for Silvertown Cord tires, 1776 decal, round, 6¼″ diameter	10.00	16.00	13.00
☐ **Ashtray,** Labatt's Stout-Lager-Ales, cream colored porcelain, round, 6½″ diameter	3.00	7.00	5.00
☐ **Bottle Opener,** Coca-Cola, cast iron	1.00	2.00	1.50
☐ **Bottle Opener,** Dr. Pepper, cast iron	1.00	2.00	1.50
☐ **Bottle Opener,** Falstaff, cast iron	1.00	2.00	1.50

	Current Price Range		Prior Year Average
☐ **Bottle Opener,** Pepsi Cola, cast iron	1.00	2.00	1.50
☐ **Bottle Opener,** Seven-Up, cast iron	1.00	2.00	1.50
☐ **Bottle Opener,** Squirt, cast iron	1.00	2.00	1.50
☐ **Box,** Barricini Candies, resembles wood, 9" x 7" x 2" with 12" x 9" base	8.00	12.00	10.00
☐ **Box,** Chandler's One-Day Tablets, 1" x 5" x 6"	.25	.50	.37
☐ **Box,** Coca-Cola, red and gold snap lid, for pencils, 1" x 3" x 8", 1937	18.00	30.00	24.00
☐ **Box,** Portola Tuna, picture of Portola and tuna, cardboard, 8½" x 14" 1929	3.50	7.00	5.00

Hires Root Beer Thermometer,
tin, lithographed, 1950,
$25.00-$37.00

	Current Price Range		Prior Year Average
Box, Solace Tobacco, blue with gold print, cardboard, 8½" x 11" x 5", 1862	35.00	45.00	40.00
Calendar, Alka Seltzer, 1942	3.50	5.75	4.25
Calendar, Blatz Beer, girl in red, 1904	135.00	175.00	155.00
Calendar, Camel Cigarettes, 1963	32.00	38.00	35.00
Calendar, Coca Cola, pictures of beautiful women, six pages, 13" x 17", 1957	20.00	25.00	22.50
Calendar, Dr. Mile's Remedies, picture of girl and boy, 1908	12.50	16.50	14.00
Calendar, Dr. Pepper, 1950	22.00	27.00	24.00
Calendar, Equitable Life Insurance, 1904 ...	20.00	28.00	24.00
Calendar, Fairy Soap, picture of Naval officer, 1899	13.00	19.00	16.00
Calendar, Farmer's Fire Insurance, 1888 ...	25.00	35.00	30.00
Calendar, Hartford Fire Insurance, 1896	9.00	14.00	12.00
Calendar, Hood's Milk, 1933	7.00	12.00	9.00
Calendar, Hood's Sasparilla, 1896	30.00	38.00	34.00
Calendar, Hupmobile, picture of sedan, people and Indian, 12" x 36", 1924	130.00	165.00	147.00
Calendar, John Busch Brewing Company, picture of beautiful woman, 6" x 16", 1917 ..	40.00	50.00	45.00
Calendar, John Hancock Insurance, 1898 ...	18.00	28.00	23.00
Calendar, McCormick-Deering, picture of boy and girl, 12" x 22", 1928	25.00	30.00	27.50
Calendar, Metropolitan Life Insurance, 1904	38.00	46.00	42.00
Calendar, Mrs. Dinsmore's Balsam, picture of a mother and child, 1901	35.00	45.00	40.00
Calendar, Nehi Soda Pop, 1904	38.00	46.00	42.00
Calendar, Richelieu Coffee, 1912	15.00	22.00	19.00
Calendar, Ruppert Breweries, 1915	25.00	35.00	30.00
Calendar, Standard Oil, 1939	15.00	21.00	18.00
Calendar, Sunshine Biscuits, 1924	15.00	21.00	18.00
Calendar, Union Pacific Tea, 1892	30.00	38.00	34.00
Calendar, Wrigley's Gum, 1927	24.00	30.00	27.00
Cannister, Sir Walter Raleigh Smoking Tobacco, round	18.00	22.00	20.00
Catalog, Lionel Trains, 8" x 11", 1958	3.00	6.00	4.50
Catalog, Williams Manufacturing Company, picture of the factory, for baskets, 1891	20.00	25.00	22.50
Catalog, Wurlitzer Juke Box, 8" x 11", 1950s	2.00	5.00	3.50
Chalkboard, Hires Root Beer, for restaurants, tin, 10" x 20", 1940s	16.00	20.00	18.00
Clicker, Butternut Break, tin cricket, 1¾" diameter, c. 1930	.75	1.75	1.25
Clock, Anheuser Busch, wood	25.00	30.00	27.50
Clock, Bardahl Petroleum, square, electric .	40.00	48.00	44.00
Clock, Canada Dry Sport Cola, 13" x 18" ...	25.00	30.00	27.50

		Current Price Range		Prior Year Average
☐	**Clock,** Coca-Cola, metal, round	35.00	45.00	40.00
☐	**Clock,** Falstaff Beer, illuminated	50.00	58.00	54.00
☐	**Clock,** Florsheim Shoes, wood, illuminated .	35.00	45.00	40.00
☐	**Clock,** General Electric, metal, refrigerator style	50.00	60.00	55.00
☐	**Clock,** Mr. Peanut, with alarm	25.00	30.00	27.50
☐	**Clock,** Pearl Beer, illuminated	30.00	40.00	35.00
☐	**Clock,** Seven-Up, metal, round	30.00	40.00	35.00
☐	**Clock,** St. Joseph's Aspirin for Children, 14″ diameter	55.00	65.00	60.00
☐	**Coaster,** Olympia Beer, metal, round, 3½″ diameter	.50	1.10	.85
☐	**Comb,** Coca-Cola, red, plastic, embossed, pocket-size, 1960s	1.00	4.00	2.50
☐	**Decal,** Bull Dog Malt Liquor, picture of a bull-dog, square, 7″, 1940s	3.00	7.00	5.00
☐	**Decal,** Planters and Clark Bar, for candy machine, 4″ x 8″, 1950s	1.25	2.00	1.62
☐	**Decal,** Red Goose Shoes, 1930s	1.00	3.00	2.00
☐	**Decal,** Seven-Up, 4″ x 4″, 1931-57	1.50	3.00	2.25
☐	**Decal,** Triple AAA, 5¢ Root Beer, picture of a girl, 6″ x 9″, 1940s	1.00	4.00	2.50
☐	**Doll,** Campbell Kid, early 1900s style clothing, rag	23.00	28.00	25.00
☐	**Door Handle,** Dandy Bread, picture of loaf and slices, metal, 3″ x 13″, 1940s	12.00	17.00	15.00
☐	**Fan,** 666 Liquid Medicine, picture of two children on a horse, wicker handle, c. 1935	1.50	2.50	2.00
☐	**Figurine,** R.C.A. Dog, "Nipper," ceramic, 3″ .	3.00	4.50	3.75
☐	**Folder,** Philadelphia Buckeye Wood Pumps, 6″ x 14″	9.00	14.00	11.50
☐	**Key Chain,** Mr. Peanut, 5″	.50	1.50	1.00
☐	**Key Holder,** Dr. Pepper, 1″ x 2″, 1930s	1.50	3.00	2.25
☐	**License Plate,** Coca-Cola, red and white, embossed, 6″ x 12″, 1970s	2.50	5.00	3.75
☐	**License Plate Top,** Ford, reflective, metal, 3″ x 10″, 1952	12.00	15.00	14.00
☐	**Lighter,** Camel Cigarettes, metal	2.50	4.50	3.50
☐	**Magazine Ad,** any automobile, 1911-1920 ...	2.50	3.50	3.50
☐	**Magazine Ad,** any automobile, 1921-1930 ...	1.50	2.00	1.75
☐	**Magazine Ad,** Coca-Cola, pre-1900	14.00	18.00	16.00
☐	**Magazine Ad,** Coca-Cola, 1901-1910	9.00	12.00	10.50
☐	**Magazine Ad,** Coca-Cola, 1911-1920	6.00	8.00	7.00
☐	**Mug,** Anheuser-Busch, crockery, embossed with eagle, 7″ tall, 1940	10.00	15.00	12.50
☐	**Pen Holders,** Falstaff Beer, for a pocket, 1960s	1.00	3.00	2.00

	Current Price Range		Prior Year Average
Pin, Coca-Cola, bottle cap style, for a lapel, enameled, 1968	3.00	5.00	4.00
Pitcher, Ambassador Scotch, white	8.00	10.00	9.00
Pitcher, Glenfiddich, black	8.00	10.00	9.00
Poster, Granger Pipe Tobacco, picture of Joe Heistand Champion trap shooter, 14″ x 20″	25.00	30.00	27.50
Poster, Planters Presents Sheindele the Chazente, cardboard, 11″ x 17″	22.00	27.00	24.00
Poster, Shoat Sale, announcing auction of 175 pigs, 12″ x 19″, c. 1920	7.00	10.00	8.50
Poster, Yeast Foam, picture of a little girl, tin rimmed, 10″ x 14″, 1920s	18.00	22.00	20.00
Pot Holders, Campbell Kid 8¼″ x 8½″, set of two	8.00	12.00	10.00
Sign, American Agriculturist, tin, embossed, 6½″ x 13½″, 1920s	7.00	10.00	8.50
Sign, Arrow Trailer Rentals, picture of U.S. map, embossed, 14″ x 18″, 1940s	12.00	16.00	14.00
Sign, Barnum's Animal Crackers, commemorative, tin 4″ diameter, 6″ tall, 1979	3.00	5.00	4.00
Sign, Bayer Aspirin, tin, 15″ x 18″	25.00	35.00	30.00
Sign, Beechnut Tobacco, rectangular	12.00	17.00	14.50
Sign, Borden, glass, 12″ x 20	62.00	72.00	68.00
Sign, Budweiser, plastic, with bottle, lighted, 5″ x 12″	12.00	18.00	15.00
Sign, Bunny Bread, red and white, tin, embossed, 3½″ x 28″, 1930s	8.00	12.00	10.00
Sign, Burma shave, wooden, 10″ x 3½″	1.50	2.50	2.00
Sign, Busch Ginger Ale, picture of eagle, porcelain, 10″ x 20″, 1920s	75.00	85.00	80.00
Sign, Coca-Cola, "Join the Friendly Circle," c. 1954	25.00	35.00	30.00
Sign, Coors Beer, picture of lake and mountain, lighted	25.00	35.00	30.00
Sign, Dr. Meyer's Foot Soap, picture of hands holding soap, cardboard, 7″ x 10″	4.00	6.00	5.00
Sign, Dr. Nutt Soda, tin, embossed, 10″ x 13″, 1920s	25.00	32.00	30.00
Sign, Dr. Pepper, red and white, tin, 6″ x 18″, 1950s	7.00	11.00	9.00
Sign, DuBois Budweiser, tin, 21″ x 13″	18.00	22.00	20.00
Sign, Dull Durham, cardboard, 14″ x 22″	35.00	45.00	40.00
Sign, Dutch Boy, "wet paint," picture of boy, cardboard, 6″ x 9″, 1930s	2.00	5.00	3.50
Sign, Fairy Soap, 5¢, for a trolley car, rectangular	85.00	115.00	100.00

	Current Price Range		Prior Year Average
☐ **Sign,** Ford Tractor, masonite, 11″ x 21″, 1942	20.00	25.00	22.50
☐ **Sign,** Free Lance Cigar, cardboard, embossed, 8″ x 10″, c. 1910	8.00	12.00	10.00
☐ **Sign,** Goodyear Tires, oval	22.00	26.00	24.00
☐ **Sign,** Hires Root Beer, paper, 28″ x 12″	40.00	50.00	45.00
☐ **Sign,** Ivory Soap, picture of child holding soap, for a trolley car, 20″ x 10″	68.00	85.00	77.00
☐ **Sign,** Kelloggs Corn Flakes, picture of infant in wicker basket, tin, rectangular	70.00	88.00	79.00
☐ **Sign,** Marvels Cigarettes, picture of two cigarette packages, tin, embossed, 3½″ x 16″, 1930s	16.00	21.00	19.00
☐ **Sign,** Smith Brothers Cough Drops, 5¢, for a trolley car	85.00	115.00	100.00
☐ **Sign,** Sun Maid Raisins, for a trolley car	40.00	50.00	45.00
☐ **Sign,** 2-Room Apartments, brass, 1½″ x 7″, c. 1940	2.00	6.00	4.00
☐ **Sign,** Uneeda Biscuits, cardboard, 10″ x 13″	25.00	35.00	30.00
☐ **Sign,** Viceroy Cigarettes, tin	22.00	33.00	27.00
☐ **Sign,** Virginia Cigarettes, picture of bathing beauty, tin, 14″ x 21″, 1930s	50.00	62.00	56.00
☐ **Sign,** White Rock Mineral Water, tin, 4″ x 12″, 1910s	8.00	12.00	10.00
☐ **Sign,** Whitman's Chocolate Candy, 13″ x 18″	50.00	68.00	59.00
☐ **Sign,** Wrigley's Gum, picture of Wrigley arrow boy, for a streetcar, 10″ x 20″, 1920s	35.00	42.00	39.00
☐ **Sign,** Wrigley's Gum, picture of Wrigley arrow man, for a streetcar, 10″ x 20″, 1920	30.00	39.00	34.00
☐ **Sign,** Woo Chong Import Co., picture of oriental women and art objects, paper, 21″ x 31″, c. 1920	30.00	40.00	35.00
☐ **Sign,** Wunder Bread, cardboard, 6″ x 9″, 1910	8.00	12.00	10.00
☐ **Silverware,** Campbell Kid, three piece place setting	14.00	18.00	16.00
☐ **Spoon,** A & P, for measuring coffee, yellow, plastic	.50	1.00	.75
☐ **Thermometer,** B-1 Soda, tin, 5″ x 16″, 1940s	16.00	21.00	19.00
☐ **Thermometer,** Carstairs, "Join the Carstairs Crowd," round	25.00	35.00	30.00
☐ **Thermometer,** Coca-Cola, tin, embossed, 16″, 1960s	5.00	8.00	6.50
☐ **Thermometer,** Coca-Cola, gold, bottle shape, 7″	20.00	30.00	25.00
☐ **Thermometer,** Coca-Cola, bottle shape, 27″	50.00	60.00	55.00
☐ **Thermometer,** Coca-Cola, "Things Go Better With Coke," 17½″	22.00	30.00	26.00

	Current Price Range		Prior Year Average
☐ **Thermometer,** Copenhagen Chewing Tobacco, 12″	12.00	18.00	15.00
☐ **Thermometer,** Dr. Pepper, 17″	25.00	35.00	30.00
☐ **Thermometer,** Gilbey's Gin, 9″	46.00	56.00	50.00
☐ **Thermometer,** Hires Root Beer, bottle shape, 27″	45.00	55.00	50.00
☐ **Thermometer,** Morton Salt, picture of girl under umbrella, metal	6.00	8.50	7.25
☐ **Tray,** Coca-Cola, girl with menu, c. 1950	20.00	30.00	25.00
☐ **Tray,** Coca-Cola, hostess, c. 1936	50.00	70.00	60.00
☐ **Tray,** Coca-Cola, Santa Claus, c. 1973	21.00	31.00	26.00
☐ **Tray,** Coors, metal, round, 13″ diameter	4.00	5.00	4.50
☐ **Tray,** Coors Beer, picture of a glass and bottle of beer	25.00	32.00	23.50
☐ **Tray,** Cracker Jack, tin	10.00	15.00	12.50
☐ **Tray,** Dr. Pepper, picture of a lion, steel, 12″ x 15″	2.00	4.00	3.00
☐ **Tray,** Falstaff Beer, picture of Sir Falstaf holding a bottle and tray, round, 12″ diameter, 1940s	22.00	28.00	25.00
☐ **Tray,** Franklin Life Insurance, for tips	22.00	28.00	25.00
☐ **Tray,** Genessee 12 Horse Ale, picture of horse team, round, 13″ diameter	35.00	45.00	40.00
☐ **Tray,** Hemmer's Ice Cream	50.00	58.00	54.00
☐ **Tray,** Hires Root Beer, c. 1910	82.00	98.00	90.00
☐ **Tray,** J. Leinenkugel Brewing Co., picture of Brewmaster testing beer	2.00	4.00	3.00
☐ **Tray,** Jenny Gasoline, for tips	38.00	48.00	40.00
☐ **Tray,** Lowenbrau, metal, round, 12″ diameter	3.00	4.50	.75
☐ **Tray,** Miller High Life, for tips	7.00	12.00	10.00
☐ **Tray,** Miller High Life, picture of girl on moon, metal, round, 12″ diameter	2.50	4.50	3.50
☐ **Tray,** Miller High Life, picture of girl on moon, round, 13″ diameter, c. 1940s	35.00	60.00	47.00
☐ **Tray,** Miller Lite, metal, round, 13″ diameter	3.00	4.50	3.75
☐ **Tray,** Old Reliable Coffee, for tips	27.00	37.00	30.00
☐ **Tray,** Pacific Beer, picture of Mount Tacoma, 12″ diameter, 1912	45.00	65.00	55.00
☐ **Tray,** Pepsi Cola, picture of Pepsi Blue Lady, for change, 4½″ x 6″	1.00	2.50	1.75
☐ **Tray,** Pepsi Cola, picture of Pepsi Blue Lady, steel, 12″ x 15″	2.00	4.00	3.00
☐ **Tray,** Pepsi Cola, "Hits the Spot," picture of children under tree	25.00	35.00	30.00
☐ **Tray,** Prudential Insurance, for tips	7.00	17.00	12.00
☐ **Tray,** R.C.A. Dog, "Nipper," steel, oval, 12″ x 15″	2.00	3.00	2.50

AUTOGRAPHS

DESCRIPTION: Original autographs of celebrities, including presidents, entertainers, writers and artists, are fairly available and always sought after.

PERIOD: Autographs that date to the middle ages exist.

COMMENTS: Autographs have established cash values though they vary greatly in price because each specimen is unique. Single signatures are generally less expensive than signatures that are part of a letter. Often values depend on buyer demand.

ADDITIONAL TIPS: A holograph letter, AL, is a letter written entirely in the person's handwriting. A letter with the body written or typed by a secretary is referred to as an L. D is for a signed document, and N is for a signed note.

Listed alphabetically by celebrity name, prices are given for ALs, Ls, signed photo, manuscript page, document and plain signatures. For further information on autographs see *The Official 1984 Price Guide to Old Books and Autographs.*

AMERICAN PRESIDENTS	ALs	Ls	Document	Signed Photo	Plain Signature
☐ Washington, George	$8000.00-	$1800.00-	$1500.00-		$450.00-
	35,000.00	9500.00	4000.00		600.00
☐ Adams, John	4000.00-	1250.00-	1000.00-		300.00-
	7000.00	4000.00	2500.00		400.00
☐ Jefferson, Thomas	6000.00-	2000.00-	1200.00-		400.00-
	30,000.00	8000.00	3000.00		500.00
☐ Madison, James	1000.00-	500.00-	200.00-		100.00-
	3000.00	1400.00	800.00		150.00
☐ Monroe, James	500.00-	450.00-	150.00-		75.00-
	1500.00	1200.00	300.00		100.00
☐ Adams, John Q.	500.00-	450.00-	150.00-		80.00-
	1500.00	1200.00	300.00		125.00
☐ Jackson, Andrew	1000.00-	700.00-	400.00-		150.00-
	3000.00	2000.00	650.00		200.00
☐ Van Buren, Martin	400.00-	200.00-	150.00-		65.00-
	900.00	600.00	200.00		85.00
☐ Harrison, William H.	700.00-	300.00-	350.00-		80.00-
	1500.00	1000.00	475.00		100.00
☐ Tyler, John	500.00-	300.00-	150.00-		60.00-
	1000.00	600.00	200.00		75.00
☐ Polk, James K.	500.00-	300.00-	150.00-		60.00-
	1000.00	600.00	200.00		70.00
☐ Taylor, Zachary	750.00-	350.00-	275.00-		60.00-
	2000.00	1100.00	600.00		100.00

	ALs	Ls	Document	Signed Photo	Plain Signature
☐ Fillmore, Millard	200.00- 400.00	150.00- 300.00	100.00- 200.00		50.00- 60.00
☐ Pierce, Franklin	200.00- 400.00	150.00- 275.00	100.00- 200.00		50.00- 60.00
☐ Buchanan, James	200.00- 400.00	150.00- 275.00	100.00- 200.00		50.00- 60.00
☐ Lincoln, Abraham	4000.00- 30,000.00	2000.00- 12,000.00	750.00- 2500.00	4000.00- 7000.00	350.00- 350.00
☐ Johnson, Andrew	800.00- 2200.00	400.00- 1000.00	150.00- 200.00	1800.00- 2500.00	50.00- 60.00
☐ Grant, U. S.	600.00- 1200.00	400.00- 750.00	85.00- 150.00	100.00- 175.00	40.00- 45.00
☐ Hayes, R. B.	250.00- 500.00	150.00- 150.00	65.00- 65.00	250.00- 300.00	30.00- 38.00
☐ Garfield, James	300.00- 600.00	200.00- 350.00	100.00- 90.00	350.00- 700.00	38.00- 50.00
☐ Arthur, Chester A.	200.00- 300.00	120.00- 250.00	60.00- 85.00	850.00- 1200.00	30.00- 38.00
☐ Cleveland, Grover	140.00- 200.00	80.00- 120.00	50.00- 70.00	100.00- 200.00	26.00- 32.00
☐ Harrison, Benjamin	300.00- 400.00	145.00 175.00	65.00- 85.00	325.00- 450.00	28.00- 32.00
☐ McKinley, William	500.00- 750.00	190.00- 300.00	95.00- 140.00	175.00- 225.00	38.00- 42.00
☐ Roosevelt, Theodore	300.00- 350.00	100.00- 190.00	60.00- 60.00	100.00- 400.00	32.00- 38.00
☐ Taft, William H.	150.00- 190.00	90.00- 100.00	45.00- 50.00	150.00- 180.00	28.00- 35.00
☐ Wilson, Woodrow	500.00- 700.00	140.00- 190.00	60.00- 70.00	160.00- 220.00	38.00- 45.00
☐ Harding, Warren G.	700.00- 900.00	250.00- 350.00	60.00- 75.00	110.00- 140.00	28.00- 35.00
☐ Coolidge, Calvin	475.00- 700.00	140.00- 180.00	75.00- 70.00	75.00- 100.00	28.00- 35.00
☐ Hoover, Herbert	4000.00- 6000.00	150.00- 190.00	45.00- 60.00	150.00- 200.00	28.00- 35.00
☐ Roosevelt, Franklin	600.00- 1000.00	100.00- 265.00	95.00- 150.00	120.00- 180.00	33.00- 39.00
☐ Truman, Harry	1200.00- 1900.00	140.00- 350.00	80.00- 120.00	150.00- 180.00	39.00- 45.00
☐ Eisenhower, Dwight	1000.00- 1500.00	200.00- 275.00	80.00- 100.00	200.00- 300.00	28.00- 35.00
☐ Kennedy, John F.	1500.00- 4000.00	450.00- 900.00	175.00- 350.00	500.00- 1000.00	80.00- 100.00
☐ Johnson, Lyndon B.	1300.00- 1800.00	300.00- 500.00	80.00- 100.00	140.00- 190.00	35.00- 48.00

	ALs		Ls Document		Signed Photo	Plain Signature
☐ Nixon, Richard M	4500.00-	450.00-	150.00-		250.00-	50.00-
	6500.00	800.00	190.00		375.00	75.00
☐ Ford, Gerald	700.00-	250.00-	80.00-		140.00-	28.00-
	1000.00	400.00	110.00		190.00	35.00
☐ Carter, James	700.00-	200.00-	70.00-		120.00-	25.00-
	1000.00	350.00	90.00		150.00	35.00
☐ Reagan, Ronald	1000.00-	175.00-	85.00-		70.00-	25.00-
	1500.00	250.00	125.00		100.00	30.00

ENTERTAINMENT FIGURES

	8x10 Black and White Photo Signed		Plain Signature	
☐ Abel, Walter	2.50-	3.50	.75-	1.00
☐ Adams, Don	2.00-	3.00	.75-	1.00
☐ Allyson, June	3.00-	4.50	.75-	1.00
☐ Altman, Robert	5.00-	7.00	1.00-	1.50
☐ Ameche, Don	3.00-	4.00	.75-	1.00
☐ Ames, Ed	2.00-	3.00	.75-	1.00
☐ Ames, Leon	3.00-	4.00	.75-	1.00
☐ Ames, Nancy	1.50-	2.50	.75	1.00
☐ Amsterdam, Morey	2.00-	3.00	.75-	1.00
☐ Anderson, Lynn	3.00-	4.00	.75-	1.00
☐ Andress, Ursula	4.00-	7.00	.75-	1.00
☐ Andrews, Julie	2.00-	3.00	.75-	1.00
☐ Ansara, Michael	2.00-	3.00	.75-	1.00
☐ Arden, Eve	3.00-	4.00	.75-	1.00
☐ Arkin, Alan	4.00-	6.00	.75-	1.00
☐ Arnaz, Desi	5.00-	8.00	.75-	1.00
☐ Arnaz, Lucie	2.00-	3.00	1.00-	1.75
☐ Arness, James	2.00-	3.00	.75-	1.00
☐ Arthur, Beatrice	3.00-	4.00	.75-	1.00
☐ Arthur, Jean	3.00-	4.00	.75-	1.00
☐ Ashley, Elizabeth	2.00-,	3.00	.75-	1.00
☐ Astin, John	1.50-	2.50	.75-	1.00
☐ Aumont, Jean-Pierre	2.00-	3.00	.75-	1.00
☐ Ayers, Lew	4.00-	6.00	.75-	1.00
☐ Aznavour, Charles	2.00-	3.00	.75-	1.00
☐ Bacall, Lauren	9.00-	15.00	1.50-	2.75
☐ Backus, Jim	2.00-	3.00	.75-	1.00
☐ Baer, Max, Jr.	1.50-	2.50	.75-	1.00
☐ Bailey, Pearl	5.00-	8.00	1.00-	1.50
☐ Beatty, Warren	3.00-	4.00	.75-	1.00
☐ Belushi, John	75.00-	100.00	10.00-	15.00
☐ Benjamin, Dick.	2.00-	3.00	.75-	1.00
☐ Benny, Jack	40.00-	50.00	5.00-	8.00
☐ Bergen, Candice.	3.00-	4.00	.75-	1.00
☐ Bergen, Polly.	2.00-	3.00	.75-	1.00

	8x10 Black and White Photo Signed		Plain Signature	
☐ Berger, Senta.	2.00-	3.00	.75-	1.00
☐ Bergman, Ingmar.	10.00-	15.00	1.00-	1.50
☐ Bergman, Ingrid.	50.00-	70.00	5.00-	8.00
☐ Berle, Milton.	4.00-	6.00	1.00-	1.50
☐ Blondell, Joan.	2.00-	3.00	.75-	1.00
☐ Bloom, Claire.	6.00-	9.00	1.00-	1.50
☐ Blyth, Ann.	2.00-	3.00	.75-	1.00
☐ Bogarde, Dirk.	3.00-	4.00	.75-	1.00
☐ Bogart, Humphrey.	85.00-	110.00	6.00-	9.00
☐ Bogdanovich, Peter.	10.00-	15.00	1.00-	1.50
☐ Boone, Richard.	4.00-	6.00	.75-	1.00
☐ Booth, Shirley.	2.00-	3.00	.75-	1.00
☐ Borge, Victor.	3.00-	4.00	.75-	1.00
☐ Borgnine, Ernest.	3.00-	4.00	.75-	1.00
☐ Bosley, Tom.	2.00-	3.00	.75-	1.00
☐ Bowman, Lee.	2.00-	3.00	.75-	1.00
☐ Boyer, Charles.	10.00-	15.00	1.00-	1.75
☐ Boyle, Peter.	2.00-	3.00	.75-	1.00
☐ Bracken, Eddie.	2.00-	3.00	.75-	1.00
☐ Brand, Neville.	1.50-	2.50	.75-	1.00
☐ Brando, Marlon.	12.00-	17.00	1.50-	2.75
☐ Burton, Richard.	14.00-	19.00	2.00-	4.00
☐ Buttons, Red.	2.00-	3.00	.75-	1.00
☐ Buzzi, Ruth.	2.00-	3.00	.75-	1.00
☐ Caan, James.	4.00-	5.00	1.00-	1.50
☐ Cabot, Sebastian.	3.50-	6.00	.75-	1.00
☐ Caesar, Sid.	3.00-	4.00	.75-	1.00
☐ Cagney, James.	12.00-	17.00	2.00-	3.75
☐ Caine, Michael.	3.00-	4.00	.75-	1.00
☐ Caldwell, Sarah.	3.00-	4.00	.75-	1.00
☐ Caldwell, Zoe.	4.00-	6.00	.75-	1.00
☐ Calhoun, Rory.	2.00-	3.00	.75-	1.00
☐ Callan, Michael.	2.00-	3.00	.75-	1.00
☐ Calvet, Corinne.	2.00-	3.00	.75-	1.00
☐ Cameron, Rod.	2.00-	3.00	.75-	1.00
☐ Cannon, Dyan.	2.00-	3.00	.75-	1.00
☐ Cantinflas.	5.00-	7.00	.75-	1.00
☐ Cantor, Eddie.	40.00-	60.00	8.00-	11.00
☐ Chaney, Lon.	60.00-	80.00	10.00-	15.00
☐ Chaplin, Charles.	75.00-	100.00	6.00-	10.00
☐ Davis, Bette.	15.00-	20.00	3.00-	5.00
☐ DeHaviland, Olivia.	7.00-	10.00	1.50-	2.00
☐ Dell, Gabriel.	2.00-	3.00	.75-	1.00
☐ Delon, Alain.	4.00-	6.00	.75-	1.00
☐ DeLuise, Dom.	2.00-	3.00	.75-	1.00
☐ Deneuve, Catherine.	4.00-	6.00	.75-	1.00
☐ DeNiro, Robert.	4.00-	6.00	.75-	1.00

	8x10 Black and White Photo Signed		Plain Signature	
☐ Dennis, Sandy.	5.00-	7.00	.75-	1.00
☐ Denver, Bob.	3.00-	4.00	.75-	1.00
☐ Derek, Bo.	8.00-	11.00	1.00-	1.75
☐ Derek, John.	2.00-	3.00	.75-	1.00
☐ Dern, Bruce.	2.00-	3.00	.75-	1.00
☐ Dewhurst, Colleen.	5.00-	7.00	.75-	1.00
☐ Douglas, Mike.	4.00-	6.00	.75-	1.00
☐ Downs, Hugh.	2.00-	3.00	.75-	1.00
☐ Drake, Alfred.	3.00-	4.00	.75-	1.00
☐ Drew, Ellen.	2.00-	3.00	.75-	1.00
☐ Dreyfuss, Richard.	5.00-	7.00	.75-	1.00
☐ Dru, Joanne.	2.00-	3.00	.75-	1.00
☐ Drury, James.	2.00-	3.00	.75-	1.00
☐ Fletcher, Louise.	2.00-	3.00	.75-	1.00
☐ Foch, Nina.	2.00-	3.00	.75-	1.00
☐ Fonda, Henry.	25.00-	32.00	2.00-	3.00
☐ Fonda, Jane.	6.00-	8.00	1.00-	1.50
☐ Fonda, Peter.	5.00-	7.00	.75-	1.00
☐ Fontaine, Frank.	2.00-	3.00	.75-	1.00
☐ Fontaine, Joan.	4.00-	6.00	.75-	1.00
☐ Fontanne, Lynn.	12.00-	20.00	2.50-	4.00
☐ Foran, Dick.	2.00-	3.00	.75-	1.00
☐ Ford, Glenn.	3.00-	4.00	.75-	1.00
☐ Forrest, Steve.	2.00-	3.00	.75-	1.00
☐ Forsythe, John.	2.00-	3.00	.75-	1.00
☐ Fosse, Bob.	2.00-	3.00	.75-	1.00
☐ Foster, Phil.	1.50-	2.50	.75-	1.00
☐ Foxx, Redd.	2.50-	4.00	.75-	1.00
☐ Franciosa, Tony.	2.00-	3.00	.75-	1.00
☐ Gable, Clark.	50.00-	70.00	4.00-	7.00
☐ Gabor, Eva.	3.00-	4.00	.75-	1.00
☐ Gabor, Zsa Zsa.	3.00-	4.00	.75-	1.00
☐ Gam, Rita.	2.00-	3.00	.75-	1.00
☐ Garbo, Greta.	150.00-	225.00	15.00-	25.00
☐ Harlow, Jean.	200.00-	300.00	20.00-	35.00
☐ Harrington, Pat, Jr.	2.00-	3.00	.75-	1.00
☐ Harris, Barbara.	4.00-	6.00	.75-	1.00
☐ Harris, Julie.	5.00-	7.00	.75-	1.00
☐ Hawn, Goldie.	4.00-	6.00	.75-	1.00
☐ Haworth, Jill.	2.00-	3.00	.75-	1.00
☐ Hayden, Sterling.	2.00-	3.00	.75-	1.00
☐ Hayes, Helen.	5.00-	7.00	1.00-	1.50
☐ Hayworth, Rita.	5.00-	7.00	.75-	1.00
☐ Healy, Mary.	2.00-	3.00	.75-	1.00
☐ Heatherton, Joey.	3.00-	4.00	.75-	1.00
☐ Heckart, Eileen.	2.00-	3.00	.75-	1.00
☐ Hemmings, David.	2.00-	3.00	.75-	1.00

	8x10 Black and White Photo Signed		Plain Signature	
☐ Henderson, Florence.	2.00-	3.00	.75-	1.00
☐ Henry, Pat.	4.00-	7.00	1.00-	1.75
☐ Hepburn, Audrey.	3.00-	4.00	.75-	1.00
☐ Hepburn, Katherine.	15.00-	28.00	2.00-	4.00
☐ Heston, Charlton.	6.00-	8.00	1.00-	1.50
☐ Heywood, Anne.	2.00-	3.00	.75-	1.00
☐ Hitchcock, Alfred.	15.00-	23.00	1.00-	1.75
☐ Hoffman, Dustin.	5.00-	7.00	.75-	1.00
☐ Holbrook, Hal.	3.00-	4.00	.75-	1.00
☐ Holden, William.	30.00-	45.00	.75-	1.00
☐ Holder, Geoffrey.	2.00-	3.00	.75-	1.00
☐ Holliman, Earl.	2.00-	3.00	.75-	1.00
☐ Holly, Buddy.	125.00-	185.00	15.00-	25.00
☐ Joplin, Janis.	65.00-	85.00	6.00-	9.00
☐ Joslyn, Allyn.	2.00-	3.00	.75-	1.00
☐ Kahn, Madeline.	6.00-	8.00	1.00-	1.50
☐ Kaplan, Gabe.	3.00-	4.00	.75-	1.00
☐ Kasznar, Kurt.	5.00-	7.00	.75-	1.00
☐ Kaye, Danny.	4.00-	6.00	1.00-	1.50
☐ Kazan, Elia.	8.00-	10.00	1.50-	2.50
☐ Keach, Stacy.	4.00-	6.00	.75-	1.00
☐ Keaton, Diane.	5.00-	7.00	.75-	1.00
☐ Keel, Howard.	3.00-	4.00	.75-	1.00
☐ Keeler, Ruby.	8.00-	10.00	1.00-	1.50
☐ Kelly, Grace.	150.00-	225.00	4.00-	7.00
☐ Kelly, Jack.	2.00-	3.00	.75-	1.00
☐ Kennedy, Arthur.	2.00-	3.00	.75-	1.00
☐ Kennedy, George.	2.00-	3.00	.75-	1.00
☐ Kerr, Deborah.	4.00-	6.00	.75-	1.00
☐ Knotts, Don.	2.00-	3.00	.75-	1.00
☐ Knowles, Patric.	2.00-	3.00	.75-	1.00
☐ Korman, Harvey.	2.00-	3.00	.75-	1.00
☐ Kramer, Stanley.	7.00-	9.00	1.00-	1.50
☐ Kristofferson, Kris.	6.00-	8.00	.75-	1.00
☐ Kubrick, Stanley.	10.00-	15.00	1.00-	1.50
☐ Kwan, Nancy.	2.00-	3.00	.75-	1.00
☐ Lamarr, Hedy.	30.00-	50.00	4.00-	7.00
☐ Lamas, Fernando.	9.00-	12.00	1.00-	2.00
☐ Lancaster, Burt.	8.00-	10.00	1.00-	1.50
☐ Lanchester, Elsa.	4.00-	6.00	.75-	1.00
☐ Lasser, Louise.	5.00-	7.00	.75-	1.00
☐ Laurie, Piper.	2.00-	3.00	.75-	1.00
☐ Lavin, Linda.	4.00-	5.00	.75-	1.00
☐ Lawford, Peter.	3.00-	4.00	.75-	1.00
☐ Lemmon, Jack.	6.00-	8.00	1.00-	1.50
☐ Lennon, John.	175.00-	250.00	20.00-	30.00
☐ Leslie, Joan.	2.00-	3.00	.75-	1.00

	8x10 Black and White Photo Signed		Plain Signature	
☐ Lester, Jerry.	2.00-	3.00	.75-	1.00
☐ Levene, Sam.	2.00-	3.00	.75-	1.00
☐ Lewis, Jerry.	2.00-	3.00	.75-	1.00
☐ Lewis, Monica.	2.00-	3.00	.75-	1.00
☐ Lewis, Robert Q.	2.00-	3.00	.75-	1.00
☐ Lewis, Shari.	3.00-	4.00	.75-	1.00
☐ Liberace.	8.00-	11.00	1.00-	2.00
☐ Lollobrigida, Gina.	10.00-	15.00	1.00-	1.50
☐ Lom, Herbert.	2.00-	3.00	.75-	1.00
☐ Lombard, Carole.	100.00-	150.00	9.00-	14.00
☐ Longet, Claudine.	8.00-	10.00	1.00-	1.50
☐ Loren, Sophia.	17.00-	23.00	2.00-	3.00
☐ Loudon, Dorothy.	2.00-	3.00	.75-	1.00
☐ Louise, Tina.	2.00-	3.00	.75-	1.00
☐ Loy, Myrna.	8.00-	10.00	1.00-	1.50
☐ Lunt, Alfred.	12.00-	20.00	2.00-	4.00
☐ Lupino, Ida.	4.00-	6.00	.75-	1.00
☐ MacMurray, Fred.	8.00-	10.00	1.00-	1.50
☐ MacRae, Gordon.	2.00-	3.00	.75-	1.00
☐ MacRae, Sheila.	2.00-	3.00	.75-	1.00
☐ Macy, Bill.	2.00-	3.00	.75-	1.00
☐ Majors, Lee.	5.00-	7.00	.75-	1.00
☐ Malden, Karl.	2.00-	3.00	.75-	1.00
☐ Malone, Dorothy.	2.00-	3.00	.75-	1.00
☐ Marceau, Marcel.	15.00-	20.00	2.00-	3.00
☐ Margolin, Janet.	2.00-	3.00	.75-	1.00
☐ Marlowe, Hugh.	2.00-	3.00	.75-	1.00
☐ Marsh, Jean.	3.00-	4.00	.75-	1.00
☐ Marshall, E. G.	3.00-	4.00	.75-	1.00
☐ Martin, Dick.	2.00-	3.00	.75-	1.00
☐ Martin, Ross.	2.00-	3.00	.75-	1.00
☐ Marx, Groucho.	40.00-	55.00	5.00-	8.00
☐ Marvin, Lee.	2.00-	3.00	.75-	1.00
☐ Mason, Jackie.	2.00-	3.00	.75-	1.00
☐ Mason, James.	3.00-	4.00	.75-	1.00
☐ Mason, Pamela.	2.00-	3.00	.75-	1.00
☐ Massey, Raymond.	4.00-	6.00	.75-	1.00
☐ Niven, David.	3.00-	4.00	.75-	1.00
☐ Nolan, Kathy.	2.00-	3.00	.75-	1.00
☐ Nolan, Lloyd.	3.00-	4.00	.75-	1.00
☐ Nolte, Nick.	2.00-	3.00	.75-	1.00
☐ North, J. Ringling.	6.00-	8.00	1.00-	1.50
☐ North, Sheree.	2.00-	3.00	.75-	1.00
☐ Novak, Kim.	5.00-	7.00	1.00-	1.50
☐ Nugent, Elliot.	2.00-	3.00	.75-	1.00
☐ Nuyen, France.	2.00-	3.00	.75-	1.00
☐ Oakie, Jack.	4.00-	6.00	.75-	1.00

	8x10 Black and White Photo Signed		Plain Signature	
☐ Oberon, Merle.	6.00-	8.00	.75-	1.00
☐ O'Brian, Hugh.	2.00-	3.00	.75-	1.00
☐ O'Brien, Edmund.	2.00-	3.00	.75-	1.00
☐ O'Brien, Margaret.	3.00-	4.00	.75-	1.00
☐ O'Connell, Helen.	3.00-	4.00	.75-	1.00
☐ O'Connor, Carroll.	4.00-	6.00	.75-	1.00
☐ O'Hara, Jill.	2.00-	3.00	.75-	1.00
☐ O'Hara, Maureen.	3.00-	4.00	.75-	1.00
☐ O'Herlihy, Dan.	2.00-	3.00	.75-	1.00
☐ Olivier, Laurence.	12.00-	18.00	2.00-	3.00
☐ Pickford, Mary.	15.00-	20.00	2.00-	3.00
☐ Picon, Molly.	3.00-	4.00	.75-	1.00
☐ Pidgeon, Walter.	3.00-	4.00	.75-	1.00
☐ Pleasance, Donald.	5.00-	7.00	.75-	1.00
☐ Pleshette, Suzanne.	3.00-	4.00	.75-	1.00
☐ Plimpton, George.	3.00-	4.00	.75-	1.00
☐ Plowright, Joan.	2.00-	3.00	.75-	1.00
☐ Plummer, Christopher.	5.00-	7.00	.75-	1.00
☐ Poitier, Sidney.	5.00-	7.00	1.00-	1.50
☐ Polanski, Roman.	10.00-	15.00	1.50-	2.50
☐ Presley, Elvis.	275.00-	375.00	20.00-	35.00
☐ Redgrave, Vanessa.	10.00-	15.00	2.00-	3.00
☐ Reed, Donna.	2.00-	3.00	.75-	1.00
☐ Reed, Rex.	1.50-	2.50	.75-	1.00
☐ Robertson, Cliff.	2.00-	3.00	.75-	1.00
☐ Robertson, Dale.	2.00-	3.00	.75-	1.00
☐ Rogers, Ginger.	8.00-	10.00	1.00-	1.50
☐ Roland, Gilbert.	5.00-	7.00	.75-	1.00
☐ Roman, Ruth.	2.00-	3.00	.75-	1.00
☐ Romero, Cesar.	2.00-	3.00	.75-	1.00
☐ Rooney, Mickey.	3.00-	4.00	.75-	1.00
☐ Ross, Katharine.	2.00-	3.00	.75-	1.00
☐ Roth, Lillian.	8.00-	10.00	1.00-	1.50
☐ Roundtree, Richard.	2.00-	3.00	.75-	1.00
☐ Rowan, Dan.	3.00-	4.00	.75-	1.00
☐ Rowlands, Gena.	2.00-	3.00	.75-	1.00
☐ Rule, Janice.	2.00-	3.00	.75-	1.00
☐ Rush, Barbara.	3.00-	4.00	.75-	1.00
☐ Russell, Jane.	5.00-	7.00	.75-	1.00
☐ Russell, Ken.	5.00-	7.00	.75-	1.00
☐ Sahl, Mort.	2.00-	3.00	.75-	1.00
☐ Saint, Eva Marie.	4.00-	6.00	.75-	1.00
☐ St. James, Susan.	2.00-	3.00	.75-	1.00
☐ St. John, Jill.	3.00-	4.00	.75-	1.00
☐ Sainte-Marie, Buffy.	6.00-	8.00	.75-	1.00
☐ Sales, Soupy.	2.00-	3.00	.75-	1.00
☐ Sand, Paul.	2.00-	3.00	.75-	1.00

	8x10 Black and White Photo Signed		Plain Signature	
☐ Sarrazin, Michael.	6.00-	8.00	.75-	1.00
☐ Savalas, Telly.	5.00-	7.00	.75-	1.00
☐ Saxon, John.	2.00-	3.00	.75-	1.00
☐ Sharif, Omar.	6.00-	8.00	.75-	1.00
☐ Shatner, William.	3.00-	4.00	.75-	1.00
☐ Shaw, Robert.	2.00-	3.00	.75-	1.00
☐ Shearer, Norma.	8.00-	10.00	1.00-	1.50
☐ Shepherd, Cybill.	6.00-	8.00	.75-	1.00
☐ Shields, Brooke.	40.00-	50.00	5.00-	8.00
☐ Stark, Koo.	75.00-	100.00	15.00-	20.00
☐ Starr, Ringo.	100.00-	150.00	15.00-	25.00
☐ Steiger, Rod.	5.00-	7.00	.75-	1.00
☐ Swanson, Gloria.	18.00-	30.00	3.00-	5.00
☐ Swit, Loretta.	9.00-	15.00	1.50-	2.75
☐ Talbot, Nita.	2.00-	3.00	.75-	1.00
☐ Tamblyn, Russ.	2.00-	3.00	.75-	1.00
☐ Tandy, Jessica.	4.00-	5.00	.75-	1.00
☐ Tate, Sharon.	100.00-	150.00	10.00-	15.00
☐ Taylor, Elizabeth.	18.00-	25.00	2.00-	3.00
☐ Taylor, Kent.	2.00-	3.00	.75-	1.00
☐ Taylor, Rod.	2.00-	3.00	.75-	1.00
☐ Temple, Shirley.	10.00-	15.00	1.50-	2.50
☐ Torn, Rip.	2.00-	3.00	.75-	1.00
☐ Totter, Audrey.	2.00-	3.00	.75-	1.00
☐ Tracy, Arthur.	3.00-	4.00	.75-	1.00
☐ Travolta, John.	12.00-	17.00	2.00-	3.00
☐ Trevor, Claire.	3.00-	4.00	.75-	1.00
☐ Tucker, Forrest.	2.00-	3.00	.75-	1.00
☐ Turner, Lana.	10.00-	15.00	1.50-	2.50
☐ Twiggy.	30.00-	40.00	4.00-	6.00
☐ Tyrell, Susan.	2.00-	3.00	.75-	1.00
☐ Tyson, Cicely.	3.00-	4.00	.75-	1.00
☐ Uggams, Leslie.	2.00-	3.00	.75-	1.00
☐ Ullman, Liv.	8.00-	10.00	1.00-	1.50
☐ Ustinov, Peter.	3.00-	4.00	.75-	1.00
☐ Vaccaro, Brenda.	2.00-	3.00	.75-	1.00
☐ Valentino, Rudolph.	225.00-	300.00	20.00-	35.00

AVON BOTTLES

DESCRIPTION: The oldest toiletry company that issues decorative bottles, Avon is the modern leader in the non-liquor bottle field.

TYPES: There are a variety of Avon bottle types, including figurals shaped as animals, people, cars, etc., cologne bottles, hand lotion bottles, among others.

PERIOD: Based on door-to-door sales, Avon began as the California Perfume Company more than 50 years ago. Since 1939 the name Avon has been used exclusively.

COMMENTS: Everything relating to Avon, including bottles, brochures and magazine ads, is highly collectible. Older Avon memorabilia is usually of more value than recent products.

ADDITIONAL TIPS: The listings in this section are alphabetized by item name, followed by date of issue, description and, when possible, issue date. For more information, consult *The Official Price Guide to Bottles, Old and New,* published by The House of Collectibles.

	Current Price Range		Prior Year Average
☐ **Baby Owl,** clear glass, gold cap, 1 oz. 1975-76. Original price $2.00	1.00	3.00	2.00
☐ **Bath Urn,** white glass and cap with gold top band under the cap, 5 oz., 1971-73	3.00	5.00	4.00
☐ **Bath Treasure Snail decanter,** clear glass, gold head, 6 oz., 1973-76. Original price $6.00	5.00	7.00	6.00
☐ **Beautiful Awakening,** clear glass, painted gold in shape of an alarm clock, with clock face on front, 3 oz., 1973-74	4.00	6.00	5.00
☐ **Betsy Ross decanter,** clear glass painted white, 4 oz., 1976. Original price $10.00	6.00	10.00	8.00
☐ **Bird of Paradise cologne,** blue glass, gold cap, 1.5 oz., 1975-76. Original price $3.00	2.00	4.00	3.00
☐ **Blue Demi-Cup bath oil,** white glass, blue cap and floral design, 3 oz., 1968-70. Original price $3.50	5.00	7.00	6.00
☐ **Blue Eyes,** kitten figurine, opal glass, blue eyes, 1.5 oz., 1975-76. Original price $3.00 . . .	3.00	5.00	4.00
☐ **Bon Bon cologne,** poodle figurine, white glass, white cap, 1 oz., 1972-73. Original price $2.00	2.00	4.00	3.00
☐ **Bon Bon cologne,** poodle figurine, black milk glass, black plastic cap, 1 oz., 1973. Original price $2.00	1.00	3.00	2.00
☐ **Bridal Moments,** clear glass painted white, figurine of a bride, gold cap, 4 oz., 1976. Original price $9.00	6.00	8.00	7.00
☐ **Candlestick cologne,** clear glass coated silver, silver cap, 3 oz., 1966. Original price $8.00	8.00	12.00	10.00

	Current Price Range		Prior Year Average
Candlestick cologne, red glass, gold cap with wide plastic collar, 4 oz., 1970-71. Original price $6.00	5.00	7.00	6.00
Candlestick cologne, clear glass painted silver, 5 oz., 1972-75	5.00	7.00	6.00
Charmlight decanter, clear glass in shape of lamp with white shade, 8.8 oz., 1975-76. Original price $7.00	6.00	8.00	7.00
Chimney Lamp cologne mist decanter, clear glass, white plastic shade with pink floral design, 2 oz., 1973-74	5.00	7.00	6.00
Christmas Bells cologne, clear glass painted red, gold cap, 1 oz., 1974-75	1.00	2.00	1.50
Christmas Tree, clear glass painted red, green, gold and silver, 4 oz., 1968-70. Original price $2.50	6.00	8.00	7.00
Classic decanter, figurine of woman with bowl on her head, white glass, gold cap, 8 oz., 1969-70	6.00	8.00	7.00
Cologne and Candlelight, clear glass, short, round bottle, gold cap and clear plastic collar, 2 oz., 1975. Original price $3.00	2.00	4.00	3.00
Dream Garden, pink frosted glass in design of a watering can, gold cap, ½ oz., 1972-73. Original price $5.00	6.00	8.00	7.00
Dr. Hoot decanter, opal white glass, black cap shaped like a graduate's cap with a gold tassel, 4 oz., 1975. Original price $5.00	4.00	6.00	5.00
Dutch Girl figurine cologne, clear glass painted blue, white plastic top, 3 oz., 1973-74	5.00	7.00	6.00
Dutch Treat Demi-Cups, white glass, floral designs on front, yellow, blue, or pink cap, 3 oz., 1971. Original price $3.50	5.00	7.00	6.00
Eiffel Tower cologne, clear glass, gold cap, 3 oz., 1970	6.00	8.00	7.00
Eighteenth Century Classic Figurine Young Boy, clear glass painted white, white plastic head, 4 oz., 1974-75. Original price $5.00	4.00	6.00	5.00
Eighteenth Century Classic Figurine Young Girl, clear glass painted white, white plastic head, 4 oz., 1974-75. Original price $5.00	4.00	6.00	5.00
Elizabethan Fashion figurine, clear glass painted pin on lower portion, top portion pink plastic, 4 oz., 1972	8.00	10.00	9.00
Enchanted Frog cream sachet, colored milk glass, plastic lid, 1.25 oz., 1973-76. Original price $3.00	2.00	4.00	3.00

	Current Price Range		Prior Year Average
☐ **Enchanted Hours,** blue glass, gold cap, 5 oz., 1972-73	6.00	8.00	7.00
☐ **French Telephone,** white milk glass base, gold cap and trim, 6 oz., 1971. Original price $22.00	18.00	24.00	21.00
☐ **Gay Nineties cologne,** clear bottle painted orange in figurine of woman, white top, orange hat, 3 oz., 1974. Original price $4.00	4.00	6.00	5.00
☐ **Golden Thimble,** clear glass on lower portion, gold cap, 2 oz., 1972-74	3.00	5.00	4.00
☐ **Good Luck Elephant,** frosted glass, gold cap, 1.5 oz., 1975-76. Original price $3.00	2.00	4.00	3.00
☐ **Graceful Giraffe,** clear glass, plastic top. 1.5 oz., 1976. Original price $4.00	3.00	5.00	4.00
☐ **Grecian Pitcher,** bust of woman with jar on her head, white glass, white stopper, 5 oz., 1972-76	4.00	6.00	5.00
☐ **Handy Frog moisturized hand lotion,** large frog with red hat, white milk glass, 8 oz., 1975-76. Original price $6.00	5.00	7.00	6.00

Avon Bottle,
owl cream sachet,
1½ oz., 1972,
$5.00-$6.50

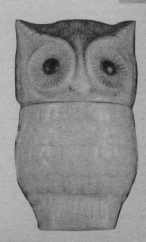

	Current Price Range		Prior Year Average
☐ **Hearth Lamp cologne decanter,** black glass, gold handle, yellow and white shade, daisies around neck, 8 oz., 1973-74	7.00	10.00	8.50
☐ **Heavenly Angel cologne,** clear glass, white top, 2 oz., 1974-75. Original price $4.00	2.00	4.00	3.00
☐ **High-Buttoned Shoe,** clear glass in shape of a shoe, gold cap, 2 oz., 1975-76. Original price $3.00	2.00	4.00	3.00
☐ **Hobnail Bell cologne decanter,** white milk glass, gold handle, gold bell clapper, 2 oz., 1973-74	3.00	5.00	4.00
☐ **Hobnail bud vase,** white milk glass, red and yellow roses on front, long neck, 4 oz., 1973-74	5.00	7.00	6.00
☐ **Hobnail decanter foaming bath oil,** white opal glass, 4 oz., 1972-74	5.00	7.00	6.00
☐ **Hurricane Lamp cologne decanter,** white glass lower portion, clear glass for top portion, gold cap, 6 oz., 1973-74	8.00	12.00	10.00
☐ **Key Note perfume,** clear glass in shape of key with gold plastic cap, ¼ oz., 1967. Original price $5.50 and $6.50	8.00	12.00	10.00
☐ **Koffee Klatch,** clear glass painted yellow in shape of coffee pot, gold top, 5 oz., 1971-74 . .	4.00	6.00	5.00
☐ **La Belle Telephone,** telephone figurine, clear glass, gold top, 1 oz., 1974-76. Original price $7.00	6.00	8.00	7.00
☐ **Lady Bug perfume decanter,** frosted glass, gold cap, ¼ oz., 1975-76. Original price $4.00	2.00	4.00	3.00
☐ **Ming Cat cologne,** tall seated cat, white glass, blue trim, neck ribbon, 6 oz., 1971	7.00	10.00	8.50
☐ **One dram perfume,** clear glass with ribbing, gold cap, 1974-76. Original price $4.25	2.00	4.00	3.00
☐ **Parisian Garden perfume,** white milk glass, in shape of pitcher with floral design on front, gold cap, 3.3 oz., 1974-75. Original price $5.00	4.00	6.00	5.00
☐ **Parlor Lamp,** lower portion in white milk glass, top portion in light amber glass, gold cap, 3 oz., 1971-72. Original price $7.00	7.00	10.00	8.50
☐ **Partridge cologne decanger,** white milk glass, white plastic lid, 5 oz., 1973-75. Original price $5.00	4.00	6.00	5.00
☐ **Perfume Petite Mouse,** frosted glass, gold head and tail, ¼ oz., 1970. Original price $7.50	14.00	16.00	15.00
☐ **Pert Penguin,** clear glass, gold cap, 1 oz., 1975-76. Original price $2.00	1.00	2.00	1.50

	Current Price Range		Prior Year Average
☐ **Petite Piglet,** clear glass, embossed, gold cap, in design of pig, 1972. Original price $5.00	7.00	9.00	8.00
☐ **Pineapple petite cologne,** clear glass in the shape of a pineapple, large gold cap, 1 oz., 1972-74	2.00	4.00	3.00
☐ **Precious Slipper,** frosted glass, gold cap as bow on shoe, .25 oz., 1973-74. Original price $4.00	4.00	6.00	5.00
☐ **Precious Swan perfume decanter,** frosted glass, gold cap, ¼ oz., 1974-76. Original price $4.00	2.00	4.00	3.00
☐ **Pretty Girl Pink,** clear glass painted pink on lower portion, top portion light pink, 6 oz., 1974-75. Original price $4.00	3.00	5.00	4.00
☐ **Queen of Scots,** white milk glass, figurine of dog, white plastic head, 1 oz., 1973-75	2.00	4.00	3.00
☐ **Regency Candlestick cologne,** clear glass, faceted, tall bottle, 4 oz., 1973-74	6.00	8.00	7.00
☐ **Remember When School Desk decanter,** black glass, light brown plastic seat and desk top, red apple for cap, 4 oz., 1972-74	6.00	8.00	7.00
☐ **Sewing Notions,** pink and white glass in design of a spool with silver cap designed as a thimble, 1 oz., 1975. Original price $3.00	2.00	4.00	3.00
☐ **Skip-A-Rope,** clear glass painted yellow, figurine of girl jumping rope, yellow top, white plastic rope, 4 oz., 1975-76. Original price $7.00	6.00	8.00	7.00
☐ **Sitting Pretty cologne,** white milk glass, in shape of easy chair, gold cap in shape of cat sitting on top of chair, 4 oz., 1971-73. Original price $5.00	6.00	8.00	7.00
☐ **Sweet Shoppe Pin Cushion cream sachet decanter,** white milk glass for lower portion of ice cream parlor chair, white plastic back, pink pin cushion for the cushion seat, 1 oz., 1972-74	4.00	6.00	5.00
☐ **Swiss Mouse,** mouse on cheese figurine, frosted glass, gold cap, 3 oz., 1974-75. Original price $4.00	3.00	5.00	4.00
☐ **Suzette decanter,** poodle figurine, milk glass, plastic head, pink ribbon, 5 oz., 1973-76	4.00	6.00	5.00
☐ **Tabatha cologne spray,** stylized cat figurine, black glass with plastic head, 1.5 oz., 1975-76. Original price $6.00	5.00	7.00	6.00

	Current Price Range		Prior Year Average
☐ **Teatime powder sachet,** frosted white, gold cap, 1.25 oz., 1974-75. Original price $4.00 . . .	3.00	5.00	4.00
☐ **Tiffany Lamp cologne,** brown glass base, pink shade, pink and green floral design on shade, 5 oz., 1972-74	8.00	10.00	9.00
☐ **To A Wild Rose Demi-Cup,** white glass, red rose on front, pink cap, 3 oz., 1969. Original price $3.50	6.00	8.00	7.00

BARBED WIRE

DESCRIPTION: Barbed wire was first used by Western farmers who installed it on their land to deter cattlemen. Railroads used it in some areas to keep cattle and buffalo off the tracks.

VARIATIONS: There are various types of barbed wire including ribbon wire, double round wire with two points and single round wire with two points.

ORIGIN: The first wire fencing was patented in 1853. Between 1868 and 1900 more than 750 patents were issued for various barbed wire styles.

COMMENTS: Barbed wire is collectible because of its historical importance during the settlement of western territories.

ADDITIONAL TIPS: Prices vary from $1 to more than $400 for a stick which is an 18 inch piece of barbed wire.

The listings in this section are alphabetical according to barbed wire type. When available, the date of manufacture is given. Along with the price range, a previous year average price is included.

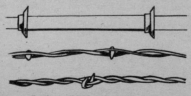

From Top to Bottom: *Brinkerhoff Ribbon wire, Daniel C. Stover two line wire and Scutt's Single Clip wire, late 1800s,* **$20.00-$30.00**

	Current Price Range		Prior Year Average

SINGLE ROUND WITH TWO POINTS

☐ Bakers Single Strand, c. 1883	3.00	5.00	3.50
☐ Charles D. Rogers, c. 1888	3.00	5.00	3.50
☐ Dobbs and Booth Single Line, c. 1875	5.00	7.00	6.00
☐ Gunderson, c. 1881	5.00	7.00	6.00
☐ Half-Hitch, c. 1877	3.25	6.50	4.75
☐ H. M. Rose Wrap Barb, c. 1877	3.00	5.00	4.00
☐ L. E. Sunderland No Kink, c. 1884	3.00	5.00	4.00
☐ Mack's Alternate, c. 1875	12.00	18.00	15.00
☐ Nelson Clip, c. 1876	80.00	100.00	90.00
☐ Putnams Flat Under Barb, c. 1877	15.00	20.00	17.00
☐ R. Emerson, c. 1876	160.00	190.00	175.00
☐ Rose Kink Line, c. 1877	3.50	5.50	4.50
☐ Single Line Wide Wrap Barb, c. 1878	80.00	100.00	90.00
☐ Sunderland Hammered Barb, c. 1884	3.50	4.50	4.00
☐ "Two Point Ripple Wire"	7.00	9.00	8.00

DOUBLE ROUND WITH TWO POINTS

☐ Australian Loose Wrap	3.50	5.50	3.50
☐ Baker's Half-Round Barb	2.50	3.50	2.00
☐ C. H. Salisbury, c. 1876	15.00	20.00	16.00
☐ Decker Parallel, c. 1884	7.00	9.00	6.00
☐ Figure 8 Barb, Wright, c. 1881	22.00	28.00	23.00
☐ "Forked Tongue", c. 1887	4.00	6.00	4.50
☐ Haish's Original "S", c. 1875	3.00	5.00	3.50
☐ Glidden Barb on Both Lines	4.50	7.50	5.00
☐ J. D. Curtis "Twisted Point"	2.50	3.50	2.50
☐ J. D. Nadlehoffer, c. 1878	45.00	60.00	50.00
☐ Kangaroo Wire c. 1876	4.00	6.50	4.50
☐ L. E. Sunderland Barb on Two Line Wire, c. 1884	110.00	140.00	115.00
☐ Missouri Hump Wire Staple Barb, c. 1876 ...	9.00	12.00	9.50
☐ Peter P. Hill Parallel, c. 1876	160.00	185.00	150.00
☐ Rose Barb on Copper Lines, c. 1877	5.50	7.50	5.50
☐ W. Edenborn	4.00	6.00	4.50
☐ W. Edenborn's Locked in Barb, c. 1885	3.00	5.00	3.50

RIBBON WIRE

☐ Allis Barbless Ribbon and Single Wire, c. 1881 .	16.00	24.00	16.00
☐ Allis Flat Ribbon Barb, c. 1892	16.00	24.00	16.00
☐ Brinkerhoff's Ribbon Barb, c. 1881	4.50	6.50	5.00
☐ Cast Iron Buckthorn	6.50	10.00	8.00
☐ Factory Splice on Thin Barbed Ribbon, c. 1892 .	40.00	55.00	40.00
☐ F. D. Ford Flat Ribbon, c. 1885	4.50	6.50	5.00
☐ John Hallner's "Greenbriar", c. 1878	1.75	4.00	2.00
☐ Harbaugh's Torn Ribbon, c. 1881	6.50	10.50	7.50
☐ Kelly's Split Ribbon, c. 1868	22.00	35.00	25.00

	Current Price Range		Prior Year Average
☐ **Kelmer Ornamental Fence**, c. 1885	16.00	20.00	16.00
☐ **"Open Face" by Brinkerhoff**, c. 1881	8.00	12.00	9.00
☐ **Scutt's Smooth Ribbon**	14.00	24.00	14.00
☐ **Scutt's Ridged Ribbon**, c. 1883	55.00	70.00	55.00
☐ **Three-Quarter Inch Ribbon**	10.00	16.00	10.00
☐ **Very Light and Narrow Ribbon**, c. 1868	60.00	70.00	60.00

BASEBALL CARDS

The baseball section features only a sampling of items. In order to accurately present the vast amount of information required by serious collectors, a special edition devoted to baseball is published by The House of Collectibles, Inc. This handy, pocket-size guide, *The Official 1985 Price Guide to Baseball Cards,* features more than 100,000 prices and valuable collecting information. It is available at bookstores for $3.95.

DESCRIPTION: Baseball cards usually have the picture of a baseball player on one side and the player's baseball record on the other. Baseball cards were made in different sizes depending on the era and the company.

ORIGIN: Baseball cards were introduced in the middle 1880s. At first they were made exclusively by tobacco companies for distribution with cigarettes or other tobacco products. Between 1900 to 1930 other firms also printed baseball cards, though not on a regular basis. The modern era of baseball cards began during the Depression when gum companies began packaging cards along with bubblegum. The motive was to boost gum sales, but as the public became more interested in the cards, they developed into a thriving industry.

TYPES: There are two types of cards — the old cards from before the 1930s and the modern cards after the 1930s.

COMPANIES: Major companies that produced baseball cards in the late 1800s and early 1900s include Goodwin and Company, Allen and Ginter, P.H. Mayo and Brothers Tobacco Company and D. Buchner.

From the early 1930s, modern card companies such as Goudey Gum Company, Delong Gum Company and Frank H. Fleer were major card producers. The Topps Chewing Gum Company, which began distributing cards in the 1970s, is perhaps the best known.

ADDITIONAL INFORMATION: For more information, consult *The Official Price Guide to Baseball Cards,* published by The House of Collectibles.

MEAT PACKERS CARDS

Hunter's Wieners, *set of 29 cards, 2"x4¾", issued in 1955, depicts players, coaches, etc. of the St. Louis Cardinals, the cards are not numbered, this set was locally distributed in the St. Louis area, had a small printing and became very scarce within a few years of its appearance, the most valuable single card is that of Stan Musial, now selling for $85-110, the rest are bringing $70-90.*

	G-VG		FINE	
☐ Complete set........................	575.00	725.00	1000.00	1300.00

Hygrade Meats, *set of nine cards, 3¾"x4½", issued in 1957, depicts members of the Seattle Pacific Coast League team, the cards are not numbered, values:*

☐ Dick Aylward.........................	22.00	29.00	40.00	55.00
☐ Bob Balcena.........................	22.00	29.00	40.00	55.00
☐ Jim Dyck	22.00	29.00	40.00	55.00
☐ Mario Fricane.......................	22.00	29.00	40.00	55.00
☐ Bill Glynn	22.00	29.00	40.00	55.00
☐ Bill Kennedy	22.00	29.00	40.00	55.00
☐ Ray Orteig	22.00	29.00	40.00	55.00
☐ Joe Taylor	22.00	29.00	40.00	55.00
☐ Maury Wills	45.00	60.00	85.00	110.00
☐ Complete set.......................	225.00	285.00	425.00	550.00

Koester's Bread, *set of 52 cards, 3½"x2", issued in 1921, depicts members of the New York Giants and New York Yankees, and is entitled "World Series Issue" (these teams met in the World Series of 1921, the first so-called "subway series" to be played in New York), the cards are unnumbered, more valuable specimens:*

☐ New York Giants · Frankie Frisch	16.00	22.00	33.00	41.00
☐ New York Giants · George Kelly	15.00	20.00	30.00	37.00
☐ New York Giants · John McGraw	17.00	24.00	36.00	45.00
☐ New York Giants · Charles D. Stengel ...	20.00	28.00	40.00	55.00
☐ New York Yankees · Waite Hoyt	14.00	19.00	28.00	35.00
☐ New York Yankees · Carl Mays	15.00	20.00	30.00	37.00
☐ New York Yankees · Babe Ruth.........	25.00	34.00	50.00	70.00
☐ Complete set.......................	700.00	900.00	1400.00	1700.00

Red Heart Dog Food, *set of 33 cards, 2½"x3¾", issued in 1954, depicts players from the American and National Leagues, the cards are not numbered, this set would appear to be somewhat scarcer than the current market value indicates.*

☐ Complete set.......................	55.00	70.00	100.00	130.00

Stahl-Meyer Frankfurters, *set of 12 cards, 3¼"x4½", issued in 1953, depicts players from the New York Yankees, New York Giants, and Brooklyn Dodgers, this set was distributed exclusively in the New York metropolitan area, the cards are not numbered, more valuable specimens:*

☐ Roy Campanella.....................	28.00	36.00	55.00	70.00
☐ Gil Hodges	38.00	49.00	70.00	90.00
☐ Monte Irvin	32.00	42.00	60.00	80.00
☐ Mickey Mantle	32.00	42.00	60.00	80.00

	G-VG		FINE	
☐ Duke Snider	28.00	36.00	55.00	70.00
☐ *Complete set*	325.00	385.00	600.00	750.00

Sugardale Meats, *set of four cards, 3¾"x5¼", issued in 1962, depicts members of the Pittsburgh Pirates, cards are lettered, values:*

	G-VG		FINE	
☐ A. Dick Groat	9.00	12.00	18.00	24.00
☐ B. Roberto Clemente	15.00	20.00	30.00	39.00
☐ C. Don Hoak	9.00	12.00	18.00	24.00
☐ D. Dick Stuart	9.00	12.00	18.00	24.00
☐ *Complete set*	60.00	80.00	115.00	135.00

TOBACCO CARDS

Fatima Cigarettes, *set of 16 cards, 5¾"x2½", issued in 1913, depicts group portraits of all the major league teams then in existence (8 National League, 8 American League), the cards are not numbered, values:*

American League

	G-VG		FINE	
☐ Boston	22.00	29.00	40.00	55.00
☐ Chicago	15.00	20.00	28.00	37.00
☐ Cleveland	15.00	20.00	28.00	37.00
☐ Detroit	33.00	45.00	60.00	80.00
☐ New York	29.00	39.00	55.00	70.00
☐ Philadelphia	15.00	20.00	28.00	37.00
☐ St. Louis	55.00	70.00	100.00	130.00
☐ Washington	15.00	20.00	28.00	37.00

National League

	G-VG		FINE	
☐ Boston	15.00	20.00	28.00	37.00
☐ Brooklyn	15.00	20.00	28.00	37.00
☐ Chicago	15.00	20.00	28.00	37.00
☐ Cincinnati	15.00	20.00	28.00	37.00
☐ New York	15.00	20.00	28.00	37.00
☐ Philadelphia	15.00	20.00	28.00	37.00
☐ Pittsburgh	15.00	20.00	28.00	37.00
☐ St. Louis	29.00	39.00	55.00	70.00
☐ *Complete set*	390.00	475.00	700.00	900.00

Fez Cigarettes, *set of 126 cards (of which 100 are baseball players, the balance boxers), entitled "Prominent Baseball Players and Athletes," 5¾"x8", issued in 1911, depicts players of the National and American Leagues, the identical set was also distributed with Old Mill cigarettes; values are the same regardless of the imprint, more valuable specimens:*

	G-VG		FINE	
☐ # 5 Sam Crawford	18.00	23.00	35.00	45.00
☐ # 6 Hal Chase	15.00	20.00	28.00	35.00
☐ # 8 Fred Clarke	16.00	21.00	30.00	37.00
☐ # 9 Ty Cobb	20.00	28.00	38.00	48.00
☐ # 23 Nap Lajoie	18.00	23.00	35.00	45.00
☐ # 26 John McGraw	18.00	23.00	35.00	45.00

		G-VG		FINE	
☐ # 27	Christy Mathewson	22.00	32.00	40.00	52.00
☐ # 35	Joe Tinker	15.00	20.00	28.00	35.00
☐ # 36	Tris Speaker	19.00	25.00	36.00	45.00
☐ # 39	Rube Waddell	21.00	31.00	39.00	49.00
☐ # 42	Cy Young	19.00	25.00	36.00	45.00
☐ # 47	Frank Chance	17.00	22.00	32.00	39.00
☐ # 80	Chief Bender	17.50	22.50	34.00	41.00
☐ # 87	Eddie Collins	18.00	23.00	35.00	43.00

Barney McCosky,
*outfielder, Philadelphia
Athletics,
No. 84 in 1951
Bowman Gum card series,*
$2.00-$2.25

BASKETS

TOPIC: The art of basketry is indeed a reflection of America's cultural past. Long before this nation's first colonization, the American Indian had achieved artistic excellence as a basket weaver. Indian baskets are said to be the world's finest. Each basket was woven for a specific purpose and with the utmost care. These baskets were not only used to hold food and water and for ceremonial purposes, but some were also used for cooking. Their works are unique because they used only materials from nature — pine needles, straw, leaves, willow, porcupine quills, vines, reeds and grass. Dyes were made from bark, roots or berries. Their distinctive designs have made them sought after by most basket enthusiasts.

TYPES: There are several types of basket construction. Wickerwork, the most common and widely used technique, is nothing more than an over and under pattern. Twining is similar except that two strands are twisted as they are woven over and under producing a finer weave. Plaiting gives a checkerboard effect and can be either a tight weave or left with some open spaces. Twillwork is much the same except that a diagonal effect is achieved by changing the number of strands over which the weaver passes. Coiling is the most desirable weave to the collector. This technique has been carefully refined since its conception around 7000 BC. Fibers are wrapped around and stitched together to form the basket's shape. Most of these pieces were either used for ceremonial purposes or for holding liquids, since the containers made in this fashion were tightly woven and leakproof.

COMMENTS: Baskets are available in a wide range of prices and types. Because of their decorative appeal they are now avidly sought by collectors. They may be collected by general category such as Indian, Appalachian, Nantucket, etc., or simply acquired in a wide variety of types and styles.

ADDITIONAL TIPS: Baskets are easy to care for but a few basic rules must be followed.

1. Never wash an Indian basket. Dust it gently using a very soft sable artist's brush.

2. Do not subject Indian baskets to the sun as it will fade the patterns.

3. Do not wash any basket made of pine needles, straw, grass or leaves.

4. Willow, oak, hickory and rattan baskets may be washed in a mild solution of Murphy's Oil Soap and dried in a sunny location.

	Current Price Range		Prior Year Average
☐ **American Indian,** 10″ Dia.	180.00	220.00	155.00
☐ **Apache burden basket,** 2½″ x 2½″	25.00	35.00	22.50
☐ **Apache burden basket,** rawhide bottom, plain, 11½″ H.	300.00	375.00	300.00
☐ **Apache burden basket,** geometric pattern, tin cones hanging from leather straps, 6½″ x 5″ . .	60.00	75.00	62.00
☐ **Apache wedding basket,** 13″ Dia., c. 1880	30.00	45.00	32.00
☐ **Bannock berry basket,** 8″ x 8½″	55.00	80.00	58.00
☐ **California,** tightly woven, light brown, diamond motif, 5¾″ Dia.	150.00	175.00	138.00

	Current Price Range		Prior Year Average
☐ **Caushatta effigy baskets,** pine cones and needles: Crawfish, 9″ x 6½″	25.00	35.00	22.50
☐ Crab, 6″ x 5″	25.00	35.00	22.50
☐ Alligator, 9″ x 2¾″	25.00	35.00	22.50
☐ Turtle, 6½″ x 3″	25.00	35.00	22.50
☐ **Cheese basket,** splint	125.00	175.00	100.00
☐ **Cheese shaker,** round, 12″ Dia.	250.00	275.00	225.00
☐ **Chehalis basket,** geometric and cross design, 4¼″ x 6¼″	200.00	250.00	160.00
☐ **Chemehuevi basket,** two concentric geometric bands, 11½″ x 2″	350.00	450.00	375.00
☐ **Clothes basket,** round with two handles	75.00	95.00	62.00
☐ **Cowlitz lidded basket,** 3″ x 4¼″	80.00	130.00	100.00
☐ **Havasupi coiled basket,** triangle design, 11¾″ Dia.	175.00	200.00	150.00
☐ **Hopi coiled basket,** rectangular body in brown, orange and yellow raincloud and thunder motif, 5⅝″	110.00	160.00	125.00
☐ **Hopi corn sifter basket,** wicker with hoop around top, spiral design	80.00	110.00	82.00
☐ **Hopi coiled bowl basket,** floral design, 9¼″ Dia.	90.00	140.00	110.00
☐ **Hopi coiled plaque,** 14½″ Dia., c. 1930	110.00	160.00	125.00
☐ **Hopi tray,** mythological motif, 11″ Dia.	80.00	130.00	100.00
☐ **Japanese,** tightly woven in brown and tan, circular, 7½″ Dia.	55.00	80.00	62.00
☐ **Karok basket,** oval, bottom inverted, 10″ x 7″	110.00	160.00	125.00
☐ **Klamath tray,** 14″ Dia., c. 1900	210.00	260.00	225.00
☐ **Lilooet basket,** 12½″ x 16″	160.00	210.00	175.00
☐ **Maidu basket tray,** 8½″ Dia.	60.00	80.00	65.00
☐ **Makah basket,** zigzag designs, 7″ Dia.	55.00	80.00	62.00
☐ **Mandan basket,** wood splint, circular	180.00	230.00	200.00
☐ **Mission basket tray,** 12″ Dia.	330.00	410.00	360.00
☐ **Miwok basket,** 7″ Dia., c. 1900	230.00	280.00	250.00
☐ **Modoc basketcap,** diamond design, 6″ Dia.	120.00	140.00	125.00
☐ **Navajo wedding basket,** 10″ Dia.	130.00	180.00	150.00
☐ **Nootka whaler's hat,** 10½″ x 10½″	230.00	280.00	250.00
☐ **Paiute coiled basket,** exterior is beaded, 5″ Dia.	180.00	210.00	182.00
☐ **Paiute lidded basket,** 10″ H., c. 1900	90.00	125.00	100.00
☐ **Paiute water jar,** horse-hair handles, 5½″ x 7½″	80.00	110.00	82.00
☐ **Panamint basket,** reverse diamond design, 10½″ x 4″	310.00	410.00	350.00
☐ **Papago basket,** geometric design, 13″ Dia.	80.00	110.00	82.00
☐ **Papago coiled basket,** body woven in dark brown with bands of swastikas, 11⅝″ Dia.	230.00	280.00	250.00
☐ **Papago plaque,** concentric square design, 15″ Dia.	130.00	180.00	150.00

	Current Price Range		Prior Year Average
☐ **Papago waste paper basket,** men and dogs motif, 10″ Dia.	100.00	130.00	110.00
☐ **Pima basket bowl,** 16″ Dia.	260.00	335.00	295.00
☐ **Pima coiled basket,** flat base, flaring body, dark brown with pattern of human figures, 11¼″ Dia.	260.00	360.00	300.00
☐ **Pima coiled basket,** shallow, dark brown with crosses in the field, 9¼″ Dia.	110.00	160.00	125.00
☐ **Pima grain barrel,** geometric design, 11″ Dia.	430.00	530.00	475.00
☐ **Pima plaque,** 11″ Dia.	180.00	230.00	200.00
☐ **Pomo basket,** decorated with feathers, 12″ Dia.	180.00	230.00	200.00
☐ **Sewing basket,** wicker	55.00	80.00	58.00
☐ **Skokomish berry basket,** 7″ x 8″	110.00	135.00	112.50
☐ **Southwest coiled storage basket,** flat base, dark brown with arrow motifs, 27″ H.	730.00	830.00	775.00
☐ **Splint collecting basket,** tightly woven, 8″ x 9″.	55.00	85.00	62.00
☐ **Splint cradle,** hooded, c. early 19th century, 19″ x 8″.	100.00	130.00	110.00
☐ **Splint hickory basket,** open handles	55.00	80.00	58.00
☐ **Splint,** oval, with wooded handles	145.00	195.00	150.00
☐ **Splint,** back pack	65.00	165.00	90.00
☐ **Split,** oak buttocks	55.00	80.00	58.00
☐ **Split,** oak buttocks, large	80.00	160.00	120.00
☐ **Tlingit basket,** geometric design, 6″ Dia.	330.00	380.00	350.00
☐ **Tlingit basket,** 5″ Dia., c. 1880	330.00	380.00	350.00
☐ **Washo basket,** geometric design, 7″	65.00	95.00	75.00
☐ **Washo coiled trinket basket,** red, blue, black and green on white ground, 4¼″ Dia.	110.00	160.00	125.00

BATMAN

This section features only a sampling of Batman items. In order to accurately present the vast amount of information required by serious collectors, a special edition devoted to comic books is published by The House of Collectibles, Inc. This handy, pocket-size guide, *The Official 1985 Price Guide to Comic Books,* features a special Batman section. It is available at bookstores for $3.95. For more in-depth information, consult *The Official 1985 Price Guide to Comic Books and Collectibles* for $10.95.

DESCRIPTION: Batman is one of the early comic strip super heroes.

VARIATIONS: Included among Batman memorabilia are comics, toy cars and toy figures.

ORIGIN: The first Batman comic was published more than 40 years ago, and "Batman" was a popular TV show in the 1960s.

ADDITIONAL TIPS: The listings for comics are in chronological order. The memorabilia section is listed alphabetically. For further information, see *The Official Price Guide to Comic Books and Collectibles*.

	Current Price Range		Prior Year Average
☐ **Bank**, ceramic figure of batman, 7″	30.00	45.00	37.50
☐ **Bank**, ceramic figures of Batman and Robin, c. 1966	65.00	85.00	75.00
☐ **Batbike**, toy, c. 1978	5.00	7.00	6.00
☐ **Batmobile**, toy, c. 1966	5.00	7.00	6.00
☐ **Batmobile and batbike**, Corgi, c. 1968	10.00	15.00	12.50
☐ **Book**, Batman and Robin, hardcover, "From The 30s to the 70s," 7½″ x 10½″, Bonanza, c. 1971 .	12.50	17.50	15.00
☐ **Bookends**, Batman and Robin, 4″ x 7″, c. 1966 .	25.00	50.00	35.00
☐ **Car set**, Corgi, c. 1977	15.00	25.00	20.00
☐ **License plate**, metal, 6″ x 12″, National Periodical Publications, c. 1966	6.00	9.00	7.50

Batman Coloring Book,
Western Publishing Company, Inc.
$4.00-$6.00

BATTLESTAR GALACTICA

TOPIC: Battlestar Galactica was originally a science fiction movie and later a television show. It starred Lorne Greene, Richard Hatch and Dirk Benedict. The story involves a group of humans whose ancestors settled a distant part of the universe. These people are attacked and nearly annihilated by hostile "Cylons" (alien creatures who control an army of robots). The survivors flee in a small fleet of spaceships led by a battlestar (fighting spaceship) called "The Galactica." The fleet's destination is earth. The Cylons are in constant pursuit.

TYPES: Memorabilia from Battlestar Galactica may come in the form of trading cards, toys, posters or other promotional items.

PERIOD: The television show ran in 1978.

COMMENTS: Although Battlestar Galactica experienced a limited run on television, it was popular and collectors still treasure memorabilia from the show.

ADDITIONAL TIPS: For more complete listings, please refer to *The Official Price Guide to Science Fiction and Fantasy Books and Collectibles*, published by the House of Collectibles.

	Current Price Range		Prior Year Average
☐ **Posters**, set of four, small	12.00	15.00	13.50
☐ **Poster**, standard size	10.00	13.00	11.50
☐ **Scripts**, group of four, "The Super Scout" and "The Night the Cyclone Landed," total of 219 pages	42.00	50.00	45.50
☐ **Trading cards**, full set of 132, Topps, 2½" x 3½", 1978	13.00	16.00	14.00
☐ **Trading card**, Topps, A Direct Hit, #116, 2½" x 3½", 1978	.10	.13	.11
☐ **Trading card**, Topps, A Planet in Peril, #101, 2½" x 3½", 1978	.10	.12	.11
☐ **Trading card**, Topps, A World in Flames, 11, 2½" x 3½", 1978	.09	.12	.10
☐ **Trading card**, Topps, Adar's Final Moments, #13, 2½" x 3½", 1978	.10	.12	.11
☐ **Trading card**, Topps, Annihilation of the Human Colonies, #19, 2½" x 3½", 1978	.10	.12	.11
☐ **Trading card**, Topps, An Ovion Warrior, #59, 2½" x 3½", 1978	.10	.12	.11
☐ **Trading card**, Topps, Conferring with Seetol, #55, 2½" x 3½", 1978	.09	.13	.11

	Current Price Range		Prior Year Average
☐ **Trading card,** Topps, Escape from Fiery Death, #57, 2½″ x 3½″, 1978	.09	.12	.10
☐ **Trading card,** Topps, For the Love of Gold Cubits, #7, 2½″ x 3½″, 1978	.10	.13	.11
☐ **Trading card,** Topps, Hitting Outrageously High Notes, #70, 2½″ x 3½″, 1978	.09	.12	.10
☐ **Trading card,** Topps, Landram to the Rescue, #123, 2½″ x 3½″, 1978	.09	.13	.11
☐ **Trading card,** Topps, Night of the Metal Monsters, #90, 2½″ x 3½″, 1978	.09	.12	.11
☐ **Trading card,** Topps, Panic in Caprica Mall, #15, 2½″ x 3½″, 1978	.10	.13	.11
☐ **Trading card,** Topps, Richard Hatch is Captain Apollo, #3, 2½″ x 3½″, 1978	.09	.12	.10
☐ **Trading card,** Topps, The President's Council, #14, 2½″ x 3½″, 1978	.09	.13	.11
☐ **Trading card,** Topps, War of the Wiles, #69, 2½″ x 3½″, 1978	.09	.12	.11
☐ **Trading card,** Topps, Where the Elite Meet, #64, 2½″ x 3½″, 1978	.10	.12	.11

THE BEATLES

This section features only a sampling of Beatles' records. In order to accurately present the vast amount of information required by serious collectors, a special edition devoted to collectible records is published by The House of Collectibles, Inc. This handy pocket-size guide, *The Official 1985 Price Guide to Collectible Records*, features a Beatles section. It is available at bookstores for $3.95. At $9.95, *The Official 1985 Price Guide to Records*, features more than 30,000 prices.

VARIATIONS: There is an unlimited variety of Beatles memorabilia. Records are quite collectible as well as buttons, posters and other souvenir items.

ORIGIN: The Beatles formed in Liverpool, England in the late 50s and early 60s. Band members included Paul McCartney, John Lennon, Ringo Starr and George Harrison. They took America by storm in 1964 when they appeared on the Ed Sullivan Show. Credited with starting the musical British invasion, The Beatles contributed much to rock and roll.

COMMENTS: The Beatles, along with Elvis Presley, are more collected than other recording artists. From the start of Beatlemania, anything Beatle related has become collectible. As the 20th anniversary of the

Beatles arrival in the U.S. is celebrated, Beatle memorabilia should be more sought after than ever before.

ADDITIONAL TIPS: The listings in this section include memorabilia and records. The memorabilia section is listed alphabetically by item. Records are also listed alphabetically by title, followed by whether the record is an LP or a 45, the record company, issue number and other pertinent information.

For further information, refer to *The Official Price Guide to Records*, or *The Official Price Guide to Music Collectibles*.

	Current Price Range		Prior Year Average
☐ **Bandaid Dispenser,** promotional item from "Help"	2.00	5.00	2.75
☐ **Bank,** date register bank, with pictures and signatures, 1964	15.00	30.00	21.00
☐ **Belt buckle,** with "Beatles" and illustrations	60.00	80.00	67.00
☐ **Books,** Beatles Monthly Books, Beat Publications, prices vary according to month	2.00	6.00	3.75
☐ **Book covers,** 20″ x 12½″, color with photos of the Beatles	3.50	7.00	5.00
☐ **Bracelet,** with Beatle picture charms	5.00	15.00	9.00
☐ **Bubble bath,** 8 oz., 1964	9.00	15.00	11.00
☐ **Button,** John Lennon Memorial button, "In Memory of a Great Beatle," 2¼″	.75	1.50	.1.10
☐ **Button,** movie promo, "I've Got My Beatles Movie Tickets, Have You?", 2¼″	.75	1.50	1.10
☐ **Car mascots,** bobbing headed Beatles, set of four	700.00	900.00	780.00
☐ **Card,** autographed wallet photo card, 2½″ x 3″, 1964	.50	1.25	.75
☐ **Cards,** gum cards, set of 65, question and answer series, color, Topps, 1964	45.00	60.00	51.00
☐ **Cards,** gum cards, set of 50, Yellow Submarine, Primrose Confectionary (Britain), 1968	90.00	120.00	105.00
☐ **Card,** individual gum card, question and answer series, color, 1964	.75	1.25	1.00
☐ **Card,** individual gum card, Yellow Submarine, Primrose Confectionary (Britain), 1968	1.25	2.00	1.60
☐ **Cards,** playing cards with picture of group, 1964	3.50	6.00	4.25
☐ **Change purse,** picture of the Beatles, 1964	2.00	4.50	3.00
☐ **Coasters,** set of six plastic coasters with illustrations and words, c. 1960s	25.00	35.00	29.00
☐ **Coloring book,** "Beatles Coloring Book," Saalfield Publishing Co., 1964	50.00	65.00	57.00
☐ **Comb,** John Lennon promotional	.75	1.50	1.05
☐ **Coin,** brass commemorative U.S. visit coin, 1964	6.00	14.00	9.00

	Current Price Range		Prior Year Average
☐ **Dolls,** blow up dolls, 16″, 1966, set of four	40.00	60.00	48.00
☐ **Doll,** John Lennon, fully dressed, base of doll is a radio, 8½″	14.00	25.00	19.00
☐ **Game,** The Beatles Flip Your Wig Game, Milton Bradley, 1964	40.00	55.00	47.00
☐ **Hair brush,** 1964	10.00	15.00	12.00
☐ **Ink stamp,** self inking stamps, set of four, 1964	10.00	20.00	14.00
☐ **Jigsaw puzzle,** for fan club members, not sold in stores, 8½″ x 11″, 1964	6.00	14.00	9.00
☐ **Key fob,** figural, promotional item for 1965 Shea Stadium Concert	.75	1.50	1.05
☐ **Key ring,** John Lennon, "Walls and Bridges" album, 1972	.75	1.50	1.05
☐ **Lunchbox,** laminated tin with color drawings of the Beatles	185.00	200.00	192.00
☐ **Magazine,** *Rolling Stone,* featuring John Lennon as "Man of the Year," 1970	30.00	45.00	37.00

Beatles, *still, if signed would be worth considerably more,* **$1.50-$2.00**

	Current Price Range		Prior Year Average
☐ **Mirror,** black and white picture pocket mirror, features picture of group playing, 1964	.75	1.50	1.05
☐ **Mirror,** color picture of the Beatles, 1964	1.00	3.50	2.00
☐ **Pencil,** picture of Beatles, set of four, 1964	3.00	4.00	3.35
☐ **Pencil case,** picture of Beatles, 1964	5.00	15.00	7.00
☐ **Pen,** magic picture pen, color photo	3.00	5.00	4.00
☐ **Pennant,** felt pennant with "Beatles" in block letters and illustrations of the group	40.00	60.00	48.00
☐ **Pin,** flasher pin flashes from group shot to four heads	1.50	3.00	2.10
☐ **Pin,** "I Like Beatles" flasher pin	1.00	2.00	1.40
☐ **Pin,** "I'm a Beatles Booster," 1965	.75	1.50	1.05
☐ **Pin,** John Lennon "Give Peace a Chance"	.75	1.50	1.05
☐ **Pin,** John Lennon "Remember Love," 1¼"	.75	1.50	1.05
☐ **Pin,** official fan pin, 2¼", 1965	.75	1.50	1.05
☐ **Pin,** tin litho picture of Beatles, 1964	.75	1.50	1.05
☐ **Pin,** Yellow Submarine, 1966	.75	1.50	1.05
☐ **Pocketbook,** canvas, illustrated with "Beatles" and pictures	40.00	50.00	44.00
☐ **Pocket knife,** John Lennon, "In Memory of a Great Beatle," 1980	1.00	3.00	2.00
☐ **Poster,** Beatles at London Paladium, full color, 20" x 27", 1963, reissued in 1975	1.00	3.00	2.00
☐ **Poster,** fan club souvenir poster, full color, 20" x 30", 1968	175.00	225.00	200.00
☐ **Poster,** features 12 full color Beatles photos, 24" x 28", 1979	1.50	3.50	2.00
☐ **Poster,** John Lennon commemorative, 1980 . . .	1.00	3.00	2.00
☐ **Poster,** John Lennon, "Imagine There's No Lennon," 17" x 25", 1980	1.00	3.50	2.00
☐ **Poster,** record shop poster advertising "A Hard Day's Night"	175.00	210.00	188.00
☐ **Press kit,** Paul McCartney, Apple, 1970	60.00	80.00	66.00
☐ **Press kit,** Paul McCartney and Wings, 1973	80.00	110.00	93.00
☐ **Program,** George Harrison, 1974 concert tour program	3.50	7.00	5.00
☐ **Record fob,** metal with faces of the Beatles, 1964	.75	1.50	1.05
☐ **Ring,** individual color flasher ring, set of four . .	.75	1.50	1.05
☐ **Ruler,** 12", with signatures, photos and information, 1965	3.00	5.00	4.00
☐ **Scarf,** colored with pictures and signatures, 1964	5.00	12.00	8.00
☐ **Strap,** for carrying schoolbooks, features "Beatles" with musical notes	15.00	20.00	17.00
☐ **Tablecloth,** printed with illustrations of the Beatles	60.00	85.00	67.00

	Current Price Range		Prior Year Average
☐ **Tickets,** concert tickets	40.00	55.00	47.00
☐ **Tie tack,** official fan club item, black and gold, 1964	1.50	3.00	2.25
☐ **Tie tack,** raised figural face, set of four, 1964 . .	8.00	16.00	11.00
☐ **Whistle,** police style from the movie "Help," 1966	1.50	4.00	2.75
☐ **Wig,** long hair Beatles wig	30.00	45.00	37.00
☐ **Wrist watch,** full color picture on dial	15.00	25.00	19.00
☐ **Writing tablet,** cover photo of the Beatles	25.00	45.00	34.00

RECORDS

	Current Price Range		Prior Year Average
☐ **Abbey Road,** LP, Apple, 383, stereo	8.00	20.00	10.00
☐ **All You Need Is Love/Baby You're A Rich Man,** 45, Capitol, 5964, promotional copy	35.00	80.00	42.00
☐ Orange label	2.00	4.50	3.00
☐ **And I Love Her/If I Fell,** 45, Capitol, 5235, orange label	2.00	4.50	3.25
☐ Picture sleeve	11.00	25.00	13.00
☐ **The Beatles,** LP, Apple, 101, stereo	13.00	30.00	19.00
☐ **The Early Beatles,** LP, Capitol, 2309, stereo, green label	7.00	13.00	9.00
☐ Black label	7.50	15.00	9.50
☐ **Eight Days A Week/I Don't Want To Spoil The Party,** 45, Capitol, 5371, orange label	2.00	4.50	3.00
☐ **From Me To You/Please Please Me,** 45, Vee Jay, 581, picture sleeve with label name in brackets	50.00	110.00	70.00
☐ **A Hard Day's Night/I Should Have Known Better,** 45, Capitol, 5222, orange label	2.00	4.50	3.25
☐ Picture sleeve	9.00	20.00	12.00
☐ **Hey Jude/Revolution,** 45, Apple, 2276	3.00	6.50	4.00
☐ **Let It Be,** LP, Apple, 3401, stereo	4.00	9.00	6.00
☐ **The Long and Winding Road/For You Blue,** 45, Apple, 2832	2.50	5.50	3.50
☐ Picture sleeve	8.50	21.00	10.00
☐ **Magical Mystery Tour,** LP, Apple, 2853, stereo .	6.00	13.00	8.00
☐ **Meet The Beatles,** LP, Apple, 2047, stereo	4.00	9.00	6.00
☐ **Meet The Beatles,** LP, Capitol, 2047, stereo, green label	7.00	13.00	9.00
☐ Black label	8.00	23.00	10.00
☐ **Please Please Me/Ask Me Why,** 45, Vee Jay, 498, Beatles is misspelled, "Beattles," and it is in thick letters	130.00	275.00	150.00
☐ **Revolver,** LP, Apple, 2576, stereo	5.00	11.00	7.00
☐ **Rubber Soul,** LP, Apple, 2442, stereo	5.00	11.00	7.00
☐ **Sergeant Pepper's Lonely Hearts Club Band,** LP, Apple, 2652, stereo	5.00	11.00	7.00

	Current Price Range		Prior Year Average
☐ **Twist And Shout/There's A Place**, 45, Capitol Starline, 6061	8.00	20.00	11.00
☐ **Yellow Submarine**, LP, Apple, 153, stereo	4.00	9.00	6.00
☐ **Yesterday/Act Naturally**, 45, Apple, 5498	2.50	5.50	3.50

BEER CANS

This section features only a sampling of collectible beer cans. In order to accurately present the vast amount of information required by serious collectors, a special edition devoted to beer cans is published by The House of Collectibles, Inc. This handy pocket-size guide, *The Official 1985 Price Guide to Beer Cans and Collectibles,* features more than 6,500 prices for all types of beer cans. It is available at bookstores for $3.95.

DESCRIPTION: Beer cans are highly collectible items. Beer cans were produced in different shapes, including flat tops, cone tops and pull tabs.

PERIOD: Cans were first produced by breweries in 1935. The first cans were called flat tops because of the shape of the can top. Cone tops were not as popular with consumers, and their production was stopped by the 1960s. Today, cans with pull tabs are produced.

ADDITIONAL TIPS: Hobbyists collect full cans, empties or unfinished cans called flats. See *The Official Price Guide to Beer Cans,* published by the House of Collectibles for more detailed information about this subject.

CONE TOPS

☐ **Altes Lager**, Tivoli, 12 oz., silver and black -CROWNTAINER	40.00	50.00	45.00
☐ **American**, American, 12 oz., red, white, blue and gold, brand name in blue script lettering .	100.00	125.00	112.00
☐ **Bavarian's Old Style**, Bavarian, 12 oz., white, gold and red, brand name in gold lettering (very ornate) with red initials	70.00	85.00	77.00
☐ **Beverwyck Ale**, Beverwyck, 12 oz., red, white and green	105.00	130.00	117.00
☐ **Beverwyck Famous**, Beverwyck, 12 oz., silver, red and bluish green, brand name in red	50.00	65.00	57.00
☐ **Pilser's Original Extra Dry Ale**, Metropolis, 12 oz., blue and white	330.00	400.00	375.00
☐ **Regent Premium**, Century, 32 oz., pink and red, slogan "Brewery Fresh"	350.00	415.00	382.00

	Current Price Range		Prior Year Average
☐ **Red Fox Premium,** Largay, 12 oz., red and yellow, brand name in red, illustration of fox carrying two glasses on tray	785.00	920.00	867.00
☐ **Royal Bru,** Union, 12 oz., purple and white, large eagle, brand name in white, "Beer" in purple	660.00	775.00	717.00
☐ **Salute Lager,** Rainier, 12 oz., light green and dark green, scenic vignette at top	800.00	950.00	875.00
☐ **Scheidt Ram's Head Ale,** Scheidt, 32 oz.	425.00	525.00	475.00
☐ **Schlitz Lager,** Schlitz, 12 oz., blue and white, slogan "The Beer that Made Milwaukee Famous," word "Beer" in larger lettering than rest of slogan	450.00	550.00	500.00
☐ **Schmidt's Cream Ale,** Schmidt, 12 oz., silver and cream white, illustration of tiger	275.00	330.00	302.00

Cone Top, Eastside Beer,
*Los Angeles Brewing Co.,
12 oz.,* **$35.00-$45.00**

*(photo courtesy of
©Rogalski Brothers,
Gainesville, FL, 1984)*

	Current Price Range		Prior Year Average

☐ **Standard Sparkling Ale,** Standard, 12 oz., orange with brand name in white on black banner **265.00** **325.00** **295.00**

FLAT TOPS

☐ **A-1 Pilsner,** Arizona, 12 oz., white with "A-1" in block characters within gold frame **37.00** **45.00** **41.00**

☐ **A-1 Pilsner,** Arizona, 12 oz., white and red, oval medallion with white lettering on red background **52.00** **65.00** **58.50**

☐ **Banner Extra Dry,** Cumberland, 12 oz., white and red, "Premium Beer" in blue **15.00** **20.00** **17.50**

☐ **Bantam,** Goebel, 8 oz. squat, white and dark green **26.00** **33.00** **29.50**

☐ **Drewry's Trophy,** Drewry, 12 oz., orange, white, black and red **48.00** **60.00** **54.00**

☐ **Duquesne Can-O-Beer,** Duquesne, 12 oz., white and red, illustration of man holding beer in raised right hand **33.00** **42.00** **37.50**

☐ **Duquesne Pilsener,** Duquesne, 12 oz., white, red and gold, man holding beer, white background on can with thin horizontal stripes .. **18.00** **23.00** **21.00**

☐ **Durst,** Atlantic, 12 oz., cream white and blue, canned at Chicago **70.00** **90.00** **80.00**

☐ **Durst,** Best, 12 oz., cream white and blue ... **48.00** **62.00** **55.00**

☐ **Falls City,** Falls City, 12 oz., red, white and gold, white is the predominant color on the front of the can **9.00** **11.75** **10.37**

☐ **Falstaff,** Falstaff, 12 oz., white, yellow and gold, gold band at bottom of can only **6.75** **9.00** **7.87**

☐ **Falstaff,** Falstaff, 12 oz., brown and gold, brand name in large lettering **19.75** **23.50** **21.57**

☐ **Falstaff,** Falstaff, 12 oz., white, yellow and gold, thin gold band at top and bottom of can **8.00** **11.00** **9.50**

☐ **Gettelman,** Gettelman, 12 oz., brown and white, brand name in white script lettering against brown flask **20.00** **25.00** **22.50**

☐ **Gettelman,** Gettelman, 12 oz., white and green, brand name in red at top, caricature illustration of smiling face **10.00** **14.00** **12.00**

☐ **Highlander Premium,** Missoula, 12 oz., red and white, white portion of can has slight greyish tinge (revised version) **13.00** **16.50** **14.75**

☐ **Hillman's Export,** Best, 12 oz., brown and black, grained effect **50.00** **65.00** **57.50**

	Current Price Range		Prior Year Average
☐ **Hillman's Superb,** Empire, 12 oz., blue and gold	62.00	78.00	69.00
☐ **Hillman's Superb,** United States Brewing, 12 oz., blue and gold	60.00	75.00	67.50
☐ **Hofbrau,** Hofbrau, 12 oz., cream white and red, illustration of German village inn	16.00	21.00	19.00
☐ **Miller Select,** Miller, 12 oz., red, white and blue, quarter-moon emblem in blue medallion	50.00	65.00	57.50
☐ **Milwaukee's Best,** Gettelman, 12 oz., blue and white, illustration of stein	16.00	21.00	19.00
☐ **Milwaukee Premium,** Waukee, 12 oz., white, red and gold	13.00	18.00	15.00
☐ **Mitchell's Premium,** Mitchell, 12 oz., red, white and blue	82.00	100.00	91.00
☐ **Old Milwaukee,** Schlitz, 12 oz., gold and red, scene within rectangular frame	25.00	33.00	29.00
☐ **Old Milwaukee,** Schlitz, 12 oz., red and white, dark printing on shield symbol	5.00	7.00	6.00
☐ **Pabst Blue Ribbon,** Pabst, 12 oz., red, white and blue	5.75	7.25	6.50
☐ **Pabst Blue Ribbon,** Pabst, 12 oz., gold, white and blue, slogan above gold band at bottom	7.00	9.50	8.50
☐ **Pabst Blue Ribbon,** Pabst, 12 oz., gold, white and blue, slogan on gold band at bottom	7.00	9.50	8.50
☐ **Pfeiffer's,** Pfeiffer, 12 oz., gold, white and red, horizontal striping	8.00	11.00	9.50
☐ **Pickwick Ale,** Haffenreffer, 12 oz., gold, black and white	100.00	130.00	115.00
☐ **Piel's,** Piel's, 12 oz., gold, silver and black, brand name in white	10.00	13.75	11.67
☐ **Schlitz,** Schlitz, 12 oz., white and brown, in slogan "The Beer That Made Milwaukee Famous," the word "Beer" is in larger lettering than the other words, and the entire slogan is printed in dark grey	5.00	6.25	5.75
☐ **Schlitz,** Schlitz, 12 oz., white and brown, in slogan "The Beer That Made Milwaukee Famous," the word "Beer" is in the same size lettering as the other words	8.00	11.00	9.50

PULL TABS

☐ **A-1 Light Pilsner,** National, 12 oz., cream white and brown	.40	.60	.50
☐ **ABC Premium,** Garden State, 16 oz., dark red and white	2.50	3.25	2.87

	Current Price Range		Prior Year Average
☐ **ABC Premium,** Wagner, 12 oz., red and white, "AGED" in rectangular frame	1.75	2.50	2.12
☐ **ABC Premium Ale,** Eastern, 12 oz., dark green with "AGED" in rectangular frame	.85	1.20	1.02
☐ **Ballantine Ale,** Falstaff, 16 oz.	1.25	1.65	1.45
☐ **Budweiser Malt Liquor,** Anheuser-Busch, 16 oz.	10.00	13.25	11.62
☐ **Buffalo,** Blitz Weinhard, 12 oz., light brown with illustration of buffalo	1.00	1.50	1.25
☐ **Busch Bavarian,** Anheuser-Busch, 12 oz., white and blue, snow-covered mountains, no clouds in background	1.75	2.50	2.12
☐ **Busch Bavarian,** Anheuser-Busch, 12 oz., white and blue, snow-covered mountains, no clouds in background, does not read "Tab Top," brand name encircled by thin red frame	. 40	.60	.50
☐ **Carling's Black Label,** Carling, 12 oz., red and black, brand name within tilted medallion, "Carling" in red within medallion, coat-of-arms in gold, gold band at top	.50	.70	.60
☐ **Carling's Tuborg,** Carling, 12 oz., dark gold and dark red	.40	.60	.50
☐ **Cascade,** Blitz Weinhard, 12 oz., blue and white, brand name in white on blue background	1.85	2.50	2.17
☐ **Cascade,** Blitz Weinhard, 16 oz., does not state "King Size"	2.00	2.50	2.25
☐ **Cascade,** Blitz Weinhard, 16 oz., states "King Size" near top	11.00	15.00	13.00
☐ **Cee Bee,** Colonial, 12 oz., white and red	10.00	13.25	11.62
☐ **Champale Malt Liquor,** Champale, 12 oz., green and white, canned at Norfolk, Virginia .	10.00	13.25	11.62
☐ **Champagne Velvet,** Heilman, 12 oz., pale blue and gold, brand name in blue lettering with red initial letters, can design forms champagne glass	.45	.65	.55
☐ **Genesee,** Genesee, 12 oz., red white, "A Little More Exciting" in black	2.50	3.25	2.87
☐ **Hamm's Draft,** Hamm, 12 oz., silver, can is shaped as beer keg with ribbing	1.85	2.50	2.17
☐ **Hamm's Preferred Stock,** Hamm, 12 oz., white and black, illustration of city scene	1.85	2.50	2.17
☐ **Hamm's Preferred stock,** Olympia, 12 oz., white and black, illustration of city scene . . .	1.00	1.50	1.25
☐ **Hampden,** Hampden Harvard, 12 oz., white and blue	.80	1.10	.95

	Current Price Range		Prior Year Average

	Current Price Range		Prior Year Average
☐ **Highlander,** Rheinlander, 12 oz., white and blue, foaming glass at center, wide silver stripe at bottom	.85	1.15	.98
☐ **High Life,** Miller, 12 oz., gold, white and red	.40	.60	.50
☐ **Hof-Brau,** General, 12 oz., red and white, brand name in grey-blue lettering	2.50	3.25	2.87
☐ **Hof-Brau,** General, 12 oz., red and white, brand name in bright blue lettering, bright blue frame around medallion	.85	1.15	1.00
☐ **Lucky Red Carpet,** General, 12 oz., red and white	.90	1.20	1.05
☐ **Maier Select,** Maier, 12 oz., red, white and blue, blue leaf near top	4.00	6.00	5.00
☐ **Malt Duck Grape,** National, 12 oz., purple and white	35.00	45.00	40.00
☐ **Manheim,** Reading, 12 oz., red and white	8.00	11.00	9.50
☐ **Mark Meister Premium Lager,** Eastern, 12 oz., blue and white	5.00	7.00	6.00
☐ **Mark V,** Pittsburgh, 12 oz., red, white and blue, brand name in black	1.75	2.35	2.05
☐ **Mark V,** Pittsburgh, 12 oz., red, white and blue, brand name in blue	.65	.85	.75
☐ **Miller High Life,** Miller, 12 oz., gold, white and red	.40	.60	.50
☐ **Old Crown,** Old Crown, 12 oz., white and red, without symbol (figure of man)	.90	1.20	1.05
☐ **Old Crown,** Old Crown, 12 oz., white and red, with symbol (figure of man)	2.00	2.50	2.25
☐ **Old Crown Bock,** Old Crown, 12 oz., brown and white, illustration of ram's head	1.75	2.50	2.12
☐ **Pabst Blue Ribbon Bock,** Pabst, 12 oz., white, red and blue, two ram heads in red at top	4.00	5.00	4.50
☐ **Pabst's Eastside,** Pabst, 16 oz., large "16" near top, does not state "Hall Quart"	2.00	2.75	2.37
☐ **Pabst Old Tankard Ale,** Pabst, 12 oz., gold, white and red, illustration of man with shield and stein	3.50	4.25	3.87
☐ **Padre Pale Lager,** General, 12 oz., various shades of brown, illustration of padre mission	2.00	2.75	2.37
☐ **Pearl Lager,** Pearl, 12 oz., white and red with pictorial illustration of stream and mountains	5.00	7.00	6.00
☐ **Schell,** Schell, 12 oz., black, illustration of moose head against silver background	.40	.60	.50
☐ **Schell,** Schell, 12 oz., white, light brown and dark brown	12.00	16.00	14.00

	Current Price Range		Prior Year Average
☐ **Schell,** Schell, 12 oz., black and multicolors, illustration of moose head, reads "It's a Good Old Beer" in pink lettering	1.85	2.20	2.02
☐ **Schell,** Schell, 12 oz., black and multicolors, illustration of moose head, reads "It's a Good Ole Beer" in white lettering	1.75	2.10	1.92
☐ **Schlitz,** Schlitz, 10 oz., white and maroon	.60	.85	.72
☐ **Standard Dry Ale,** Standard Rochester, 12 oz., blue, white and gold	3.75	4.75	4.25
☐ **Stegmaier Bock,** Stegmaier, 12 oz., brown and white, slogan "Truly Brewed"	1.00	1.50	1.25
☐ **Stegmaier Gold Medal,** Stegmaier, 12 oz., gold and white	.90	1.20	1.05
☐ **Winchester Malt Liquor,** Walter, 12 oz., pale blue	4.50	5.75	5.12
☐ **Winchester Malt Liquor,** Walter, 16 oz.	12.00	16.00	14.00
☐ **Wisconsin Club Premium Pilsner,** Huber, 12 oz., white and gold, brand name in white	1.00	1.35	1.17

BELLS

TOPIC: Bells have been used for thousands of years to signal important events such as births, weddings, enemy attacks and holidays.

TYPES: Bells can be divided into many categories, including closed and open mouth bells, figurine bells, jingle bells, chimes and gongs.

PERIODS: Bells have existed for thousands of years, although they were introduced to Europe about 1500 years ago.

MATERIALS: Brass, iron, silver, gold, bronze, wood, glass and porcelain are frequently used to make bells.

COMMENTS: Bells are very popular among collectors because of their interesting shapes and musical qualities.

☐ **Alaska bell,** colored totem handle, original	42.00	58.00	48.00
☐ **Alexander's helmet bell,** no clapper, 5½ " Dia. .	13.00	18.00	14.00
☐ **Bayreuther bell,** hand painted porcelain, lilies of the valley	72.00	92.00	80.00
☐ **Brass bell,** stork	34.00	50.00	38.00
☐ **Brass clapper bell**	110.00	130.00	112.50
☐ **Brass dinner bell**	8.00	12.00	7.50
☐ **Brass hotel call bell,** 4 " Dia.	50.00	65.00	52.00
☐ **Brass musical chime bell**	32.00	68.00	42.00
☐ **Brass school bell,** 4⅞ " Dia., c. 1910	20.00	28.00	21.00

	Current Price Range		Prior Year Average
☐ **Brass bell,** wooden handle, 4"	12.00	18.00	12.50
☐ **Brass bell,** wooden handle, 6"	18.00	22.00	20.00
☐ **Brass bell,** wooden handle, 7"	28.00	38.00	30.00
☐ **Brass bell,** wooden handle, 8"	28.00	38.00	30.00
☐ **Bronze art figurine bells,** very detailed, rare ...	210.00	360.00	275.00
☐ **Bronze bell,** angel holder	95.00	115.00	100.00
☐ **Cast iron bell,** mechanical	130.00	160.00	138.00
☐ **Charlie Chaplin bell,** solid brass, cane and typical pose	18.00	22.00	17.50
☐ **China bell,** cobalt, 5"	50.00	63.00	52.00
☐ **China bell,** German, painted clown	68.00	82.00	72.00
☐ **Chinese brass gong bell,** 9"	45.00	60.00	48.00
☐ **Church bell,** solid brass, single tier	110.00	135.00	112.50
☐ **Church bell,** solid brass, triple tier	180.00	220.00	195.00
☐ **Church bell,** old, 1100 pounds	575.00	675.00	600.00
☐ **Church bell,** without wheel	130.00	160.00	138.00
☐ **Conestoga,** graduated on strap (4), brass	210.00	260.00	225.00
☐ **Cow bell,** iron ring with strap attachment	32.00	48.00	38.00
☐ **Cow bell,** leather collar	12.00	16.00	12.50
☐ **Cow bell,** clapper	28.00	38.00	30.00
☐ **Cow bells,** hand riveted	28.00	38.00	30.00
☐ **Crystal bell,** faceted drummer boy handle, Blair-Reubel	35.00	50.00	38.00
☐ **Cutter bells,** 4 bells, 2½" - 2¾" Dia.	45.00	60.00	48.00
☐ **Cutter-type bell,** iron strap	80.00	110.00	82.00
☐ **Damascus bell,** bronze, inlaid gold and green leaves with red berries	55.00	75.00	60.00
☐ **Dinner bell,** crystal	55.00	75.00	60.00
☐ **Dinner bell,** enamel on metal	55.00	75.00	60.00
☐ **Dinner bell,** nickel	13.00	17.00	12.50
☐ **Dinner bell,** ornate sterling silver	65.00	90.00	72.00
☐ **Dog bells,** sculptured handles, pair, 4"	80.00	110.00	87.50
☐ **Doorbell,** Abbe's patent double strike	35.00	50.00	38.00
☐ **Doorbell,** brass	55.00	75.00	60.00
☐ **Early American thumbprint bell,** design around skirt	50.00	65.00	48.00
☐ **Elephant bell,** brass	45.00	60.00	48.00
☐ **Elephant bell,** cloisonne	110.00	130.00	112.00
☐ **Fire Alarm bell**	48.00	58.00	48.00
☐ **French flint glass bell,** coordinated handle and clapper	420.00	495.00	430.00
☐ **Glass bell,** amber, glass	120.00	185.00	112.00
☐ **Glass bell,** bristol, 11½"	120.00	185.00	112.00
☐ **Glass bell,** bristol wedding bell, 14"	130.00	160.00	138.00
☐ **Glass bell,** carnival	18.00	22.00	17.50
☐ **Glass bell,** cranberry glass, clear handle	160.00	200.00	170.00
☐ **Mission bell,** min. clapper	80.00	110.00	82.00

	Current Price Range		Prior Year Average
☐ **Mission bell**, Spanish	110.00	135.00	112.50
☐ **Pewter sterling bell**	22.00	32.00	25.00
☐ **Pressed glass bell**, smokey	6.00	12.00	7.50
☐ **Quimper lady bell**, colored, 8″	75.00	95.00	80.00
☐ **Roeland Ghend**, bronze, sand cast, crusade handle	65.00	85.00	70.00
☐ **Saddle chimes**, set of 3 with pinwheel on each	145.00	175.00	150.00
☐ **School bell**, bronze, 20″ iron yoke, Jones and Hitchcock, c. 1856	860.00	960.00	900.00
☐ **School bell**, metal, wooden handles, small	80.00	110.00	82.00
☐ **School bell**, metal, wooden handle, large	90.00	110.00	90.00
☐ **School bell**, 5″	50.00	65.00	52.00
☐ **School bell**, 6½″	72.00	92.00	80.00
☐ **School bell**, 8¼″	95.00	115.00	100.00
☐ **School bell**, 9½″	95.00	115.00	100.00
☐ **Sculptured bell**, lady 4″	55.00	75.00	60.00
☐ **Sculptured bell**, little boy on a coal pile, original clapper, detailed	155.00	190.00	170.00
☐ **Sculptured bell**, old woman on the green from "Canterbury Tales", detailed	110.00	160.00	125.00
☐ **Sheep bell**	55.00	75.00	60.00
☐ **Ship bell**, brass, c. 1845	210.00	260.00	235.00
☐ **Ship bell**, brass dolphin	225.00	250.00	235.00
☐ **Silver-plated bell**, wooden handle, 7″ H.	40.00	50.00	45.00
☐ **Silver-plated call bell**, foot operated, embossed trim, 36″ H.	80.00	92.00	85.00
☐ **Sleigh bells**, leather strap of 17 bells	210.00	260.00	225.00
☐ **Sleigh bells**, leather strap of 20 bells	260.00	285.00	262.00
☐ **Sleigh bells**, iron string of 25 bells	280.00	330.00	300.00
☐ **Sleigh bells**, brass string of 25 bells	230.00	280.00	250.00
☐ **Sleigh bells**, all brass, 29 bells mounted on a jointed brass strap, old	170.00	205.00	178.00
☐ **Soldier**, roman	55.00	75.00	60.00
☐ **Sterling silver bell**, Reed & Barton, "Pointed Antique"	25.00	32.00	29.00
☐ **Sterling silver bell**, twisted handle, engraved scroll design	30.00	36.00	33.00
☐ **Sterling silver bell**, woman	120.00	150.00	132.00
☐ **Swedish bell**, heavy brass, double throated, 2¾″ Dia.	20.00	26.00	20.50
☐ **Swedish bell**, heavy brass, triple throated, 3″ Dia.	22.00	32.00	25.00
☐ **Town Crier**, long with wooden handle	110.00	135.00	112.50
☐ **Trolley car**, 8″ Dia.	80.00	110.00	82.00
☐ **Turtle**, German mechanical	80.00	110.00	82.00
☐ **Waterford crystal bell**	60.00	80.00	65.00
☐ **Wedgwood**, porcelain, c. 1979	30.00	40.00	30.00

BICENTENNIAL

DESCRIPTION: The bicentennial, celebrated on July 4, 1976, was the 200th birthday of the United States as an independent nation. It was on July 4, 1776 that the Declaration of Independence was signed in Philadelphia, PA and the U.S. declared its freedom from England.

PERIOD: Bicentennial memorabilia was produced from the early 1970s until 1976.

COMMENTS: A variety of bicentennial commemoratives were made, from inexpensive trinkets to fine plates and silver.

ADDITIONAL TIPS: The listings are alphabetical by item. Other information includes, when possible, a description of the item, manufacturer, country of manufacture, production quantity and date. The first price listed is the issue price of the item; the second price is the current value of the item.

For more information on bicentennial memorabilia refer to *The Official Price Guide to Collector Plates* and *The Official Price Guide to American Silver and Silver Plate.*

	Current Price Range		Prior Year Average
☐ **Knife,** The American Eagle Bicentennial Series, commemorative set of five knives, handcrafted, solid nickel silver bolsters, brass linings, stainless steel blades	160.00	190.00	5.00
☐ **Medal,** July 4, 1976, set of 12, sterling silver, 39 mm., Franklin Mint, U.S., production quantity 4,675, 1976 . . . . each	20.00	40.00	30.00
☐ . . . . set	240.00	300.00	270.00
☐ **Medal,** sterling silver, 64 mm., Franklin Mint, U.S., production quantity 18,849, 1975-1976 . .	75.00	100.00	87.00
☐ **Medal,** sterling silver, 32 mm., Franklin Mint, U.S., production quantity 238,192, 1976	12.00	25.00	19.00
☐ **Medal,** thirteen original states, set of 13 medals, sterling silver, 39 mm., Franklin Mint, U.S., production quantity, 10,264 . . . . . . each	19.00	20.00	19.50
☐ . . . . set	247.00	300.00	273.00
☐ **Plate,** Across the Delaware, Wedgwood, Great Britain, 1975	45.00	86.00	65.50
☐ **Plate,** Boston Tea Party, silver, Gorham Collection, U.S., production quantity 750, 1973 . .	550.00	625.00	587.00
☐ **Plate,** Burning of the Gaspee, pewter, Gorham Collection, U.S., production quantity 5,000, 1971	35.00	38.00	36.50
☐ **Plate,** Calm Before the Storm, Armstrong's, U.S., production quantity 250, 1971	250.00	275.00	262.00

	Current Price Range		Prior Year Average
☐ **Plate,** Constellation, Kirk, U.S., production quantity 825, 1972	75.00	80.00	77.50
☐ **Plate,** Crossing the Delaware, Stieff, U.S., production quantity 10,000, 1975	50.00	53.00	51.50
☐ **Plate,** The Declaration, Castleton China, U.S., production quantity 7,600, 1973	60.00	62.00	61.00
☐ **Plate,** The Declaration, porcelain, scalloped border, 9¾", Haviland, France, production quantity 10,000, 1976	39.95	48.00	44.00
☐ **Plate,** Declaration Signed, Wedgwood, Great Britain, 1976	45.00	60.00	52.00
☐ **Plate,** E. Pluribus Unum, Bing and Grondahl, Denmark, 1976	50.00	55.00	52.50
☐ **Plate,** Eagle, blue satin glass, Fenton Art Glass, U.S., 1974	15.00	28.00	21.00
☐ **Plate,** Eagle, chocolate glass, Fenton Art Glass, U.S., 1976	17.50	30.00	24.50
☐ **Plate,** Eagle, red satin glass, Fenton Art Glass, U.S., 1975	15.00	28.00	21.00
☐ **Plate,** Eagle, white satin glass, Fenton Art Glass, U.S., 1976	15.00	28.00	21.00
☐ **Plate,** First in War, Ridgewood, U.S., production quantity 12,500, 1974	40.00	42.00	41.00
☐ **Plate,** Gaspee Incident, Armstrong's, U.S., production quantity 175, 1972	250.00	265.00	257.00
☐ **Plate,** Independence Hall, Bayel of France, France, production quantity 500, 1975	60.00	63.00	61.50
☐ **Plate,** John Hancock Signs the Declaration of Independence, sterling silver, bas-relief, 24kt gold inlaid and electro plated, 8", Franklin Mint, U.S., production quantity 10,166, 1976	175.00	210.00	192.00
☐ **Plate,** Liberty Bell, Bayel of France, France, production quantity 500, 1974	50.00	52.00	51.00
☐ **Plate,** Monticello, damascene silver, Reed and Barton, U.S., production quantity 1,000, 1972	75.00	80.00	77.50
☐ **Plate,** Mt. Vernon, damascene silver, Reed and Barton, U.S., 1973	75.00	80.00	77.50
☐ **Plate,** A New Dawn, Castleton China, U.S., production quantity 7,600, 1972	60.00	62.00	61.00
☐ **Plate,** One Nation, Castleton China, U.S., production quantity 7,600, 1974	60.00	62.00	61.00
☐ **Plate,** Paul Revere, porcelain, scalloped border, 9¾", Haviland, France, production quantity 10,000, 1975	39.95	53.00	45.00

BLACK MEMORABILIA

DESCRIPTION: A wide variety of items depicting blacks was produced from 1900 to 1960. Many were advertising promotions featuring Uncle Remus and Aunt Jemima type characters. Figural mammy kitchenware, slavery postcards, cast iron banks and doorstops, chalkware statues, dolls, figurines, etc., were very popular.

COMMENTS: Many of these items were extremely derogatory in nature and depicted blacks as slovenly and ignorant. The civil rights movement of the 1960s put an end to the production of racist depictions of blacks.

	Current Price Range		Year Average
☐ **Bank,** Aunt Jemima, cast iron, 8″	8.00	10.00	
☐ **Bell,** Mammy, bisque, red and yellow dress with white apron, holding mixing bowl	4.00	5.00	4.50
☐ **Booklet,** advertising, Excelsier Improved Varnish, 1940s, cover depicts black boy, read "Won't Turn White," eight pages long .	1.00	2.00	1.50
☐ **Broom Holder,** Mammy, cast iron	140.00	145.00	142.00
☐ **Button,** advertising, black boy holding raccoon, Two Coons Axle Grease, color, 2¼″ . .	1.00	2.00	1.50
☐ **Button,** advertising, Black Man, Georgia Cane Syrup, color, 2¼″	1.00	1.50	1.25
☐ **Button,** advertising, Pickaninny Girl with Watermelon, color, 2¼″	1.00	1.50	1.25
☐ **Candy Box,** Amos n' Andy	75.00	80.00	77.00
☐ **Cookie Jar,** Mammy, bisque, very colorful, 9½″	15.50	18.50	16.50
☐ **Cookie Jar,** Mammy, Rockingham Pottery, lid is on belly, brown and red with white trim, 9″	16.50	18.50	17.00
☐ **Doll,** Aunt Jemima Pancake Flour, cloth, uncut	65.00	70.00	67.00
☐ **Doll,** baby, bisque, jointed arms and legs, three braided pigtails, red polka dot dress, 3½″	5.00	6.00	5.00
☐ **Doll,** Bye-Lo Baby, black bisque head, arms and legs, lace trimmed gown and bonnet, 11″	9.00	11.00	10.00
☐ **Doll,** girl, bisque, jointed arms and legs, three braided pigtails, red polka dot dress, 6″	7.00	8.00	7.50
☐ **Doll,** Mammy, bisque head, arms, legs, stuffed body, fully dressed in colorful outfit with apron and bandana 16″	11.00	15.00	12.00

	Current Price Range		Prior Year Average
☐ **Doll,** Mammy, rag, Mammy flips over to Southern Belle doll, 14″	6.50	8.50	7.50
☐ **Doll,** Uncle Mose, cloth, uncut	65.00	70.00	67.00
☐ **Fugurine,** Black Boy Eating Watermelon, bisque, colorful, 2″	.250	3.50	2.75
☐ **Figurine,** Black Boy on Potty, bisque, dressed in yellow nightgown and red night cap, holding a slice of watermelon	4.00	6.00	4.75
☐ **Figurines,** set of five, New Orleans Jazz Band, bisque, five musicians dressed in tuxedos playing banjo, clarinet, horn, saxophone and drums, 3″	17.00	20.00	18.50
☐ **Kewpie,** vinyl, Rose O'Neill wings, 4½″	1.50	2.50	1.75
☐ **Label** cane syrup, Uncle Remus, 1924, stone lithograph, says "Dis' Sho' Am Good," 6¾″ x 2″	8.00	8.50	8.25
☐ **Mirror,** advertising, Merrick Thread, depicts black boy hanging by thread over open mouthed alligator, saying "Fooled Dis Time Cully Dis Cotton Ain't Gwine To Break," 2″ x 3″	1.50	2.50	1.75
☐ **Mirror,** Aunt Jemima, round, color	1.00	1.50	1.25
☐ **Oven Paddle,** Mammy, wooden, full color picture of Mammy 15½″	2.50	4.50	2.75
☐ **Pail,** peanut butter, pickaninny	20.00	25.00	22.00
☐ **Pin Back,** Aunt Jemima, color, 2¼″	1.00	1.50	1.25
☐ **Postcards,** set of twelve, shows different scenes of slavery, color	6.00	8.00	6.50
☐ **Postcards,** 1940s, set of 25 assorted, Ashville Postcard Company, full color, variety of subjects including comical, Mammy, plantation, pickaninnies, etc	12.00	15.00	13.00
☐ **Salt and Pepper Shakers,** Aunt Jemima and Uncle Mose, ceramic, colorful, pair, 3¾″	4.00	5.00	4.50
☐ **Salt and Pepper Shakers,** Mammy and Chef, porcelain, colorful, pair, 4½″	4.00	5.00	4.50
☐ **Salt and Pepper Shakers,** Mammy bisque, colorful, pair, 3″	4.00	5.00	4.50
☐ **Salt and Pepper Shakers,** Mammy, celluloid, colorful, pair, 5″	3.50	5.50	4.50
☐ **String Holder,** Mammy, chalkware, wall mounted	8.00	9.00	8.50
☐ **Thermometer,** Mammy, metal picture of Mammy cooking, mint in box, 7½″	2.00	3.00	2.50
☐ **Thimble,** Mammy, bisque, figural, very colorful	2.00	3.00	2.50

	Current Price Range		Prior Year Average
☐ **Toothpick Holder,** Mammy, bisque, colorful, 3″	2.00	3.00	2.50
☐ **Tape Measure,** Aunt Jemima, retractable, colorful	1.50	2.50	1.75
☐ **Wall Plaques,** Mammy and Chef chalkware, with hooks for hanging pot holders, 6″	7.00	8.00	7.50
☐ **Wall Plaques,** set of two, black boy and girl with umbrellas, chalkware, 8″	9.00	10.00	9.50

BOOKPLATES

TOPIC: Bookplates are printed paper labels which identify the owner a book.

PERIOD: These items were produced primarily during the 1600s and 170.

ORIGIN: The first bookplates were printed in Germany in the 15th century.

MATERIALS: Paper was used to make bookplates.

COMMENTS: Many enthusiasts collect bookplates that have similar designs, while others do not limit themselves. In Europe, where bookplate collecting is presently very popular, it is common to buy mixed packets of bookplates, much as mixed packets of stamps are offered to stamp collectors in the United States.

ADDITIONAL TIPS: The following listings are organized by artist.

☐ **Bell, Robert,** design for Fanny Nicholson, c. 1900	7.50	8.75	8.00
☐ **Gill, Eric,** design for Scott Cunningham	7.25	9.50	8.00
☐ **Kent, Rockwell,** most designs	6.25	8.50	6.90
☐ **Parrish, Maxfield**	10.00	15.00	12.00
☐ **American Bookplates,** 18th century, except Revere or Hurd	5.25	7.50	6.25
☐ **Armorials,** 18th century, not done for famous people	5.00	7.25	6.00
☐ **Mixed Packet,** 50 different, 18th century	12.50	17.50	14.50
☐ **Mixed Packet,** 100 different, 18th century	27.00	37.00	31.00
☐ **Mixed Packet,** 50 different, 19th century	7.50	10.50	9.00
☐ **Mixed Packet,** 100 different, 19th century	13.00	16.50	14.75

Left to Right: *bookplate, English, armorial design; bookplate, English, pictorial landscape, Latin motto, both early 1800s.* **$1.00-$2.50**

BOOKS

TOPIC: Books have been extremely important in man's history, for they allow him to record information and distribute it to others in unaltered form.

TYPES: Books fall into two categories, fiction and non-fiction. The non-fiction books can be further subdivided by the subjects they deal with, such as medicine or natural history.

PERIOD: Books first began to be printed around 1450, although handwritten books were in existence earlier than that.

MATERIALS: Paper was used almost exclusively in producing books.

COMMENTS: Many book collectors limit themselves to one or two favorite writers or a favorite subject, since the field of book collecting is vast. A collection is judged on quality rather than quantity, since the number of books that would be appropriate in a collection is so large.

CONDITION: It is important that the book be in good condition. Books with water damage, fire damage, broken bindings or missing pages are worth significantly less than similar books in good condition.

TIPS: For further information please refer to *The Official Price Guide to Old Books and Autographs,* published by The House of Collectibles.

	Current Price Range		Prior Year Average
☐ **Bronte, Charlotte.** *Jane Eyre.* London, 1847, three vols.	1000.00	1350.00	1150.00
☐ **Bronte, Charlotte.** *Shirley.* London, 1849, three vols.	1500.00	1900.00	1700.00
☐ **Bronte, Charlotte.** *The Professor.* London, 1857, two vols.	150.00	185.00	165.00
☐ **Bronte, Emily.** *Wuthering Heights.* London, 1847, three vols. The third volume was titled *Agnes Grey.* Only 1,000 copies were printed, though this was not a "limited edition" in the true sense of the term	9000.00	12000.00	10500.00
☐ **Browning, Elizabeth B.** *Two Poems.* London, 1854, softbound	40.00	55.00	46.00
☐ **Browning, Elizabeth B.** *Aurora Leigh.* N.Y., 1857, first American edition	40.00	55.00	46.00
☐ **Browning, Elizabeth B.** *Poems Before Congress.* London, 1860, blindstamped cloth	120.00	150.00	133.00
☐ **Browning, Elizabeth B.** *Last Poems.* London, 1862, purple cloth	60.00	80.00	69.00
☐ **Browning, Elizabeth B.** *Psyche Apocalype.* London, 1876, softbound	50.00	70.00	59.00
☐ **Browning, Elizabeth B.** *Sonnets from the Portuguese.* London, 1887, one of eight copies on vellum	450.00	575.00	500.00
☐ **Browning, Robert.** *Paracelsus.* London, 1835, boards with paper label	450.00	525.00	480.00
☐ **Browning, Robert.** *The Ring and the Book.* London, 1868, four vols., green cloth	110.00	140.00	125.00
☐ **Browning, Robert.** *Balaustion's Adventure.* London, 1871	14.00	18.00	15.50

	Current Price Range		Prior Year Average

- **Browning, Robert.** *Aristophanes' Apology.* London, 1875 .... 18.00 / 23.00 / 20.00
- **Browning, Robert.** *Dramatic Idyls.* London, 1879 .... 14.00 / 18.00 / 16.00
- **Browning, Robert.** *Parleyings With Certain People.* London, 1887, brown cloth .... 32.00 / 40.00 / 36.00
- **Browning, Robert.** *Men and Women.* London, 1908, two vols., vellum, limited edition ..... 900.00 / 1200.00 / 1050.00
- **Clemens, Samuel Langhorne.** *"Mark Twain" The Celebrated Jumping Frog of Calaveras County and Other Sketches.* Edited by John Paul. The first issue has traditionally been identified by a page of yellow ads before the title page, and a normal letter "i" in "this" on page 198, last line. An effort is now under way to fix priority on basis of binding. The bindings are in assorted colors, but in some the gold-stamped frog adorning the front cover is at the center, in others at the lower left. It is believed (cautiously) the former represents an earlier or at least scarcer state. N.Y., 1867 .... 2175.00 / 2700.00 / 2400.00
- **Dickens, Charles.** *The Adventures of Oliver Twist.* London, 1846, third edition, ten parts, green wrappers .... 900.00 / 1200.00 / 1050.00
- **Dickens, Charles.** *The Adventures of Oliver Twist.* London, 1846, hard covers .... 250.00 / 300.00 / 265.00
- **Dickens, Charles.** *Nicholas Nickleby.* First issue. has misspelling "vister" for "sister," page 123, line 17 of Part Four. London, 1838-1939, 19 parts, green wrappers .... 425.00 / 500.00 / 460.00
- **Dickinson, Emily.** *Poems.* Edited by M.L. Todd and T.W. Higginson. Boston, 1890 .... 325.00 / 400.00 / 355.00
- **Dickinson, Emily.** *Poems.* London, 1891, first English edition .... 325.00 / 400.00 / 355.00
- **Dickinson, Emily.** *Poems.* Second Series. Boston, 1891, grey cloth, or white with green spine .... 120.00 / 160.00 / 135.00
- **Dickinson, Emily.** *Poems.* Third Series. Bindings vary; first state copies have "Roberts Brothers" stamped on spine. Boston, 1891 . 250.00 / 300.00 / 270.00
- **Eliot, T.S.** *The Sacred Wood.* London, 1920 .. 60.00 / 80.00 / 70.00
- **Eliot, T.S.** *Marina.* London, n.d., softbound .. 110.00 / 150.00 / 130.00
- **Eliot, T.S.** *Andrew Marvell.* London, 1922 ... 22.00 / 28.00 / 25.00
- **Eliot, T.S.** *Poems.* London, 1925 .... 80.00 / 100.00 / 90.00
- **Eliot, T.S.** *A Song for Simeon.* London, 1928, limited edition .... 170.00 / 200.00 / 185.00

	Current Price Range		Prior Year Average
☐ Eliot, T.S. *Ash Wednesday.* London, 1930 ...	18.00	23.00	20.00
☐ Eliot, T.S. *Charles Whibley.* London, 1931, softbound	40.00	55.00	47.00
☐ Eliot, T.S. *After Strange Gods.* London, 1934	60.00	80.00	70.00
☐ Eliot, T.S. *The Rock.* London, 1934	35.00	45.00	40.00
☐ Eliot, T.S. *Murder in the Cathedral.* London, 1935	28.00	35.00	31.00
☐ Eliot, T.S. *Four Quartets.* N.Y., 1943	1250.00	1600.00	1400.00
☐ Faulkner, William. *Mosquitoes.* N.Y., 1927, blue cloth	1400.00	1900.00	1600.00
Faulkner, William. *Sartoris.* N.Y., n.d., 1929 .	600.00	800.00	700.00
Faulkner, William. *These Thirteen.* N.Y., n.d., 1931	50.00	65.00	56.00
☐ Faulkner, William. *Idyll in the Desert.* N.Y., 1931, limited signed edition	600.00	800.00	700.00
☐ Faulkner, William. *Sanctuary.* N.Y., n.d., 1931	1000.00	1475.00	1200.00
☐ Hemingway, Ernest. *The Sun Also Rises.* First state copies have misspelling "stopped" on page 181, line 26. N.Y., 1926, black cloth	600.00	800.00	700.00
☐ Hemingway, Ernest. *Men Without Women.* N.Y., 1927, weighs 15 to 15½ ounces in the first state	225.00	300.00	260.00
☐ Hemingway, Ernest. *Death in the Afternoon.* N.Y., 1932, black cloth. For fine copy in dust-jacket	400.00	500.00	450.00
☐ Hemingway, Ernest. *Winner Take Nothing.* N.Y., 1933, black cloth	150.00	200.00	170.00
☐ Hemingway, Ernest. *God Rest You Merry Gentlemen.* N.Y., 1933, red cloth	350.00	425.00	380.00
☐ Hemingway, Ernest. *Green Hills of Africa.* N.Y., 1935, green cloth	110.00	140.00	127.00
☐ James, Henry. *Notes of a Son and a Brother.* N.Y., 1914	40.00	55.00	46.00
☐ James, Henry. *Notes on Novelists.* N.Y., 1914, brown cloth	100.00	135.00	115.00
☐ Joyce, James. *Anna Livia Plurabelle.* N.Y., 1928, limited to 850 signed copies	450.00	600.00	525.00
☐ Joyce, James. *Collected Poems.* N.Y., 1936, limited to 750 copies. There was also an edition on vellum, limited to 50 copies, signed by Joyce. These are boxed and worth up to $750	150.00	200.00	175.00
☐ Joyce, James. *Finnegan's Wake.* London, 1939, limited to 425 on large paper, signed and boxed	2500.00	3250.00	2850.00

	Current Price Range		Prior Year Average
☐ **London, Jack.** *White Fang.* N.Y., 1906, blue cloth	20.00	25.00	22.00
☐ **London, Jack.** *The Cruise of the Dazzler.* London, n.d., 1906	600.00	800.00	700.00
☐ **London, Jack.** *The Road.* N.Y., 1907	20.00	25.00	22.00
☐ **Poe, Edgar A.** *Tamerlane and Other Poems.* "By a Bostonian." Boston, 1827, softbound	130000.00	175000.00	145000.00

The most valuable American first edition in the field of literature, and the most valuable book of the 19th-century excepting Audubon's "Birds of America." Unknown at the time and despairing to find a publisher, Poe brought out the work himself, with predictable results: it failed to sell.

	Current Price Range		Prior Year Average
☐ Steinbeck, John. *Saint Katy the Virgin.* N.p., n.d. (N.Y., 1936), limited to 199 signed copies, rare	1200.00	1500.00	1350.00
☐ **Steinbeck, John.** *Nothing So Monstrous.* N.Y., 1936, limited to 370 copies	300.00	375.00	330.00
☐ **Steinbeck, John.** *In Dubious Battle.* N.Y., n.d., 1936, orange cloth	125.00	160.00	136.00
☐ **Steinbeck, John.** *The Red Pony.* N.Y., 1937, limited to 699 signed copies, boxed	150.00	180.00	166.00
☐ **Steinbeck, John.** *Of Men and Mice.* N.Y., n.d., 19.., beige cloth	90.00	115.00	100.00
☐ **Wilder, Thornton.** *The Angel That Troubled the Waters.* N.Y., 1928, limited, signed	35.00	45.00	40.00
☐ **Wilder, Thornton.** *The Long Christmas Dinner.* N.Y., 1931	35.00	45.00	40.00
☐ **Wilder, Thornton.** *The Ides of March.* N.Y., 1948, limited to 750, signed	85.00	110.00	95.00
☐ **Williams, Tennessee.** *The Glass Menagerie.* N.Y., 1945	125.00	150.00	133.00
☐ **Williams, Tennessee.** *A Streetcar Named Desire.* N.p., n.d., (Norfolk, 1947)	125.00	150.00	133.00
☐ **Williams, Tennessee.** *The Roman Spring of Mrs. Stone.* N.p., n.d., (N.Y., 1950), limited to 500, signed	185.00	235.00	205.00
☐ **Williams, Tennessee.** *Cat on a Hot Tin Roof.* N.p., n.d., (N.Y., 1955)	40.00	50.00	45.00
☐ **Wolfe, Thomas.** *Look Homeward Angel.* N.Y., 1929, blue cloth. First state has Scribner logo on verso of title	600.00	750.00	675.00
☐ **Wolfe, Thomas.** *Of Time and the River.* N.Y., 1935	85.00	110.00	95.00
☐ **Wolfe, Thomas.** *From Death to Morning.* N.Y., 1935	85.00	110.00	95.00

	Current Price Range		Prior Year Average
☐ **Wolfe, Thomas.** *The Face of a Nation.* N.Y., 1939, cloth	40.00	55.00	47.00
☐ **Wolfe, Thomas.** *You Can't Go Home Again.* N.Y., n.d., 1940	60.00	80.00	70.00
☐ **Wolfe, Thomas.** *The Hills Beyond.* N.Y., n.d., 1941	90.00	110.00	100.00
☐ **Wolfe, Thomas.** *Gentlemen of the Press.* Chicago, n.d., 1942, limited to 350	130.00	160.00	145.00
☐ **Woolf, Virginia.** *The Years.* London, 1937	225.00	275.00	250.00
☐ **Woolf, Virginia.** *Three Guineas.* London, 1937	110.00	140.00	120.00
☐ **Woolf, Virginia.** *Between the Acts.* London, 1941	60.00	80.00	70.00
☐ **Woolf, Virginia.** *A Writer's Diary.* London, 1953	60.00	80.00	70.00
☐ **Woolf, Virginia.** *Hours in a Library.* N.Y., 1957	60.00	80.00	70.00
☐ **Wordsworth, William.** *Poems.* London, 1807, two vols. The first state is identified by a pair of points: a period after the word "Sonnets" on page 103 of Volume One and the misspelling "fnuction" for "function" on page 98 of Volume Two. The publisher's binding is plain boards with paper label	1200.00	1500.00	1350.00
☐ **Yeats. W.B.** *Stories From Carleton.* London, n.d., 1889, blue cloth with paper label	90.00	115.00	100.00
☐ **Yeats, W.B.** *The Tables of the Law.* London, 1904	30.00	38.00	34.00
☐ **Yeats, W.B.** *The Hour Glass.* London, 1904	35.00	45.00	40.00

BOTTLES

This section features only a sampling of bottles. In order to accurately present the vast amount of information required by serious collectors, a special edition devoted to bottles is published by The House of Collectibles, Inc. This handy, pocket-size guide, *The Official Price Guide to Bottles,* features values for a variety of old and new bottles. It is available at bookstores for $3.95. For more in-depth information refer to *The Official Price Guide to Bottles Old and New* for $10.95.

DESCRIPTION: With the availability of cheaper containers made of plastic, aluminum and paper, glass bottles are declining rapidly as a form of storage. With the decline of bottle production, more collectors are realizing how important old bottles are especially as they relate to history.

TYPES: There are many types of bottles found on the collectible market including ale and gin, beer, cosmetic, bitters, crocks, cure, food, ink, medicine, mineral water, poison, pontil, soda and spirits.

ADDITIONAL TIPS: This section is organized alphabetically by bottle type. For additional information on bottles, consult *The Official Price Guide to Bottles Old & New* published by The House of Collectibles.

	Current Price Range		Prior Year Average
☐ **Bitters,** Dr. Boyce's Tonic label, sample size, twelve panels, aqua, 4½″	13.00	17.00	14.75
☐ **Bitters,** The Bitters Pharmacy on label, clear, 4½″	4.00	6.00	5.00
☐ **Bitters,** Caroni, pint, amber	19.00	28.00	22.50
☐ **Bitter,** Celery & Chamonile on label, square, amber, 10″	18.00	23.00	20.00
☐ **Bitters,** Dr. E. Chyder Stomach Bitters, N.O., amber, 10″	18.00	23.00	20.00
☐ **Bitters,** Compound Calisaya Bitters in two lines, tapered top, square, amber, 9½″	14.00	18.00	15.75
☐ **Bitters,** Fer-Kina Galeno on shoulder, beer type bottle, brown, machine made, 10⅛″ . . .	14.00	18.00	15.75
☐ **Cure,** Sample Shiloh's Cure printed vertical on front, rectangular, aqua, 4¼″	7.00	10.00	8.00
☐ **Cure,** Speedy Cure for Coughs And Colds, printed on one side Jones & Primely Co., other side Elkhart, Ind., ring top, clear, 8″ . .	15.00	20.00	17.00
☐ **Cure,** Dr. Taylor's Sure Chill Cure, on side Richardson Taylor Med. Co., ring top, aqua, 5½″	5.00	10.00	7.00
☐ **Cure,** Twenty-Four Hour Cure Guaranteed, ring top, clear, 5″	8.00	12.00	9.50
☐ **Cure,** Veno's Lightning Cough Cure, double ring top, aqua, 7¼″	7.00	10.00	8.25
☐ **Cure,** White's Quick Healing Cure, amber, 6¼″	9.00	12.00	10.25
☐ **Cure,** Wood's Great Peppermint Cure for Coughs and Colds, clear, 6½″	7.00	10.00	8.50
☐ **Cure,** Zemo Cures Exzema, E.W. Rose Med. Co. St. Louis printed on one side, reverse side is Zemo Cures Pimples and all Diseases of the Skin and Scalp, fancy bottle, ring top, clear, 6½″	9.00	12.00	10.00
☐ **Food,** The Abner Royce Co., The Abner Royce Co. Pure Fruit Flavor, Cleveland, Ohio on back, clear, 5¼″	5.00	10.00	7.00
☐ **Food,** The A-1 Sauce, aqua, 7¾″	4.00	6.00	4.75

	Current Price Range		Prior Year Average
☐ **Food,** Armour & Co., aqua, 4″	3.00	5.00	4.20
☐ **Food,** Baker's Flavoring Extracts, Baker Extracts Co. printed on one side Strength & Purity, on the other Full Measure, machine made, clear	3.00	4.00	3.70
☐ **Food,** Candy Bros MFG. Co. Confectioners, label, aqua, 12″	6.00	8.00	7.00
☐ **Food,** Carnation's Fresh Milk, Chicago Sealed 1 qt., milk bottle, amber	5.00	7.00	6.00
☐ **Food,** Geo M. Curtis, Pure Olive Oil, slim, round	1.50	2.00	1.60
☐ **Food,** Dawson's Pickles, ten panels, clear or amethyst, 7½″	4.00	6.00	4.60
☐ **Food,** Eno's Fruit Salt, W on bottom, 7″	5.00	7.00	5.90
☐ **Food,** Extract Tabasco on bottom, clear, 4¾″	2.00	4.00	2.40
☐ **Ink,** Angus & Co., cone, aqua, 3½″	4.00	6.00	4.75
☐ **Ink,** Arnold's round, clear or amethyst, 2½″	5.00	7.00	5.75
☐ **Ink,** B&B, pottery bottle, tan, 7½″	5.00	8.00	6.50
☐ **Ink,** Billing & Co., Banker's Writing Ink, aqua, 2″	10.00	15.00	12.00
☐ **Medicine,** Dr. Mile's Medical Co. printed on front panel, rectangular, aqua, 8½″	3.00	4.00	3.25
☐ **Medicine,** George Moore, clear, 5¾″	4.00	6.00	4.50
☐ **Medicine,** Nervine prepared by the Catarrhozone Co., Kinston, Ont. printed vertical on front in oval sunken panel, square collar, rectangular, amethyst, 5¼″	6.00	9.00	6.75
☐ **Medicine,** Norton, clear or amethyst, 5″	3.00	5.00	3.75
☐ **Medicine,** The Oakland Chemical Co., amber, 4¾″	3.00	5.00	3.50
☐ **Medicine,** Olive Oil, open pontil, no embossing, 10½″	9.00	12.00	10.25
☐ **Medicine,** Palace Drug Store, clear, 4½″ ...	4.00	6.00	4.75
☐ **Medicine,** Parker printed on one side, New York on other, 17 on bottom, amber, 7″	3.00	5.00	3.75
☐ **Medicine,** P.D. & Co., on bottom, amber 3¼″	3.00	4.00	3.25
☐ **Medicine,** Platt's Chloride, clear or amethyst	5.00	8.00	5.75
☐ **Mineral,** Abilena Natural Cathartic Water printed on bottom, amber or brown, 11½″ ..	7.00	9.00	7.75
☐ **Mineral,** Aetna Mineral Water, aqua, 11½″ .	6.00	9.00	7.25
☐ **Mineral,** Bear Lithia Water, aqua, 10″	6.00	9.00	7.25
☐ **Mineral,** Beford Water, label in back, aqua, 14″	5.00	9.00	6.75
☐ **Mineral,** Buffalo Lick Springs, clear or amethyst, 10″	6.00	9.00	7.25

	Current Price Range		Prior Year Average
☐ **Mineral,** Carlsbad L.S., sheared collar, cylindrical, ground top, clear, 4″	6.00	9.00	6.75
☐ **Mineral,** Clark & White printed in U shape, under it New York, in center C Mineral Water, olive green, 9¼″	18.00	25.00	21.00
☐ **Mineral,** Columbia Mineral Water Co., St. Louis, Mo., aqua, 7¼″	9.00	12.00	10.50
☐ **Poison,** F.S. & Co. on base, Poison vertically, surrounded by dots, two sides plain, ring top, amber, 2¾″	11.00	16.00	13.00
☐ **Poison,** R.C. Millings Bed Bug Poison, Charleston, S.C. shoulder strap on side, clear, 6¼″	12.00	17.00	14.00
☐ **Poison,** Rat Poison printed horizontal on round bottle, clear or amethyst, 2½″	18.00	26.00	21.00
☐ **Poison,** Tincture Iodine printed in three lines under skull and crossbones, square, amber	6.00	9.00	7.50
☐ **Poison,** Triloids printed on one panel of bottle, Poison on another, cobalt, 3¼″	6.00	9.00	7.50
☐ **Poison,** Wyeth Poison printed vertical on back, round ring base and top, cobalt, 2¼″	10.00	15.00	12.00
☐ **Pontil,** Allen Mrs. S.A. printed on one side, on front World's Hair Balsam, 355 Broone St printed in three lines, aqua, 6½″	19.00	27.00	22.00
☐ **Pontil,** Bake's Dr. printed on front, tapered top, pale aqua, 5″	24.00	37.00	29.00
☐ **Pontil,** Balsam of Honey printed on three lines, round bottle, ring top, aqua, 3″	19.00	27.00	23.00
☐ **Pontil,** Brown's, F., Ess of Jamaica Ginger, Philad. printed on four lines, tapered top, oval, aqua, 5½″	10.00	15.00	12.00

Berkshire Bitters Bottle, *pig, 9½″*

Left to Right: National Bitters Bottle, *ear of corn design, burgundy, 12½"*; **S.T. Drake's Plantation Bitters Jar,** *square body, expanded lip, golden amber, 9½"*

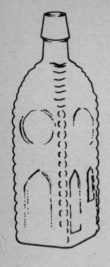

American Life Bitters Bottle,
cabin design, amber, 9"

	Current Price Range		Prior Year Average
☐ **Pontil,** Cannington Shaw & Co., St. Helens on top of L.D. beaded decoration around shoulder	14.00	21.00	17.00
☐ **Spirits,** Acker Merrall, label, A9 on bottom, amber, 11"	8.00	11.00	9.50
☐ **Spirits,** Bailey's Whiskey, clear or amethyst, 9¾"	8.00	11.00	9.75
☐ **Spirits,** B&B, clear or amber	4.00	6.00	4.75
☐ **Spirits,** Belle of Nelson, label, whiskey, M.M. on bottom, clear, 12"	6.00	9.00	7.25
☐ **Spirits,** E.R. Betterton & Co., distillers Chattanooga, Tenn. printed on three lines in sunken panel on back, raised panel plain, flask, three ribs on each side, twenty ribs around neck, on bottom a diamond with letter Y, brown	7.00	10.00	8.75

	Current Price Range		Prior Year Average
☐ **Spirits,** Red Chief, Fort Hood, Indiana, Ballina Rye, clear, 12″	14.00	19.00	16.00
☐ **Spirits,** H.H. Robinson, Boston, label, Guaranteed Full Pt printed on back, clear or amethyst, 8¾″	3.00	5.00	4.00
☐ **Spirits,** L. Rose & Co., rose and vine bottle, applied crown, tapered, aqua, 7½″	7.00	10.00	8.00

BOXES

DESCRIPTION: Versatile and charming, boxes not only have a variety of uses but they are also quite collectible.

MATERIALS: Boxes are made using a variety of materials including straw, wood, china and glass.

COMMENTS: In the 18th and 19th centuries boxes were mostly for utilitarian use such as perishable food storage. Special boxes were made to hold such items as wedding dresses. Small boxes, for trinkets, matches or cigarettes, seem to be especially intricate and collectible.

ADDITIONAL TIPS: The listings in this section are alphabetical according to type of box, followed by descriptions and date.

	Current Price Range		Prior Year Average
☐ **Apple Box,** footed, smoked finish	260.00	310.00	275.00
☐ **Apple Box,** pine, painted, 11″ x 8½″	55.00	80.00	62.00
☐ **Ballot Box,** maple, oblong, sliding top	105.00	135.00	120.00
☐ **Band Box,** oval, painted, schoolhouse, flowers and trees on lid, 9″ x 6″	1400.00	1900.00	1600.00
☐ **Band Box,** man and woman with flowers on lid, flowers on sides	1300.00	1800.00	1500.00
☐ **Band Box,** hunter shooting deer	600.00	700.00	585.00
☐ **Bible Box,** carved oak, English, mid 1600's . .	430.00	480.00	450.00
☐ **Book-shaped Box,** inlaid, large	85.00	110.00	90.00
☐ **Book-shaped Box,** with name and dated 1861	325.00	375.00	350.00
☐ **Book-shaped Box,** Pennsylvania German, painted wood	55.00	110.00	75.00
☐ **Book-shaped Box,** inlaid colored wax hearts, stars	30.00	45.00	38.00
☐ **Box,** Wilcox, quadruple plate, scrolls, pointer dogs, lock lion's paw feet, 9″ x 5″ . .	185.00	210.00	182.00
☐ **Brass Box,** covered with leather, shape of coffin	50.00	70.00	55.00
☐ **Bride's Box,** painted flowers, dark green, c. 1817	275.00	325.00	275.00

	Current Price Range		Prior Year Average
☐ **Bride's Box,** oval, painted bride and groom with floral motif, 18″	385.00	435.00	400.00
☐ **Bride's Box,** German or Pennsylvania German, oval, 19th c.	210.00	260.00	225.00
☐ **Butter Box,** six individual containers	110.00	145.00	118.00
☐ **Candle Box,** cherry, carved, scalloped arch	410.00	460.00	425.00
☐ **Candle Box,** geometric design, carved and inlaid, 8″	110.00	145.00	118.00
☐ **Candle Box,** pine, sliding lid, red border, knob on lid, 14″	385.00	430.00	400.00
☐ **Candle Box,** tin, hanging, round	180.00	230.00	200.00
☐ **Cheese Box,** tree and leaf design, inlaid mahogany, 7″ Dia.	380.00	430.00	400.00
☐ **Cigar Box,** coromandel with brass fittings, mid 19th c.	180.00	230.00	200.00
☐ **Cigarette Box,** "Wavecrest," cream, blue, white, pink forget-me-nots, word "Cigarettes," 4″ H.	260.00	310.00	275.00
☐ **Cigarette Box,** cloisonne, cylindrical, unmarked	65.00	110.00	80.00
☐ **Cigarette or Chocolate Box,** brass, Princess Mary, WW1, with Mary, and names of Allies around lid	38.00	48.00	40.00
☐ **Cigarette Box,** green, Lenox wreath mark, Lenox	29.00	33.00	31.00
☐ **Cigarette Box,** pink daisy design, square with lid, 4½″, Southern Potteries	6.00	8.00	7.00
☐ **Cigarette Box,** rounded corners, ribbing, relief apple blossom design, green with white flowers, Lenox wreath mark, Lenox	49.00	55.00	52.00
☐ **Cigarette Box,** rounded corners, ribbing, relief apple blossom design, Lenox wreath mark, Lenox	34.00	38.00	36.00
☐ **Miniature Box,** antique Satsuma, rectangular, children, and swans on cover and interior, 3½″, 18th century	300.00	360.00	330.00
☐ **Pantry Box,** Scandinavian Bentwood	110.00	150.00	125.00
☐ **Pantry Box,** varnished, 10″	28.00	42.00	32.00
☐ **Pantry Box,** two-fingered round, small size	110.00	150.00	120.00
☐ **Pantry Box,** three-fingered oval, painted red (possibly Shaker)	135.00	180.00	150.00
☐ **Pantry Box,** oval, two-fingered, c. 1820	135.00	180.00	150.00
☐ **Pantry Boxes,** five graduated, round, painted	160.00	210.00	180.00
☐ **Patch Box,** Royal Bayreuth tapestry, five sheep on lid, gray mark, 2½″ x 1½″	140.00	180.00	150.00
☐ **Pencil Box,** sliding lid, dovetailed	22.00	32.00	25.00
☐ **Pipe Box,** pine, drawer, dovetailed	330.00	360.00	338.00

	Current Price Range		Prior Year Average
☐ **Pottery Box,** covered, oval, all white with shell molded base, shell finial on lid, 5¾", Bennington	80.00	95.00	84.00
☐ **Pottery Box,** square with Lion of Lucerne figure, Bennington	120.00	130.00	124.00
☐ **Rouge Box,** round, embossed rims and ornate finial, undecorated, C.A.C. green palette mark, Lenox	40.00	50.00	44.00
☐ **Salt Box,** curved front, flat black, painted red	55.00	70.00	62.00
☐ **Salt Box,** maple and cherry, striped wood, hinged cover	110.00	135.00	112.00
☐ **Salt Box,** pine, dovetailed, open, hanging	90.00	110.00	92.00
☐ **Salt Box,** walnut, dovetailed, slant lid, hanging	140.00	170.00	150.00
☐ **Salt Box,** Pennsylvania Dutch design, two compartments, open	180.00	210.00	182.00
☐ **Seed Box,** compartments, sliding lid	135.00	160.00	138.00
☐ **Shaving Box,** brush	45.00	55.00	45.00
☐ **Snuff Box,** Austrian silver gilt, musical with sectional comb, 9 cm., hallmarked Vienna, c. 1828	2300.00	2700.00	2460.00
☐ **Snuff Box,** French tortoiseshell, musical with sectional comb, 9 cm., c. 1810	1200.00	1800.00	1450.00
☐ **Snuff Box,** Mauchline ware, boxwood, 3½" W.	55.00	80.00	62.00
☐ **Snuff Box,** horn, acorn-shaped, screw-on top, 1¾"	28.00	38.00	30.00
☐ **Snuff Box,** pewter	38.00	48.00	40.00
☐ **Snuff Box,** treenware, 2¾" Dia.	18.00	24.00	18.00
☐ **Spice Box,** cherry, nine drawers, original, 13" H.	150.00	175.00	152.00
☐ **Spice Box,** curly maple, twelve drawers, brass pulls	315.00	365.00	325.00
☐ **Spice Box,** oak, eight drawers, wooden pulls, hanging	80.00	110.00	82.00
☐ **Spice Box,** pine, eight drawers, porcelain pulls, hanging	100.00	130.00	102.00
☐ **Spice Box,** tin, eight drawers, painted black	100.00	130.00	102.00
☐ **Spice Box,** walnut, two drawers, carved back, dovetailed	280.00	330.00	300.00
☐ **Stamp Box,** brass, footed, covered	45.00	55.00	45.00
☐ **Stamp Box,** pewter, hinged top	65.00	85.00	70.00
☐ **Stamp Box,** sterling with enameled lid, chair and finger ring	28.00	38.00	30.00
☐ **Stationery Box,** walnut with brass and ivory decoration, 7" H., late 19th c.	120.00	170.00	135.00
☐ **Tea caddy,** Marguetry, English, c. 1780	550.00	650.00	562.00

	Current Price Range		Prior Year Average
☐ **Tea caddy,** imitation tortoise shell, green, English, early 19th c.	230.00	280.00	250.00
☐ **Tin Box,** with brass rings, hand embossed arch and bullseye, c. 1880	30.00	40.00	33.00
☐ **Tin Box,** "Breethem" breath sweetener box, picture of a woman and product slogan	1.50	3.00	2.10
☐ **Tobacco Box,** Pennsylvania Dutch design, 19" H.	55.00	70.00	62.00
☐ **Tool Box,** oak	28.00	32.00	30.00
☐ **Tool Box,** child's, with tools, c. 1930	45.00	55.00	45.00
☐ **Tramp Art Box,** footed, geometic design, hinged top, 14" x 15"	185.00	210.00	182.00
☐ **Tramp Art Wall Boxes,** small	32.00	48.00	38.00
☐ **Trinket Box,** Art Deco, woman on cover, 6½", Fulper Pottery	195.00	205.00	199.00
☐ **Trinket Box,** painted, one drawer	325.00	375.00	325.00
☐ **Trinket Box,** papier mache and antique sulphide, design features four women, 2¾", 18th century	350.00	400.00	360.00
☐ **Trinket Box,** rectangle, hand painted red roses with gold trim, 2" x 4", Lenox palette mark, Lenox	75.00	85.00	77.00
☐ **Trinket Box,** round, Ming pattern, 3¾", Lenox wreath mark, Lenox	115.00	125.00	119.00
☐ **Trinket Box,** round, undecorated, 3¾", Lenox pallete mark, Lenox	42.00	48.00	44.00
☐ **Trinket Box,** wooden, carved, painted flowers, 6" H.	325.00	375.00	325.00
☐ **Wall Box,** open top, painted brown, 19th c.	160.00	210.00	175.00
☐ **Writing Box,** oak, English, 13½" W., 18th c.	135.00	185.00	150.00
☐ **Writing Box,** Shaker, two drawers	135.00	185.00	150.00

BRASS

DESCRIPTION: Brass is an alloy of copper and zinc and has been used since antiquity. Because of its malleable nature it can be fashioned into a wide variety of utensils, tools and decorative objects.

COMMENTS: Decorative brassware has been imported from the orient since the turn of the century. These wares feature very intricate engraving and tooling. Brass is very durable and although it tarnishes quickly it can be polished and restored to its lovely golden color very easily. Brassware can often be found in garage sales very cheaply as many people are unwilling to polish it regularly.

	Current Price Range		Prior Year Average
☐ **Andirons,** pair, solid brass fluted column and ball finial with solid brass feet, 20½ " ..	110.00	120.00	112.50
☐ **Ashtray,** brass dog standing on edge, marked China, 4½ "	18.00	20.00	18.50
☐ **Ashtray,** fashioned from World War II artillery shell, very heavy, marked FSC 8/19/43, 7-V 50 cal., 4½ "	10.00	15.00	10.50
☐ **Ashtray,** ivy leaf shape, marked English Ivy by Cambron, 5¾ " x 4½ "	12.00	15.00	12.50
☐ **Ashtray,** shaped like coal scuttle, enameled with scene of men studying books around table, marked China	10.00	12.00	10.50
☐ **Ashtray,** shaped like handled bowl, enameled in floral, geometric, and scenic motifs, marked China	13.00	15.00	13.50
☐ **Ashtray,** square, cast oriental characters, 3 "	4.00	5.00	4.25
☐ **Ashtray,** tooled and enameled, marked India Benares Brass, 3⅝ " x 1⅞ "	7.00	8.00	7.25
☐ **Ashtrays,** pair, slipper shape, floral engraving, marked India	5.00	6.00	5.25
☐ **Ashtrays,** set of four, nesting, scalloped, engraved flowers, marked China, 3½ " x 2¾ "	10.00	12.00	10.75
☐ **Bell,** cow shape, 3¼ "	6.00	8.00	6.50
☐ **Bell,** lady in ruffled skirt holds fan, shawl around shoulders, 3¼ "	20.00	25.00	22.50
☐ **Bell,** lady in ruffled skirt holds parasol, 4½ "	28.00	32.00	30.00
☐ **Bowl,** sits on brass stand, marked China, 4½ "	21.00	24.00	22.00
☐ **Bowl,** tooled flowers and leaves, marked India, 6½ " x 1¾ "	9.00	11.00	9.25
☐ **Box,** oval, pierced hinged lid and sides, top handle hasp, marked India, 4" x 2½ " x7" ...	5.00	6.00	5.25
☐ **Candelabra,** five arms, marked China, 15½ " x 14"	45.00	50.00	47.50
☐ **Candelabra,** pair, each has three arms, elaborate styles, 15"	140.00	160.00	145.00
☐ **Candle Sconces,** pair, pierced 6" arm with hinge, engraved wall plate, marked China ..	28.00	33.00	29.50
☐ **Candleholders,** pair, spiral shaft, marked China, 10"	65.00	70.00	67.50
☐ **Candlestick,** heavy, teardrop and saucer turning, square footed base, 9¾ "	32.00	38.00	32.50
☐ **Candlesticks,** pair, heavy, 3"	10.00	12.00	10.50
☐ **Centerpiece,** shaped like Viking ship on stand with columns, hand hammered and footed, 17" long x 11" tall x 7" deep	34.00	40.00	35.00

	Current Price Range		Prior Year Average
☐ **Cigarette Jar with Lid,** cylindrical, dome lid, floral engraving, marked China, 3½ " x 3 " ..	12.00	15.00	12.50
☐ **Cigarette Set,** three pieces, includes cigarette box, match box cover, ashtray, enameled, marked China	60.00	65.00	58.50
☐ **Coal Scuttle,** engraved, marked China, 4" x 3½ "	6.00	7.00	6.25
☐ **Coaster,** heavy, engraved flowers and leaves, marked China, 3½ "	4.00	5.00	4.25
☐ **Desk Lamp,** marble base	30.00	38.00	32.50
☐ **Desk Set,** eight pieces, floral scroll design, pen tray, covered stamp safe, calendar, letter holder, ink well with glass insert and hinged cover, rolling blotter, spring clip paper holder, Bradley and Hubbard, 1890s ..	285.00	315.00	290.00
☐ **Dish,** animal relief border, 4"	4.00	6.00	4.25
☐ **Dish,** footed, tooled and enameled decoration, marked Banares Brass, 2" x 6"	9.00	11.00	9.50
☐ **Dish,** hammered, 4"	3.00	4.00	3.25
☐ **Dish,** heavy cast brass with elaborate scrolled surface, tri-footed, 4¼ "	4.50	6.50	4.75
☐ **Dish,** pedestal, incised dragon, 4½ " x 3¼ " .	7.00	9.00	7.25
☐ **Door Knocker,** lion, 3½ " x 2½ ", marked with impressed C & A	20.00	25.00	22.50
☐ **Figurine,** Art Deco style, nude dancer, domed base, very heavy, 8½ "	120.00	130.00	125.00
☐ **Fireplace Tools and Stand,** small, stand is 16" tall, tools are 11" to 12" tall and include hearth broom, poker, shovel, engraved heraldic crests, marked Made in England ..	120.00	130.00	125.00
☐ **Gong,** with stand and wooden striker, 7" ...	8.00	10.00	8.50
☐ **Incense Burner,** lid pierced with I Ching symbols, two tall pierced ear handles, three legs, 4½ " x 7"	22.00	28.00	23.50
☐ **Incense Burner,** pierced lid and tooled base, 2" x 2"	2.00	4.00	2.25
☐ **Incense Burner,** pierced lid, tooled, scalloped rim, marked India, 1½ " x 2¼ " ..	3.50	5.00	3.75
☐ **Incense Burner,** pierced lid, tooling, tri-footed, marked India, 3¼ " x 2"	4.00	6.00	4.25
☐ **Jar,** cylindrical, open, engraved trees, marked China, 1¾ "	4.00	5.00	4.25
☐ **Jardiniere,** floral basket frieze around rim, ring handles, tri-footed, 9" x 10½ "	28.00	36.00	28.50
☐ **Jardiniere,** hammered texture, 2½ " band of sculptured roses in heavy relief around rim, 9¾ " x 11½ "	32.00	38.00	33.50

	Current Price Range		Prior Year Average
Jelly Pot, iron basket handle, 15″ x 5¾″	55.00	65.00	57.50
Keys, group of seven, old	12.00	15.00	12.50
Letter Holder, depicts jockey on horse in front of horseshoe, 6⅝″ x 4½″	32.00	38.00	35.00
Miniature Andirons, pair, 1¾″	5.00	6.00	5.25
Miniature Bottle, solid with screw in stopper, 1¾″	8.00	10.00	8.50
Miniature Candlestick, solid base, 1¼″	3.00	4.00	3.25
Miniature Candlesticks, very heavy, 1¾″ ..	10.00	12.00	10.50
Miniature Decanter, very heavy, 1¾″	8.00	10.00	8.50
Miniature Incense Burner, pair, shaped like candlesticks, 2½″	4.00	5.00	4.25
Miniature Pestle, 1¼″	3.50	4.50	3.75
Miniature Slipper, pair, 1½″	4.00	5.00	4.25
Mint Dish, hand tooled floral and leaf band and center, pedestal base, marked India, 5″ x 2″	8.00	10.00	8.50
Mug, no handle, 3″ x 3″	3.00	4.00	3.25
Pig, solid, 2½″	10.00	12.00	11.00
Pig, solid, 3″	15.00	17.00	16.00
Pig, solid, 4¼″	24.00	28.00	25.00
Plate, covered with tooled leaf engraving, 4¾″	4.00	5.00	4.25
Plate, heavy cast brass with scalloped rim, features people in elaborate relief at center and around rim	6.00	8.00	6.50
Platter, pedestal, marked China, 8″	19.00	21.00	18.50
Soap Dish, Victorian bath tub with four curved feet, 5½″ x 2⅜″	9.00	11.00	10.00
Spittoon, 6⅝″ x 4¾″	32.00	35.00	33.00

Ice Cream Server,
nickeled brass,
1930s, **$23.00-$30.00**

	Current Price Range		Prior Year Average
☐ **Table Lighter,** engraved leaves, marked India, 4½"	8.00	10.00	8.50
☐ **Table Top,** round, brass clad, covered with intricate Mid-Eastern engraving and caligraphy, 24" diameter x 1⅝" thick	130.00	150.00	140.00
☐ **Tongs,** claw end, hanging ring, 11"	15.00	18.00	16.50
☐ **Tray,** hammered, 5½"	4.00	5.00	4.25
☐ **Tray,** octagonal, hammered, 15" x 10"	15.00	18.00	15.50
☐ **Tray,** two handles, engraved peacocks and flowers, marked India, 29" x 8"	24.00	28.00	25.00
☐ **Vase,** bronze birds and flowers, marked China, 6"	28.00	32.00	28.50
☐ **Vase,** heavy, square top, two Foo dog handles, marked China, 9½"	65.00	75.00	67.50
☐ **Wall Brush Set,** includes mirror, and two bristle brushes with leaf scroll tooling, brushes hang from two hooks below mirror	45.00	48.00	46.00
☐ **Wax Seal,** bee shape	3.00	4.00	3.25
☐ **Wax Seal,** leaf shape	3.00	4.00	3.25

BREWERIANA

This section features only a sampling of breweriana. In order to accurately present the vast amount of information required by serious collectors, a special edition devoted to beer collectibles is published by The House of Collectibles, Inc. This handy, pocket-size guide, *The Official 1985 Price Guide to Beer Cans and Collectibles,* features much valuable information. It is available at bookstores for $3.95.

TOPIC: Breweriana is beer related memorabilia.

TYPES: Popular types of breweriana include serving trays, coasters, bottle and can openers and advertising signs.

PERIOD: Breweriana that dates back to 17th century England can be found, but most collectible breweriana was made after 1800. Contemporary products such as advertising mirrors are presently quite popular.

COMMENTS: Although some breweriana enthusiasts collect beer cans and beer bottles also, many limit themselves to breweriana and a specific company. Others collect certain items such as ashtrays.

ADDITIONAL TIPS: The following listings are arranged by company. For more extensive listings, refer to *The Official Price Guide to Beer Cans,* published by The House of Collectibles.

MISCELLANEOUS

	Current Price Range		Prior Year Average
☐ **Albion,** mirror, "Gold Medal Award from the 1924 Breweries Exhibition, To Albion Brewery, Championship Cup and Gold Medal Ales," 7" x 9"	130.00	170.00	150.00
☐ **American,** non-illuminated sign, glass and wood, "Brewer's Best Premium," 13" x 13"	22.00	28.00	25.00
☐ **American,** poster, "Salute to National Tavern Month," 11¼" x 14"	.40	.60	.50
☐ **Ballantine,** coaster, circular, red and black, "We Serve Ballantine Ale and Beer," probably late 1940's, 4¼"	4.00	6.00	5.00
☐ **Ballantine,** foam scraper, white and red, smile mug with logo and "Ballantine Draught Beer," dated 1964, 9"	8.50	11.50	10.00
☐ **Barbey's Sunshine,** tray, "Since 1861," gold with blue background, rounded sizes	31.00	39.00	36.00
☐ **Bavarian,** coaster, circular, red and black, "Bavarian Type Beer, Mount Carbon Brewery, Pottsville, Pa., Union Made," 1940's, 4¼"	3.50	4.50	4.00
☐ **Blatz,** illuminated sign, octagonal, brand name at center, mounted on pillar-type decorative bar with brass finial, gold and brown, 14" x 7"	8.00	10.00	9.00
☐ **Blatz,** miniature bottle, 4"	13.00	17.00	15.00
☐ **Braumeister,** coaster, oval, red, blue and yellow, "Braumeister Special Pilsner Beer, Milwaukee's Choicest, Independent Milwaukee Brewery," World War II era, 4¼"	4.00	6.00	5.00
☐ **Black Horse Ale,** tap marker	6.50	8.50	7.50
☐ **Brunswick Bock,** poster, "Brunswick Bock Beer," ram's head in white against green background, 1930's-40's, 23" x 34"	60.00	80.00	70.00
☐ **Budweiser,** opener, wooden bottle with Bud label	10.00	14.00	12.00
☐ **Budweiser,** paper hat, white with red lettering, "We Feature Budweiser Beer," c. 1950-60	8.50	11.50	10.00
☐ **Budweiser,** tip tray, Budweiser logo and "King of Beers," red with white lettering, rectangular, 3" x 7"	10.00	14.00	12.00
☐ **Columbia,** tray, hops and stars, multicolored with gold, 11¾"	19.00	25.00	22.00
☐ **Columbia Five Star,** tray, Shenandoah, Pennsylvania, grain, hops and shield in multicolors and gold	22.00	28.00	26.00
☐ **Coors,** tray, "America's Fine Light Beer," white lion, red striped background, 13¼"	8.00	10.00	9.00

	Current Price Range		Prior Year Average

☐ **Coors,** poster, reprint, "Coors Golden Brewery, Golden, Colo.," Gibson girl, 14″ x 19″ .. 8.50 11.50 10.00

☐ **Dinkel Acker,** plastic, white with black and yellow border, logo and brand name 90 1.20 1.05

☐ **Edelweiss,** non-illuminated sign, "Stop Here for Edelwiss Light Beer," thick cardboard in black, red, yellow and white, has circle marked "Special" with space for price to be written, c. 1950-60 . . . . 22.00 28.00 25.00

☐ **Esslinger,** salt and pepper set, 4″ 21.00 27.00 24.00

☐ **Esslinger's,** opener, "Esslinger's Premium Beer, Over the Top" 8.00 10.00 9.00

☐ **Falls City,** tray, "70th Anniversary," illustration of brewery, multicolors, 11¾″ 19.00 25.00 22.00

☐ **F and S Beer and Ale,** tray, multicolored drum major 22.00 29.00 25.00

☐ **Genesee,** tray, "Ask for Jenny," illustration of Jenny, white, black and yellow against reddish background, 11¾″ 14.00 18.00 16.00

☐ **Genesee,** tray, still life with pheasant on table, multicolored, 11¾″ 15.00 19.00 17.00

☐ **Gibbons Mellow–Pure Beer and Ale,** tray, white, black and red, 11¾″ 13.00 17.00 15.00

☐ **Gibbons Premium,** tray, "Gibbons is Good," white with black and red lettering, 13¼″ . . . 8.00 10.00 9.00

☐ **Grain Belt,** tray, logo with grain, hops, mug and lake in background, multicolored, 13¼″ 12.00 16.00 14.00

☐ **Hamm's,** tray, bear with lake in woodland scene, multicolored, 11¾″ 14.00 18.00 16.00

☐ **Hamm's,** tray, canoer on lake, multicolored, 13¼″ 15.00 19.00 17.00

☐ **Hamm's,** tray, lion crest in gold with white lettering on red background, 13¼″ 8.00 10.00 9.00

☐ **Hamm's,** tray, woodland scene with hiker and bear, multicolored, 13¼″ 15.00 19.00 17.00

☐ **Hamm's Preferred Stock,** tray, view of brewery on front and reverse of tray, red and black against white background, 13¼″ 24.00 32.00 28.00

☐ **Heineken,** pocket knife-opener combination, brand name on handle, "Solingen, Germany" on base of blade 44.00 52.00 49.00

☐ **Heineken,** shoe, wood, "Heineken Beer," yellow with illustration of Dutch boy and windmill, 10″ 22.00 28.00 25.00

☐ **Hofbrau Bavaria,** mug, ceramic 4.00 6.00 5.00

	Current Price Range		Prior Year Average
☐ **Holsten,** ashtray, ceramic, circular, "Holsten Beer" in black lettering on white, made in Germany, 4"	17.00	23.00	20.00
☐ **Iroquois,** coaster, red and white, head of Indian chief, "Iroquois Indian Head Beer and Ale, Iroquois Beverage Corp., Buffalo, N.Y.," c. 1940-50, 4"	5.00	7.00	6.00
☐ **Iroquois,** tip tray, Indian chief trademark with "Iroquois Brewery, Buffalo," circular, c. 1930-40, 4½"	100.00	140.00	120.00
☐ **Jacob Ruppert,** non-illuminated sign, oval, wire stand-up device on back, "Ruppert Beer and Ale, New York," reverse-painted on glass, black with silver lettering, imitation wood frame, 18" x 12"	50.00	70.00	60.00
☐ **Knickerbocker,** opener, "Jacob Ruppert Brewery, New York, The Brew that Satisfies, Save this Opener, Order by the Case"	17.00	23.00	20.00

Iroquois Tray, *made by Charles Snowk, 1905, scarce, 12",* **$350.00-$400.00**
(photo courtesy of ©Paul Michel, Buffalo, NY, 1984)

	Current Price Range		Prior Year Average
☐ **Kuebler,** tip tray, "Kuebler Beer, Easton, Pa., 1852," black and orange, illustration of top-hatted man with mug, circular, believed to date from late 1940's, 4½"	35.00	45.00	40.00
☐ **Lone Star,** tray, star logo in gold and red against white background, 13¼"	11.00	15.00	13.00
☐ **Lowenbrau,** tray, gold heraldic lion, blue background, 13¼"	5.00	7.00	6.00
☐ **McSorley's Cream Stock Ale,** tray, tavern interior scene, dated 1936, 11¾"	40.00	50.00	45.00
☐ **Michelob,** coaster, circular, red and black, emblem on front, on back: "Have a Michelob, It's an Unexpected Pleasure," c. 1970-80, 3½"	.90	1.20	1.05
☐ **Miller Lite,** non-illuminated sign, plastic, white with blue lettering, 18" x 14"	4.00	5.00	4.50
☐ **Old German,** thermometer, circular, 10" diameter	22.00	28.00	25.00
☐ **Old German,** tie clip, "Herman"	13.00	17.00	15.00
☐ **Old Shay Ale,** ashtray, metallic, silver color, "Old Shay Ale, Product of Fort Pitt Brewing Co., Jeannette, Pa. Plant" in black lettering	13.00	17.00	15.00
☐ **Old Style,** illuminated sign, octagonal, brand name at center, mounted on pillar-type decorative bar with brass finial, gold and brown, 14" x 7"	8.00	10.00	9.00
☐ **Pabst Blue Ribbon,** illuminated sign, standard logo,raised seal and lettering in a plaque-like frame, blue and white, 15" x 20"	16.00	20.00	18.00
☐ **Pabst Blue Ribbon,** illuminated sign, circular, silver and gold mug with large brand name at top of frame, logo at bottom, 15" x 15"	10.00	14.00	12.00
☐ **Pabst Blue Ribbon,** tray, girl in flapper outfit, multicolored, 13¼"	7.00	9.00	8.00
☐ **Pabst Blue Ribbon,** tray, 1976 Bicentennial tray with view of old brewery, 13¼"	7.00	9.00	8.00
☐ **Piel's** tray, "Enjoy Piel's Beer," multicolored caricatures of Bert and Harry Piel, white background, 13¼"	15.00	19.00	17.00
☐ **Piel's Light,** tray, elf carrying tray, multicolored against gold background, 11¾"	15.00	19.00	17.00
☐ **Rheingold Extra Dry,** tray, Liebman, black and white on red background, 11¾"	7.00	9.00	8.00
☐ **Rheingold Extra Dry Lager,** tray, logo in black and red against white background, red sides, 13¼"	8.00	10.00	9.00

	Current Price Range		Prior Year Average
☐ **Ruppert Knickerbocker**, tray, Father Knickerbocker, multicolored, 13¼"	10.00	14.00	12.00
☐ **Ruppert Old Knickerbocker**, tray, eagle in gold and white, gold and red on red background, 13¼"	18.00	24.00	21.00
☐ **Schaefer**, tray, logo and grain symbol in red, white and gold, repeated on reverse, 13¼" . .	7.00	9.00	8.00
☐ **Schaefer**, tray, red and white with mottos, 11¾"	9.00	13.00	11.00
☐ **Schlitz**, illuminated sign, shield-shaped, "Light Beer" with word "Light" in very large lettering, decorative molding, gold and yellow, 20" x 18"	21.00	27.00	24.00
☐ **Schmidt's**, non-illuminated sign, "Schmidt's of Philadelphia, Beer and Ale," small sign on black wooden stand, black with silver lettering, c. 1940-50, 8" x 6"	43.00	57.00	50.00
☐ **Whitebread**, astray, plastic, circular, blue, "Whitebread Tankard Helps me Excel," made in Great Britain, 9"	4.00	6.00	5.00
☐ **Yuengling**, coaster, circular, green and red, front: "Yuengling Premium Beer, Since 1829," reverse: "America's Oldest Breweries," 3¼"	1.85	2.30	2.10
☐ **Yuengling**, opener, "Drink Yuengling's Beer and Ale, D.G. Yuengling & Son, Inc., Pottsville, Pa."	8.00	10.00	9.00

BUCK ROGERS

DESCRIPTION: Buck Rogers began as a futuristic comic strip conceived by Philip Nowlan in 1929. Since then, comic books, radio programs, television series and movies have been produced about this space hero.

TYPES: Because of its popularity among children, all types of items including premiums, toys, school supplies and dishes have featured Buck Rogers characters.

COMMENTS: Collectors of Buck Rogers memorabilia will find that items produced in its early years are usually more valuable then recent objects.

☐ **Badge**, Buck Rogers Solar Scout badge, Cream of Wheat premium, dated 1935	35.00	45.00	40.00
☐ **Button**, Buck Rogers in the 25th Century, celluloid, multicolored	35.00	45.00	40.00

	Current Price Range		Prior Year Average
☐ **Button,** Buck Rogers Satellite Pioneer, lithographed tin in red, white and black, illustration of space vehicle with balcony encircling it, astronauts walking on balcony, words, "Rocket Rangers" in small letters	95.00	115.00	110.00
☐ **Button,** Buck Rogers Solar Scout membership button, Cream of Wheat premium, celluloid, 1935	20.00	25.00	22.50
☐ **Figure,** Buck Rogers in the 25th Century, Ardella, Mego, plastic, 1979	9.00	12.00	10.50
☐ **Figure,** Buck Rogers in the 25th Century, Draco, Mego, plastic, 1979	9.00	12.00	10.50
☐ **Figure,** Buck Rogers in the 25th Century, Killer Kane, Mego, plastic, 1979	9.00	12.00	10.50
☐ **Gun,** Buck Rogers Atomic Pistol, Daisy Manufacturing Co., Plymouth, Michigan, cast pot metal with chrome plating, beaded grip	50.00	70.00	60.00
☐ **Gun,** Buck Rogers Copper Disintegrator Cap gun, cast iron, picture of Buck Rogers with wording "Buck Rogers in the 25th Century"	120.00	150.00	135.00
☐ **Gun,** Buck Rogers Pocket Pistol, Daisy Manufacturing Co., lithographed tin	100.00	130.00	120.00
☐ **Gun,** Buck Rogers Rubber Band Gun, Onward School Supply Co., large lithographed cardboard card from which the gun and targets punch out	35.00	45.00	40.00
☐ **Gun,** Buck Rogers Sonic Ray Gun, Norton Engineering and Manufacturing Co., Chicago, plastic, battery powered	30.00	40.00	35.00
☐ **Holster,** Buck Rogers combat set holster, 1934	100.00	120.00	110.00
☐ **Kite,** Buck Rogers Strato-Kite, Aero Kite Co., 1946	45.00	55.00	40.00
☐ **Matchbook Cover,** Buck Rogers, carries ad for ice cream with ad for Buck Rogers radio network program	7.00	10.00	8.50
☐ **Pencil Case,** Buck Rogers Pencil Case, cardboard, multicolored, top has picture of Buck Rogers, 1938	25.00	35.00	30.00
☐ **Printing Set,** Buck Rogers, set of 22 stamps used to create comic book stories	115.00	135.00	125.00
☐ **Rocket Ships,** Buck Rogers Battlecruiser, Tootsie Toy Co., lithographed tin, blue and yellow, moves on string or wire, 1937	60.00	80.00	70.00
☐ **Rocket Ship,** Buck Rogers Laserscope Fighter, Mego, plastic, complex design, 1979	20.00	25.00	22.50

	Current Price Range		Prior Year Average

Rocket Ship, Buck Rogers Tootsietoy Rocket Ship #1033, Attack Ship, cast metal, white and red **130.00 160.00   145.00**

BUMPER STICKERS

TOPIC: Bumper stickers were put on the bumpers of cars to make a statement or to promote something.

TYPES: Bumper stickers may be humorous, political or promotional, or they may simply declare an interesting thought.

PERIOD: These items were very popular during the 1960s and early 1970s.

COMMENTS: Bumper stickers are collectible, but few dealers carry them. Collectors usually rely on swapping or trading with other enthusiasts.

☐ **Bear Mountain State Park,** 4½" x 18", c. 1962 .... **1.25   1.50   1.30**

Bumper Stickers, *World War II,* each, **$8.00–$15.00**

	Current Price Range		Prior Year Average
☐ **Boston Red Sox**, team symbol, blue and white, c. 1968	2.00	2.50	2.25
☐ **Chicago Bears**, team symbol, 5″ x 16″, c. 1960	2.25	2.75	2.50
☐ **I Brake For Animals**, 5½″ x 17″, c. 1970 . . .	1.25	1.50	1.37
☐ **If You Can Read This You're Too Close**, black lettering, white background, 4″ x 12″, late 1950s	1.75	2.25	2.00
☐ **Impeach Early Warren**, 5″ x 17″, c. 1960	11.00	16.00	13.50
☐ **Jesus Saves**, various versions of accompanying text, some with no accompanying text, mid to late 1960s	1.25	1.50	1.33
☐ **Kennedy For President**, 4½″ x 14″, white letters on red and blue background, 1960	15.00	20.00	17.00
☐ **Kennedy/Johnson**, caricatures, green and black, 1960	17.00	22.00	19.00
☐ **Make Love Not War**, various designs, some with peace symbol, mid 1960s	2.75	3.50	3.10
☐ Most other novelty of humorous themes . . .	1.25	2.50	1.75
☐ Presidential campaign, 1972 (most varieties)	5.00	6.50	5.60
☐ Presidential campaign, 1976 (most varieties)	3.25	4.50	3.90
☐ **Watch My Tail, Not Hers**, 4⅞″ x 15½″, c. 1958	1.75	2.75	2.20

BUTTONS

DESCRIPTION: Dating to the 13th century, buttons were first used for decoration. Early buttons had very elaborate and exquisite designs. Later buttons were more commonly used as fasteners. Both types are collectible.

VARIATIONS: A variety of button types have been made including, heads of famous people, animals, picture buttons, story buttons, sporting buttons, among others. "Realistics" were plastic buttons made in the 1930s and 1940s that looked like everyday items in miniature. Examples include fruit, animals and food.

MAKER: Most antique and collectible buttons on the market today are American, French or English made.

MATERIALS: Buttons have been made from materials including painted tin, metal, mother-of-pearl, pewter, brass, glass, gilt, plastic, ivory, ceramic, cloisonne and celluloid.

MARKS: Some early buttons, from the 18th and 19th centuries, had backmarks which identify the maker. Some collectors collect by backmark rather than by button design.

COMMENTS: Currently buttons from the 18th century to the present are the most available and collectible. They are a lovely and usually inexpensive collectible.

ADDITIONAL TIPS: The listings are arranged alphabetically by button material. A description follows.

For further button information, contact: The National Button Society, Box 39, Eastwood, Kentucky 40018.

	Current Price Range		Prior Year Average
☐ **Black Glass,** cameo head	12.50	20.00	14.00
☐ **Black Glass,** elephant under palm tree	7.50	13.00	8.50
☐ **Black Glass,** faceted ball, gold foil top	35.00	45.00	37.00
☐ **Black Glass,** mountain with house scene, beaded gilt edge	35.00	45.00	37.00
☐ **Black Glass,** shape of a slipper	10.00	15.00	12.00
☐ **Black Onyx,** with 14K gold, ball shaped, 19th century	60.00	70.00	63.00

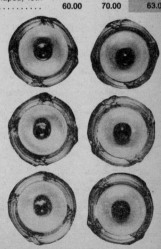

Buttons,
mother of pearl,
sapphire inset,
Tiffany & Co., 1915,
$675.00-$800.00

	Current Price Range		Prior Year Average
☐ **Black Onyx,** gold filled, ball shaped, 19th century	20.00	25.00	21.00
☐ **Brass,** Aesop's Fable, frog and rabbit	21.50	30.00	24.00
☐ **Brass,** Aesop's Fable, two mice	35.00	45.00	37.00
☐ **Brass,** angry rooster	10.00	15.00	12.00
☐ **Brass,** cherubs with cornucopia and goat	4.50	8.00	6.50
☐ **Brass,** children playing game, Victorian era	21.00	30.00	24.00
☐ **Brass,** dancing gypsy girl with goat	48.00	60.00	53.00
☐ **Brass Disc,** bridge and river scene, black and white	75.00	105.00	84.00
☐ **Brass,** Indian hunter	35.00	45.00	37.00
☐ **Brass,** mother feeding child, high relief	21.50	30.00	25.00
☐ **Brass,** rooster standing on wheat shaft	16.00	25.00	18.00
☐ **Celluloid,** angel head, gold background, gilt rims	35.00	45.00	37.00
☐ **Celluloid,** Count Fersen, floral brass frame	21.00	30.00	22.00
☐ **Celluloid,** Duchess of Devonshire, pastel colors	42.00	55.00	47.00
☐ **Celluloid,** Marie Antonette	10.00	15.00	12.00
☐ **Ceramic,** bird, black and white	25.00	35.00	28.00
☐ **Ceramic,** bird with branch in beak, scalloped border	35.00	45.00	37.00
☐ **Ceramic,** cupid, scroll design on edge	45.00	55.00	47.00
☐ **Cloisonne,** birds flying, brass, black and white on red background	82.00	115.00	95.00
☐ **Enamel,** lighthouse with boat scene	47.00	58.00	50.00
☐ **Enamel,** lady riding bicycle, cut steel border	62.00	77.00	65.00
☐ **Enamel,** maiden, blue and white, diamond paste border	52.00	67.00	55.00
☐ **Enamel,** rose colored scene on white, embossed scroll border	200.00	245.00	220.00
☐ **Enamel,** with seed pearls and 14K gold, ladybug design, 19th century	575.00	600.00	580.00
☐ **Enamel,** shepherdess, light purple, diamond paste border	47.00	58.00	50.00
☐ **Enamel,** star shape decorated with cut steels	16.00	25.00	20.00
☐ **Enamel,** woman at fountain	55.00	75.00	60.00
☐ **Glass,** black liberty cap and flag, silver frame, 18th c.	55.00	75.00	60.00
☐ **Glass,** French Revolution motif, copper rim	70.00	88.00	74.00
☐ **Glass,** molded opaque, brown bird design	25.00	35.00	28.00
☐ **Gold,** 14K, ball shape with ribbing, 19th century	60.00	70.00	63.00
☐ **Gold,** 14K, button set with chain, 19th century	50.00	60.00	52.00

	Current Price Range		Prior Year Average
☐ **Gold,** 14K, engraved collar button, 19th century	30.00	35.00	31.00
☐ **Gold,** 14K, pearl shape, 19th century	60.00	70.00	63.00
☐ **Gold,** 14K, scrolled edge design, 19th century	60.00	70.00	63.00
☐ **Gold,** woven hair under swirls, cartwheel design, 19th century	110.00	130.00	118.00
☐ **Gold,** woven hair under swirls, cartwheel design with scalloped edge, 19th century ...	130.00	150.00	138.00
☐ **Gold Plated,** dragon	7.50	13.00	8.00
☐ **Ivory,** carved Royal Salamander	30.00	40.00	34.00
☐ **Ivory,** cut-out girl and bird, blue background	150.00	180.00	155.00
☐ **Ivory,** painted cherub in chariot drawn by two horses	90.00	110.00	95.00
☐ **Ivory,** painted girl and dog chasing butterflies	90.00	110.00	95.00
☐ **Ivory,** painted lady and dog, silver rim	48.00	60.00	53.00
☐ **Ivory,** painted Oriental head	35.00	45.00	40.00
☐ **Mother-of-pearl,** 14K gold, simple button, 19th century	75.00	85.00	80.00
☐ **Oriental,** fan design, multicolored, scalloped border	30.00	40.00	33.00
☐ **Oriental,** floral motif, enameled	35.00	45.00	37.00
☐ **Pewter,** owl's head	4.50	8.00	5.50
☐ **Pierced Brass,** Little Red Riding Hood	13.00	20.00	15.00
☐ **Porcelain,** cherub catching butterflies, pink, black and white	20.00	30.00	23.00
☐ **Porcelain,** cupid, scroll design on edge	48.00	65.00	52.00
☐ **Porcelain,** flowers and butterfly, 18th c.	17.50	30.00	20.00
☐ **Porcelain,** pasture scene with children	30.00	40.00	34.00
☐ **Porcelain,** with gold, painted angels, 19th century	520.00	540.00	528.00
☐ **Silver,** Bacchus, God of Wine, etched design	25.00	35.00	27.00
☐ **Stamped Brass,** two children fighting and pulling hair	21.00	30.00	24.00
☐ **Steel,** floral design	4.50	8.00	5.50
☐ **Turquoise,** with 14K gold, button set with chain, 19th century	95.00	105.00	98.00
☐ **Victorian,** figure, black glass disc	8.50	14.00	9.00
☐ **Wedgwood,** classic figures, white relief on blue, cut steel border, 18th c.	250.00	295.00	270.00
☐ **Wedgwood,** classic figure, white on royal blue, gilt rim, 18th c.	235.00	275.00	245.00
☐ **Wedgwood,** classical figures, white relief on light blue	52.00	70.00	60.00
☐ **Wedgwood,** floral design, diamond paste border, silver frame	200.00	250.00	215.00

	Current Price Range		Prior Year Average
☐ **Wedgwood,** warrior, white relief on royal blue, copper border	225.00	275.00	230.00

CAMERAS

DESCRIPTION: Camera collecting is a small but strong field.

TYPES: Box, folding, panoramic, miniature and 35 mm cameras are all favorite types to collect.

ORIGIN: Although the photographic process was invented by Louis Jacques Mande Daguerre of Paris in 1839, it wasn't until the late 1800s that photography was accessible to the masses. An American, George Eastman, was the first major camera manufacturer.

COMMENTS: Since Kodak was the first company to sucessfully produce cameras for the public, Kodak cameras are quite sought after.

ADDITIONAL INFORMATION: For more information about camera collectibles, consult *The Official Price Guide to Collectible Cameras,* published by The House of Collectibles.

	Current Price Range		Prior Year Average
☐ **Kodak,** Autographic Junior No.1, F77/100 mm lens, 1915	15.00	25.00	20.00
☐ **Kodak,** Brownie, No.2, 50th Anniversary box camera giveaway, 1930	15.00	20.00	17.50
☐ **Kodak,** Bulls-Eye No.3, uses 124 film, 1910 .	40.00	50.00	45.00
☐ **Kodak,** Duo-620 Series II folding camera, f3.5/75 mm lens, 1940	50.00	60.00	55.00
☐ **Kodak,** Eureka No.4, uses 109 film, 1899	85.00	95.00	80.00
☐ **Kodak,** Folding Pocket No.3, uses 122 film, 1905	30.00	50.00	40.00
☐ **Kodak,** Ordinary, box, wooden, 4″ x 5″, 1890s	800.00	1200.00	1000.00
☐ **Kodak,** Premo, box camera, achromatic lens, automatic shutter, 4″ x 5″, 1910	20.00	30.00	25.00
☐ **Kodak,** Quick Focus, achromatic lens, rotary shutter, 3¼″ x 5½″, 1908	125.00	150.00	137.00
☐ **Kodak,** Vest Pocket Kodak Model B, rotary shutter, 1930s	80.00	120.00	100.00
☐ **Leica,** model IIc, highest shutter speed 500, 1940s	150.00	200.00	175.00
☐ **Minolta,** Semi-Automatic, folding, Promar lens, 1937	40.00	60.00	50.00
☐ **Nikon,** Model S, later replaced by Model S2, 1951	100.00	125.00	112.00
☐ **Pentacon,** model FBM, exposure meter, 1957	55.00	80.00	67.00

	Current Price Range		Prior Year Average
☐ **Peerless,** box camera, uses glass plates ...	60.00	80.00	70.00
☐ **Rex Magazine Camera, Co.,** 4″ x 5″, 1899 ...	175.00	220.00	200.00
☐ **Teddy Camera Co.,** Model A, takes direct positive prints, developing tank below camera, 1924	325.00	425.00	375.00

CANES AND WALKING STICKS

TOPIC: Canes and walking sticks were popular accessories in the 17th and 18th centuries. They were both fashionable and utilitarian because they could be used for protection if needed.

TYPES: Canes are either simple walking sticks or "gadget" canes which conceal a sword, pistol, musical instrument or other device.

PERIOD: Canes are descendants of the sticks early man used to defend himself, and as such date back into early human history. The stylish canes of Europe came into vogue in the 17th and 18th centuries, while the 19th century saw gadget canes reaching a peak of popularity.

MATERIAL: Wood is used for the shafts of almost all canes. Handles amy be made out of wood, ivory, bone or metal.

COMMENTS: Canes are fascinating collectibles whether they contain concealed devices or not. The ones that do are particularly interesting because ingenious guns or other weapons may be hidden in them. It is advisable to use caution when handling old canes because a concealed weapon might be inadvertently triggered.

ADDITIONAL TIPS: When buying a cane or walking stick, examine it closely for indications of hidden compartments. Many devices are so well concealed in canes that they go undiscovered for years.

	Current Price Range		Prior Year Average
☐ **Amethyst,** cut glass handle	172.00	205.00	188.00
☐ **Bamboo,** curved handle	14.00	18.00	16.00
☐ **Blown Glass,** green	65.00	80.00	72.00
☐ **Bottle Cane,** glass liner holds liquor, 36″ ...	145.00	175.00	157.00
☐ **Clenched Hand,** ivory	160.00	320.00	240.00
☐ **Dog's Head,** Fox Terrier, painted and carved wood	205.00	225.00	212.00
☐ **Dog's Head,** wood with brown eyes, c. 1900 .	32.00	52.00	42.00
☐ **Dog's Head,** glass eyes, c. 1900	48.00	55.00	51.00
☐ **Hound's Head,** ivory	55.00	110.00	80.00
☐ **Monkey,** hand carved	90.00	115.00	102.00

	Current Price Range		Prior Year Average
☐ **Mother-Of-Pearl,** gold	55.00	75.00	65.00
☐ **Parade Cane,** china clown head	30.00	40.00	35.00
☐ **Umbrella Cane,** wood case, 34"	85.00	115.00	100.00
☐ **Walking Stick,** gold head	100.00	125.00	112.00
☐ **Walking Stick,** sterling	43.00	58.00	50.00

CARNIVAL GLASS

This section features only a sampling of carnival glass. In order to accurately present the vast amount of information required by serious collectors, a special edition devoted to glassware has been published by The House of Collectibles, Inc. For more in-depth information refer to *The Official Price Guide to Glassware* for 10.95.

DESCRIPTION: In 1905, Taffeta, or Carnival glass as it has come to be known, was born out of the turn of the century craze for iridescent art glass. Using mass production and new chemical techniques, Carnival glass was widely produced toward the end of the Art Nouveau period. Tastes changed, however, ushering in the streamlined Art Deco period. Even though it continued to be produced until 1930, by 1925 Carnival glass was on the way out. With a dwindling market, this glass was sold by the trainload to fairs and carnivals to be given away as prizes. Hence, it has come to be called Carnival glass.

ADDITIONAL TIPS: Intense collector interest has already driven the prices of Carnival glass into the astronomical range. An amethyst Carnival farmyard plate sold for $8,000 just this year. The talbes have really been turned in this field over the years as this originally cheap imitation of Art glass now far exceeds in value the high quality glass it sought to imitate. Long regarded with disdain by serious dealers, collectors and auction houses, Carnival glass is now turning up on the most prestigious auction blocks in the country. Carnival glass auctions demonstrated one thing clearly — Carnival glass continues to command higher and higher prices with no ceiling in sight. Examples of auction results are: are, one-of-a-kind Acan Burrs aqua-opalescent punch bowl, base and five cups, $12,500; purple Christmas compote, $1550; large green Hobstar and Feather rosebowl, $1150; amethyst Inverted Thistle pitcher, $2100; teal blue Grape and Cable plate, $1150; and amethyst Farmyard bowl, $1400.

RECOMMENDED READING: For more in-depth information on Carnival glass, you may refer to *The Official Price Guide to Glassware* and *The Official Identification Guide to Glassware*, published by The House of Collectibles.

ACORN — *Fenton*

	Current Price Range		Prior Year Average
Bowl, diameter 7″ - 8½″			
☐ marigold	20.00	30.00	25.00
☐ purple	28.50	50.00	30.00
☐ green	28.50	50.00	30.00
☐ blue	28.50	50.00	30.00
☐ amethyst	28.50	50.00	30.00
☐ peach opalescent	120.00	135.00	125.00
☐ vaseline	110.00	125.00	115.00
☐ red	225.00	325.00	260.00
Plate, diameter 9″			
☐ marigold	120.00	135.00	125.00
☐ purple	285.00	340.00	300.00
☐ green	285.00	340.00	300.00
☐ blue	285.00	340.00	300.00
☐ amethyst	285.00	340.00	300.00

Bowl, *Marigold Carnival Glass, Luster Rose pattern, three footed, marked,* **$85.00-$100.00**
(photo courtesy of ©BJ Warner, Surfside Beach, SC, 1984)

APPLE BLOSSOMS — *Dugan*

	Current Price Range		Prior Year Average
Bowl, diameter 7″ - 9″			
☐ marigold	35.00	45.00	37.50
☐ purple	40.00	50.00	42.00
☐ green	40.00	50.00	42.00
☐ blue	40.00	50.00	42.00
☐ amethyst	40.00	50.00	42.00
☐ white	60.00	80.00	65.00
☐ ices	60.00	80.00	65.00
Plate, diameter 8½″			
☐ marigold	45.00	57.50	48.50
☐ purple	65.00	85.00	70.00
☐ green	65.00	85.00	70.00
☐ blue	65.00	85.00	70.00
☐ amethyst	65.00	85.00	70.00
☐ white	85.00	110.00	90.00
☐ ice blue	85.00	110.00	90.00
☐ ice green	85.00	110.00	90.00

BANDED DRAPE — *Fenton*

Tumbler			
☐ marigold	15.00	20.00	17.00
☐ blue	28.00	32.00	29.00
☐ amethyst	28.00	32.00	29.00
☐ ice green	35.00	41.00	37.00
☐ white	35.00	41.00	37.00
Water Pitcher			
☐ marigold	70.00	85.00	72.00
☐ blue	185.00	200.00	190.00
☐ amethyst	185.00	200.00	190.00
☐ ice green	240.00	275.00	245.00
☐ white	240.00	275.00	245.00

CHRYSANTHEMUM — *Fenton*

Bowl, flat, diameter 10″			
☐ marigold	33.00	37.00	35.00
☐ blue	47.00	55.00	50.00
☐ green	47.00	55.00	50.00
☐ ice green	95.00	110.00	100.00
☐ white	95.00	110.00	100.00
☐ red	500.00	600.00	550.00
Bowl, footed, diameter 10″			
☐ marigold	33.00	37.00	35.00
☐ blue	47.00	55.00	50.00
☐ green	47.00	55.00	50.00

	Current Price Range		Prior Year Average
☐ ice green	95.00	110.00	100.00
☐ white	95.00	110.00	100.00
☐ red	500.00	600.00	525.00

ELKS — Fenton

Bowl, Detroit

☐ purple	325.00	375.00	330.00
☐ green	325.00	375.00	330.00
☐ blue	325.00	375.00	330.09
☐ amethyst	325.00	375.00	330.00

Bowl, Parkersburg

☐ purple	350.00	425.00	360.00
☐ green	350.00	425.00	360.00
☐ blue	350.00	425.00	360.00
☐ amethyst	350.00	425.00	360.00

GRAPE DELIGHT — Dugan

Nut Bowl

☐ purple	60.00	75.00	62.00

Rose Bowl

☐ marigold	40.00	50.00	42.00
☐ purple	50.00	65.00	52.00
☐ green	50.00	65.00	52.00
☐ blue	50.00	65.00	52.00
☐ amethyst	50.00	65.00	52.00

HEADDRESS — Imperial

Bowl, diameter 9″

☐ marigold	16.00	18.00	17.00
☐ purple	25.00	30.00	28.00
☐ green	25.00	30.00	28.00
☐ blue	25.00	30.00	28.00
☐ ice blue	38.00	42.00	40.00
☐ ice green	38.00	42.00	40.00
☐ vaseline	38.00	42.00	40.00
☐ clambroth	38.00	42.00	40.00

HOBSTAR AND ARCHES — Imperial

Bowl, diameter 9″

☐ marigold	32.00	36.00	34.00
☐ amethyst	42.00	46.00	43.00
☐ green	42.00	46.00	43.00
☐ smoke	52.00	66.00	54.00

	Current Price Range		Prior Year Average
Fruit Bowl, two piece			
☐ marigold	70.00	85.00	73.00
☐ amethyst	90.00	100.00	94.00
☐ green	90.00	100.00	94.00
☐ smoke	110.00	120.00	115.00

ORANGE TREE AND SCROLL — *Fenton*

Pitcher			
☐ marigold	250.00	300.00	275.00
☐ green	350.00	450.00	360.00
☐ amethyst	350.00	450.00	360.00
Tumbler			
☐ marigold	40.00	45.00	42.00
☐ green	55.00	65.00	57.00
☐ amethyst	55.00	65.00	57.00

ROSALIND — *Millersburg*

Bowl			
☐ marigold	60.00	70.00	65.00
☐ green	80.00	90.00	85.00
☐ purple	80.00	90.00	85.00
☐ blue	80.00	90.00	85.00
☐ amethyst	80.00	90.00	85.00
Plate			
☐ green	200.00	225.00	215.00
☐ purple	200.00	225.00	215.00
☐ blue	200.00	225.00	215.00
☐ amethyst	200.00	225.00	215.00

SWIRL HOBNAIL — *Millersburg*

Rose Bowl			
☐ marigold	135.00	165.00	140.00
☐ purple	260.00	320.00	270.00
☐ green	260.00	320.00	270.00
☐ blue	500.00	650.00	525.00
☐ amethyst	260.00	320.00	270.00
Spittoon			
☐ marigold	360.00	430.00	370.00
☐ purple	420.00	480.00	425.00
☐ green	420.00	480.00	425.00
☐ blue	900.00	1100.00	910.00
☐ amethyst	420.00	480.00	425.00

TAFFETA LUSTRE — Fostoria	Current Price Range		Prior Year Average
Bowl, diameter 10"			
☐ blue	110.00	130.00	115.00
☐ green	110.00	130.00	115.00
☐ amber	90.00	110.00	95.00
☐ orchid	90.00	110.00	95.00
Candlesticks			
☐ blue	250.00	260.00	255.00
☐ green	250.00	260.00	255.00
☐ amber	230.00	240.00	235.00
☐ orchid	230.00	240.00	235.00

CARS

In order to accurately present the vast amount of information required by serious collectors, a special edition devoted to cars and trucks is published by The House of Collectibles. This handy pocket-size guide features more than 10,000 prices for antique, classic and collector cars. It is available at most bookstores. For more extensive car and truck information, refer to the $10.95 *Official 1985 Price Guide to Collector Cars* featuring more than 37,000 prices.

CASH REGISTERS

ORIGIN: The cash register was introduced in 1884 by James Ritty. Its primary purpose was to deter sales clerks from stealing money. One of Ritty's customers bought controlling interest in Ritty's business and eventually started the National Cash Register Company.

MAKER: National Cash Register Company is the best known maker of cash registers. Others include such companies as St. Louis, Ideal and Michigan.

MATERIALS: Prior to World War I, cash registers were ornately made and decorated. Popular materials used were oak, brass and bronze.

COMMENTS: Registers made before 1916 are the most sought after because of their decoration. Age, rarity and beauty of the machine are the top factors when buying a cash register. Size is also important.

ADDITIONAL TIPS: The following listings are alphabetical according to manufacturers.

	Current Price Range		Prior Year Average
☐ **Hallwood**, aluminum, c. 1890	720.00	800.00	750.00
☐ **Michigan**, nickel plated, 20th century	560.00	650.00	600.00
☐ **Monitor**, model 1A, oak with decal, c. 1900 . .	380.00	460.00	405.00
☐ **National**, brass and mahogany	500.00	600.00	550.00
☐ **National**, brass and oak	900.00	1000.00	950.00
☐ **National**, brass, oak, floor model with drawers	2400.00	3000.00	2500.00
☐ **National**, brass, ornate	560.00	650.00	600.00
☐ **National**, brass, side box	538.00	600.00	550.00
☐ **National**, brass with marble	400.00	550.00	450.00
☐ **National**, model 15, oak	250.00	350.00	300.00
☐ **National**, model 47, c. 1901	1000.00	1300.00	1200.00
☐ **National**, model 452, brass, hand crank	750.00	900.00	825.00
☐ **National**, model 130	950.00	1200.00	1000.00
☐ **National**, nickel plated, embossed, lock box	285.00	350.00	300.00
☐ **National**, nickel plated, brass, oak base, c. 1913	1900.00	2500.00	1950.00
☐ **National**, oak brass, inlaid, double drawers, c. 1908	1500.00	1700.00	1575.00
☐ **Premier Junior**	325.00	395.00	360.00
☐ **St. Louis**, nickel plated	380.00	470.00	420.00
☐ **St. Louis**, brass	612.00	675.00	630.00

CHALKWARE

DESCRIPTION: Items made from plaster of paris and painted in bright colors are called chalkware.

TYPES: Animal figurines are the most common chalkware items.

PERIOD: Chalkware, which was produced as a cheap imitation of Staffordshire and Bennington ware, was found in middle class homes during the 1800s.

COMMENTS: Chalkware is now associated with Folk Art and can be found in antiques stores specializing in that area.

ADDITIONAL TIPS: Animals with nodding heads are especially rare. Few were produced and even fewer have survived through the years.

☐ **Bank**, apple with red cheeks	28.00	32.00	27.50
☐ **Basket**, fruit filled	310.00	360.00	325.00
☐ **Bird**, nesting	260.00	310.00	280.00
☐ **Black Boy with Watermelon**, 4″	18.00	22.00	17.50
☐ **Bookends**, pirates, painted, pair	42.00	48.00	42.00
☐ **Boy**, reading books, 10½″	90.00	110.00	92.00
☐ **Cat**, 4½″	160.00	185.00	162.00

	Current Price Range		Prior Year Average
☐ **Cat**, 10½ "	185.00	235.00	200.00
☐ **Charley McCarthy**, 15"	22.00	28.00	22.50
☐ **Dancing Lady**, 14"	18.00	32.00	22.00
☐ **Deer**, 9½ "	435.00	485.00	450.00
☐ **Dog**, 8½ "	135.00	155.00	138.00
☐ **Dove**, green with blue wings, 12"	210.00	235.00	212.00
☐ **Dove**, green and yellow wings, 6"	260.00	310.00	275.00
☐ **Duck**	140.00	165.00	142.00
☐ **Eagle**, spread, 9½ "	285.00	335.00	300.00
☐ **Gnome**, German, 11", 1930s	22.00	28.00	22.50
☐ **Horn of Plenty**, 14"	18.00	32.00	22.00
☐ **Indian**, Cigar Store, reclining, 23"	210.00	235.00	212.00
☐ **Lamb**, gray body, 8½ "	260.00	310.00	275.00
☐ **Lamb**, rectangular base, 6½ "	135.00	160.00	138.00
☐ **Owl**, 12"	185.00	210.00	182.00
☐ **Parrot**, 10½ "	1300.00	1600.00	1400.00
☐ **Pigeon**, 10"	135.00	160.00	138.00
☐ **Poodles**, 7¾ "	185.00	235.00	200.00
☐ **Rabbit**, sitting, 8"	160.00	185.00	162.00
☐ **Rooster**, 6"	335.00	385.00	350.00
☐ **Santa Claus**, 24"	155.00	180.00	160.00
☐ **Sheep**, mother with babies, 7"	185.00	210.00	182.00
☐ **Shepherd**, German, 17½ "	85.00	105.00	85.00
☐ **Squirrel**, 10"	185.00	210.00	182.00
☐ **Stag**, rectangular base, 15"	260.00	310.00	275.00

CHILDREN'S BOOKS

VALUE: Condition and author play important roles in determining value of children's books. Books by well-known authors, such as Lewis Carroll, are quite valuable and command high prices.

COMMENTS: Children's books of the 1800s are especially collectible.

☐ Abbott, Jacob. *Rollo's Correspondence.* Boston, 1841	100.00	150.00	125.00
☐ **Abbott, Jacob.** *Marco Baul's Travels and Adventures: Erie Canal.* Boston, 1848, colored frontispiece and four colored plates	55.00	75.00	65.00
☐ Abbott, Jacob. *Rollo at School.* Boston, 1849	175.00	225.00	200.00
☐ **Adams, Hannah.** *An Abridgement of the History of New England for the Use of Young Persons.* Boston, 1807, second edition	20.00	30.00	25.00
☐ **Aikin, Lucy.** *Juvenile Correspondence, or Letters ... for Children of Both Sexes.* Boston, 1822, calf	30.00	40.00	35.00

	Current Price Range		Prior Year Average
☐ **Alcott, Louisa M.** *Little Women.* Boston, 1869, second issue	70.00	90.00	80.00
☐ **Alcott, Louisa M.** *Little Men.* Boston, 1871	240.00	315.00	277.00
☐ **Alcott, Louisa M.** *Silver Pitchers.* Boston, 1876	35.00	42.00	38.00
☐ **Alcott, Louisa M.** *Jo's Boys.* Boston, 1886	35.00	42.00	38.00
☐ **Brereton, Captain F. S.** *In the Grip of the Mullah.* A tail of adventure in Somililand. London, 1904	8.00	10.00	9.00
☐ **Brereton, Captain F. S.** *The Hero of Panama.* A tale of the great canal. London, 1912	8.00	10.00	9.00
☐ **Browning, Robert.** *The Pied Piper of Hamelin.* London, n.d.	25.00	30.00	27.50
☐ **Burnett, Francis H.** *Little Lord Fauntleroy.* N.Y., 1886	150.00	200.00	175.00
☐ **Burnett, Francis H.** *Editha's Burglar.* Boston, 1888, second issue	15.00	20.00	17.50

East Of The Sun And Of The Moon,
illustrated by Kay Nielsen, Garden City Publishing Company,
1914, **$10.00-$15.00**

	Current Price Range		Prior Year Average
☐ **Butterworth, Hezekiah.** *Zip-Zag Journeys in Europe.* Boston, 1880, first edition	40.00	50.00	45.00
☐ **Caldecott, Randolph.** *The House that Jack Built.* London, n.d., 1878	25.00	30.00	27.50
☐ **Carroll, Lewis.** *Phantasmagoria and Other Poems.* London, 1869, blue cloth	100.00	130.00	115.00
☐ **Carroll, Lewis.** *Through the Looking-Glass, and What Alice Found There.* London, 1872, with 50 drawings by Tenniel, red cloth	350.00	425.00	387.00
☐ **Carroll, Lewis.** *The Hunting of the Shark.* London, 1876	175.00	225.00	200.00
☐ **Carroll, Lewis.** *Rhyme? and Reason?* London, 1883, green cloth	80.00	110.00	95.00
☐ **Carroll, Lewis.** *A Tangled Tale.* London, 1885	80.00	110.00	95.00
☐ **Carroll, Lewis.** *Sylvie and Bruno.* London, 1889	120.00	150.00	135.00
☐ **Carroll, Lewis.** *Sylvie and Bruno Concluded.* London, 1893	120.00	150.00	135.00
☐ **Carter, Nicholas ("Nick Carter").** *The Chain of Clues.* ¢N.Y., n.d., 1907	18.00	23.00	20.00
☐ **Examples of Goodness.** *Narrated for the Young.* Philadelphia, 1853	50.00	60.00	55.00
☐ **Faithful Fritz.** Troy, N.Y., n.d., 1888?, colored frontispiece	22.00	28.00	25.00
☐ **Famous Story Book.** Boston, n.d., c. 1890, colored pictorial boards and frontispiece . .	18.00	23.00	20.00
☐ **Federer, Charles.** *Yorkshire Chap Books.* London, 1889, marbled boards with vellum spine	80.00	100.00	90.00
☐ **Field Eugene.** *Little Willie.* N.p., n.d., oblong 6½" x 4", softbound	30.00	35.00	32.50
☐ **Field, Rachel.** *Hitty, Her First Hundred Years.* Illustrated by Dorothy P. Lathrop, N.Y., 1929	60.00	75.00	67.00
☐ **Florian, Chevalier de.** *William Tell or Switzerland Delivered.* Translated from the French. Exeter, N.H., 1826	40.00	50.00	45.00
☐ **Frost, John.** *Easy Exercises in Composition: Designed for use of Beginners.* Philadelphia, 1839, first edition	60.00	75.00	67.00
☐ **Kingsley, Charles.** *The Water-Babies.* Boston, 1864, first American edition	70.00	90.00	80.00
☐ **Kingston, W.H.G.** *Round the World.* A tale for boys, London, 1859	30.00	38.00	34.00
☐ **Kingston, W.H.G.** *In New Granada or heroes and patriots.* With 36 engravings. London, 1880, first edition	38.00	47.00	43.00

	Current Price Range		Prior Year Average
☐ **Lanier, Sidney.** *The Boy's King Arthur.* N.Y., 1880	38.00	47.00	43.00
☐ **Lear, Edward.** *A Book of Nonsense.* London, 1861	275.00	350.00	312.00
☐ **Lear, Edward.** *Calico Pie.* London, n.d., boards	120.00	150.00	135.00
☐ **Lear, Edward.** *Nonsense Songs.* London, 1871	300.00	375.00	337.00
☐ **Leech, John.** *Little Tour in Ireland.* London, 1859	70.00	90.00	80.00
☐ **Leigh, Percival.** *The Comic english Grammar.* London, 1856, upwards of 50 illustrations by John Leech	40.00	55.00	47.00
☐ *Little Ann and Other Stories.* Worcester, n.d., c. 1845	40.00	50.00	45.00
☐ *Little Book of Trades.* New Haven, n.d., c. 1835, softbound	120.00	150.00	135.00
☐ *Little Red Riding Hood.* N.Y., n.d., c. 1855, softbound	40.00	55.00	47.00
☐ **Lofting, Hugh.** *The Story of Doctor Dolittle.* N.Y., 1923, 12th printing	18.00	23.00	21.00
☐ **Lofting, Hugh.** *Dr. Dolittle's Circus.* N.Y., 1924	110.00	140.00	125.00
☐ **Lofting, Hugh.** *Dr. Dolittle's Garden.* N.Y.	32.00	38.00	35.50
☐ **Lofting, Hugh.** *Dr. Dolittle and the Secret Lake.* Philadelphia and N.Y., 1958	32.00	38.00	35.50
☐ *Lulu Tales, The Boat Builders, The Little Artist and other stories.* N.Y., 1855, decorated boards	18.00	23.00	20.50
☐ *Marmaduke Multiply.* N.Y. and Boston, n.d., c. 1840	65.00	80.00	72.00
☐ *Mary's Little Lamb.* Dearborn, Mich., 1928	25.00	32.00	28.50
☐ **May, Sophie.** *Dotty Dimple (Little Prudy Series).* Boston, 1856	34.00	40.00	37.00
☐ *Merry's Book of Travel and Adventure.* N.Y., 1860	18.00	23.00	20.50
☐ **Milne, A.A.** *Fourteen Songs from When We Were Very Young.* N.Y., 1925, first American edition	22.00	28.00	25.00
☐ **Milne, A.A.** *A Gallery of Children.* Philadelphia, n.d., 1925, first American edition	55.00	70.00	62.00
☐ **Milne, A.A.** *Winnie-the-Pooh.* London, 1926	200.00	250.00	225.00
☐ **New-England Primer.** Brookfield, Mass, 1822	90.00	120.00	105.00
☐ *Night Before Christmas.* London, n.d., c. 1905, softbound	23.00	30.00	26.00
☐ **Old Ironside.** *The Story of a Shipwreck.* Salem, 1855	18.00	23.00	20.50

	Current Price Range		Prior Year Average
☐ **Optic, Oliver.** *The Prisoners of the Cave.* N.Y., n.d., 1915, softbound	8.00	10.00	9.00
☐ **Otis, James.** *Toby Tyler or Ten Weeks with a Circus.* N.Y., 1881	165.00	195.00	180.00
☐ **Otis, James.** *Jennry Wren's Boarding House.* Boston, n.d., 1893, first edition	65.00	85.00	75.00
☐ **Otis, James.** *The Cruise of the Comet.* Boston, 1898	40.00	55.00	47.00
☐ **Page, Thomas N.** *Two Little Confederates.* N.Y., 1888	65.00	85.00	75.00
☐ **Phillips, E.O.** *Birdie and Her Dog.* London, n.d., c. 1885	14.00	18.00	15.50
☐ **Pinchard, Mrs.** *The Blind Child or Anecdotes of the Wyndham Family.* London, n.d., c. 1818	50.00	65.00	57.00
☐ *Poetical Geography.* Cincinnati, 1852	30.00	35.00	32.50
☐ *Poetry without Fiction for Children Between the Ages of Three and Seven.* By a Mother. Boxton, 1825	45.00	60.00	52.00
☐ **Porter, Eleanor H.** *Pollyana.* Boston, 1913	160.00	190.00	175.00
☐ **Porter, Eleanor H.** *Pollyana Grows Up.* Boston, 1915	40.00	50.00	45.00
☐ **Potter, Beatrix.** *The Tale of Benjamin Bunny.* London, 1904, boards	90.00	130.00	110.00
☐ **Potter, Beatrix.** *The Pie and the Patty-Pan.* London, 1905, boards	90.00	130.00	110.00
☐ **Potter, Beatrix.** *The Tale of Mrs. Tiggy-Winkle.* London, 1905, boards	85.00	120.00	102.00
☐ **Smith, Jessie Wilcox.** *The Water Babies.* N.Y., n.d., 1916	60.00	75.00	67.00
☐ **Smith, Joshua.** *The Northmen in New England.* Boston, 1829. Early work on Viking explorations of North America, for children	70.00	85.00	77.00
☐ **Sonvestre.** *Popular Legends of Brittany.* Boston, 1856, with 16 hand colored plates	80.00	100.00	90.00
☐ **Wiggin, Kate Douglas.** *The Story of Patsy.* Boston, 1890	18.00	23.00	20.50
☐ **Wiggin, Kate Douglas.** *Rebecca of Sunnybrook Farm.* Boston, 1903	45.00	60.00	52.00
☐ **Willard, Samuel.** *The Franklin Primer ... Adorned with Elegant Cuts Calculated to Strike a Lasting Impression on the Tender Minds of Children.* Boston, 1803	170.00	200.00	185.00
☐ *Woodbridge and Willard's Geography.* Hartford, 1820	22.00	27.00	24.00
☐ **Worcester, J.E.** *Elements of Geography, Ancient and Modern.* Boston, 1830	24.00	29.00	26.00
☐ *Young Child's A.B.C. Or, First Book.* Baltimore, n.d., c. 1816, 13 pp., softbound	150.00	190.00	170.00

CHILDREN'S DISHES

DESCRIPTION: This chapter includes both toy dishes and children's tableware. These items were produced extensively throughout America, Europe and the Orient from the 1880s through the 1950s. They are found in every material that full size dishes and tablewares are made of. Indeed, they were intended to be miniatures of "Mother's" dishes and many are accurate down to the smallest detail.

ADDITIONAL TIPS: This area is gaining rapidly in popularity and prices are going up accordingly.

For further information on children's dishes, refer to *The Official Price Guide to Depression Glassware* published by The House of Collectibles.

	Current Price Range		Prior Year Average
☐ **Bowl,** Blue Marble, England, oval, 4½"	28.00	33.00	30.00
☐ **Bowl,** Blue Willow, Made in Japan, 3½"	10.00	15.00	12.00
☐ **Bowl,** glass, Hopalong Cassidy, white milk glass with black enameled pictures of Hopalong Cassidy, 5"	10.00	15.00	12.00
☐ **Bowl,** glass, Shirley Temple, blue, 6½"	50.00	65.00	55.00
☐ **Butter Dish,** pattern glass, Bead and Scroll, clear, with dome lid, 4"	135.00	155.00	140.00
☐ **Casserole,** Blue Willow, Made in Japan, 4¾"	15.00	20.00	17.50
☐ **Casserole,** Blue Willow, Made in Japan, 5"..	15.00	20.00	17.50
☐ **Casserole,** Blue Willow, Occupied Japan	15.00	20.00	17.50
☐ **Casserole,** graniteware, blue and white, with lid, 2⅞"	42.00	50.00	43.00
☐ **Cup And Saucer,** Blue Willow, Made in Japan, 1⅛" cup, 3⅜" diameter saucer	6.00	8.00	6.50
☐ **Cup And Saucer,** Blue Willow, Made in Japan, 3½" cup, 3¾" diameter saucer	6.50	10.00	7.50
☐ **Cup And Saucer,** Blue Willow, Occupied Japan	10.00	12.00	11.00
☐ **Cup And Saucer,** depression glass, Cherry Blossom, pink, 1½" cup, diameter of saucer is 4½"	25.00	28.00	26.00
☐ **Cup And Saucer,** depression glass, Doric and Pansy, ultramarine, 1½" cup, diameter of saucer is 4½"	25.00	30.00	22.00
☐ **Cup And Saucer,** Water Hen, England, 2" cup, 4½" diameter saucer	15.00	18.00	16.50
☐ **Dishpan,** aluminum, flat sides, rolled edge, loop handles, 4"	4.00	8.00	5.00
☐ **Frying Pan,** graniteware, blue and white, 4½"	28.00	35.00	30.00
☐ **Grater,** graniteware, blue and white, 4"	50.00	55.00	52.00

	Current Price Range		Prior Year Average
☐ **Gravy Boat,** Blue Marble, England, 1½"	28.00	33.00	30.00
☐ **Gravy Boat,** Blue Willow, Made in Japan	15.00	20.00	17.50
☐ **Grill Plate,** Blue Willow, Made in Japan, 5" ..	15.00	20.00	17.50
☐ **Mold,** graniteware, blue and white, fluted, 2¾"	30.00	35.00	32.00
☐ **Mug,** glass, Hopalong Cassidy, white milk glass with black enameled picture of Hopalong Cassidy, 3"	5.00	7.00	5.50
☐ **Penny Candy Tray,** with spoon, pressed tin, shaped like cream skimmer, originally sold in 1920s filled with candy, 3" x 1" x ⅛"	5.00	10.00	7.50
☐ **Pitcher And Wash Bowl,** ironstone, white background with pastel green shading, 24 Kt gold bands, roses, scalloped edges, scroll handle, 4", 1890	25.00	30.00	27.50
☐ **Plate,** glass, Akro Agate, Concentric Rib, green opaque, 3¼"	1.50	2.50	1.75
☐ **Plate,** glass, Hopalong Cassidy, white milk glass with black enameled picture of Hopalong Cassidy and his horse, 7"	14.00	18.00	15.00
☐ **Plate,** Noritake, Bluebird, 4¼"	3.50	5.00	4.00
☐ **Plate,** Pagodas, England, 4½"	10.00	12.00	10.00
☐ **Plate,** Sunset, Made in Japan, 4¼"	1.00	2.00	1.25

Roy Rogers Plate And Bowl, *set,* **$10.00-$15.00**
(photo courtesy of ©Hake's Americana, York, PA, 1984)

	Current Price Range		Prior Year Average
☐ **Platter,** Blue Marble, England, 4½ "	25.00	30.00	27.00
☐ **Platter,** Blue Willow, Made in Japan, 4⅝ " . . .	7.00	10.00	7.50
☐ **Platter,** Blue Willow, Made in Japan, 6"	7.00	10.00	7.50
☐ **Platter,** Blue Willow, Occupied Japan	10.00	15.00	12.00
☐ **Platter,** Noritake, Bluebird, 7⅛ "	10.00	15.00	12.00
☐ **Platter,** Pagodas, England, 7⅛ "	25.00	32.00	27.00
☐ **Presentation Cup,** porcelain, "To My Sister," pink roses, 24 Kt scrolling, closed loop handle, 2⅜ ", 1890	15.00	20.00	17.50
☐ **Sugar Bowl,** Blue Willow, Made in Japan, with lid, 2"	7.00	10.00	8.50
☐ **Sugar Bowl,** Blue Willow, Made in Japan, with lid, 2¾ "	5.00	10.00	6.00
☐ **Sugar Bowl,** Blue Willow, Occupied Japan, with lid	10.00	15.00	12.00
☐ **Teapot,** Blue Willow, Occupied Japan, with lid	20.00	25.00	17.50
☐ **Teapot,** glass, Akro Agate, J.P., Transparent green, with lid, 1½ "	25.00	30.00	26.50
☐ **Teapot,** Noritake, Bluebird, with lid, 3½ " . . .	30.00	40.00	35.00
☐ **Teapot,** Noritake, Silhouette, pale lavender with black silhouette of little girl pushing a doll buggy, 3½ "	30.00	40.00	32.00
☐ **Teapot,** Silhouette, Made in Japan, with lid, 4"	6.00	8.00	6.50
☐ **Teapot,** Sunset, Made in Japan, with lid, 3¾ "	5.00	7.00	5.50
☐ **Teapot,** Water Hen, England, with lid, 5¼ " . .	35.00	40.00	36.50

CHRISTMAS DECORATIONS

DESCRIPTION: Christmas tree ornaments were first manufactured and sold to consumers in the 1870s. Replacing homemade decorations, most of these early ones were simple shapes made in small German villages. Dresden ornaments are the rarest and most valuable. Being made of embossed cardboard and covered with metallic paper, these intricate handcrafted specimens were soon superceded by easily produced blown glass items. It is estimated that by the 1920s, over 5,000 different designs were used for ornaments.

COMMENTS: Age, rarity and, therefore, value are determined by the ornament's construction, design, patina and the material of which it is made. The best place to find old ornaments at a reasonable price is most likely in great-grandma's attic. Since they are in great demand at the moment, dealer prices are high, even for specimens in average condition.

ADDITIONAL TIPS: Also quite collectible are Christmas tree lights dating from the 1920s and 1930s, even if they no longer work. The most collectible of these are the blown glass ones made in molds in Occupied Japan. A variety of shapes and sizes are available.

	Current Price Range		Prior Year Average
☐ **Light,** Andy Gump, milk glass	15.00	17.00	16.00
☐ **Light,** bear with guitar, milk glass	15.00	17.00	16.00
☐ **Light,** blue bird, milk glass	15.00	17.00	16.00
☐ **Light,** clock	15.00	17.00	16.00
☐ **Light,** clown, milk glass	20.00	24.00	22.00
☐ **Light,** elephant, milk glass	7.00	9.00	8.00
☐ **Light,** fish, milk glass	13.00	15.00	14.00
☐ **Light,** gingerbread man	13.00	15.00	14.00
☐ **Light,** grapes, milk glass	8.00	10.00	9.00
☐ **Light,** house, milk glass	13.00	15.00	14.00
☐ **Light,** Humpty Dumpty, milk glass	15.00	17.00	16.00
☐ **Light,** lantern	13.00	15.00	14.00
☐ **Light,** parrot, milk glass	7.00	9.00	8.00
☐ **Light,** Pinocchio	20.00	22.00	21.00
☐ **Light,** Puss N' Boots, milk glass	20.00	22.00	21.00
☐ **Light,** Santa, painted	20.00	22.00	21.00
☐ **Light,** snowman, milk glass	13.00	15.00	14.00
☐ **Light,** zeppelin with flag	20.00	22.00	21.00
☐ **Ornament,** ball, amber	23.00	25.00	24.00
☐ **Ornament,** ball, canary, blown glass	20.00	22.00	21.00
☐ **Ornament,** basket, fruit filled, blown glass	23.00	25.00	24.00
☐ **Ornament,** bear with muff, blown glass	48.00	50.00	49.00
☐ **Ornament,** camel, Dresden	30.00	32.00	31.00
☐ **Ornament,** child, milk glass	10.00	12.00	11.00
☐ **Ornament,** church, blown glass	30.00	32.00	31.00
☐ **Ornament,** clown head, blown glass	53.00	55.00	54.00
☐ **Ornament,** fence, wood	23.00	25.00	24.00
☐ **Ornament,** fish, blown glass	53.00	55.00	54.00
☐ **Ornament,** football player, milk glass	20.00	22.00	21.00
☐ **Ornament,** girl, blown glass	34.00	36.00	35.00
☐ **Ornament,** heart, blown glass, large	35.00	37.00	36.00
☐ **Ornament,** icicle, glass	20.00	24.00	22.00
☐ **Ornament,** lamp	55.00	57.00	56.00
☐ **Ornament,** lion, Dresden	20.00	22.00	21.00
☐ **Ornament,** musical instrument	20.00	22.00	21.00
☐ **Ornament,** peacock, blown glass, brush tail	20.00	22.00	21.00
☐ **Ornament,** pinecone, blown glass	7.00	9.00	8.00
☐ **Ornament,** pipe, blown glass	23.00	25.00	24.00
☐ **Ornament,** purse, blown glass	33.00	35.00	34.00
☐ **Ornament,** Santa, celluloid	33.00	35.00	34.00
☐ **Ornament,** Santa, with plaster face	23.00	25.00	24.00

	Current Price Range		Prior Year Average
☐ **Ornament,** star, Dresden	20.00	22.00	21.00
☐ **Ornament,** swan, blown glass	23.00	25.00	24.00
☐ **Ornament,** teapot	23.00	25.00	24.00
☐ **Ornament,** umbrella, tinsel	23.00	25.00	24.00

CHROME

DESCRIPTION: A glossy metal, chrome is most often used as decorative trim on cars, trucks, boats, etc.

TYPES: Chrome collectibles include auto items as well as a wide variety of decorative household objects and novelties.

PERIOD: Chrome came into extensive use in the 1920s. It was one of the more important substances of the Art Deco era.

CARE AND CONDITION: Clean with any metal cleaning polish recommended for use on chrome. Do not use an abrasive tool, nor even steel wool, as this will result in fine scratches that mar the surface. As chrome is very durable, it presents no problem in storage or display.

☐ **Bud Vase,** chased, 4½″ cylinder resting on a 3½″ base	16.00	20.00	18.00
☐ **Cocktail Set,** shaker with six matching flared goblets, height of goblets 7″, set	30.00	35.00	32.00
☐ **Cocktail Shaker,** footed, etched banding with grape leaf cluster motif, red plastic handle, 11¾″	10.00	14.00	12.00
☐ **Cocktail Shaker,** grape etching, with cap and lid	9.00	12.00	10.25
☐ **Cordial Dispenser,** clear glass and chrome, plunger type with six jiggers, the glass decorated with horizontal ribbing, jiggers have plastic belts, set	22.00	28.00	24.00
☐ **Cordial Dispenser,** keg resting on pedestal with six small mugs, price for full set	14.00	18.00	16.00
☐ **Farber Cocktail Shaker And Six Glasses,** hammered texture, shaker with plastic handle (black), height of glasses 6¼″, set	27.00	34.00	30.00
☐ **Lazy Susan,** 2-tier bar, green plastic central handle, top has six small jiggers with green and yellow striping, bottle has twelve jiggers, set	32.00	40.00	35.00

	Current Price Range		Prior Year Average
Liquer Dispenser, decorative sphere with six shot glasses, set	20.00	25.00	22.00
Tray, large, ceramic with chrome trim and chrome handles, the ceramic painted with purple grapes, 13¾" diameter	21.00	28.00	23.00

CIRCUS MEMORABILIA

VARIATIONS: All circus-related items are considered collectible, including posters, photographs, ticket stubs, programs as well as large items such as cages and tents.

ORIGIN: The first American circus opened in 1793 in Philadelphia. The show was modeled after already established English circuses. The show traveled from town to town in order to entertain rural communities. About 30 years after the first American circus, tents and big tops were introduced. In 1919 the top three competing circuses, P. T. Barnum, James A. Bailey and Ringling Brothers combined their shows.

COMMENTS: The year 1984 marks the centennial for Ringling Brothers. This special celebration may add to the already high interest in circus memorabilia.

ADDITIONAL TIPS: The following listings are alphabetical according to title. A description and price range follows.

Book, *The Man of the Mountain,* by Frederic Farnsworth, Boston, c. 1818	150.00	180.00	160.00
Book, *Tom Thumb,* life of Charles S. Stratton, 28" high and 15 pounds, 24 pp. booklet, published by Barnum, New York, c. 1847	200.00	280.00	224.00
Booklet, *Barnum and Bailey Circus,* color cover, features biographies, pictures and descriptions of the circus, c. 1910	65.00	85.00	70.00
Booklet, *Forepaugh and Sells Circus,* color cover, features biographies, pictures and descriptions of the circus, c. 1910	55.00	75.00	60.00
Booklet, *Walter L. Main Circus,* 8 pp., color, wraps	16.00	25.00	18.00
Broadside Handbills, illustrated, 10" x 28", c. 1920s	20.00	30.00	23.00
Courier, *Illustrated News,* by P. T. Barnum, 16 pp., c. 1897	42.00	58.00	44.00
Lithograph, *The Tigers Are Ferocious and They Bite,* by Adam Forepaugh, c. 1880	135.00	175.00	160.00

	Current Price Range		Prior Year Average
☐ **Lithograph,** *The Circus Kings of All Time,* window card, 14″ x 22″, mid 1830s	32.50	40.00	35.00
☐ **Herald Or Handbill,** *Sparks Circus,* c. 1921 . .	16.00	25.00	18.00
☐ **Magazine,** *Barnum and Bailey Circus,* bright color cover, c. 1918	55.00	75.00	60.00
☐ **Magazine,** *Magazine of Wonders and Daily Review,* by Ringling Brothers, color, c. 1914 .	60.00	80.00	70.00
☐ **Photograph,** Downie Brothers Circus, groups of photos features various artists, 5″ x 7″, c. 1930	35.00	50.00	40.00
☐ **Photograph,** Russell Brothers Circus, groups of photos features various artists, 5″ x 7″, c. 1930	15.00	25.00	18.00
☐ **Poster,** Adam Forepaugh Circus and Roman Hippodrome, 7 part composite, 30½″ x 40″, c. 1885	185.00	215.00	195.00
☐ **Poster,** Adam Forepaugh's "Queen of The Ring," 30″ x 40½″c. 1885	135.00	175.00	145.00
☐ **Poster,** Adam Forepaugh and Sells circus, pictures Aurora Zoaves	52.00	70.00	58.00
☐ **Poster,** Barnum and Bailey Circus, color, depicts naval battle against Spanish fleet, 25″ x 36″, c. 1898	180.00	220.00	195.00
☐ **Poster,** Clyde Beatty Circus, action scene, 21″ x 28″, c. 1930	75.00	100.00	80.00
☐ **Poster,** Clyde Beatty, training lions and tigers, c. 1930	80.00	100.00	89.00
☐ **Poster,** Dale's animal three-ring circus	15.50	25.00	18.00
☐ **Poster,** "Lady Viola, The Most Beautiful Tattoed Woman in The World," painted in oils over large photo, 40″ x 40″, New York, c. 1925	450.00	495.00	460.00
☐ **Poster,** "Lilla," high-wire act, 34″ x 45″, c. 1895	230.00	250.00	237.00
☐ **Poster,** "Princess Topaze, Star of The Casino de Paris," female midget, 35″ x 48″	300.00	340.00	310.00
☐ **Poster,** P. T. Barnum and Co., Lake Front, Chicago, Monday, July 19th	20.00	28.00	23.00
☐ **Poster,** "Terrell Jacobs The Liong King," 28″ x 40″, c. 1935	60.00	70.00	63.00
☐ **Poster,** Terrell Jacobs in Big Top, surrounded by lions, 28″ x 40″, c. 1934	75.00	85.00	77.00
☐ **Program,** Ringling Brothers, Barnum and Bailey, c. 1948	15.00	23.00	17.00
☐ **Program,** Hagenbeck-Wallas	20.00	28.00	23.00
☐ **Sheet Music,** Children At The Circus, c. 1909	25.00	35.00	28.00
☐ **Sheet Music,** Whe It's Circus Day Back Home, c. 1917	25.00	35.00	27.00

	Current Price Range		Prior Year Average
☐ **Song Book,** Barnum and London Musical Album, large size	25.00	35.00	27.00
☐ **Stationery,** Sparton Brothers, ornate, unused	4.50	8.00	6.00
☐ **Tickets,** Barnum's Circus, c. 1890	15.00	24.00	17.00
☐ **Tickets,** Hunts Brothers, illustrated with clown, 100 large, c. 1940s	10.00	15.00	12.00
☐ **Ticket,** P. T. Barnum Circus, c. 1890	15.00	25.00	17.00
☐ **Toy,** Barnum and Bailey circus cage, elephant drawn, painted, stained and lithographed wood, c. 1930	180.00	280.00	220.00

CIVIL WAR MEMORABILIA

DESCRIPTION: The Civil War produced some of the most collectible antiques in today's marketplace. Items are available all over the world. Collecting Civil War memorabilia can be a most gratifying hobby for the collector as he delves into the history of each item and discovers the principles upon which this country has grown.

COMMENTS: The most sought-after collectible in this category is firearms. This period in time marked a technological transition from a single shot gun to one that would shoot several times, including the first machine gun. Other collectible areas include uniforms, buttons, belt buckles, canteens, knapsacks, insignias and personal effects, such as diaries, letters, and photographs.

ADDITIONAL TIPS: Auctions are a great place to pick up such items as well as dealer shops. Prices are as varied as the items so even the novice can afford to begin this type of collection.

RECOMMENDED READING: For more in-depth information and listings, you may refer to *The Official Price Guide to Military Collectibles* by Colonel Robert H. Rankin, published by The House of Collectibles.

☐ **Belt,** Union, infantry, oval belt plate marked SNY, issued by the state of New York early in the war, black bridle leather belt	325.00	350.00	337.50
☐ **Belt,** Union, infantry, standard issue leather belt with U.S. oval buckle	75.00	80.00	77.50
☐ **Blanket,** Union, Regular Army issue, medium brown, very fine condition	300.00	325.00	312.50
☐ **Books,** *Millers Photographic History,* set of ten volumes, contains original photographs on nearly every page, 8″ x 11″, each is around 350 pages, excellent condition, published in 1911, the classic Civil War reference work . . .	330.00	350.00	340.00

	Current Price Range		Prior Year Average

☐ **Buckle,** Confederate, forked tongue, found buried near Fredericksburg, Virginia, 3⅝" x 2¼" .... 190.00 | 200.00 | 195.00

☐ **Bugle,** cavalry, solid brass, 8½" .... 365.00 | 385.00 | 375.00

☐ **Bugle,** infantry, 17¾" .... 320.00 | 330.00 | 325.00

☐ **Candleholder,** camp, spike on bottom and side, cast iron, 4½" .... 45.00 | 50.00 | 47.50

☐ **Drummers Plate,** solid brass, worn on drum sling, iron wire hooks, stamped in back is C.L. Carrington/AP/4th, excellent condition, 3¼" wide by 3½" high .... 225.00 | 250.00 | 237.50

☐ **Drumsticks,** rosewood, pair .... 90.00 | 100.00 | 95.00

☐ **Flag,** Confederate, regimental battle flag of the Confederate Army of Northern Virginia, infantry size, 4' x 4', superb condition, very rare .... 9500.00 | — | —

☐ **Flag,** Confederate, small version used to show patriotism during parades and rallies, polished cotton on wooden stick, 6" x 8", excellent condition, 1863 .... 65.00 | 75.00 | 70.00

☐ **Flask,** whiskey, Confederate, glass body with pewter top and cup which slides over lower half of flask, engraved, 7", marked on bottom by hand Richmond/1863/B.A./1st VA. REG. .. 175.00 | 195.00 | 185.00

☐ **Holster,** Confederate, full flap holster for dragoon sized revolver, brass stud closure, single wide belt loop on back, typical reddish brown Richmond leather, excellent condition .... 475.00 | 500.00 | 487.50

☐ **Jacket,** Union, artillery shell, regulation issue, dark blue with red piping, twenty eagle buttons, fully lined, small to medium, excellent condition .... 475.00 | 500.00 | 487.50

☐ **Kit,** boot care, black japanned tin hinged case lid, contains three compartments which hold cake of saddle soap, chamois, and four brushes, marked Tiffany & Co. in gold letters on lid .... 185.00 | 205.00 | 195.00

☐ **Knapsack,** Confederate, box style, black oil cloth over wood frame with leather reinforced corners, white buff straps, imported from England, marked "S.Isaacs Campbell/London." .... 150.00 | 170.00 | 160.00

☐ **Lantern,** camp and signal, tin, japanned finish, scalloped peaked roof, cylindrical body with large glass lens on door, oil burner, wire loop handles, wire belt hook, 6½", excellent condition .... 65.00 | 85.00 | 75.00

	Current Price Range		Prior Year Average
☐ **Letter,** Confederate, written by General John Bell Hood, commander of the Texas Cavalry, 8″ x 10″, dated March 2, 1864, framed	175.00	185.00	180.00
☐ **Lincoln Portrait Bust,** stamped on copper sheet with very detailed relief, coated with frosted silver plate, applied to velvetized tin background and mounted in a circular frame of gilded plaster over wood, bust is 7″ high, frame is 16″ in diameter, done at the end of the Civil War, signed and dated, J. Powell, Patented 1865	250.00	270.00	260.00
☐ **Map,** Confederate, pocket map of Virginia published by West & Johnston in Richmond, 1862	325.00	350.00	337.50
☐ **Musket,** Confederate, 3 band rifled, marked Potts & Hunt, London, good condition	775.00	825.00	800.00
☐ **Officers Frock Coat,** Union, field grade officers model, regulation army, finest quality materials and workmanship, double breasted with eighteen buttons bearing the Rhode Island state seal, excellent condition	600.00	650.00	625.00
☐ **Picket Pin,** Confederate Cavalry, 14½″ long steel rod, pointed at tip and flattened at top through which a 2½″ ring fastened, ⅝″ thick, dug near Richmond, Virginia, for tethering horses	95.00	100.00	97.50
☐ **Rifle,** Burnside carbine, good condition	435.00	455.00	445.00
☐ **Sword Belt,** Confederate, consists of two piece sword belt plate on original belt, plate marked CS	975.00	1000.00	987.50
☐ **Sword,** officers, staff and field, rayskin grips, Horstmann blade, etched eagle, scabbard is brass mounted steel	650.00	660.00	655.00

CLOTHING

DESCRIPTION: Vintage clothing is collected by those who add it to their wardrobes as well as by collectors who display it.

VARIATIONS: Clothes of all ages are collectible. Currently, the most sought after are Victorian era clothes as well as clothes from the 1920s, 1930s and 1940s.

	Current Price Range		Prior Year Average
☐ **Apron,** embroidered, Hungarian, c. 1930	32.00	45.00	38.00
☐ **Baby Shoes,** hand stitched satin shoes with mocassin style lowers and double ribbon drawstring through uppers	10.00	20.00	13.00

	Current Price Range		Prior Year Average
☐ **Baby Shoes,** kidskin leather button shoes, three buttons on uppers, c. 1880	35.00	65.00	45.00
☐ **Baby Shoes,** velvet top button shoes, leather lowers, five buttons on uppers, c. 1880	50.00	75.00	60.00
☐ **Baby Slippers,** white kid Mary Janes, strap, fastened with mother-of-pearl button, soft leather sole	30.00	50.00	40.00
☐ **Bonnet,** for Christening, lace with white silk tie ribbons	25.00	45.00	35.00
☐ **Coin Purse,** nickel plated metal with mother-of-pearl panels, compartments in red leatherette	12.00	20.00	14.00
☐ **Dress,** black faille damask, cap sleeves, tie belt, c. 1940	50.00	90.00	60.00
☐ **Dress,** floor length, horizontal stripes and metallic thread, tiered	60.00	100.00	80.00
☐ **Dress,** for child, tucked bib, lace trim, embroidered	30.00	60.00	40.00
☐ **Dress,** handmade traveling dress, c. 1890s . .	200.00	240.00	210.00
☐ **Dress,** for infant, lace, long sleeves	20.00	50.00	35.00
☐ **Dress,** for infant, scalloped collar, embroidered	25.00	50.00	37.00
☐ **Dress and Jacket,** blue lace over rose, velvet ribbon straps, short jacket	40.00	75.00	55.00
☐ **Evening Bag,** Victorian, crochet flowers, metal beads	115.00	130.00	120.00
☐ **Evening Bag,** Victorian, petit point flowers on silk	115.00	130.00	122.00
☐ **Gloves,** cotton crochet, c. 1890	14.50	22.00	16.00
☐ **Gloves,** long, brown suede	8.00	16.00	11.00
☐ **Gloves,** short, white kid	8.00	16.00	13.00
☐ **Gloves,** white cotton	8.00	16.00	13.00
☐ **Hat,** fox fur	15.00	30.00	18.00
☐ **Hat,** man's beaver top hat	45.00	65.00	55.00
☐ **Mantilla,** Blonde de Caen lace, cream colored, c. 1820	120.00	160.00	130.00
☐ **Mantilla,** black lace	45.00	60.00	53.00
☐ **Purse,** clear crystal beads, white cloth liner, drawstring, beaded decoration, c. 1920s . .	20.00	40.00	30.00
☐ **Robe,** embroidered silk, Japanese, c. 1890 . .	282.00	350.00	300.00
☐ **Shawl,** peach silk, bright silk embroidered flowers, c. 1920s	165.00	225.00	180.00
☐ **Skirt,** crocheted, floor length, fringed bottom	30.00	50.00	40.00
☐ **Wedding Gown,** lace, satin, pearls and white beaded flowers, high neck, cap sleeves, train, c. 1960s	75.00	150.00	100.00

COCA-COLA COLLECTIBLES

ORIGIN: Atlanta pharmacist, John Pemberton produced the first Coca-Cola in 1886 in Atlanta, GA. The familiar Coca-Cola logo was created by Pemberton's bookkeeper, Frank Robinson.

	Current Price Range		Prior Year Average
☐ **Ashtray,** aluminum, c. 1955	3.00	6.00	3.00
☐ **Ashtray And Match Holder,** c. 1940	180.00	200.00	177.00
☐ **Ashtray,** metal, c. 1963	18.00	22.00	17.50
☐ **Ashtray,** Mexican, painted aluminum	3.00	4.00	2.50
☐ **Ashtray,** picture of Atlanta plant	18.00	22.00	20.00
☐ **Ashtray,** set of card suites, c. 1940	55.00	60.00	52.00
☐ **Badge,** Coca-Cola Vendor's License, brass 1¾"	1.00	4.00	3.00
☐ **Bank,** Coca-Cola, metal cap	1.00	2.00	1.50
☐ **Calendar,** lady with roses, c. 1902	610.00	660.00	625.00
☐ **Calendar,** modern image dancing, c. 1970 . .	7.00	9.00	6.50
☐ **Calendar,** old man with boat, c. 1936	110.00	125.00	108.00
☐ **Calendar,** pearl white, c. 1916	240.00	260.00	235.00
☐ **Calendar,** snowman and girl, c. 1958	12.00	18.00	12.50
☐ **Calendar,** two models, c. 1912	285.00	310.00	382.00
☐ **Calendar,** U.S. Army Nurse Corp., c. 1943 . . .	28.00	32.00	27.50
☐ **Calendar,** Victorian lady cloth replica, c. 1972	9.00	13.00	10.00
☐ **Calendar,** World War I girl, c. 1917	210.00	230.00	210.00
☐ **Calendar,** 1973 reproduction of 1899 Valentine, c. 1973	12.00	18.00	12.50
☐ **Car Bottle Holder,** c. 1950	18.00	22.00	17.50
☐ **Cards,** set of 50, nature motif, c. 1930	38.00	58.00	45.00
☐ **Cards,** two complete decks in tin lithographed box	2.00	4.00	3.00
☐ **Carrier,** first paper carton, c. 1924	28.00	32.00	27.50
☐ **Carrier,** foil-covered carton, c. 1941	18.00	22.00	17.50
☐ **Carrier,** July Fourth six-box wrapper, c. 1935	38.00	52.00	42.00
☐ **Carrier,** Santa Claus carton, c. 1931	22.00	28.00	22.50
☐ **Carrier,** vendor's holder, c. 1940	62.00	78.00	68.00
☐ **Carrier,** wooden home type, c. 1940	20.00	26.00	20.00
☐ **Carrier,** yellow wooden, c. 1939	22.00	28.00	22.00
☐ **Case,** miniature, display type, 24 bottles . . .	6.00	10.00	7.00
☐ **Case,** miniature, plastic bottles and case, c. 1973	6.00	10.00	7.00
☐ **Case,** miniature, 28 bottles, gold finish	32.00	42.00	35.00
☐ **Case,** shipping type, c. 1906	130.00	150.00	125.00
☐ **Case,** wooden, 24 bottle type, c. 1924	40.00	55.00	42.00
☐ **Change Purse,** c. 1915	42.00	58.00	52.00
☐ **Cigar Band,** c. 1931	150.00	170.00	152.00

	Current Price Range		Prior Year Average
☐ **Cigarette Case**, frosted glass, 50th Anniversary, c. 1936	100.00	120.00	100.00
☐ **Cutouts**, uncut, c. 1932	55.00	80.00	62.00
☐ **Dice**, white and red imprint, pair	1.00	2.00	1.50
☐ **Door Pull**, bottle shape	48.00	58.00	50.00
☐ **Flashlight**, bottle shaped plastic	6.00	8.00	6.00
☐ **Fountain Dispenser**	85.00	120.00	85.00
☐ **Glass**, 5¢ with arrow, c. 1905	130.00	155.00	132.00
☐ **Glass**, flair type, c. 1900	185.00	195.00	180.00
☐ **Glass**, flair type, c. 1923	35.00	45.00	35.00
☐ **Glass**, fountain type with syrup line, c. 1900	52.00	62.00	55.00
☐ **Glass**, fountain type, no syrup line	8.00	12.00	8.50
☐ **Glass**, home promotion type, red and white	4.00	6.00	4.00
☐ **Glass**, pewter, c. 1930	72.00	82.00	75.00
☐ **Ice Pick And Opener**, c. 1940	8.00	12.00	8.50
☐ **Key Chain**, amber replica bottle with brass chain, c. 1964	6.00	8.00	6.00
☐ **Key Chain**, car key style, c. 1950	28.00	32.00	27.50
☐ **Key Chain**, red with gold bottle, c. 1955	18.00	28.00	20.00
☐ **Key Chain**, 50th Anniversary Celebration, c. 1936	12.00	18.00	12.50
☐ **Knife**, pocket, "Enjoy Coca-Cola"	80.00	110.00	82.00
☐ **Knife**, pocket, two blades	12.00	18.00	12.50
☐ **Menu Board**, tin, c. 1940	42.00	62.00	50.00
☐ **Milk Glass**, light shade, c. 1920	385.00	410.00	382.00
☐ **Mirror**, pocket-size, "Bathing Beauty," c. 1918	285.00	300.00	282.00
☐ **Mirror**, pocket-size, "Betty," c. 1914	110.00	130.00	110.00
☐ **Mirror**, pocket-size, "Coca-Cola Girl," c. 1909	130.00	150.00	135.00
☐ **Mirror**, pocket-size, "Coca-Cola Girl," c. 1911	130.00	150.00	130.00
☐ **Mirror**, pocket-size, "Drink Coca-Cola 5¢," c. 1914	260.00	285.00	262.00
☐ **Opener**, bone handle knife, c. 1908	140.00	160.00	140.00
☐ **Opener**, Nashville Anniversary, c. 1952	55.00	70.00	58.00
☐ **Opener**, skate key style, c. 1935	38.00	48.00	40.00
☐ **Opener**, "Starr X," c. 1925	3.00	5.00	3.00
☐ **Opener**, stationary wall model, c. 1900	22.00	28.00	22.00
☐ **Paperweight**, Coca-Cola gum, c. 1916	80.00	90.00	80.00
☐ **Paperweight**, "Coke is Coca-Cola," c. 1948	75.00	95.00	80.00
☐ **Paperweight**, hollow glass, tin bottom, c. 1909	260.00	285.00	262.00
☐ **Pen**, ball point with telephone dialer	6.00	8.00	6.00
☐ **Pen**, baseball bat, c. 1940	22.00	33.00	25.00
☐ **Poster**, "Bathing Beauty," c. 1918	410.00	435.00	412.00
☐ **Poster**, "Betty," c. 1914	260.00	280.00	260.00
☐ **Poster**, "Early Display with Young Lovers," c. 1891	460.00	490.00	465.00

	Current Price Range		Prior Year Average
☐ Poster, "Flapper Girl," c. 1929	160.00	180.00	160.00
☐ Poster, "Florine McKinney," c. 1936	40.00	50.00	40.00
☐ Poster, "Girl in Hammock," c. 1900	435.00	460.00	438.00
☐ Poster, "Hilda Clark Cuban," c. 1901	310.00	335.00	312.00
☐ Poster, "Soldier and Girl," c. 1943	28.00	32.00	27.50
☐ Pretzel Bowl, metal, c. 1935	50.00	62.00	52.00
☐ Radio, Coke bottle shaped, c. 1930	310.00	350.00	320.00
☐ Radio, Coke can shaped, c. 1971	14.00	20.00	15.00
☐ Radio, Coke cooler shaped, c. 1949	145.00	160.00	142.00
☐ Radio, crystal, c. 1950	100.00	110.00	100.00
☐ Radio, transistor, vending machine shaped, c. 1963	60.00	80.00	70.00
☐ Sign, bottle tray, tin, c. 1900	310.00	350.00	320.00
☐ Sign, "Coca-Cola Girls," cardboard, c. 1922	80.00	90.00	80.00
☐ Sign, Coke bottle, tin	100.00	115.00	105.00
☐ Sign, "Drink Coca-Cola"	70.00	85.00	72.00
☐ Sign, "Elaine," tin, c. 1917	485.00	510.00	582.00
☐ Sign, "Hilda Clark," paper, c. 1900	260.00	290.00	262.00
☐ Sign, "Hilda Clark," tin, c. 1904	285.00	300.00	285.00
☐ Sign, "Lillian Russell," oval, tin, c. 1904	775.00	825.00	775.00
☐ Sign, "Please Pay Cashier," c. 1940	62.00	78.00	68.00
☐ Shoe Shine Kit	150.00	170.00	155.00
☐ Tape Measure, Drink Coca Cola in Bottles	2.00	4.00	3.00
☐ Thermometer, Coca Cola, metal	2.00	4.00	3.00
☐ Thimble, red, pictures Coke bottle, gold trim	2.00	4.00	3.00
☐ Token, brass, oval shape	1.00	2.00	1.50
☐ Toy, train set (Lionel), c. 1974	105.00	115.00	100.00
☐ Toy, Volkswagen van, c. 1950	22.00	33.00	25.00
☐ Toy, whistle, c. 1945	5.50	8.50	6.50
☐ Toy, yo-yo, c. 1955	4.00	7.00	5.00
☐ Tray, "Autumn Girl," c. 1922	160.00	210.00	175.00
☐ Tray, "Bathing Beauty," c. 1930	105.00	125.00	115.00
☐ Tray, "Betty," c. 1912	85.00	110.00	88.00
☐ Tray, "Betty," oval, c. 1914	80.00	110.00	88.00
☐ Tray, ceramic "Change Receiver," c. 1900	485.00	560.00	512.00
☐ Tray, "Coca-Cola Girl," oval, c. 1909	105.00	125.00	105.00
☐ Tray, "Curb Service," c. 1927	85.00	180.00	125.00
☐ Tray, "Elaine," c. 1917	55.00	85.00	70.00
☐ Tray, "Farm Boy with Dog," c. 1931	100.00	120.00	100.00
☐ Tray, "Flapper Girl," c. 1923	80.00	110.00	82.00
☐ Tray, "Frances Dee," c. 1933	20.00	28.00	21.00
☐ Tray, "Girl at Party," c. 1925	80.00	110.00	82.00
☐ Tray, "Girl in the Afternoon," c. 1938	38.00	48.00	40.00
☐ Tray, "Girl with Fox Fur," c. 1925	70.00	90.00	75.00
☐ Tray, "Girl with French Menu," c. 1950	70.00	90.00	75.00
☐ Tray, "Girl with Umbrella," c. 1957	65.00	80.00	68.00
☐ Tray, "Hilda Clark," c. 1904	260.00	285.00	262.00

	Current Price Range		Prior Year Average
☐ **Tray,** "Johnny Weismuller and Maureen O'Sullivan," c. 1934	185.00	210.00	188.00
☐ **Tray,** "Juanita," round, c. 1905	150.00	175.00	158.00
☐ **Tray,** "Olympic Games," 15″ x 11″, c. 1976	12.00	18.00	12.50
☐ **Tray** (serving), plastic, c. 1971	50.00	60.00	52.00
☐ **Tray,** replica of "Duster Girl," c. 1972	28.00	42.00	32.00
☐ **Tray,** "Sailor Girl," c. 1940	28.00	42.00	32.00
☐ **Tray,** "Saint Louis Fair," oval, c. 1904	160.00	190.00	170.00
☐ **Tray,** "Santa Claus," 15″ x 11″, c. 1973	22.00	32.00	25.00
☐ **Tray,** "Soda Fountain Clerk," c. 1927	80.00	110.00	82.00
☐ **Tray,** "Springboard Girl," c. 1939	45.00	60.00	46.00
☐ **Tray,** "Summer Girl," c. 1921	185.00	235.00	200.00
☐ **Tray,** T.V., candle design, c. 1972	20.00	28.00	21.00
☐ **Tray,** T.V., picnic basket	28.00	38.00	30.00
☐ **Tray,** T.V., Thanksgiving motif, c. 1961	20.00	28.00	21.00
☐ **Tray,** "Topless," c. 1908	510.00	710.00	600.00
☐ **Tray,** "Two Girls at Car," c. 1942	32.00	42.00	35.00
☐ **Tray,** "Vienna Art Nude," c. 1905	210.00	285.00	238.00
☐ **Tray,** "Western Bottling Co.," c. 1905	110.00	160.00	125.00
☐ **Vendor's Umbrella,** "Pause that Refreshes"	135.00	160.00	138.00
☐ **Wallet,** Coke bottle emblem, c. 1915	75.00	85.00	75.00
☐ **Wallet,** Coca-Cola script, c. 1922	88.00	98.00	90.00
☐ **Wallet,** embossed coin purse, c. 1906	150.00	165.00	148.00
☐ **Watch Fob,** bulldog, c. 1925	55.00	85.00	65.00
☐ **Watch Fob,** "Drink Coca-Cola in Bottles"	60.00	80.00	65.00

COINS

In order to accurately present the vast amount of information required by serious collectors, a special edition devoted to coins is published by The House of Collectibles, Inc. This handy, pocket-size guide, *The Official 1985 Blackbook Price Guide to U.S. Coins*, features listings, prices, photographs and expert advice. It is available at bookstores for $3.95.

COMBS

DESCRIPTION: Since the 18th century, beautiful and decorative combs have adorned milady's hair. These ornate combs were originally designed to serve as jewelry pieces and were passed down in the family as prized possessions.

COMMENTS: Combs are categorized by how they are used, back or side, and by the material of which they are made, such as silver, ivory, bone, tortoise shell, steel, pewter and celluloid. The collector must beware of celluloid that can be made to look like tortoise shell or ivory. Markings in genuine materials tend to be more irregular in comparison to the even and more regular patterns in celluloid.

ADDITIONAL TIPS: Combs in good condition are rare since most are scratched, cracked, and have missing teeth. It is important to note, however, that a damaged comb may be worth more than an excellent one simply because of its design and workmanship.

RECOMMENDED READING: For more in-depth information on combs, you may refer to *The Official Price Guide to Antique Jewelry* published by The House of Collectibles.

Left to Right: *Tortoiseshell hair comb, openwork motif, gold, 1870s,* **$375.00-$400.00;** *tortoise hair comb, floral swirl motif, gold, 1890s,* **$375.00-$400.00;** *tortoise hair ornament, floral swirl motif, gold, 1900s,* **$225.00-$250.00**

	Current Price Range		Prior Year Average
☐ **Bakelite**, back comb with coral, 5″ L., c. 1880	85.00	90.00	97.50
☐ **Celluloid**, back comb, Art Deco, c. 1920	53.00	55.00	54.00
☐ **Celluloid**, back comb, Art Nouveau, c. 1900 .	45.00	50.00	47.50
☐ **Celluloid**, back comb, feather design, c. 1930	98.00	102.00	100.00
☐ **Celluloid**, back comb, rhinestones, c. 1940 ..	70.00	75.00	72.50
☐ **Celluloid**, hairpins, rhinestones, c. 1930	20.00	24.00	22.00
☐ **Celluloid**, side comb, Victorian, c. 1880	23.00	25.00	24.00
☐ **Ivory**, carved	40.00	42.00	41.00
☐ **Ivory**, inlaid rhinestones	20.00	24.00	22.00
☐ **Russian**, amber	55.00	57.00	56.00
☐ **Silver**, back comb, rhinestones, 5″ L., c. 1890	140.00	150.00	145.00
☐ **Sterling Silver**, elaborate carving	38.00	40.00	39.00
☐ **Tortoise**, back comb, coral, 6″ L., c. 1880 ...	165.00	175.00	170.00
☐ **Tortoise**, back comb, 7½″ L., c. 1840	115.00	120.00	117.50
☐ **Tortoise**, back comb, English, rhinestones, c. 1890	135.00	145.00	140.00
☐ **Tortoise**, hairpin, Art Nouveau, c. 1910	35.00	40.00	37.50

COMIC BOOKS

This section features just a sampling of comic book prices. In order to accurately present the vast amount of information required by serious collectors, a special edition devoted to comic books is published by The House of Collectibles, Inc. This handy, pocket-size guide, *The Official Price Guide to Comic Books*, features more than 10,000 comic book prices. It is available at bookstores for $3.95. For more in-depth information, refer to *The Official Price Guide to Comic Books and Collectibles*. It is $10.95.

TOPIC: Comic books are collections of sequential cartoons that tell a story. Each illustrated frame progresses the story line.

TYPES: Comic books are categorized by publisher; for instance, D-C/ National Periodical, Fawcett and Marvel.

PERIOD: Most collectible comic books were published from 1940 to the early 1970s.

COMMENTS: Comic books make wonderful collectibles because they are both historic and artistic.

ADDITIONAL TIPS: The following listings are organized by publisher. The order of the remaining information is: name and date of the series, name of the issue, issue number, main characters and descriptive information. For more information and extensive listings, please refer to *The Official Price Guide to Comic Books and Collectibles,* published by The House of Collectibles.

	Current Price Range		Prior Year Average
☐ **Columbia, Joe Palooka, #3,** Joe Palooka Ko's The Nazis	25.00	32.00	27.00
☐ **D.C., Adventure, #32,** Federal Men	135.00	165.00	145.00
☐ **D.C., Adventure, #62,** Starman vs. The Light	250.00	300.00	265.00
☐ **D.C., Adventure, #65,** Cotton Carver	240.00	285.00	250.00
☐ **D.C., Batman, #1,** All New Adventures Of The Batman And Robin The Boy Wonder	**Very Rare**		
☐ **D.C., Batman, #2,** The Crime Master	1150.00	1375.00	1230.00
☐ **D.C., Batman, #17,** Adventure Of The Vitamin Vandals	140.00	170.00	152.75
☐ **D.C., Batman, #21,** Batman And Robin Whoop It Up In Four Whirlwind Action Stories	140.00	170.00	148.00
☐ **D.C., Detective, #29,** Batman Meets Dr. Death	1750.00	2150.00	1875.00
☐ **D.C., Detective, #63,** A Gentleman In Gotham	120.00	145.00	127.75
☐ **D.C., Detective, #86,** Danger Strikes Three	67.00	81.75	69.00
☐ **D.C., Green Lantern, #1,** Origin Of The Green Lantern	1100.00	1350.00	1175.00
☐ **D.C., Green Lantern, #29,** "All Harlequin" Issue	125.00	165.00	135.00
☐ **D.C., Joker, #1,** First Sensational Issue Of The Clown Prince Of Crime In His Own Magazine!	.75	1.00	.75
☐ **D.C., World's Finest, #2,** The Man Who Couldn't Remember	500.00	600.00	560.00
☐ **D.C., World's Finest, #13,** The Curse Of Isis	175.00	225.00	190.00
☐ **D.C., World's Finest, #46,** Bruce Wayne, Riveter	75.00	90.00	81.75
☐ **Dell, Uncle Scrooge, #4,** Menehunes	120.00	150.00	122.00
☐ **Dell, Uncle Scrooge, #14,** The Lost Crown Of Genghis Khan	115.00	140.00	119.00
☐ **Fiction House, Jumbo, #1,** Sheena, Queen Of The Jungle	625.00	750.00	655.00
☐ **Marvel Comics Group, Plus Timely/Atlas, Amazing Spiderman, #1,** Origin Retold	1100.00	1350.00	1175.00
☐ **Marvel Comics Group, Plus Timely/Atlas, Amazing Spiderman, #4,** Nothing Can Stop The Sandman	170.00	200.00	182.00
☐ **Marvel Comics Group, Plus Timely/Atlas, Amazing Spiderman, #14,** Green Goblin	80.00	100.00	87.00

	Current Price Range		Prior Year Average
☐ **Marvel Comics Group, Plus Timely/Atlas, Avengers, #1,** Coming Of The Avengers	420.00	470.00	430.00
☐ **Marvel Comics Group, Plus Timely/Atlas, Avengers, #15,** Now By My Hand Shall Perish A Villain	20.00	25.00	21.50
☐ **Marvel Comics Group, Plus Timely/Atlas, Fantastic Four, #1,** Origin Of The Fantastic Four	2000.00	2500.00	2175.00
☐ **Marvel Comics Group, Plus Timely/Atlas, Fantastic Four, #11,** Visit With The Fantastic Four	110.00	130.00	115.00
☐ **Marvel Comics Group, Plus Timely/Atlas, Incredible Hulk, #2,** Terror Of The Toad Men .	310.00	370.00	325.00
☐ **Marvel Comics Group, Plus Timely/Atlas, Incredible Hulk, #6,** The Incredible Hulk vs. Metal Master	135.00	160.00	140.00
☐ **Marvel Comics Group, Plus Timely/Atlas, Iron Man, #1,** Alone Against AIM	70.00	100.00	75.00
☐ **Marvel Comics Group, Plus Timely/Atlas, Marvel Team-Up, #1,** Amazing Spiderman, The Human Torch	21.50	25.00	23.00
☐ **Marvel Comics Group, Plus Timely/Atlas, Sergeant Fury, #1,** Sgt. Fury And His Howling Commandos	100.00	120.00	105.00
☐ **Marvel Comics Group, Plus Timely/Atlas, Strange Tales, #101,** The Human Torch	140.00	175.00	145.00
☐ **Marvel Comics Group, Plus Timely/Atlas, Strange Tales, #105,** Return Of The Wizard . .	25.00	33.00	27.00
☐ **Marvel Comics Group, Plus Timely/Atlas, Sub-Mariner, #1,** Origin Retold	13.00	17.00	14.50
☐ **Marvel Comics Group, Plus Timely/Atlas, Tales Of Suspense, #39,** Birth Of Iron Man . .	280.00	335.00	300.00
☐ **Marvel Comics Group, Plus Timely/Atlas, Tales Of Suspense, #45,** Icy Fingers Of Jack Frost	20.00	25.00	21.75
☐ **Marvel Comics Group, Plus Timely/Atlas, Tales To Astonish, #27,** The Man In The Anthill	635.00	715.00	660.00

COOKBOOKS

PERIOD: Cookbooks have been published for close to 500 years.

ORIGIN: European in origin, the earliest cookbooks often featured recipes for medicine.

COMMENTS: Rare first edition cookbooks, and those published before 1850, can be very expensive. However, most collectible cookbooks are reasonably priced. Many cookbooks from the early 20th century were given away as advertising premiums.

CONDITION: Cookbooks were used heavily so they are not expected to be in mint condition. Notations in margins are common.

ADDITIONAL TIPS: The following listings are alphabetical according to title of book. Following the title are the author's name, brief description, city of publisher, date and price range.

For further information, refer to *The Official Price Guide to Kitchen and Household Collectibles,* or *The Official Price Guide to Old Books and Autographs,* published by The House of Collectibles.

	Current Price Range		Prior Year Average
☐ **Adulterations Detected; or, Plain Instructions for the Discovery of Frauds in Food and Medicine,** by A.H. Hassall, clothbound, London, 1857	70.00	90.00	77.00
☐ **American Family Cookbook, The,** by Juliet Carson, Chicago, 1898	44.00	60.00	50.00
☐ **Archdeacon's Kitchen Cabinet,** Chicago, 1876	245.00	280.00	250.00
☐ **Art of Cookery made plain and easy, by a Lady, The,** by Mrs. Hannah Glasse, this is the most valuable cookbook in the English language, the price for a first edition published in 1747, London 1747	18,000.00	20,000.00	19,000.00
☐ **Aunt Jenny's Favorite Recipes,** 1930	2.50	5.00	2.50
☐ **Cookery For The Many As Well As For The "Upper Ten Thousand,"** colored frontis and three colored plates, London, 1864	110.00	140.00	120.00
☐ **Cookery From Experience,** by Mrs. Sara T. Paul, Philadelphia, 1875	28.00	35.00	30.00
☐ **Cre-Frdd's Family Fare, The Young Housewife's Daily Assistant On All Matters Relating Cookery And Housekeeping,** London, 1864	55.00	75.00	60.00
☐ **Culture And Cooking,** by Catherine Owen, New York, 1881	32.00	43.00	35.00
☐ **Dainty Dishes For Slender Incomes,** New York, 1900	25.00	35.00	25.00
☐ **Dining And Its Amenities,** by "A Lover Of Good Cheer," New York, 1907	28.00	37.00	32.00
☐ **Direction For Cookery,** by Miss Leslie, Philadelphia, 1863	23.00	30.00	25.00

	Current Price Range		Prior Year Average
☐ **Fatal Friendship, or The Drunkard's Misery,** by Richard Ames, London, 1693	245.00	275.00	240.00
☐ **Gold Medal Flour Cookbook,** 1910	13.00	18.00	13.00
☐ **Good Cheer, The Romance Of Food And Feasting,** by Frederick W. Hackwood, London, 1911	55.00	70.00	60.00
☐ **Good Cook, The, by A Practical Housekeeper,** New York, 1853	55.00	75.00	60.00
☐ **Just For Two,** by Amelie Langdon, Minneapolis, 1907	12.00	16.00	14.00
☐ **Kitchen Directory And American Housewife,** softbound, New York, 1844	80.00	100.00	88.00
☐ **London Art Of Cookery And Housekeeper's Complete Assistant,** by John Farley, London: John Fielding, J. Scatcherd and J. Whitacker, 1796	190.00	240.00	195.00
☐ **Luncheons,** by Mary Ronald, New York, 1902	12.00	16.00	14.00
☐ **Magic Chef Cooking,** 1937	2.00	4.50	3.00
☐ **Modern Domestic Cookery And Useful Receipts Book,** by W.A. Henderson, Boston, 1844	150.00	175.00	160.00
☐ **Modern Priscilla Cookbook,** 1924	11.00	17.00	11.00
☐ **Mrs. Hill's Cook Book,** 1881	65.00	85.00	65.00
☐ **Mrs. Rohrer's New Cookbook,** 1902	8.00	12.00	8.00
☐ **New Book Of Designs For Cake Bakers,** by H. Heug, 1893	28.00	35.00	30.00
☐ **New System Of Domestic Cookery,** by "A Lady," London, 1849	150.00	180.00	150.00
☐ **Practical Guide To French Wines,** by William Bird, includes 2 maps, softbound, c.1926 . . .	14.00	18.00	15.00
☐ **Principles Of Cookery,** by Anna Barows, Chicago, 1910	19.00	25.00	20.00
☐ **Record War-Time Cook Book,** by Nevada D. Hitchcock, Philadelphia, 1918	10.00	15.00	12.00
☐ **Rhymed Receipts For Any Occasion,** by Imogen Clark, Boston, 1912	23.00	30.00	25.00
☐ **Rocky Mountain Cook Book, The,** by Caroline T. Norton, Denver, 1903	32.00	45.00	37.00
☐ **Royal Baking Powder Biscuit Booklet,** 1927 .	2.50	5.00	2.50
☐ **Rumford Baking Powder Booklet**	2.50	5.00	2.50
☐ **Scientific Cooking With Scientific Methods,** by Sarah Craig, 1911	8.00	15.00	8.00
☐ **Sherry,** by Warner H. Allen, clothbound, London, 1934	14.00	19.00	15.00
☐ **Standard Cookbook For All Occasions,** by Marion Lockhart, New York, 1925	15.00	18.00	16.00

	Current Price Range		Prior Year Average
☐ **Through Good Cook, The,** by George A. Sala, New York, 1896	85.00	105.00	93.00
☐ **Universal Cook And City And Country Housekeeper,** by Francis Collingwood and John Woollams, London: printed by C. Whittingham for J. Scatcherd, 1792	160.00	220.00	170.00
☐ **Vinegars And Catsup,** by R.O. Brooks, New York, 1912	16.00	20.00	17.00
☐ **Virginia Housewife Methodical Cook,** by Mary Randolph, 1831	280.00	320.00	280.00
☐ **What To Do & What Not To Do In Cooking,** by Mrs. Lincoln, Boston, 1886	55.00	75.00	55.00
☐ **Young Housekeeper's Friend,** by Mrs. Cornelius, Boston and New York, 1846	140.00	180.00	150.00
☐ **Young Woman's Guide To Virtue, Economy And Happiness With A Complete And Elegant System Of Domestic Cookery, The,** John Armstrong, England, c. 1819	120.00	140.00	125.00

COOKIE CUTTERS

TOPIC: Cookie cutters are outlines or molds that shape cookie dough into a specific design.

TYPES: Cookie cutters are generally divided into the hand-crafted variety and the manufactured variety. They can also be categorized according to shape or design.

PERIOD: Cookie cutters have been widely used since at least the 16th century. There is evidence that they have existed in some form for thousands of years.

ORIGIN: Cookie cutters are thought to have originated in Europe.

MATERIAL: The oldest cookie cutters are made of wood. These are seldom seen on the market today. Aluminum became popular around 1920, and plastic usurped aluminum around 1940. Other metals, especially tin, were also used to make cutters.

COMMENTS: Backplates can sometimes be used to approximate the date of manufacture of a cookie cutter. In the late 1800s, these backings were trimmed to echo the shape of the cutter design. After the turn of the century, backplates were usually rectangular.

ADDITIONAL TIPS: Scarcity and age are not good indicators of cutter prices. In general, the price depends on the quality of the piece and the interest the individual collector has in it. Cutters with names on them are often more valuable than similar nameless ones. The following listings are organized by design.

	Current Price Range		Prior Year Average
☐ **Acorn**, metal, European	4.00	7.00	6.00
☐ **Animals**, tin	8.00	15.00	8.50
☐ **Bear**, metal, oval backplate, holes form a star	12.00	18.00	15.00
☐ **Bear**, metal, trimmed backplate, two holes, 6¼″	75.00	100.00	83.00
☐ **Bear**, tin, 4″ high	15.00	25.00	16.00
☐ **Bird**, aluminum, 4¾″	1.00	2.50	1.75
☐ **Bird**, metal, flying, handle, 2¾″ x 5¼″	20.00	29.00	24.50
☐ **Bird**, metal, flying, two holes, 4¾″	100.00	125.00	112.50
☐ **Bird**, metal, standing, one hole, 3¾″	20.00	30.00	25.00
☐ **Bird**, tin, 3″ long	20.00	35.00	19.00
☐ **Butterfly**, tin	15.00	26.00	19.00

Cookie Cutter, *tin, early 1900s,* **$8.00-$12.00**

	Current Price Range		Prior Year Average
☐ **Cat**, metal, sitting, curling tail, one hole, handle, 5″	110.00	125.00	117.00
☐ **Cat**, metal, sitting, French	20.00	30.00	25.00
☐ **Chick**, metal, holes form a star, 4″	17.00	25.00	21.00
☐ **Chick**, tin	10.00	20.00	10.50
☐ **Christmas Tree**, metal, thick trunk, handle, 4⅝″	80.00	95.00	87.50
☐ **Christmas Tree**, tin, 4¾″	4.00	6.50	5.25
☐ **Circle**, aluminum, open handle, late 1800s	7.00	10.00	8.50
☐ **Circle**, metal, crimped, handle, 4″	5.00	8.00	6.50
☐ **Circle**, tin, handle, 3″ diameter	2.00	4.00	3.00
☐ **Club (of cards)**, tin, 3½″ long, 1¾″ high	1.00	3.00	2.00
☐ **Deer**, tin, jumping	30.00	42.00	31.00
☐ **Diamond**, metal, painted wood handle	.50	1.50	1.00
☐ **Dog**, metal, Husky, one hole, 3⅝″ x 4⅞″	35.00	50.00	42.50
☐ **Donkey**, tin, lying down	16.00	26.00	19.00
☐ **Duck**, metal, 4″	5.00	8.00	7.00
☐ **Duck**, metal, embossed, "Davis Baking Powder"	4.00	8.00	6.00
☐ **Elephant**, metal, one hole, 4½″	100.00	115.00	107.50
☐ **Fish**, metal, handle, 6″	20.00	35.00	27.50
☐ **Gingerbread Man**, aluminum, 6″	3.50	6.50	5.00
☐ **Gingerbread Man**, plastic, with crown, yellow	1.00	3.50	2.25
☐ **Goose**, tin, flying	32.00	47.00	37.00
☐ **Guitar**, tin	20.00	30.00	21.00
☐ **Heart**, metal, painted wood handle	.50	1.50	1.00
☐ **Heart**, metal, two holes, handle, 4½″	40.00	65.00	47.50
☐ **Heart**, tin	4.00	10.00	5.50
☐ **Horse**, metal, prancing, three holes, 5¼″	135.00	160.00	148.00
☐ **Horse**, tin	12.00	24.00	13.00
☐ **Lamb**, aluminum, 4″	1.00	3.50	2.25
☐ **Leaf**, metal, crimped border, interior design	12.00	20.00	16.00
☐ **Lion**, metal, standing, two holes, 4½″	10.00	15.00	12.50
☐ **Man on Horseback**, tin	15.00	21.00	17.00
☐ **Man**, tin, stylized	20.00	30.00	21.00
☐ **Multiple Forms (animals)**, metal, Mexican	3.00	7.00	5.00
☐ **Peacock**, tin	18.00	30.00	21.00
☐ **Pig**, tin	33.00	46.00	37.00
☐ **Pitcher**, metal, two holes, handle, 5¼″	90.00	110.00	100.00
☐ **Rabbit**, metal, handle, 3″	5.00	15.00	10.00
☐ **Rabbit**, tin	10.00	25.00	13.00
☐ **Santa Claus**, tin	11.00	18.00	13.00
☐ **Set**, tin, "Junior Card Party Cake Cutters," a heart, spade, diamond and club, 2″	10.00	15.00	12.50
☐ **Spade**, tin, handle, 3½″	2.00	4.00	3.00
☐ **Star in Crescent Moon**, metal, 2¾″	15.00	28.00	21.50
☐ **Star**, tin, six points	22.00	37.00	27.00

	Current Price Range		Prior Year Average
☐ **Swan**, metal, standing, two holes, 3¼″	25.00	40.00	32.50
☐ **Tulip**, metal, crimped border, contemporary ..	10.00	20.00	15.00
☐ **Whale**, metal, multiple holes, 3¾″	20.00	35.00	27.50
☐ **Woman**, aluminum, 5¼″	2.50	4.00	3.25
☐ **Woman**, metal, stylized, 3″	10.00	20.00	15.00

COOKIE JARS

MAKER: A variety of pottery and glassware companies have made cookie jars. It is sometimes difficult to identify the maker because different companies often used similar molds.

COMMENTS: Cookie jars are collected by those interested in pottery as well as those interested in kitchen items. Prices on cookie jars, unless very rare or very old, are usually moderate.

ADDITIONAL TIPS: The listings are alphabetical according to cookie jar shape. When available, a description, color, height and company are listed.

RECOMMENDED READING: For more information, see *The Official 1984 Price Guide to Pottery and Porcelain*.

☐ **Alice in Wonderland**	26.00	38.00	30.00
☐ **Animals**, "Cookies," in relief	19.00	36.00	24.00
☐ **Antique Wall Phone**, Cardinal pottery	15.00	25.00	28.00
☐ **Apple**, yellow, red, green, with lid	10.00	15.00	12.00
☐ **Autumn Leaf**, Hall China Company, c. 1936, 1939	75.00	80.00	77.00
☐ **Bananas**, McCoy pottery	16.00	24.00	18.00
☐ **Bear**, cookies in pocket, McCoy pottery	22.00	26.00	23.00
☐ **Bear**, McCoy pottery	20.00	26.00	22.00
☐ **Bell**, "Ring Fo Cookies," with lid	15.00	24.00	28.00
☐ **Bird**, flying, 9″ diameter	341.00	380.00	350.00
☐ **Cat**, seated, yellow, black, pink, white	18.00	37.00	22.00
☐ **Chick**, on chicken	19.00	39.00	25.00
☐ **Chick**, wearing a blue jacket	13.50	18.00	15.00
☐ **Clown**, head only, with black boater hat, lid is formed by hat, McCoy pottery	18.00	23.00	20.00
☐ **Clown**, in barrel, tan and white, McCoy pottery	16.00	24.00	18.00
☐ **Coffee Grinder**, with lid, McCoy pottery	18.00	25.00	20.00
☐ **Coffee Pot**, imprinted cookies and cup, white	14.00	20.00	16.00
☐ **Cookie Garage**	16.00	22.00	18.00
☐ **Coors USA**	25.00	35.00	30.00
☐ **Covered Wagon**, with lid, McCoy pottery	25.00	35.00	30.00
☐ **Daffodil**, gold trim, Hall China Company	27.00	33.00	30.00

	Current Price Range		Prior Year Average
☐ **Dog,** in basket	11.00	22.00	14.00
☐ **Donald Duck,** with nephews, Disney	32.00	40.00	35.00
☐ **Dutch Boy,** American Bisque	14.00	28.00	17.00
☐ **Dutch Girl,** tulips on skirt	19.00	40.00	24.00
☐ **Dutch Windmill**	16.00	34.00	20.00
☐ **Elephant,** grinning, blond, in blue bonnet and jacket, ice cream cone in trunk, with lid	16.00	24.00	18.00
☐ **Elephant,** honking, crossed legs	21.00	28.00	23.00
☐ **Grandma,** red skirt, glasses, hair bun forms lid	27.00	32.00	29.00
☐ **Humpty Dumpty,** yellow, with lid	12.00	16.00	14.00
☐ **Kitten,** in basket, McCoy pottery	22.00	26.00	24.00
☐ **Mammy,** red kerchief, "Mammy," Pearl china	18.00	25.00	20.00
☐ **Monk,** "Thou Shalt Not Steal"	26.00	50.00	35.00
☐ **Owl,** glossy brown, McCoy pottery	15.00	25.00	18.00
☐ **Owl,** white and brown, one eye closed, Shawnee Pottery Company	11.00	15.00	13.00
☐ **Penguins,** kissing, McCoy pottery	24.00	28.00	26.00
☐ **Picnic Basket,** McCoy pottery	30.00	35.00	32.00
☐ **Pig,** dressed as farmer, white, Shawnee Pottery Company	32.00	36.00	34.00
☐ **Pig,** Smiley, red bandana, flowers, Shawnee Pottery Company, with lid	30.00	40.00	35.00
☐ **Pineapple,** McCoy pottery	22.00	25.00	23.00
☐ **Pot Belly Stove,** black, McCoy pottery	10.00	16.00	12.00
☐ **Red and White,** with lid, 10″ diameter	26.00	50.00	35.00
☐ **Red Riding Hood,** with lid, Hull Pottery	30.00	40.00	33.00
☐ **Rooster,** tail is handle, with lid, pale green, Red Wing pottery	26.00	32.00	28.00
☐ **School Girl's Face,** glasses and pigtails, "Cooky," Abingdon pottery	15.00	25.00	20.00
☐ **Strawberry,** McCoy pottery	22.00	28.00	24.00
☐ **Sunset Scene,** house and church in background, jeweling on three legs and finial, 7½″	160.00	180.00	168.00
☐ **Teapot,** copper and bronze, McCoy pottery	22.00	28.00	24.00
☐ **Truck,** with perched bird, yellow	14.00	20.00	16.00
☐ **Wishing Well,** McCoy pottery	16.00	24.00	18.00

COPPER

DESCRIPTION: This versatile metal has been used extensively by mankind in every conceivable way. Copper is an excellent conductor of heat and electricity and is also very malleable. It has been made into wire, cooking utensils, coins, decorative objects and countless other useful items.

RECOMMENDED READING: For more in-depth information on copper you may refer to *From Hearth to Cookstove* by Linda Campbell Franklin and *The Official Price Guide to Kitchen Collectibles,* published by The House of Collectibles.

	Current Price Range		Prior Year Average
☐ **Ashtray,** decorated with enameled bird of paradise	3.00	5.00	4.00
☐ **Ashtray,** sombrero shape, hand crafted, 5½ " x 2"	9.00	11.00	10.00
☐ **Basin,** side handle, tin lined, 14" diameter x 5" high	75.00	85.00	80.00
☐ **Bedwarmer,** floral engraving on lid, 12" diameter	255.00	285.00	270.00
☐ **Hanging Planter,** cauldron shape, copper chain and wall bracket, 3½ " diameter	6.00	8.00	7.00
☐ **Lamp,** miner's cap, copper, brass and tin, marked "Crown", never used	60.00	64.00	62.00
☐ **Measure,** pint	38.00	42.00	40.00
☐ **Measure,** quart	48.00	52.00	50.00
☐ **Measure,** with hood and pouring spout, 1½ " wide copper handle in back, 10" high, 5½ " diameter at base, tinned, very old	22.00	26.00	24.00
☐ **Miniature Fireplace,** kettle hangs over hearth, flanked by two buckets, nicely tooled and soldered, wood base, 8½ " x 3½ "	10.00	12.00	11.00
☐ **Teakettle,** features Delft porcelain on bail handle and finial, tinned interior, marked Made in Portugal	18.00	22.00	20.00
☐ **Teapot,** spouted vessel with hinged lid, tall finial, silver wash, hand tooled leaves and scrolls, unusual shape, Middle Eastern	28.00	32.00	30.00

CRACKER JACK MEMORABILIA

ORIGIN: This famous mixture of popcorn, peanuts, and molasses was developed in 1893 and sold at the Columbian Exposition in Chicago where it was an overnight sensation. In 1896 it was named Cracker Jack and in 1910 the prizes were introduced. At first coupons were used which the customer could trade for various prizes. The company began putting the actual prize in each box in 1912.

MATERIAL: Cracker Jack prizes have been made of lead, paper, porcelain, plastic, tin and wood.

	Current Price Range		Prior Year Average
☐ **Air Corps Wings,** metal, embossed	25.00	50.00	37.50
☐ **Badge,** junior detective, metal, embossed, 1¼"	5.00	25.00	15.00
☐ **Baseball Card,** #124, Earl Moore, Buffalo Federals, red, white and black	25.00	75.00	50.00
☐ **Baseball Card,** #150, W.R. Johnston, Cleveland Americans, red, white, blue and black	25.00	75.00	50.00
☐ **Card,** #95, Victoria Cross Heroes series, 3" x 2½", made by Lowney	5.00	25.00	15.00
☐ **Clicker,** metal, black and silver, instructions on front, 2⅛" H	5.00	25.00	15.00
☐ **Clicker, Whistle,** metal, embossed CJ, 2". . .	15.00	25.00	20.00
☐ **Corkscrew,** Angelus, metal, 3¾" wide	25.00	50.00	37.50
☐ **Flip Book,** Charlie Chaplin, pre-1922	50.00	75.00	62.50
☐ **Fortune Teller,** 2" H.	25.00	50.00	37.50
☐ **Game #1,** red, white and blue, 2½"	20.00	50.00	35.00
☐ **Horse And Wagon,** metal, 2" long	50.00	100.00	75.00
☐ **Hummer Band,** metal, embossed, 1" diameter	15.00	25.00	20.00
☐ **Magazine Advertisement,** *Saturday Evening Post,* June, 1919, red, white and blue	5.00	15.00	10.00
☐ **Magic Puzzle,** donkey, paper and plastic, 1½"	5.00	15.00	10.00
☐ **Magic Puzzle,** fish	5.00	15.00	10.00
☐ **Magic Puzzle,** man with cigar, marked CJ Co. on reverse	5.00	15.00	10.00
☐ **Paper Booklet,** #12, Bess and Bill, 2½"	15.00	50.00	32.50
☐ **Paper Frog,** outside is green black and white, opens to red and tan inside	15.00	25.00	20.00
☐ **Paper Golf Top,** red, white and blue, rules back, intact	15.00	50.00	32.50
☐ **Paper Prize,** Jack at the blackboard, turn dial and Jack writes and erases his name from blackboard, black, white, red, blue, and brown, 2" square	25.00	75.00	50.00
☐ **Pin,** Lady	15.00	25.00	20.00
☐ **Pin,** Lady, celluloid, paper insert in back for "CJ 5 Cents"	15.00	25.00	20.00
☐ **Pocket Watch,** tin, gold, black, and white, 1½" diameter	15.00	25.00	20.00
☐ **Postcard,** bears, #13	5.00	25.00	15.00
☐ **Postcard,** bears, #15	5.00	25.00	15.00
☐ **Puzzle Book,** #1, 4", copyright 1917	15.00	50.00	32.50
☐ **Puzzles,** #1-15, complete set	100.00	200.00	150.00

	Current Price Range		Prior Year Average
☐ **Rainbow Spinner,** blue and white on one side, other side is red, blue and yellow, 2½" long, 1940s	15.00	25.00	20.00
☐ **Sign,** cardboard, string at top for hanging, red, white and blue box on blue background, 11" x 15"	· 200.00	500.00	350.00
☐ **Tin Stand-Up,** Harold Teen	25.00	50.00	37.50
☐ **Tin Stand-Up,** Orphan Annie	5.00	50.00	37.50
☐ **Tin Stand-Up,** Perry	25.00	50.00	37.50
☐ **Tin Top**	5.00	25.00	15.00
☐ **Tin Top,** fortune teller	25.00	50.00	37.50
☐ **Truck,** plastic, embossed on all four sides, gold, 1⅝" long, late 1940s	5.00	15.00	10.00
☐ **Truck,** tin, red, white and black, one side says Cracker Jack, the other says Angelus, 1⅝" long	15.00	25.00	20.00
☐ **Whistle,** metal, embossed CJ	15.00	50.00	32.50
☐ **Whistle,** paper, red and white, reverse marked CJ Whistle, 2" H	15.00	25.00	20.00
☐ **Whistle,** paper, 2⅜", rare	15.00	50.00	30.00
☐ **Whistle,** plastic, red and white, embossed, 1½", 1950s	5.00	15.00	10.00

CRECHES

DESCRIPTION: Creches are miniature manger scenes used at Christmas time to depict the birth of Christ. During the 18th century, craftsmen from all over Europe produced as many kinds of creches as their own imagination would allow. Creches have been made in nearly every country of the world and of nearly every imaginable material. Figures may be free standing or the entire scene may be in one piece.

☐ **American,** wood and painted plaster, six piece set, c. 1920	43.00	45.00	44.00
☐ **French,** hand painted, angel 12" L., single piece, c. 1875	300.00	320.00	310.00
☐ **French,** hand painted, wooden, 12 piece set, c. 1890	275.00	295.00	285.00
☐ **German,** ceramic, 12 piece set, c. 1900	200.00	250.00	225.00
☐ **German,** hand carved, 14 piece set, c. 1880	250.00	300.00	275.00
☐ **Guatemalan,** hand carved, 15 piece set, c. 1900	100.00	110.00	105.00
☐ **Hummel,** nativity set #214, 11 china pieces	700.00	750.00	725.00

Nativity Set, Hummel, *figurines number 214/A through 214/O, excluding 214/I, trademark Goebel,* **$888.00-$975.00**

	Current Price Range		Prior Year Average
☐ **Hummel,** Ferrandiz creche set #375, 13 china pieces	500.00	550.00	525.00
☐ **Mexican,** hand painted clay, 18 piece set, c. 1920	100.00	120.00	110.00
☐ **Mexican,** red clay, 10 piece set, c. 1910	85.00	95.00	90.00
☐ **Polish,** hand carved, wood, nativity scene, one piece, c. 1890	200.00	220.00	210.0

CURRENCY

In order to accurately present the vast amount of information required by serious collectors, a special edition devoted to currency is published by The House of Collectibles, Inc. This handy, pocket-size guide, *The Official 1985 Blackbook Price Guide to U.S. Paper Money*, features listings, prices, photographs and expert advice. It is available at bookstores for $3.95.

CUT GLASS

This section features only a sampling of cut glass. In order to accurately present the vast amount of information required by serious collectors, a special edition devoted to glassware has been published by The House of Collectibles, Inc. This handy pocket-size guide, *The Official 1985 Price Guide to Glassware,* contains a variety of glassware information. It is available at bookstores for $3.95. For more detailed glassware information and prices, refer to *The Official 1985 Price Guide to Glassware* for $10.95.

DESCRIPTION: Cut glass features deep prismatic cutting in elaborate, often geometrical designs. The edges are very sharp, thus allowing light to be refracted easily. Its high lead content makes it heavier than most blown glass. It also has a distinct bell tone when struck.

ORIGIN: It developed during the 16th century in Bohemia and was very popular until the invention of molded pressed glass, in America about 1825, which was an inexpensive imitation of cut glass. It enjoyed a revival during the Brilliant period of cut glass in America which dated from 1876-1916.

PROCESS: The making of cut glass was a time consuming process requiring the patience and talent of master craftsmen. The glass was handblown of the finest 35-45% lead crystal and poured into molds to produce the shaped piece, called a blank. These blanks were anywhere from ¼" - ½" thick in order to permit the deep cutting which distinguished this glass from later periods. The resulting finished product was, therefore exceedingly heavy.

The cutting and polishing was accomplished in four steps. The first step involved making the desired pattern on the blank with crayons or paint. Next the deepest cuts were made by rough cutting. This was accomplished by pressing the blank on an abrasive cutting wheel of metal or stone which was lubricated by a small stream of water and sand. In the third step, the rough cuts were smoothed with a finer stone wheel and water only. Finally, polishing or "coloring" was done on a wooden wheel with putty powder or pumice, in order to produce the gleaming brilliant finish.

RECOMMENDED READING: For more in-depth information on cut glass, you may refer to *The Official Price Guide to Glassware,* and *The Official Identification Guide to Glassware,* published by The House of Collectibles.

	Current Price Range		Prior Year Average
☐ **Ashtray,** rectangular	55.00	80.00	62.00
☐ **Ashtray,** richly cut, signed	80.00	110.00	88.00
☐ **Basket,** floral design, handle, 10″	210.00	260.00	225.00

	Current Price Range		Prior Year Average
☐ **Basket,** scalloped edge, handle, 6″	160.00	210.00	175.00
☐ **Basket,** floral and miter cut, twisted handle, 8″	170.00	195.00	172.00
☐ **Bell,** diamond and fan	110.00	135.00	112.00
☐ **Bell,** star design	135.00	160.00	138.00
☐ **Bonbon,** diamond shape, 6″	70.00	95.00	78.00
☐ **Bonbon,** heart shape, 6″	80.00	110.00	88.00
☐ **Bonbon,** oval, 5¼″	28.00	38.00	30.00
☐ **Bonbon,** pedestal, pair	460.00	510.00	475.00
☐ **Bonbon,** Plymouth, 5″	50.00	65.00	52.00
☐ **Bonbon,** Royal, square	80.00	110.00	88.00
☐ **Bonbon,** scalloped edge	38.00	48.00	40.00
☐ **Bottle,** bitters, silver plate stopper	160.00	185.00	162.00
☐ **Bottle,** cologne, butterfly design, 8 oz.	80.00	110.00	88.00
☐ **Bottle,** cologne, diamond and fan, 4 oz.	50.00	65.00	52.00
☐ **Bottle,** cologne, globe shape, pinwheel, 2 oz.	38.00	48.00	40.00
☐ **Bottle,** cologne, hobstar, 6 oz.	28.00	38.00	30.00
☐ **Bottle,** cordial, bell shape, pinwheel stopper .	110.00	135.00	112.00
☐ **Carafe,** water, hobstar and notched prism ...	80.00	110.00	88.00
☐ **Carafe,** water, pinwheel, crosscut diamond and flasked fan	90.00	120.00	98.00
☐ **Carafe,** water, pinwheel cut flowers	80.00	110.00	88.00
☐ **Carafe,** wine, hobstar and fan, sterling collar	135.00	160.00	138.00
☐ **Celery,** Harvard, Libbey	260.00	310.00	275.00
☐ **Celery,** hobstar and fan, signed Hawkes	135.00	160.00	138.00
☐ **Celery,** strawberry, diamond and fan, Hawkes	185.00	210.00	188.00
☐ **Champagne,** Russian, rayed star base	80.00	110.00	88.00
☐ **Compote,** Harvard, hobstar base, intaglio cut, 9″	310.00	360.00	325.00
☐ **Compote,** hobstar, strawberry, diamond and fan, 8″	360.00	410.00	375.00
☐ **Compote,** pinwheel, hobstar, prism cut, 7½″	135.00	160.00	138.00
☐ **Compote,** square, signed Hoare	510.00	585.00	538.00
☐ **Cordial,** crystal and silver, pair	760.00	835.00	780.00
☐ **Cordial,** Russian	80.00	110.00	88.00
☐ **Cordial,** sterling, blown glass	135.00	185.00	150.00
☐ **Creamer,** hobstar	80.00	95.00	82.00
☐ **Creamer,** pinwheel	55.00	70.00	58.00
☐ **Creamer,** Waterford, c. 1930's	45.00	65.00	50.00
☐ **Cruet,** Harvard, signed Hoare	160.00	185.00	162.00
☐ **Cruet,** Middlesex	75.00	95.00	80.00
☐ **Cruet,** prism, signed Libbey	155.00	175.00	155.00
☐ **Cruet,** pyramid shape, 7½″	55.00	80.00	62.00
☐ **Decanter,** Art Deco, pressed pattern of Chrysler Building	110.00	160.00	125.00
☐ **Decanter,** Harvard, 8″	95.00	140.00	110.00

	Current Price Range		Prior Year Average
☐ **Decanter**, hobstar, diamond and fan, cut stopper	160.00	185.00	162.00
☐ **Decanter**, original stopper, numbered	185.00	210.00	188.00
☐ **Decanter**, pineapple cut	110.00	135.00	112.00
☐ **Decanter**, pineapple fan, brilliant cut	80.00	130.00	100.00
☐ **Decanter**, pinwheel	185.00	210.00	188.00
☐ **Dish**, cheese and cracker, signed Hoare	310.00	410.00	350.00
☐ **Dish**, cheese and cracker, hobstar, strawberry and diamond	100.00	125.00	105.00
☐ **Goblet**, prism cut, signed Hawkes	60.00	85.00	68.00
☐ **Goblet**, Russian	110.00	135.00	112.00
☐ **Goblet**, spiral pinwheel	40.00	55.00	42.00
☐ **Goblet**, Vintage	55.00	80.00	62.00
☐ **Inkwell**, crystal	235.00	310.00	262.00
☐ **Inkwell**, silver and crystal	535.00	610.00	562.00
☐ **Inkwell**, sterling lid, 2″	40.00	55.00	42.00
☐ **Jar**, Art Nouveau, sterling lid	45.00	65.00	50.00
☐ **Jar**, candy, Hawkes, 11″	210.00	260.00	225.00
☐ **Jar**, mustard, signed Webb	55.00	80.00	62.00
☐ **Jar**, powder, Art Nouveau, hobstar and fan	110.00	135.00	112.00
☐ **Jar**, powder, Reine Des Fleurs	80.00	110.00	88.00
☐ **Jar**, powder, sterling lid, 3″ x 3″	80.00	110.00	88.00
☐ **Jar**, tobacco, sterling top, 7″	135.00	160.00	138.00
☐ **Jug**, whiskey, Clarke	285.00	335.00	300.00
☐ **Knife Rest**, c. 1920's	22.00	32.00	25.00
☐ **Knife Rest**, ball ends, diamond cut	28.00	38.00	30.00
☐ **Knife Rest**, signed Hawkes	45.00	65.00	50.00
☐ **Lamp**, diamond cut, 17″	385.00	485.00	425.00
☐ **Lamp**, table, mushroom shade, 18″	485.00	585.00	525.00
☐ **Matchstrikes**, antique, pair	210.00	260.00	225.00
☐ **Muffineer**, sterling, cone shaped	80.00	130.00	100.00
☐ **Nappy**, hobstar and fan, signed Clarke	65.00	80.00	68.00
☐ **Nappy**, pinwheel	50.00	65.00	52.00
☐ **Nappy**, strawberry and diamond	45.00	60.00	48.00
☐ **Pitcher**, cider, prism and bull's eye, hobstar base, 8″	160.00	185.00	162.00
☐ **Pitcher**, claret, Encore by Strauss, 12″	260.00	310.00	275.00
☐ **Pitcher**, Harvard, signed Libbey, 8″	160.00	210.00	175.00
☐ **Pitcher**, hobstar and fan, 8″	160.00	210.00	175.00
☐ **Pitcher**, milk, Russian, starred buttons, 5″	360.00	435.00	380.00
☐ **Pitcher**, milk, deep cutting, twelve point star base, signed Hawkes, 5½″	185.00	235.00	200.00
☐ **Pitcher**, pinwheel, strawberry and diamond, 9″	135.00	160.00	138.00
☐ **Syrup**, silver plate, strawberry, diamond and fan	70.00	95.00	78.00
☐ **Syrup**, sterling, Hawkes	160.00	210.00	175.00

	Current Price Range		Prior Year Average
☐ **Toothpick Holder,** diamond and fan	55.00	80.00	62.00
☐ **Toothpick Holder,** pinwheel	40.00	60.00	45.00
☐ **Tray,** bread, cane, intaglio florals	80.00	100.00	88.00
☐ **Tray,** card, Russian, starred buttons	75.00	95.00	80.00
☐ **Tray,** Harvard, floral and leaves, 11″ x 6¼″ .	95.00	130.00	110.00
☐ **Tray,** hobstar and fan, signed Clarke, 14″ x 7½″	235.00	285.00	250.00
☐ **Vase,** dahlias and leaves, 8″	135.00	160.00	138.00
☐ **Vase,** English, graceful shape, 16″	285.00	385.00	325.00
☐ **Vase,** floral and leaf, intaglio cut, Libbey 9½″	260.00	310.00	275.00
☐ **Vase,** flower, signed Hawkes, 16″	260.00	335.00	280.00
☐ **Vase,** grapes and leaves, Libbey, 12″	160.00	185.00	162.00
☐ **Vase,** Hawkes, 18″	160.00	185.00	162.00

DAIRY COLLECTIBLES

DESCRIPTION: All items pertaining to the American dairy industry.

TYPES: Dairy collectibles include articles used on dairy farms such as pails, milking devices and churns, containers to transport and retail milk and other dairy products, as well as advertising items, brochures and signs.

PERIOD: Though dairy farming in America dates to the early colonial era, collectibles available on the market date from the 1700s. Most of them are of the period from about 1850 to the early 1900s. This era ushered in large scale factory production of such items as milk cans and store bottles.

COMMENTS: This is another of various fields of collecting in which charm and historical appeal take precedence over immaculate condition.

☐ **Bottle Filler,** three wooden legs, glass window at front, brass spigot, 36″ tall	27.00	34.00	30.00
☐ **Butter Churn,** Dazy Churn and Manufacturing Co., glass, model No. 40, made in St. Louis, square, four quart capacity, wood paddles	43.00	57.00	48.00
☐ **Centrifugal Butter Fat Tester,** Vermont Farm Machinery Co., Bellows Falls, Vermont, 100 revolutions per minute, embossed cover, brass gears and brass bottle holders, galvanized rack and tank, 8½″ x 6″ x 7″	90.00	115.00	98.00
☐ **Metal Sign,** Turner Centre Ice Cream, reads "It's Frozen Health," embossed black letters on yellow background, nailhole at top, 1928	90.00	105.00	95.00

	Current Price Range		Prior Year Average
☐ **Milk Bottle,** B & S Pasteurizing Co., Tamaque, Pennsylvania, glass, quart, round, slug plate	6.00	8.00	7.00
☐ **Milk Bottle,** Bloomingdale Dairy Co., Inc., 136 to 40 Hunterdon St., Newark, New Jersey, glass, quart, round	7.00	10.00	8.20
☐ **Milk Bottle,** Chestnut Farm Chevy Chase Dairy, Washington, D.C., reads "Milk for Babies," glass, quart, round	6.00	8.00	7.00
☐ **Milk Bottle,** D.A. Delano, Norway, Maine, "Tel. 6-24," glass, quart, round, slug plate . .	7.00	10.00	8.50
☐ **Milk Bottle,** Edward Carlson, East Walpole, glass, quart, round	6.00	8.00	7.00
☐ **Milk Bottle,** Granite Farm Pure Milk and Cream, Brunswick, Maine, glass, quart, round, slug plate	7.00	10.00	8.50
☐ **Milk Bottle,** Laudholm Farms, Wells, Maine, glass, quart, round	7.00	10.00	8.50
☐ **Milk Bottle,** The Lawson Milk Co., Akron, Ohio, glass, quart, round, slug plate	6.00	8.00	7.00
☐ **Milk Bottle,** Petersburg Creamery, Petersburg, Ohio, reads "Safe Milk Every Morning," glass, quart, round	9.00	12.00	10.20
☐ **Milk Bottle,** R.O. Stockman, Portland, Maine, glass, quart, round	6.00	8.00	7.00
☐ **Milk Bottle,** Wonder Brook Farm, A.F. Smith, Kennebunk, Maine, glass, quart, round stubby style	9.00	12.00	10.25
☐ **Milk Bottle Cap,** Parson's Jersey Dairy, plug type, 56 mm.	.10	.15	.12
☐ **Milk Bottle Cover,** National Milk Co., Boston, aluminum with pouring lip.	9.00	12.00	10.20
☐ **Milk Strainer,** filter type, homemade filter holder	4.00	6.00	5.00
☐ **Porch Box,** Blais Dairy, Lewiston, Maine, stenciled name, double box, holds eight milk bottles	22.00	28.00	24.00
☐ **Porch Box,** Needham Dairy Inc., embossed double box, holds six milk bottles	20.00	26.00	22.00

DECOYS

TOPIC: A decoy is a representation of some animal used to lure others of that species within shooting range.

TYPES: Decoys most often represent waterfowl, but frog, fish, owl and crow decoys are not uncommon. Decoys can be solid, hollow or slat-bodied. They can be either of the floating variety or the "stick-up" variety, which is driven into the ground.

PERIOD: Decoys produced after the mid-nineteenth century are most popular among collectors.

ORIGIN: American Indians have made and used decoys since 1000 A.D.

MAKERS: Famous decoy carvers include Ira Hudson, Charles Wheeler, Albert Laing and Mark Whipple.

MATERIALS: Decoys are usually carved out of wood, although metal and other materials are found.

COMMENTS: Enthusiasts usually collect decoys by carver, species or fly-way (the path of migration). Decoys made for actual use are more favored by collectors than those intended only for show.

TIPS: The condition of the paint on a decoy is a good indicator of age. Many cracked layers of paint mean that the decoy is probably old. Original paint is favored by collectors.

	Current Price Range		Prior Year Average
B.W. Teal, P. Wilcoxen	80.00	130.00	105.00
B.W. Teal, glass eyes, pre-1900	1300.00	1700.00	1500.00
B.W. Teal, preening, Ohio	75.00	100.00	87.50
Beach Duck, papier-mache, paper label, Mackey	170.00	220.00	195.00
Beach Duck, cork body, Thomas H. Gelston	125.00	175.00	150.00
Black Duck, August mock drake, c. 1900	200.00	250.00	225.00
Black Duck, Cobb Island, carved wing tips	175.00	225.00	200.00
Black Duck, Dan English	525.00	575.00	550.00
Brant, Long Island, cork body	175.00	225.00	200.00
Brant, Mason's	190.00	230.00	210.00
Brant, swimming, carved wings	200.00	240.00	220.00
Broadbill, Chauncey Wheeler	300.00	360.00	330.00
Bufflehead, drake, Doug Jester	115.00	145.00	130.00
Bufflehead, drake, Ira Hudson	300.00	425.00	362.50
Bufflehead, drake, California	75.00	125.00	100.00
Bufflehead, glass eyes	600.00	900.00	750.00
Bufflehead, drake, hollow, carved, Charles Parker	300.00	360.00	330.00
Bufflehead, drake, primitive, Oscar Ayers	115.00	145.00	130.00
Canada Goose, Nathan Cobb	450.00	500.00	475.00
Canada Goose, Hurley Conklin	650.00	750.00	700.00
Canada Goose, John Furlow	275.00	325.00	300.00
Canada Goose, solid, Madison Mitchell	160.00	200.00	180.00

	Current Price Range		Prior Year Average
☐ Canada Goose, L. Parker	275.00	325.00	300.00
☐ Canada Goose, Harvey V. Shourds	380.00	420.00	400.00
☐ Canada Goose, swimming, signed, c. 1880	1900.00	2100.00	2000.00
☐ Canvasback, drake, balsa wood, Harry Megargy	90.00	120.00	105.00
☐ Canvasback, drake, feeding, A. Elmer Crowell	415.00	475.00	430.00
☐ Canvasback, drake, Lohrman	130.00	180.00	155.00
☐ Canvasback, drake, Madison Mitchell	100.00	170.00	135.00
☐ Canvasback, drake, Michigan bobtail	190.00	220.00	205.00
☐ Canvasback, drake, Samuel Denny	245.00	285.00	260.00
☐ Canvasback, hen, Mason's	90.00	120.00	205.00
☐ Canvasback, hen, Frank Schmidt	270.00	330.00	300.00
☐ Canvasback, Michael Pavolich	150.00	200.00	175.00
☐ Coot, J.W. Johnson, 1960	60.00	100.00	80.00
☐ Coot, Mason's	300.00	330.00	315.00
☐ Coot, Benjamin J. Schmidt	170.00	200.00	185.00
☐ Crow, hollow, late 1800s	325.00	425.00	375.00
☐ Crow, hollow, carved, Charles H. Perdew Co.	325.00	375.00	350.00
☐ Crow, wooden, glass eyes, c. 1900	475.00	525.00	500.00
☐ Curlew, Barnegat	615.00	645.00	630.00
☐ Curlew, Cobb Island, running	760.00	790.00	775.00
☐ Curlew, Eskimo, carved wings, signed	740.00	780.00	760.00
☐ Curlew, Mason's	2800.00	3000.00	2900.00
☐ Curlew, sickle-billed, Harry Shourds, contemporary	225.00	325.00	275.00
☐ Dowitcher, Long Island	275.00	325.00	300.00
☐ Duck, J. H. Whitney	90.00	120.00	105.00
☐ Duck, Labrador	770.00	790.00	780.00
☐ Duck, Pacific Northwest	45.00	75.00	60.00
☐ Duck, papier-mache	35.00	55.00	45.00
☐ Eider duck, primitive	160.00	180.00	170.00
☐ Fish, carved and painted, pair, 19th c.	340.00	360.00	350.00
☐ Gadwell, hen, Ken Anger	270.00	290.00	280.00
☐ Golden Eye, drake, Doug Jester	125.00	200.00	161.50
☐ Golden Eye, drake, Mason's	290.00	320.00	305.00
☐ Golden Eye, drake, Steven's Decoy Factory	400.00	440.00	420.00
☐ Golden Eye, hen, Harry Shourds	160.00	180.00	170.00
☐ Golden Eye, hen, Bob White	325.00	375.00	350.00
☐ Golden Plover	75.00	90.00	82.50
☐ Goose, standing, aggressive stance, hollow, Prince Edward Island	400.00	550.00	475.00
☐ Great Blue Heron, sheet metal, painted	375.00	425.00	400.00
☐ Gull, with iron weight, J. W. Carter	2500.00	2700.00	2600.00
☐ Heron, primitive	650.00	750.00	700.00
☐ Lesser Yellowlegs, Bay Head	250.00	280.00	265.00
☐ Lesser Yellowlegs, Mason's	650.00	700.00	675.00
☐ Lesser Yellowlegs, William Matthews	315.00	335.00	325.00

		Current Price Range		Prior Year Average
☐ **Lesser Yellowlegs**, c. 1896		300.00	320.00	210.00
☐ **Mallard**, drake, J. N. Dodge Decory Factory .		75.00	95.00	85.00
☐ **Mallard**, drake, Elliston		2400.00	2800.00	2600.00
☐ **Mallard**, drake, Old Illinois River		360.00	380.00	370.00
☐ **Mallard**, drake, Charles H. Perdew Co.		550.00	580.00	565.00
☐ **Mallard**, hen, Mason's		80.00	100.00	90.00
☐ **Mallard**, hen, Ward Brothers, c. 1920		220.00	250.00	235.00
☐ **Mallard**, papier-mache		25.00	30.00	27.50
☐ **Mallard**, drake, cork body		28.00	32.00	30.00
☐ **Mallard**, crude, Kansas		30.00	45.00	37.50
☐ **Merganser**, drake, red-breasted, Hurley Conklin		170.00	190.00	180.00
☐ **Merganser**, hen, Doug Jester		500.00	540.00	520.00
☐ **Merganser**, Long Island		370.00	400.00	385.00
☐ **Merganser**, Harold Haertel		2900.00	3000.00	2950.00
☐ **Merganser**, primitive, American		150.00	200.00	175.00
☐ **Merganser**, red-breasted, drake		125.00	225.00	175.00
☐ **Merganser**, tack eyes		700.00	1000.00	850.00
☐ **Old-Squaw**, drake, Mark English		850.00	890.00	870.00
☐ **Owl**, balsa wood, glass eyes		480.00	500.00	490.00
☐ **Owl**, 19th c.		225.00	275.00	250.00
☐ **Pigeon**, English wood, Austin Johnson		275.00	350.00	311.50
☐ **Pigeon**, Lou Schifferell		275.00	295.00	285.00
☐ **Pintail**, drake, carved cedar		280.00	300.00	290.00
☐ **Pintail**, drake, carved wings and feathers . . .		275.00	325.00	300.00
☐ **Redhead**, drake, sleeping, Mason's		340.00	370.00	355.00
☐ **Redhead**, hen, Nate Quillen		530.00	590.00	560.00
☐ **Ruddy Duck**, hen, L. T. Ward		150.00	170.00	160.00
☐ **Sanderling**, A. Elmer Crowell		830.00	860.00	845.00
☐ **Sanderling**, Taylor Johnson		280.00	300.00	290.00
☐ **Sandpiper**, Cobb Island		260.00	280.00	270.00

DEPRESSION GLASS

This section features only a sampling of Depression Glass. In order to accurately present the vast amount of information required by serious collectors, a special edition devoted to glassware has been published by the House of Collectibles, Inc. This handy, pocket-size guide, *The Official Price Guide to Glassware*, contains a variety of glassware information. It is available at bookstores for $3.95. For detailed, in-depth Depression Glass information, refer to *The Official Price Guide to Depression Glass* for $9.95.

DESCRIPTION: Colored glassware was machine made during the Depression years of the late 1920s and early 1930s. The glass was available in ten cent stores, given away at filling stations, theatres, and used for promotional purposes. There are approximately 150,000 collectors and the popularity is steadily increasing each year. There are over 80 Depression Glass clubs which sponsor shows with attendance in the thousands.

COMMENTS: Of the approximately 100 different patterns and colors produced, rose pink remains the favorite color. Luncheon sets of 16 pieces sold new for as low as $1.29. Today a dinner service, depending on the scarcity of the pattern, may cost from $100.00 to $1000.00.

RECOMMENDED READING: For more in-depth information on Depression Glass you may refer to *The Official Price Guide to Glassware* and *The Official Identification Guide to Glassware,* published by The House of Collectibles.

Depression Glass, Miss America Pattern, *pink, 10¼", made from 1933 to 1936,* **$16.50-$19.50**

AMERICAN SWEETHEART (Pink, Monax — MacBeth-Evans Glass Co.)

	Current Price Range		Prior Year Average
☐ Bowl, 4½″	25.00	35.00	30.00
☐ Bowl, 6″	9.00	10.00	9.50
☐ Bowl, 9″	16.00	33.00	23.00
☐ Bowl, oval, 11″	28.00	38.00	33.00
☐ Creamer	7.00	8.00	7.50
☐ Cup and Saucer	10.00	13.00	11.50
☐ Plate, 6″	2.00	4.00	3.00
☐ Plate, 8″	6.00	7.00	6.50
☐ Plate, 9¾″	12.00	15.00	13.50
☐ Platter, oval, 13″	17.00	38.00	27.50
☐ Sherbet, footed, 4¼″	9.00	14.00	11.50
☐ Sugar, footed	6.00	8.00	7.00
☐ Tumbler, 3½″ (pink only)	32.00	33.00	32.50
☐ Tumbler, 4½″ (pink only)	40.00	42.00	41.00

AUNT POLLY (Green, Blue — U.S. Glass Co.)

☐ Bowl, 4¾″	8.00	11.00	10.00
☐ Bowl, 7⅞″	11.00	18.00	14.50
☐ Bowl, oval, 7¼″	18.00	33.00	22.00
☐ Bowl, oval, 8⅜″	19.00	33.00	26.00
☐ Butter, covered	145.00	190.00	167.50
☐ Candy Dish, covered	35.00	48.00	41.50
☐ Creamer	16.00	26.00	21.00
☐ Plate, 6″	3.00	5.00	4.00
☐ Plate, 8″	8.00	9.00	8.50
☐ Pitcher, 8″	115.00	120.00	117.50
☐ Salt and Pepper	145.00	150.00	147.50
☐ Sugar	11.00	17.00	14.00
☐ Tumbler, 3⅝″	13.00	15.00	14.00
☐ Vase, 6½″	22.00	28.00	25.00

BLOCK OPTIC (Pink, Green — Hocking Glass Co.)

☐ Bowl, 4¼″	4.00	6.00	5.00
☐ Bowl, 7″	8.00	14.00	11.00
☐ Butter, covered	35.00	40.00	37.50
☐ Candy Dish, covered	25.00	40.00	32.50
☐ Creamer	8.00	10.00	9.00
☐ Cup and Saucer	9.00	14.00	11.50
☐ Goblet, 5¾″	11.00	14.00	12.50
☐ Goblet, 7¼″	12.00	19.00	15.50
☐ Pitcher, 8″	32.00	38.00	35.00
☐ Plate, 8″	2.50	4.00	3.25
☐ Plate, 9″	10.00	15.00	12.50

	Current Price Range		Prior Year Average
☐ Salt and Pepper	20.00	43.00	31.50
☐ Sherbet	4.00	10.00	7.00
☐ Sugar	8.00	9.00	8.50
☐ Tumbler, 5 oz.	11.00	12.00	11.50
☐ Tumbler, 9 oz.	8.00	13.00	10.50
☐ Tumbler, 10 oz.	9.00	12.00	10.50

CAMEO (Green — Hocking Glass Co.)

☐ Bowl, 5½"	20.00	22.00	21.00
☐ Bowl, 8¼"	24.00	26.00	25.00
☐ Bowl, oval, 10"	13.00	14.00	13.50
☐ Bowl, three feet	39.00	41.00	40.00
☐ Butter, covered	128.00	132.00	130.00
☐ Candlesticks, pair, 4"	72.00	75.00	73.50
☐ Candy Dish, covered	40.00	42.00	41.00
☐ Cookie Jar	36.00	38.00	37.00
☐ Creamer	16.00	17.00	16.50
☐ Cup and Saucer	13.00	15.00	14.00
☐ Decanter	82.00	85.00	83.50
☐ Goblet, 4"	46.00	48.00	47.00
☐ Goblet, 6"	34.00	36.00	35.00
☐ Pitcher, 6"	38.00	42.00	40.00
☐ Pitcher, 8½"	35.00	40.00	37.50
☐ Plate, 8"	7.00	8.00	7.50
☐ Plate, 9½"	13.00	14.00	13.50
☐ Plate, 10½"	7.00	8.00	7.50
☐ Plate, cake, three feet	14.00	15.00	14.50
☐ Platter, 12"	13.00	14.00	13.50
☐ Salt and Pepper	48.00	52.00	50.00
☐ Sugar	11.00	17.00	14.00
☐ Tumbler, 3¾"	18.00	19.00	18.50
☐ Tumbler, 4¾"	20.00	22.00	21.00
☐ Tumbler, 5"	20.00	22.00	21.00
☐ Vase, 8"	18.00	19.00	18.50

DOGWOOD (Pink — MacBeth Evans Glass Co.)

☐ Bowl, 5½"	14.00	15.00	14.50
☐ Bowl, 8½"	33.00	35.00	34.00
☐ Creamer	11.00	14.00	12.50
☐ Cup and Saucer	13.00	15.00	14.00
☐ Plate, 8"	4.00	5.00	4.50
☐ Plate, 9¼"	18.00	19.00	18.50
☐ Plate, 10½"	13.00	14.00	13.50
☐ Sherbet	17.00	19.00	18.00
☐ Sugar	9.00	12.00	10.50

	Current Price Range		Prior Year Average
☐ Tumbler, 4″	22.00	23.00	22.50
☐ Tumbler, 5″	35.00	37.00	36.00

ENGLISH HOBNAIL (Pink, Green — Westmoreland Glass Co.)

☐ Bowl, 6″	10.00	12.00	11.00
☐ Bowl, 8″	16.00	18.00	17.00
☐ Bowl, footed and handled, 8″	38.00	40.00	39.00
☐ Bowl, square, 5″	10.00	11.00	10.50
☐ Candlesticks, pair, 3½″	30.00	32.00	31.00
☐ Candy Dish, covered, three feet	55.00	60.00	57.50
☐ Celery Dish	16.00	18.00	17.00
☐ Creamer	15.00	16.00	15.50
☐ Cup and Saucer	15.00	16.00	15.50
☐ Goblet, 2 oz.	13.00	15.00	14.00
☐ Goblet, 8 oz.	17.00	19.00	18.00
☐ Pitcher, 23 oz.	115.00	120.00	117.50
☐ Plate, 6½″	3.00	5.00	4.00
☐ Plate, 8″	7.00	9.00	8.00
☐ Relish, oval, 12″	17.00	19.00	18.00
☐ Salt and Pepper	65.00	70.00	67.50
☐ Sherbet	12.00	14.00	13.00
☐ Sugar	15.00	16.00	15.50
☐ Tumbler, 3¾″	13.00	14.00	13.50
☐ Tumbler, 5″	18.00	19.00	18.50

LACE EDGE (Pink — Hocking Glass Co.)

☐ Bowl, 6⅜″	13.00	14.00	13.50
☐ Bowl, 9½″	13.00	14.00	13.00
☐ Bowl, three feet, 10½″	125.00	130.00	127.50
☐ Butter, covered	45.00	49.00	47.00
☐ Candlesticks, pair	115.00	120.00	117.50
☐ Candy Dish, covered	33.00	35.00	34.00
☐ Compote, 7″	15.00	17.00	16.00
☐ Cookie Jar	40.00	42.00	41.00
☐ Creamer	15.00	17.00	16.00
☐ Cup and Saucer	14.00	15.00	14.50
☐ Plate, 7¼″	13.00	14.00	13.50
☐ Plate, 10½″	18.00	19.00	18.50
☐ Platter, 12¾″	17.00	19.00	18.00
☐ Relish, divided	38.00	40.00	39.00
☐ Sherbet	48.00	50.00	49.00
☐ Sugar	15.00	17.00	16.00
☐ Tumbler, 5″	40.00	42.00	41.00

MAYFAIR — OPEN ROSE (Pink — Hocking Glass Co.)

	Current Price Range		Prior Year Average
☐ Bowl, 5½″	15.00	17.00	16.00
☐ Bowl, 7″	15.00	17.00	16.00
☐ Bowl, covered, 10″	60.00	64.00	62.00
☐ Bowl, oval, 9½″	16.00	18.00	17.00
☐ Bowl, 12″	38.00	39.00	38.50
☐ Butter, covered	45.00	47.00	46.00
☐ Candy Dish, covered	36.00	38.00	37.00
☐ Celery Dish, 10″	18.00	20.00	19.00
☐ Cookie Jar	30.00	32.00	31.00
☐ Creamer	15.00	17.00	16.00
☐ Cup and Saucer	31.00	33.00	32.00
☐ Decanter	90.00	100.00	95.00
☐ Goblet, 4″	52.00	54.00	53.00
☐ Goblet, 5¾″	40.00	44.00	42.00
☐ Goblet, 7¼″	128.00	130.00	129.00
☐ Pitcher, 8″	35.00	37.00	36.00
☐ Plate, 8½″	16.00	18.00	17.00
☐ Plate, 9½″	40.00	44.00	42.00
☐ Plate, cake, 12″	18.00	20.00	19.00
☐ Platter, oval, 12″	15.00	17.00	16.00
☐ Relish, 8⅜″	18.00	20.00	19.00
☐ Salt and Pepper	40.00	44.00	42.00
☐ Sherbet, 3″	13.00	14.00	13.50
☐ Sherbet, 4¾″	55.00	59.00	57.00
☐ Sugar	15.00	17.00	16.00
☐ Tumbler, 3½″	28.00	32.00	30.00
☐ Tumbler, 4¾″	88.00	90.00	89.00
☐ Tumbler, 5¼″	30.00	32.00	31.00
☐ Tumbler, 6½″	29.00	31.00	30.00

MISS AMERICA (Crystal, Pink — Hocking Glass Co.)

☐ Bowl, 6¼″	6.00	15.00	10.50
☐ Bowl, 8″	30.00	47.00	38.50
☐ Bowl, oval, 10″	11.00	18.00	14.50
☐ Butter, covered	188.00	380.00	284.00
☐ Candy Dish, covered	50.00	100.00	75.00
☐ Celery Dish, oval, 10½″	8.00	16.00	12.00
☐ Compote, 5″	10.00	16.00	13.00
☐ Creamer	7.00	15.00	11.00
☐ Cup and Saucer	10.00	20.00	15.00
☐ Goblet, 3¾″	15.00	50.00	32.50
☐ Goblet, 5½″	18.00	38.00	28.00
☐ Pitcher, 8″	50.00	90.00	70.00
☐ Plate, 8½″	5.00	15.00	10.00

	Current Price Range		Prior Year Average
☐ Plate, 10¼"	10.00	20.00	15.00
☐ Platter, oval, 12"	10.00	16.00	13.00
☐ Relish, 8¾"	8.00	14.00	11.00
☐ Salt and Pepper	25.00	45.00	35.00
☐ Sherbet	7.00	14.00	11.00
☐ Sugar	6.00	14.00	10.00
☐ Tumbler, 4"	14.00	38.00	26.00
☐ Tumbler, 6¾"	22.00	48.00	35.00

PRINCESS (Pink, Green — Hocking Glass Co.)

	Current Price Range		Prior Year Average
☐ Bowl, 4½"	10.00	18.00	14.00
☐ Bowl, 9"	17.00	24.00	20.50
☐ Bowl, oval, 10"	15.00	18.00	16.50
☐ Butter, covered	65.00	70.00	67.50
☐ Candy Dish, covered	35.00	40.00	37.50
☐ Cookie Jar	35.00	42.00	38.50
☐ Creamer	9.00	11.00	10.00
☐ Cup and Saucer	11.00	15.00	13.00
☐ Pitcher, 6"	25.00	38.00	31.50
☐ Pitcher, 8"	35.00	40.00	37.50
☐ Plate, 8"	7.00	9.00	8.00
☐ Plate, 11½"	6.00	8.00	7.00
☐ Platter, 12"	11.00	14.00	12.50
☐ Relish, divided, 7½"	13.00	18.00	15.50
☐ Salt and Pepper	30.00	40.00	35.00
☐ Sherbet	12.00	15.00	13.50
☐ Sugar	7.00	9.00	8.00
☐ Tumbler, 3"	15.00	21.00	18.00
☐ Tumbler, 4"	13.00	20.00	16.50
☐ Tumbler, 6½"	30.00	50.00	40.00
☐ Vase, 8"	18.00	23.00	20.50

DISNEYANA

DESCRIPTION: Disneyana refers to all items made by or for Walt Disney Productions such as Mickey Mouse, Donald Duck, Snow White and a host of other cartoon characters.

TYPE: Disney characters have been reproduced on every item from animated cels to dishes.

COMMENTS: Some hobbyists collect Disneyana by character or item, while others collect anything which features a Disney character. Older Mickey Mouse items are especially valuable, since this was the first character produced by the company.

ADDITIONAL TIPS: For more information, consult *The Official Price Guide to Collectible Toys,* published by The House of Collectibles.

	Current Price Range		Prior Year Average
☐ **Aristocats, The,** Schmid, Walt Disney Prod., set of five figural music boxes, all play different tunes, height 6″	100.00	125.00	112.00
☐ **Baloo,** Walt Disney Prod., c. 1965, ceramic figurine of the "Jungle Book" bear, height 5½″	16.00	20.00	15.00
☐ **Bambi,** Anri, c. 1971, wooden music box, figures of Bambi and Thumper revolve on this Italian Disney item	80.00	105.00	90.00
☐ **Bambi And Thumper,** Schmid, pair of two pewter figurines, recent	25.00	35.00	30.00
☐ **Cinderella,** c. 1950, drinking glass, #8, red, yellow, and blue, shows her being fitted for shoe, height 4⅝″	4.50	7.50	6.50
☐ **Donald Duck,** c. 1935, bisque "Long-Bill" with hands on hips, Japan, height 4½″	200.00	250.00	230.00
☐ **Donald Duck,** Morris Plastics, c. 1955, "The Bubble Duck," mouth clacks, blows bubbles, in original box	11.00	17.00	15.00
☐ **Donald Duck,** California Originals, c. 1970, ceramic cannister cookie jar, Donald's Cookie Express, height 10″	13.00	17.00	15.00
☐ **Donald Duck,** c. 1940, ceramic figural cowboy bank, height 6½″	42.00	47.00	45.00
☐ **Donald Duck,** c. 1940, ceramic figural milk pitcher, height 6½″	24.00	30.00	28.00
☐ **Dumbo,** California Originals, ceramic figural cookie jar, says "Dumbo's Greatest Cookies On Earth," height 12″	20.00	38.00	22.50
☐ **Dumbo,** ceramic figural toothbrush holder, height 4″, c. 1940	22.00	30.00	27.50
☐ **Dumbo,** ceramic planter, height 3¾″, c. 1940	16.00	20.00	18.00
☐ **Dumbo,** Cameo Doll Co., composition figure, swiveling trunk and "Googlie Eyes," height 9″, c. 1941	100.00	150.00	125.00
☐ **Dumbo,** Gare Mold Co., glazed figurine, height 9″	30.00	35.00	32.50
☐ **Dumbo,** Schmid, pewter figurine	23.00	27.00	25.00

	Current Price Range		Prior Year Average
☐ **Dumbo,** American Pottery, c. 1940, seated version of "Baby" Dumbo with Bonnet, #41 on bottom, height 5½ "	50.00	60.00	55.00
☐ **Dumbo And Timothy,** Gare Mold Co., pair of figurines, height 9"	30.00	37.00	35.00
☐ **Jiminy Cricket,** Gund, vinyl and cloth hand puppet, in original box, c. 1960	7.00	12.00	9.50
☐ **Jiminy Cricket,** oval "cameonyx" jewelry box, showing him in poses raised on cover, white on blue, height 6", c. 1980	36.00	43.00	39.00
☐ **Lady And Tramp,** double bisque figurine, having spaghetti dinner over candlelight, height 7", c. 1970	25.00	30.00	28.50
☐ **Lady And The Tramp,** Grolier bisque Christmas figurine in original box, c. 1980	38.00	42.00	40.00
☐ **Mickey Mouse,** Schmid, 50th birthday globe ornament, in box	12.00	17.00	15.00
☐ **Mickey Mouse and Donald Duck,** J. Chein And Co., tin sand pail, also shows Daisy and nephews at the zoo, height 4½ ", c. 1940 . . .	24.00	32.00	27.50
☐ **Mickey Mouse, Donald Duck And Goofy,** Masterwork, Bicentennial belt buckle, item laminated with colorful scene of the three of them marching and carrying flag as "Minutemen," c. 1976	6.00	10.00	9.00
☐ **Mickey Mouse, Donald Duck And Goofy,** Schmid, ceramic Christmas ornament, height 3½ "	13.00	17.00	15.00
☐ **Mickey Mouse, Donald Duck And Goofy,** "Triple Bisque" Bicentennial figurine, depicting the three of them dressed as "Minutemen," marching and playing instruments, c. 1976 . .	300.00	420.00	385.00
☐ **Mickey Mouse, Donald Duck And Goofy,** Mattel, "Skediddlers" toys, set of three in original boxes, c. 1960	40.00	48.00	45.00
☐ **Mickey Mouse, Donald Duck And Pluto,** "Patriot China" cup, shows them in a tug of war scene, c. 1930	6.00	8.00	7.00
☐ **Mickey Mouse And Goofy,** Schmid, Christmas ceramic figural "Happy Holidays" music box, Mickey and Goofy are holding wreaths around their necks, plays "Rudolph The Red Nosed Reindeer," height 7", c. 1981	30.00	38.00	35.00

	Current Price Range		Prior Year Average

☐ **Mickey Mouse And Minnie Mouse,** Royal Orleans, bisque figurine with stocking caps, she's holding Christmas sock with Christmas package in it, he's holding a big Christmas package, c. 1980 . . . . 20.00   24.00   22.00

☐ **Mickey Mouse And Minnie Mouse,** bisque toothbrush holder, they're standing arm-in-arm, height 4½", c. 1930 . . . . 85.00   95.00   90.00

☐ **Mickey Mouse And Minnie Mouse,** Schmid, "Caroling" pewter figurines, they're holding book marked "Noel" 25.00   31.00   27.50

☐ **Mickey Mouse And Minnie Mouse,** Dan Brechner, ceramic salt and pepper shakers, seated on a wooden park bench, height 4½", c. 1950 . . . . 30.00   40.00   35.00

☐ **Mickey Mouse And Minnie Mouse,** drinking glass, full figures in black on pink, height 5⅞", c. 1950 . . . . 8.00   10.00   8.50

☐ **Mickey Mouse And Minnie Mouse,** "Nifty Nineties" double bisque figurine, Mickey's sporting striped coat, straw hat, bow-tie and cane, Minnie in polka dot dress with bow in hair 27.00   32.00   30.00

☐ **Pluto,** Walt Disney Productions, composition figural bank, sitting down with tongue hanging out, height 6½" 8.00   12.00   10.00

☐ **Pluto And Goofy,** Radnor, c. 1970, set of two bone china thimbles, in box 13.00   16.00   15.00

☐ **Pluto And Mickey Mouse,** Patriot China, c. 1930, ceramic cup, seated Pluto 45.00   50.00   45.00

☐ **Professor Ludwig Von Drake,** Dell, c. 1960, figural vinyl squeeze toy, height 7½" 18.00   22.00   20.00

☐ **Professor Ludwig Von Drake,** Gund, c. 1961, plush and vinyl doll, height 15" 40.00   42.00   45.00

☐ **Snow White And Seven Dwarfs,** c. 1938, souvenir song album, from movie 30.00   42.00   37.50

☐ **Snow White And Seven Dwarfs,** c. 1939, Disney All Star Parade drinking glass, dark blue and light blue, height 4⅞" 20.00   26.00   22.50

☐ **Song Of The South,** triple bisque figurine, featuring Brer Rabbit, Brer Fox and Brer Bear, height 6½" 28.00   36.00   32.00

☐ **Stromboli,** c. 1940, drinking glass, full figure in green, with poem on back, height 4⅞" . . . 10.00   14.00   12.50

☐ **Three Pigs, The,** Walt Disney Enterprises, tin sand pail, "Ohio Art," playing at beach with Big Bad Wolf lurking behind post, height 3" . 40.00   45.00   42.50

DOLLHOUSES

PERIOD: Dollhouses have been manufactured by toy companies since the Industrial Revolution. The most elaborate American dollhouses date from the Victorian period which is considered to be the "golden age" of toys.

COMMENTS: Many of the loveliest examples are handmade. Traditionally fathers and grandfathers have made dollhouses for their little girls, often a miniature version of their actual house.

ADDITIONAL TIPS: Because of the tremendous popularity of all types of miniature collectibles the demand for vintage dollhouses is at its greatest peak ever.

	Current Price Range		Prior Year Average
☐ **Dollhouse,** Bliss, 13″	155.00	175.00	165.00
☐ **Dollhouse,** fireplaces in all rooms, simulated carved shingles, stucco exterior, late 1920's .	730.00	830.00	780.00
☐ **Dollhouse,** lithographed, c. 1930	80.00	100.00	90.00
☐ **Dollhouse,** lithographed, wood, 2 wooden figures, 13″ L.	275.00	325.00	300.00
☐ **Dollhouse,** wood, faced with paper, painted, brick styled chimney, 17½″ L.	90.00	110.00	100.00
☐ **Dutch Colonial,** wood, accessories, c. 1925 . .	475.00	575.00	520.00
☐ **English,** four rooms with staircase, two fireplaces, original, late 1800	850.00	950.00	900.00
☐ **French Chateau Style,** windows on three sides, working door, c. 1890	650.00	750.00	700.00
☐ **German,** curtained windows, attic, steps leading to front door, c. 1890	1475.00	1575.00	1525.00
☐ **German Castle,** ½″ to 1′ scale, molded after a late Gothic castle, c. 1875	2200.00	3200.00	2250.00
☐ **German,** small, embossed paper railing on second floor, unfurnished, c. 1900	310.00	360.00	335.00
☐ **Nineteenth Century Style,** roof shingled, clapboard sides, four rooms with hallways and staircase, two fireplaces, Victorian furnishings	3000.00	4000.00	3500.00
☐ **Swiss Chalet Style,** oak base on wheels, stenciled design on exterior, five rooms, Victorian furnishings, fourteen figures	2600.00	3600.00	3100.00
☐ **Tootsietoy**	35.00	45.00	40.00
☐ **Tudor Style,** Schoenhut	300.00	340.00	320.00
☐ **Twentieth Century Style,** four rooms with hallways and staircase, conventional furnishings	270.00	370.00	325.00
☐ **Walt Disney,** six-room, metal	60.00	90.00	75.00

DOLLHOUSE FURNITURE

	Current Price Range		Prior Year Average
☐ **Bathtub,** tin, paint worn, 2½", late 19th c. . . .	25.00	35.00	30.00
☐ **Bedroom Suite,** four pieces: chairs, bureau . .	40.00	50.00	45.00
☐ **Bedroom Suite,** three pieces, painted, c. 1920	50.00	80.00	65.00
☐ **Bowfront Chest,** Tynietoy, scale	55.00	65.00	60.00
☐ **Broom Holder,** tin, with brooms and dust pan	50.00	60.00	55.00
☐ **Dining Table,** golden oak, scale 1" to 1'	70.00	90.00	80.00
☐ **Drum Table,** rosewood, top tilts, edge lines in velvet, 3" Dia.	45.00	50.00	47.50
☐ **Fireplace,** open hearth, pine mantel	25.00	35.00	30.00
☐ **Hepplewhite Sofa,** Tynietoy, scale	70.00	90.00	80.00
☐ **Ice Cream Parlor Set,** 2 chairs with wire mesh seats, table 3½"	50.00	55.00	52.50
☐ **Rope Bed,** ticking mattress and pillow, 15½" x 10½"	30.00	40.00	35.00
☐ **Rug,** needlepoint, 3½" Dia.	12.00	16.00	14.00
☐ **Shaving Mirror,** mahogany frame and stand, mirror beveled glass, 4"	35.00	45.00	40.00
☐ **Stove,** cast iron	70.00	90.00	80.00
☐ **Stove,** tin kitchen, with utensils 11" H.	115.00	125.00	120.00
☐ **Teakettle,** brass with trivet	55.00	75.00	65.00
☐ **Victrola,** four-legs, painted wood, 4½"	55.00	75.00	65.00

FINE MINIATURE FURNITURE

	Current Price Range		Prior Year Average
☐ **Chest Of Drawers,** George III, mahogany, late 18th c., 14" H.	365.00	465.00	420.00
☐ **Chest Of Drawers,** George III style, mahogany, 10" H.	110.00	120.00	115.00
☐ **Tea Caddy,** George III, 4½" H., 18th c.	110.00	150.00	130.00
☐ **Victorian Dining Room Set,** walnut table and sideboard with marble tops, upholstered chairs	240.00	290.00	265.00
☐ **Wing Chair,** Federal, upholstered in brocade, 8¼" H.	265.00	285.00	275.00

DOLLS

This section features only a sampling of collectible doll prices. In order to accurately present the vast amount of information required by serious doll collectors, a special edition devoted to dolls is published by The House of Collectibles, Inc. This handy, pocket-size guide, *The Official 1985 Price Guide to Dolls,* features more than 5,000 prices for all types of dolls and manufacturers. It is available at bookstores for $3.95. For more in-depth doll information, refer to *The Official 1985 Price Guide to Antique and Modern Dolls* for $9.95.

COMMENTS: Doll collecting has grown phenomenally in the last 25 years to become one of the top hobbies in the United States. Individual appeal seems to be the magic ingredient in the world of doll collecting. Some dolls made of common materials show exquisite workmanship and detailing, while others made of fine porcelain bisque are crudely fashioned.

ADDITIONAL TIPS: The prices of dolls cover such a wide range that any collector can find specimens to fit his budget. While the French and German fashion dolls are out of the financial reach of many collectors, most of the more recent composition dolls are relatively plentiful and inexpensive. Interesting and varied collections may be assembled by specializing in dolls of a certain era, a certain construction material, those dressed in similar nationalistic costumes, or all the various dolls made by a single manufacturer. Prices given are for dolls in excellent to mint original condition. Deductions must be made for any missing parts, worn-out or faded clothes, and broken or cracked heads.

RECOMMENDED READING: For more extensive information, see *The Official Price Guide to Dolls,* published by The House of Collectibles.

ALEXANDER

	Current Price Range		Prior Year Average
☐ **Alexanderkin,** hard plastic, wears bathing suit, sandals, robe, square sunglasses, carries beach bag, 8″	75.00	95.00	85.00
☐ **Amy,** plastic sleep eyes, blonde looped curls, 14″	100.00	115.00	107.50
☐ **Cissy,** hard plastic, jointed at knees and elbows, long flowing yellow cape-style coat, sleep eyes, high heel open dress shoes, 21″ .	95.00	120.00	107.50
☐ **Laurie,** vinyl head, sleep eyes, sad, long eyelashes, black hair, wears double-breasted jacket, plaid trousers, 12″	20.00	25.00	22.50
☐ **Scarlett O'Hara,** vinyl, sleep eyes, long black glossy hair, satin gown with trimming, satin bonnet, wears cameo on a chain at the neck, marked Alexander 1961, 21″	115.00	145.00	130.00
☐ **Sleeping Beauty,** Disney special edition, 1959, 9″	225.00	475.00	325.00
☐ **M.I.B.**	475.00	525.00	500.00
☐ **Wendy,** hard plastic, sleep eyes, dressed as tennis player with racquet, skirt, opentoe shoes, 8″	100.00	120.00	110.00
☐ **Wendy Ann,** hard plastic, sleep eyes, puffy cheeks, blond hair, wears jacket and skirt of matching style, two buttons on jacket, 8″ . . .	80.00	100.00	90.00

	Current Price Range		Prior Year Average

ARRANBEE

- ☐ **Army Boy,** composition head and limbs, body stuffed with excelsior, molded hair, painted eyes, wears U.S. soldier's uniform of post-World War I era, featuring reproductions (in reduced size) of Lincoln cents for jacket buttons, 15″ 100.00 110.00 105.00
- ☐ **Baby Marie,** vinyl head, vinyl arms and legs, plastic body, sleep eyes, molded hair, partially open mouth, shaped for insertion of nursing bottle, wears diaper, quilt jacket, 8¼″ 7.00 9.00 8.00
- ☐ **Scarlet,** composition head, composition arms, legs and body, sleep eyes (green), long eyelashes, closed mouth, wears long ball gown of U.S. Civil War era and large bonnet, gown is trimmed with silk ribbons, marked R & B, 15″ 65.00 75.00 70.00
- ☐ **Sonja Heinie,** composition head and body, brunette wig attached by adhesive, sleep eyes (brown), marked R & B, made in 1945, 21¼″ 55.00 65.00 60.00
- ☐ **Taffy,** plastic, sleep eyes (green), marked R & B, made in 1954, 16½″ 60.00 70.00 65.00

FISHER PRICE

- ☐ **Audrey,** vinyl head, cloth body, rooted hair, painted eyes, blouse with small heart pattern, marked 168240, 1973, Fisher Price Toys, 14″ . 15.00 18.00 16.50
- ☐ **Baby Ann,** vinyl head, cloth body, rooted blond hair, painted eyes, floral print dress with large sash ribbon, marked 60, 188460, 1973, Fisher Price Toys, 13½″ 12.00 16.00 14.00
- ☐ **Elizabeth,** black, vinyl head, cloth body, rooted hair, closed mouth in semi-smile, painted eyes, marked 18, 168630, 1973, Fisher Price Toys, 13½″ 12.00 16.00 14.00
- ☐ **Mary,** vinyl head, cloth body, rooted hair, upturned eyes (painted), angelic facial expression, wears print dress and white apron, marked 168420, 1973, Fisher Price Toys, 14″ 12.00 16.00 14.00
- ☐ **Natalie,** vinyl head, cloth body, rooted hair, upturned eyes (painted), grinning smile, marked 168320, 1973, Fisher Price Toys, 13½″ 12.00 16.00 14.00

HASBRO

	Current Price Range		Prior Year Average

☐ **Baby Ruth,** vinyl head, stuffed body, vinyl hands, molded and painted features, blonde hair, rooted, sold originally with a tag reading Baby Ruth 1971, used as a premium by the Curtis Candy Co., 10″ **6.00 8.00 7.00**

☐ **Flying Nun,** vinyl, brunette hair, rooted, molded and painted features, marked 1967 Hasbro, Hong Kong, 5″ **12.00 14.00 13.00**

☐ **G.I. Joe,** Action Marine, plastic, molded hair, brown, brown eyes, painted, marked 7700, G.I. Joe TM Copyright by Hasbro Patent Pending, made in U.S.A., made in 1964, 11½″ **40.00 45.00 42.50**

☐ **G.I. Joe,** Action Marine, plastic, molded hair, brown, brown eyes, painted, marked 7500, G.I. Joe, Copyright 1964 by Hasbro, Pat. No. 3,277,602, made in U.S.A., no problem distinguishing this 1967 version from the previous: the patent is no longer pending, a patent number is shown, 11½″ **25.00 30.00 27.50**

IDEAL

☐ **Baby, Baby,** vinyl, rooted hair (blonde), fixed eyes (blue), nursing mouth, marked 115 Ideal, made in Hong Kong in 1974, 7″ **8.00 10.00 9.00**

☐ **Baby Belly Button,** black, vinyl, black hair (rooted), painted features, brown eyes, smiling closed mouth, in the likeness of an infant, Baby Belly Button has a knob at its stomach which, when turned, makes the arms, legs and head move, dressed in a diaper and white lace-edged smock, marked Ideal Toy Corp., E9-2-H-165, made in Hong Kong in 1970, 9″ . . **6.00 8.00 7.00**

☐ **Baby Big Eyes,** vinyl, blonde hair (rooted), sleep eyes (blue), closed mouth, marked Ideal Doll, made in 1954, 21″ **50.00 60.00 55.00**

☐ **Shirley Temple,** vinyl head, vinyl arms, legs and body, blonde wig, open mouth, dressed as Heidi from a motion picture role (but the doll is of considerably later date than the movie), marked Ideal Doll, ST17, 17″ **30.00 35.00 32.50**

☐ **Shirley Temple,** vinyl head, vinyl arms, legs and body, open mouth (big smile), white stockings, patent leather shoes, marked Ideal Doll, ST-35-38-2, 35″ **120.00 140.00 130.00**

	Current Price Range		Prior Year Average
☐ **Snow White,** composition head, arms and legs, cloth body, molded and painted hair, molded and painted features, open mouth, eyes turned to side, marked Ideal, made c. 1939, 17½″	75.00	95.00	85.00
☐ **Tressy,** plastic/vinyl, black hair (rooted), sleep eyes (blue), pug nose, closed mouth, hair has "grow" feature (portion of wig is fitted inside head; when hair is pulled gently, it gives the appearance of "growing" out of the scalp), marked 1969, Ideal Toy Corp., GH-18, also marked (on hip) with Patent No. 3162976, made in Hong Kong	9.00	11.00	10.00

MATTEL

BARBIE AND BARBIE-RELATED

☐ **Barbie,** plastic, molded and painted features, bubble hairdo, wears red swimsuit (one piece), marked 850, made in 1962, 11½″	330.00	430.00	380.00
☐ **Barbie's Friend Christie,** black, plastic, molded and painted features, talker, brown hair (parted), wears knitted green shirt and red shorts, marked 1126, sold in 1968, 11½″	130.00	140.00	135.00
☐ **Bendable Ken,** plastic, molded and painted features, bendable legs, wears blue jacket and red trunks, marked 1020, sold in 1965, 12″	15.00	19.00	17.00
☐ **Busy Barbie,** plastic, molded and painted features, wears checked skirt and denim sunsuit, marked 3311, sold in 1972, 11½″	9.00	11.00	10.00
☐ **Chef Boy-Ar-Dee Barbie,** plastic, molded and painted features, painted lashes, wears green and red suit (one piece), marked 1190, sold in 1971, 11½″	9.00	12.00	10.50

PAPER DOLLS

☐ **Annie Oakley**	10.00	12.00	11.00
☐ **Beatles,** Yellow Submarine	13.00	16.00	14.50
☐ **Betty Grable**	25.00	30.00	27.50
☐ **Betsy McCall**	2.00	3.00	2.50
☐ **Betty Field**	17.00	23.00	20.00
☐ **Bremner's Biscuits,** 6 dolls, c. 1895	45.00	55.00	50.00
☐ **Captain Marvel**	15.00	19.00	17.00
☐ **Cleverest Fit Together Cutouts,** 9 dolls, c. 1923	60.00	80.00	70.00
☐ **Dolly Dimple**	6.00	9.00	7.50
☐ **Donna Reed**	18.00	22.00	20.00

	Current Price Range		Prior Year Average
☐ Elizabeth Taylor	20.00	24.00	22.00
☐ Esther Williams	15.00	18.00	16.50
☐ Flying Captain Marvel	5.00	7.00	6.00
☐ F. W. Rueckheim Brothers, 4 dolls, c. 1895	20.00	25.00	22.50
☐ J. and P. Coats, 7 dolls, c. 1895	45.00	55.00	50.00
☐ Jane Russell	10.00	14.00	12.00
☐ Jolly Hane	10.00	14.00	12.00
☐ Katzenjammer Kids	9.00	12.00	10.50
☐ Linda Darnell	18.00	22.00	20.00
☐ Little Miss Sunbeam	22.00	26.00	24.00
☐ Mary Poppins	6.00	8.00	7.00
☐ Our Gang	55.00	65.00	60.00
☐ Palmer Cox, Brownies, Irishman, Scotsman, etc., c. 1888	45.00	55.00	50.00
☐ Princess Elizabeth	30.00	34.00	32.00
☐ Rabbit Family	8.00	12.00	10.00

DOORSTOPS

DESCRIPTION: Doorstops are small, heavy figures, usually made of iron, that are used to hold open doors.

ORIGIN: While things such as stones have always been used to prop open doors, the use of decorative figures for such a purpose dates to late 18th century England.

MATERIALS: Doorstops are usually made of cast iron that has been painted or bronzed. Some are made of other metals, and those made of brass tend to be the most valuable.

COMMENTS: Doorstops made prior to 1920 are the most collectible. Age, rarity and condition affect the price.

ADDITIONAL TIPS: The listings are alphabetical according to the figure. Measurements and descriptions follow as available. Unless otherwise noted, the doorstops are made of cast iron.

☐ Airedale	35.00	45.00	37.00
☐ American Eagle	50.00	65.00	53.00
☐ Aunt Jemima	65.00	75.00	67.00
☐ Basket of Flowers, height 6¼"	17.00	26.00	19.00
☐ Basket of Red Poppies, height 8", Hubley	25.00	35.00	28.00
☐ Basket of Fruit, height 10", aluminum	20.00	28.00	22.50
☐ Black Bear	40.00	50.00	43.00
☐ Boxer	30.00	42.00	33.00
☐ Bull	35.00	45.00	37.00

	Current Price Range		Prior Year Average
☐ **Bulldog**	37.50	47.00	40.00
☐ **Campbell Kid**, with teddy bear	170.00	210.00	185.00
☐ **Cat**, black	28.00	35.00	30.00
☐ **Cat**, black, green eyes	40.00	50.00	43.00
☐ **Cat**, height 7″, seated, black body with green eyes, red mouth and yellow whiskers	80.00	100.00	87.00
☐ **Cat**, white, blue eyes, bell at throat, Hubley	80.00	100.00	87.00
☐ **Cockatoo**, height 7½″, red, yellow and green paint, B. Noyes & Co.	55.00	75.00	62.00
☐ **Cockatoo**	28.00	34.00	29.00
☐ **Colonial Lady**, height 11½″, black dress, holding yellow hat	40.00	55.00	42.00
☐ **Conestoga Wagon**, height 10″	60.00	80.00	67.00
☐ **Court Jester**, with animal	50.00	60.00	53.00
☐ **Dog**, Boston Terrier, height 8½″, length 7″	40.00	58.00	45.00
☐ **Dog**, Boston Terrier, height 9½″, length 8″, facing left	65.00	80.00	70.00
☐ **Dog**, Cocker Spaniel	40.00	50.00	43.00
☐ **Dog**, German Shepherd	35.00	50.00	40.00
☐ **Dog**, Russian Wolf Hound, height 9½″, length 15½″	130.00	155.00	138.00
☐ **Dog**, Scotty, length 10¼″	70.00	85.00	75.00
☐ **Doll**, with toy	40.00	50.00	43.00
☐ **Drum Major**	115.00	140.00	125.00
☐ **Elephant**	30.00	40.00	32.00
☐ **Fiddler**, with violin	33.00	40.00	34.00
☐ **Flowers**, in basket, solid brass	60.00	75.00	63.00
☐ **Fox**, brass	70.00	80.00	72.00
☐ **Frog**, solid bronze	92.00	115.00	95.00
☐ **Fruit**, in bowl	28.00	35.00	30.00
☐ **General Robert E. Lee**, height 7¼″	70.00	95.00	75.00
☐ **Girl**, height 11¾″, standing, bonnet on head, holding skirt by hem, white and blue paint, B&H	100.00	120.00	105.00
☐ **Boy and Girl**, Dutch, Hubley	80.00	97.00	85.00
☐ **Golfer**, in knickers	140.00	165.00	150.00
☐ **Horses**	45.00	55.00	47.00
☐ **Indian**, riding horse	78.00	90.00	80.00
☐ **Jenny Lind**, height 4½″	60.00	75.00	65.00
☐ **Kitten**	38.00	45.00	40.00
☐ **Lamb**, black	48.00	55.00	50.00
☐ **Lighthouse**	68.00	80.00	70.00
☐ **Lion**	45.00	55.00	47.00
☐ **Little Red Riding Hood and The Wolf**, pair	68.00	80.00	70.00
☐ **Mail Coach**	50.00	60.00	52.00
☐ **Mammy**, height 9″	110.00	135.00	115.00
☐ **Monkey**	40.00	50.00	42.00

	Current Price Range		Prior Year Average
☐ **Parrot**	28.00	35.00	29.00
☐ **Peacock**	78.00	95.00	85.00
☐ **Penguin**, height 10½″, black and white paint	73.00	90.00	79.00
☐ **Peter Rabbit**, height 11¾″	58.00	73.00	65.00
☐ **Popeye**	50.00	60.00	53.00

EGGS

DESCRIPTION: Eggs are considered very beautiful art objects and are quite collectible.

VARIATIONS: Eggs are made for various purposes, from simple wooden darning eggs to jeweled egg boxes.

Minton Emperor's Garden,
of the egg series,
1982, **$95.00-$110.00**

COMMENTS: The most famous eggs, prized for their beauty and rarity, are the Russian eggs created by Peter Carl Faberge. Today the decorated Easter egg is the most sought after by collectors. Prices tend to be reasonable.

ADDITIONAL TIPS: The listings are alphabetical according to type of egg, followed by description, manufacturer, year and price range.

For further information on eggs, contact The Egg Art Guild, 1174 Glenwood Dale, Cape St. Claire, MD 21408.

	Current Price Range		Prior Year Average
☐ **Art Glass Egg,** iridescent, large, Vanderbelt .	35.00	45.00	37.00
☐ **Art Glass Egg,** pink, gold flowers	138.00	165.00	145.00
☐ **Box,** china, painted with flowers and birds, hinged lid, brass fittings, 9½ "	140.00	180.00	145.00
☐ **Easter Candy Container,** papier-mache, egg being drawn by rabbit, 4"	12.50	20.00	14.00
☐ **Easter Egg,** baby chick, Goebel, c. 1978	17.50	25.00	19.00
☐ **Easter Egg,** dove on cover, Wedgwood, c. 1977	60.00	75.00	63.00
☐ **Easter Egg,** glass, raised lettering	40.00	50.00	44.00
☐ **Easter Egg,** glass, undecorated, large, set of four	40.00	50.00	44.00
☐ **Easter Egg,** porcelain, Royal Bayreuth, c. 1979	25.00	35.00	28.00
☐ **Easter Egg,** porcelain, floral decoration, Furstenberg, c. 1974	20.00	30.00	23.00
☐ **Easter Egg,** silver and enamel, lilies and forget-me-nots, Faberge, by Ruckert, c. 1900	11750.00	14000.00	12000.00
☐ **Jewel case,** mother-of-pearl, gilded metal, egg "wheelbarrow"	68.00	85.00	72.00
☐ **Mary Gregory Glass Egg,** raised lettering and design	25.00	35.00	27.00
☐ **Milk Glass Egg,** raised lettering and design .	30.00	40.00	32.00
☐ **Minton Emperor's Garden,** Royal Doulton, edition size 3500, 1982	100.00	115.00	103.00
☐ **Minton 19th Century,** Royal Doulton, edition size 3500, 1979	80.00	100.00	85.00
☐ **Rouge Flambe,** Royal Doulton, edition size 3500, 1980	110.00	120.00	112.00
☐ **Vinaigrette,** ivory, screw lid with grill inside, English	175.00	250.00	185.00
☐ **Vinaigrette,** silver and enamel, figure of a woman, French	700.00	800.00	720.00
☐ **Vinaigrette,** silver and enamel, purple, gold, white, French	950.00	1300.00	1050.00
☐ **Wooden Egg,** pine, hen, painted	7.50	12.00	8.00

ELVIS PRESLEY MEMORABILIA

This section features only a sampling of Elvis Presley memorabilia. In order to accurately present the vast amount of information required by serious collectors, a special edition devoted to collectible records is published by The House of Collectibles, Inc. This handy, pocket-size guide, *The Official 1985 Price Guide to Collectible Records,* features an Elvis Presley section. It is available at bookstores for $3.95. For more detailed information and more than 30,000 prices, refer to *The Official 1985 Price Guide to Records* for $9.95.

DESCRIPTION: Elvis Presley, a rock and roll legend, exerted a tremendous influence on modern music. His phenomenal career began in 1956 and continued until his untimely death in 1977. Because of the millions of Elvis Presley fans throughout the world, any items relating to the "King of Rock and Roll" are valuable among collectors.

TYPES: There are all kinds of Elvis memorabilia from clothes, cars and contracts to autographed photos and school items. One of the largest collecting areas is his records.

COMMENTS: Some Elvis fans collect only his records while others collect all types of his memorabilia.

ADDITIONAL TIPS: For more information, consult *The Official Price Guide to Music Collectibles,* published by The House of Collectibles.

	Current Price Range		Prior Year Average
☐ **Elvis Presley Child's Guitar**, plastic.	23.00	36.00	29.00
☐ **Elvis Presley School Bag.**	30.00	47.00	39.00
☐ **8 x 10 Photo With Guitar**, signed and inscribed, 1957.	260.00	340.00	300.00
☐ **Printed Postcard Photo**, facsimile signature.	5.00	8.00	6.50
☐ **Lifesize Cardboard Figure of Elvis**, c. 1961, used for theater promotion, full color.	300.00	400.00	350.00
☐ **8 x 10 Color Photo**, signed.	350.00	500.00	425.00
☐ **Elvis Presley Drinking Mug**, ceramic, picture on side.	20.00	29.00	24.50
☐ **Handkerchief**, colored silk, illustrated.	17.00	25.00	21.00
☐ **Typewritten Note by Col. Tom Parker (his manager)**, signed.	7.00	10.00	8.50
☐ **8 x 10 Photo**, unsigned, black and white.	2.00	4.00	3.00
☐ **8 x 10 Motion Picture Still**, unsigned, black and white.	1.50	3.00	2.25

	Current Price Range		Prior Year Average
☐ 8 x 10 Motion Picture Still, unsigned, color. . .	5.00	8.00	6.50
☐ 8 x 10 Motion Picture Still, black and white, signed.	225.00	350.00	237.00
☐ 8 x 10 Motion Picture Still, color, signed.	275.00	400.00	337.00
☐ Typewritten Letter, signed, ½ page	130.00	200.00	165.00
☐ Typewritten Letter, signed, 1 page	160.00	230.00	200.00
☐ Typewritten Letter, signed, 2 pages	240.00	320.00	280.00
☐ Handwritten Letter, signed, ½ page	240.00	320.00	280.00
☐ Handwritten Letter, signed, 1 page	375.00	500.00	437.00
☐ Handwritten Letter, signed, 2 pages	500.00	750.00	625.00
☐ Handwritten Letter, signed, 3 pages	600.00	1000.00	800.00
☐ Note in His Handwriting, one line.	120.00	180.00	140.00
☐ Signature on an Otherwise Blank Sheet of Paper or Card.	60.00	85.00	72.00
☐ Typewritten Letter to him from record company executive.	33.00	46.00	39.00
☐ Typewritten Letter to him from motion picture executive.	35.00	49.00	42.00
☐ Typewritten Letter to him from TV producer. .	31.00	42.00	36.00
☐ Typewritten Letter to him from music agent. .	29.00	39.00	34.00
☐ Typewritten Letter to him from U.S. Armed Forces.	235.00	310.00	242.00
☐ Typewritten Letter to him from author seeking an interview.	9.00	14.00	11.50
☐ Typewritten Letter to him from Ed Sullivan. . .	140.00	200.00	170.00
☐ Draft Card, issued to him by Selective Service.	1750.00	3000.00	2375.00
☐ Magazine Cover with full color photo.	.50	1.00	.75
☐ News Cuttings (most).	.50	2.00	1.25

EMBROIDERY

DESCRIPTION: Embroidery is decorative needlework using diverse threads such as silk, gold, wool or cotton stitched into any type of fabric including cloth or leather.

PERIOD: The most valuable and rarest embroidery work is from the 1700s. Embroidery pieces from the 1800s and 1900s are more readily available.

VALUE: The condition, workmanship, materials, design and age of a piece are equally important in determing value.

Tea Cloth, *royal blue with white embroidery and crocheted trim, 1930s,* **$10.00-$15.00**

COMMENTS: Many hobbyists collect all types of embroidery while others collect by motif, stitch or country.

	Current Price Range		Prior Year Average
☐ **Embroidered Picture,** titled "Cornelia's Jewels," signed by Mary Beach of Saunders and Beach Academy, Dorchester, Massachusetts, embroidered and painted on silk, five figures in semi-classical style, inscription beneath, undated, c. 1830, 16½" x 16½"	1800.00	2175.00	1975.00
☐ **Embroidered Picture,** titled "Spring," anonymous, showing two women and a man in a field, one of the women seated, an overhanging tree nearby, place of origin not known, probably late 18th century or early 19th century, 16½" x 18"	625.00	750.00	670.00

	Current Price Range		Prior Year Average
☐ **Embroidered Picture on Silk,** titled "Timoclea," signed by Harriet Valentine, a classical scene from the legend of Timoclea with numerous figures clad in robes, the embroidery done in chenille and silk thread, undated, c. 1840, 26″ x 36″	850.00	1075.00	920.00
☐ **Embroidered Picture on Silk,** untitled, an American eagle with spread wings near the top, in the central portion a vignette of a World War I naval gunnery ship surrounded by flags, also cannon and anchor devices, probably made in the Orient for sale on the U.S. market at the time of World War I, c. 1918, 42″ x 25½″	450.00	575.00	500.00
☐ **Needlework Map of Maryland,** also showing portions of New Jersey and Pennsylvania, signed by Harriet Beall, done in a variety of stitches and colors, undated, probably very early 19th century, 13″ x 17½″	800.00	1000.00	875.00
☐ **Silk and Chenille Embroidered Floral Picture,** signed with initials "G.M.," worked in various colors of chenille thread against solid beige silk background, picturing a basket filled with an assortment of flowers, place of origin unknown, c. 1820, 22″ x 19″ .	375.00	450.00	410.00
☐ **Tent-Stitched Picture,** titled "Fishing Lady," shows lady at pond hooking fish while man stands by with hat in hand, various colors of wool thread woven into a canvas backing, Connecticut origin, mid 1700s, 16″ x 20″ ...	4475.00	5600.00	4800.00
☐ **Yarn-sewn Wall Picture,** untitled, signed by Christine Wuerpel, showing a male and female rider in a sleigh being drawn across a snow-covered field by a light and dark horse, undated, c. 1880, 22″ x 33″	325.00	425.00	365.00

FANS

ORIGIN: Folding fans were popular and fashionable accessories for women of means during the 18th, 19th and even into the early 20th centuries. Aside from the obvious function of being used to cool oneself, fans were used to show not only one's social position and wealth, but also for coquetry or flirting.

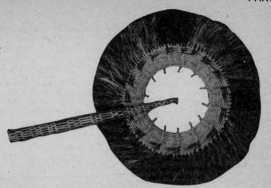

Fan, *woven straw with tortoiseshell, 1920s,* **$8.00-$10.00**

The Oriental version — like all Oriental artifacts — was a symbolic and functional device, essential to the proper code of daily living. Men as well as women utilized them, from the scented fans of the elderly, to the black and red implements of the military. A popular export item (particularly the delicate ivory fans, carved under water and much sought after as wedding gifts), fans served many functions in Oriental society. They were used for cooling of course, but also as an essential fashion accessory, for fanning flames, to direct military troops, as message carriers, in dances, stories, games and wrestling matches.

CONSTRUCTION: Folding fans were constructed in one of two ways. The more common method was the insertion of sticks into a pleated piece of material called a "leaf." Leaves were made of silk, lace, paper, or even vellum (very thin goatskin). The other type of folding fan was called a "brise." The brise fan was made up of wide, overlapping sticks and joined by a ribbon. Nearly all fans of both types have scenes or designs painted on them.

Another type, considered quite stylish from the 1870s until about 1910, was the feather fan. Usually made of ostrich feathers, this type was quite perishable and is now relatively rare.

Beautifully drawn, painted, or inscribed, Oriental fans fell into two main structural categories. Women's fans were usually non-folding, consisting of a roundish piece of paper glued to a flat bamboo handle. Folding fans, used more extensively in ritual ceremonies, or by high born citizens, were made of paper or silk, with wooden, bamboo, ivory, or mother-of-pearl ribs.

ADDITIONAL TIPS: Because fans are not durable collectibles, their numbers tend to be rather low and prices accordingly high. Once a beautiful fan is acquired, the methods of display and preservation are vital factors. Special attention should be paid to store the item in an airtight container that screens out damaging ultraviolet rays. Most specimens do well when placed in a protective frame.

RECOMMENDED READING: For more in-depth information on fans you may refer to *The Official Price Guide to Oriental Collectibles,* published by The House of Collectibles.

	Current Price Range		Prior Year Average
☐ **Advertising,** Hire's Root Beer, 6½ ″, c. 1930 ..	10.00	15.00	12.50
☐ **Advertising,** Homer's 5 Cigar, 7″, c. 1910	10.00	15.00	12.50
☐ **Advertising,** lithographed, late 19th c.	10.00	15.00	12.50
☐ **Black net,** with sequins	20.00	30.00	25.00
☐ **Bride's,** lace, hand painted	20.00	30.00	25.00
☐ **Bride's,** lace, sequins, ivory sticks	35.00	45.00	37.50
☐ **Brise,** child's, painted, ribbon and floral design	65.00	75.00	70.00
☐ **Brise,** gilded, painted with three vignettes, loop	130.00	160.00	145.00
☐ **Brise,** Regency, painted floral design, amber guards	120.00	130.00	125.00
☐ **Brise,** Regency, painted vase of flowers	40.00	60.00	50.00
☐ **Celluloid,** carved flower	40.00	60.00	50.00
☐ **Celluloid,** miniature	40.00	60.00	50.00
☐ **Celluloid,** Oriental design	20.00	30.00	25.00
☐ **Celluloid,** sequins, chiffon	45.00	50.00	47.50
☐ **Cockade,** silver and cut steel pique, middle quizzing glass	275.00	300.00	237.50
☐ **Feather,** celluloid sticks	45.00	55.00	50.00
☐ **Feather,** ivory sticks	100.00	140.00	120.00
☐ **Feather,** painted, c. 1870	100.00	110.00	105.00
☐ **Feather,** tortoiseshell sticks	100.00	110.00	105.00
☐ **Feather,** small, late 19th c.	120.00	130.00	125.00
☐ **Feather,** signed Duvelleroy, 19th c.	500.00	600.00	550.00
☐ **French,** painted, ivory sticks	175.00	185.00	170.00
☐ **French,** painted, tortoise sticks, sequins ...	175.00	185.00	170.00
☐ **French,** painted, signed Jolivet, 19th c.	500.00	700.00	600.00
☐ **French,** painted, carved, signed	75.00	85.00	80.00

	Current Price Range		Prior Year Average
☐ **George Washington and Cherry Smash,** lithographed	20.00	30.00	25.00
☐ **Gold edge,** pink silk, ebony ribs	30.00	35.00	32.50
☐ **Hand painted,** floral design, wood	20.00	30.00	25.00
☐ **Horn,** carved, painted pansies, blue ribbon .	100.00	130.00	115.00
☐ **Lacquered,** black, silver flower	75.00	85.00	80.00
☐ **Lacquered,** white, silver handle	55.00	65.00	60.00
☐ **Marabou feathers,** satin, hand painted, 20″.	125.00	145.00	135.00
☐ **Oriental,** straw, lacquered handle	15.00	20.00	17.50
☐ **Oriental,** silk, Geisha figure	10.00	15.00	12.50
☐ **Ostrich plume,** tortoise shell sticks	50.00	60.00	55.00
☐ **Pearl sticks,** sequin design, 8″	35.00	45.00	40.00
☐ **Puzzle,** four scenes, two-way opening	150.00	170.00	160.00
☐ **Satin flower center,** carved, ivory sticks	150.00	170.00	160.00
☐ **Silk,** embroidered, ivory sticks	75.00	85.00	80.00
☐ **Silk,** hand painted animal figure and books .	25.00	35.00	30.00
☐ **Silk,** hand painted figures and floral designs, original storage container	65.00	75.00	70.00
☐ **Silk,** Oriental design, ivory and bamboo	45.00	55.00	50.00
☐ **Souvenir Centennial,** historical buildings, 12″	100.00	110.00	105.00
☐ **Wedding,** ivory sticks, lace	65.00	75.00	70.00

FIESTA WARE

DESCRIPTION: Fiesta Ware is a line of brightly colored pottery tableware introduced in 1935 by the Homer Laughlin China Company of East Liverpool, Ohio.

DESIGN: The design is a series of rings which graduate in size, with the smallest ring at the center and the greatest width between rings also at the center. This design is mostly used on the rims and at the center of items such as plates, bowls, etc. It is also used on pieces with small pedestal bases and on lids.

COLOR: The colors used for these wares are Fiesta red, rose, dark green, medium green, light green, chartreuse, yellow, old ivory, gray, turquoise and dark blue. Red is the most valuable.

COMMENTS: Fiesta began to be actively collected in the 1960s and a big surge of popularity followed in the next decade. Prices on the secondhand market zoomed from an average of 25¢ to 35¢ to the $5 to $10 range. This seemed unbelievable, because everyone knew Fiesta ware was very common — it had been one of the most widely manufactured tablewares of the 20th century. Nevertheless, buyer demand was strong, and with this kind of demand anything can happen to retail prices.

MARKS: Each piece, except a very few, is marked with the Fiesta trademark, either in the mold or an ink handstamped mark.

RECOMMENDED READING: For more in-depth information on Fiesta Ware you may refer to *The Official Price Guide to Pottery and Porcelain* and *The Official Identification Guide to Pottery and Porcelain,* published by The House of Collectibles.

	Current Price Range		Prior Year Average
☐ **Ashtray,** red	18.50	26.50	22.00
☐ **Ashtray,** yellow, with three impressions, c. 1936	17.00	22.00	20.00
☐ **Bowl,** dessert, 4½", turquoise	7.50	9.50	8.50
☐ **Bowl,** dessert, 4½", gray	8.00	12.00	10.00
☐ **Bowl,** dessert, 6", blue, c. 1959	9.00	11.00	10.00
☐ **Bowl,** dessert, medium green, 1959	22.00	27.00	24.50
☐ **Bowl,** fruit, 5½", gray	8.00	12.00	10.00
☐ **Bowl,** fruit, 5½", light green	6.00	8.00	7.00
☐ **Bowl,** fruit, 5½", yellow	5.25	8.50	7.00
☐ **Bowl,** nested, 5", numbered "1" on the bottom	19.00	23.00	21.00
☐ **Bowl,** nested, 6", numbered "2" on the bottom	11.00	16.00	13.50
☐ **Bowl,** nested, 7", numbered "3" on the bottom	16.00	22.00	19.00
☐ **Bowl,** nested, 8", numbered "4" on the bottom	22.00	27.00	24.50
☐ **Bowl,** nested, 9", numbered "5" on the bottom	22.00	27.00	24.50
☐ **Bowl,** nested, 10", numbered "6" on the bottom	27.00	32.00	29.50
☐ **Bowl,** nested, 11", numbered "7" on the bottom	32.00	37.00	34.50
☐ **Bowl,** salad, 9½", yellow, with pronounced rim	27.00	32.00	29.50
☐ **Bowl,** salad, 10", footed, cobalt blue	65.00	75.00	70.00
☐ **Bowl,** salad, 10", footed, red	100.00	120.00	110.00
☐ **Bud Vase,** tubular shape, on small pedestal base	22.00	27.00	24.50
☐ **Candleholders,** blue, pair, spherical body on square base, c. 1936	62.00	72.00	67.00
☐ **Candleholders,** bulb shaped, red, pair	40.00	50.00	45.00
☐ **Candleholders,** yellow, pair, tripod	32.00	34.00	33.00
☐ **Carafe,** cobalt blue	28.00	32.00	30.00

	Current Price Range		Prior Year Average
☐ **Carafe,** three-pint, old ivory, cork seal top, c. 1941	29.00	34.00	31.50
☐ **Carafe,** turquoise	32.50	38.00	35.00
☐ **Casserole,** yellow, "French Baker"	60.00	70.00	65.00
☐ **Casserole,** French, yellow, with notched lid and plug handle	66.00	82.00	70.00
☐ **Coffeepot,** ivory, with lid	25.00	30.00	27.50
☐ **Coffeepot,** light green with lid	25.00	30.00	27.50
☐ **Coffeepot,** red, with notched lid and handle, c. 1936	52.00	62.00	57.00
☐ **Coffeepot,** yellow, with lid	40.00	80.00	60.00
☐ **Creamer,** ivory	4.50	6.50	5.50
☐ **Creamer,** light green with ring handle, on small pedestal base	6.00	8.00	7.00
☐ **Creamer,** red with plug handle, on small pedestal base	32.00	37.00	34.50
☐ **Creamer,** turquoise	52.00	67.00	61.50
☐ **Creamer,** yellow	5.00	7.00	6.00
☐ **Creamer,** yellow, experimental, with ring handle	22.00	27.00	24.50
☐ **Creamer,** yellow, with plug, on small pedestal base	9.00	12.00	10.50
☐ **Cup And Saucer,** light green	10.00	15.00	12.50
☐ **Cup And Saucer,** medium green	20.00	30.00	25.00
☐ **Cup And Saucer,** red	13.00	16.00	14.50
☐ **Cup and Saucer,** yellow	10.00	15.00	12.50
☐ **Gravy Boat,** forest green	20.00	30.00	25.00
☐ **Gravy Boat,** ivory	9.00	11.00	10.00
☐ **Mug,** turquoise	22.00	27.00	24.50
☐ **Mug,** yellow	22.00	27.00	24.50
☐ **Pitcher,** ice, two-quart, red, with handle, on small pedestal base	27.00	32.00	29.00
☐ **Pitcher,** juice, disk shape, 30 ounces, yellow, with handle	9.00	11.00	10.00
☐ **Pitcher,** juice, red	20.00	30.00	25.00
☐ **Pitcher,** juice, yellow	15.00	20.00	17.50
☐ **Pitcher,** water, yellow	20.00	30.00	25.00
☐ **Plate,** 6", ivory	3.00	5.00	4.00
☐ **Plate,** 6", red	4.00	6.00	5.00
☐ **Plate,** 6", rose	5.00	7.00	6.00
☐ **Plate,** 6", turquoise	3.00	5.00	4.00
☐ **Plate,** 6", yellow	4.00	6.00	5.00
☐ **Plate,** 7"	2.00	3.00	2.50
☐ **Plate,** 9"	2.00	3.00	2.50
☐ **Plate,** 9½", ivory	6.00	8.00	7.00
☐ **Plate,** 9½", gray	7.00	9.00	8.00

	Current Price Range		Prior Year Average
☐ Plate, 10½″, ivory	18.00	22.00	20.00
☐ Plate, 11″, light green	8.00	10.00	9.00
☐ Plate, 11″, red	10.00	15.00	12.50
☐ Plate, 13″, blue	15.00	20.00	17.50
☐ Plate, 13″, dark green	15.00	20.00	17.50
☐ Plate, 13″, ivory	9.00	15.00	12.00
☐ Plate, 13″, yellow	12.00	16.00	14.00
☐ Plate, chop, 6″, yellow	6.00	8.00	7.00
☐ Plate, dessert, 6″, yellow	6.00	8.00	7.00
☐ Plate, dinner, 10″, rose, c. 1936	5.00	9.00	7.00
☐ Platter, 12″, light green	9.00	12.00	10.50
☐ Platter, 12″, turquoise, oval, with extended rim, c. 1939	8.00	11.00	9.50
☐ Platter, 12″, yellow, oval	11.00	14.00	12.50
☐ Relish, three compartments, ivory	40.00	50.00	45.00
☐ Relish, three compartments, turquoise	45.00	55.00	50.00
☐ Salt And Pepper, green	9.00	12.00	10.50
☐ Sauceboat, green, with handle, on small pedestal base, c. 1939	11.00	14.00	12.50
☐ Soup Plate, scalloped rim, ivory	9.00	12.00	10.50
☐ Soup Plate, scalloped rim, yellow	9.00	12.00	10.50
☐ Soup Plate, scalloped rim, turquoise	9.00	12.00	10.50
☐ Soup Plate, scalloped rim, yellow	16.00	18.00	17.00
☐ Sugar Bowl, turquoise, with lid	10.00	14.00	12.50
☐ Sugar Bowl, yellow, with cover	9.00	12.00	10.50
☐ Sugar And Creamer, red, c. 1941	13.00	17.00	15.00
☐ Teapot, large, red, holds eight cups, with ring handle, c. 1936	27.00	32.00	29.50
☐ Teapot, red, with lid, small	50.00	60.00	55.00
☐ Teapot, yellow, with lid	35.00	45.00	40.00
☐ Tray, turquoise	52.00	62.00	57.00
☐ Tray, yellow	52.00	62.00	57.00
☐ Tray, relish, green base, red center, multi-color inserts	37.00	42.00	39.50
☐ Tray, relish, old ivory, c. 1939	37.00	42.00	39.50
☐ Tray, utility, green, oblong, with extended rim	11.00	14.00	12.50
☐ Tray, utility, yellow, c. 1941	8.00	11.00	9.50
☐ Tumbler, red, footed	15.00	17.00	16.00
☐ Tumbler, turquoise, footed	11.00	14.00	12.50
☐ Tumbler, cobalt blue, footed	18.00	22.00	20.00
☐ Tumbler, 5 ounces, cylindrical, ivory, turquoise, yellow	11.00	14.00	12.50

FISHING TACKLE

DESCRIPTION: Rods, reels, flies and lures comprise the majority of collectible fishing tackle. The manufacture of fishing tackle did not begin in the United States until around 1810. Prior to that time, all fishing supplies were imported from Europe.

MAKERS: Reels made by J. F. and B. F. Meeks, B. Milam and Pfleuger are favored, as are rods made by Hiram Leonard. Flies, fake bait made by tying feathers, fur or other materials around the shaft of a hook, are also popular. There are over 5,000 patterns and sizes of flies, each with its own name. The manufacturer, or tier, of individual flies is very difficult to discern, unless the fly is in its original marked container.

	Current Price Range		Prior Year Average
☐ **Casting rod,** Heddon, split bamboo, 6', c. 1920	85.00	100.00	115.00
☐ **Casting rod,** split bamboo, straight handle, 5', c. 1800	45.00	55.00	50.00
☐ **Casting rod,** Tonkin, cane, 5½', c. 1900	55.00	65.00	60.00
☐ **Casting rod,** Union Hardware, 5', c. 1920	20.00	30.00	25.00
☐ **Casting rod,** Winchester, split bamboo, c. 1925	20.00	30.00	25.00
☐ **Creel fishing basket,** splint weave, pine lid, c. 1900	85.00	125.00	105.00
☐ **Creel fishing basket,** wicker with leather straps, c. 1880	115.00	165.00	140.00
☐ **Fishhooks,** set of 50, c. 1910	20.00	24.00	22.00
☐ **Flies,** English, set of 12, c. 1880	420.00	440.00	430.00
☐ **Fly box,** metal, round, c. 1910	25.00	35.00	30.00
☐ **Fly box,** wooden, 6" x 10", c. 1900	55.00	65.00	60.00
☐ **Fly rod,** Heddon, split bamboo, 9½', c. 1922	65.00	75.00	70.00
☐ **Fly rod,** H. L. Leonard, 8½', c. 1890	165.00	185.00	175.00
☐ **Fly rod,** H. L. Leonard, 7', c. 1885	320.00	340.00	330.00
☐ **Lure,** Heddon, wooden plug, Heddon's Minnow, #100 series	10.00	12.00	11.00
☐ **Lure,** Heddon, wooden plug, Meadow Mouse, #4000 series	8.00	10.00	9.00
☐ **Lure,** Shakespeare, wooden plug, Darting Shrimp #135 series	13.00	15.00	14.00
☐ **Reel,** Billinghurst, fly, nickel plated, c. 1869	190.00	250.00	220.00
☐ **Reel,** Coxe, casting, aluminum, c. 1940	120.00	140.00	130.00
☐ **Reel,** English fly, silver, c. 1850	520.00	620.00	570.00
☐ **Reel,** Heddon, casting, silver, c. 1925	55.00	85.00	70.00
☐ **Reel,** Hendryx, fly, brass, c. 1890	25.00	35.00	30.00
☐ **Reel,** Leonard, fly, bronze, silver trim, c. 1878	470.00	570.00	520.00
☐ **Reel,** Leonard, fly, silver, c. 1925	270.00	300.00	285.00
☐ **Reel,** Meek, casting, brass, c. 1855	520.00	620.00	570.00

	Current Price Range		Prior Year Average
☐ Reel, Meek, casting, silver, c. 1930	145.00	185.00	165.00
☐ Reel, Meisselbach, casting, c. 1920	55.00	75.00	65.00
☐ Reel, Meisselbach, fly, nickel plated, c. 1895 .	50.00	70.00	60.00
☐ Reel, Meisselbach, trolling, wood, c. 1910 . . .	25.00	35.00	30.00
☐ Reel, Milam, casting, brass, c. 1865	420.00	520.00	470.00
☐ Reel, Milam, casting, silver, c. 1898	170.00	230.00	200.00
☐ Reel, Mills, fly, nickel, c. 1895	120.00	170.00	145.00
☐ Reel, Orvis, fly, nickel plated, c. 1874	120.00	170.00	145.00
☐ Reel, Orvis, fly, solid silver, c. 1874	620.00	720.00	670.00
☐ Reel, Pennell, casting, nickel plated, c. 1920	40.00	60.00	50.00
☐ Reel, Pfleuger, casting, brass, c. 1910	25.00	35.00	30.00
☐ Reel, Pfleuger, casting, silver, c. 1925	60.00	110.00	85.00
☐ Reel, Pfleuger, fly, rubber, c. 1905	120.00	170.00	145.00
☐ Reel, Pfleuger, trolling, brass, c. 1915	30.00	40.00	35.00
☐ Reel, Pfleuger, trolling, rubber, c. 1890	40.00	60.00	50.00
☐ Reel, Sage, fly, solid silver, c. 1848	770.00	870.00	820.00
☐ Reel, Shakespeare, casting, plastic, c. 1940	50.00	70.00	60.00
☐ Reel, Shakespeare, casting, level wind, c. 1922	40.00	60.00	50.00
☐ Reel, Shakespeare, universal, take down, c. 1922	40.00	60.00	50.00
☐ Reel, Shipley, casting, brass, c. 1885	190.00	270.00	230.00
☐ Reel, Snyder, casting, brass, c. 1820	520.00	670.00	595.00
☐ Reel, South Bend, fly, aluminum, c. 1940 . . .	45.00	65.00	55.00
☐ Reel, Talbot, casting, silver, c. 1920	95.00	145.00	120.00
☐ Reel, Union Hardware, fly, nickel plated, c. 1920	35.00	55.00	45.00
☐ Reel, Vom Hofe, fly, nickel, small, c. 1890 . . .	145.00	195.00	165.00
☐ Reel, Vom Hofe, trolling, rubber, c. 1918	170.00	240.00	195.00
☐ Reel, Yawman and Erbe, fly, aluminum, c. 1889	120.00	170.00	145.00
☐ Reel, Zwarg, trolling, rubber, c. 1950	195.00	275.00	235.00
☐ Rod case, wood, brass trim, 5', c. 1880	100.00	120.00	110.00
☐ Steel casting rod, Wards, telescopic, 9", c. 1922	35.00	45.00	40.00
☐ Steel casting rod, Wards, with case, agate guides, 5½', c. 1922	35.00	45.00	40.00
☐ Tackle box, wooden and brass trim, 14", c. 1910	55.00	65.00	60.00
☐ Tackle box, metal and brass trim, 16", c. 1925	55.00	65.00	60.00

FOOTBALL CARDS

This section features only a sampling of football items. In order to accurately present the vast amount of infc.mation required by serious collectors, a special edition devoted to football is published by The House of Collectibles, Inc. This handy, pocket-size guide *The Official 1985 Guide to Football Cards,* features more than 50,000 card prices and valuable collecting information. It is available at bookstores for $3.95.

DESCRIPTION: Football cards usually have the picture of a football player on one side and his statistics or biography on the other.

ORIGIN: The first football cards we produced by Goudey Gum in 1933.

MAKER: There are several companies who have produced football cards including Topps, Fleer, O-Pee-Chee and Bowman.

COMMENTS: Although the popularity of collecting football cards lags behind the well established baseball card hobby, football's tremendous popularity assures the growth of football card collecting.

ADDITIONAL TIPS: The most valuable cards to watch for are old sets, famous player cards and rookie cards. For more information, consult *The Official Price Guide to Football Cards,* published by The House of Collectibles.

BOWMAN — 1950
(2¹⁄₁₆″ x 2½″, Numbered 1-144, Color)

			Current Prior Year	Price Range Average
☐		Complete Set	375.00	225.00	227.00
☐	1	Doak Walker, Detroit Lions back	5.20	4.20	4.70
☐	5	Y.A. Tittle, Baltimore Colts, quarterback	11.00	7.00	7.48
☐	6	Lou Groza, Cleveland Browns, tackle	10.00	6.00	5.35
☐	16	Glenn Davis, Los Angeles Rams, back	5.10	4.10	4.60
☐	27	Sid Luckman, Chicago Bears, quarterback	10.75	6.75	5.53
☐	45	Otto Graham, Cleveland Browns, quarterback	12.00	8.00	11.98
☐	78	Dante Lavelli, Cleveland Browns, end	4.40	3.40	3.90
☐	100	Sammy Baugh, Washington Redskins, quarterback	14.00	9.50	11.75
☐	132	Chuck Bednarik, Philadelphia Eagles, center	5.00	3.00	4.95

BOWMAN — 1951
(2¹⁄₁₆″ x 3⅛″, Numbered 1-144, Color)

☐		Complete Set	425.00	275.00	235.00
☐	2	Otto Graham, Cleveland Browns, quarterback	10.50	6.50	10.65

		Current Price Range		Prior Year Average
☐	4 **Norm VanBrocklin**, Los Angeles Rams, quarterback	7.00	4.50	6.60
☐	12 **Chuck Bednarik**, Philadelphia Eagles, center	6.50	4.00	5.05
☐	20 **Tom Landry**, New York Giants, back . . .	12.50	8.80	10.65
☐	34 **Sammy Baugh**, Washington Redskins, quarterback	16.00	10.00	10.65
☐	75 **Lou Groza**, Cleveland Browns, tackle . .	8.00	5.00	8.18
☐	76 **Elroy Hirsch**, Los Angeles Rams, back .	7.00	4.00	5.05
☐	102 **Bobby Layne**, Detroit Lions, quarterback	10.20	7.70	8.95
☐	105 **Joe Perry**, San Francisco 49ers, back . .	3.50	2.00	5.10

FLEER — 1960
(2½ ″ x 3½ ″, Numbered 1-132, Color)

☐	Complete Set	75.00	50.00	56.50
☐	7 **Sid Gillman**, Los Angeles Chargers (AFL), coach	1.00	.60	.74
☐	20 **Sammy Baugh**, New York Titans (AFL), coach	5.00	4.00	4.55
☐	58 **George Blanda**, Houston Oilers (AFL), quarterback/kicker	4.00	3.00	3.53
☐	66 **Billy Cannon**, Houston Oilers (AFL), back/end	1.50	.90	1.90
☐	73 **Abner Haynes**, Dallas Texans (AFL), back	1.50	.90	1.90
☐	76 **Paul Lowe**, Los Angeles Chargers (AFL), back	1.25	1.00	1.13
☐	116 **Hank Stram**, Los Angeles Chargers (AFL), back	2.20	1.60	1.90
☐	118 **Ron Mix**, Los Angeles Chargers (AFL), tackle	2.20	1.60	1.90
☐	124 **John Kemp**, Los Angeles Chargers (AFL), quarterback	7.75	5.00	4.55

FLEER — 1961
(2½ ″ x 3½ ″, Numbered 1-220, Color)

☐	Complete Set	135.00	80.00	113.00
☐	11 **Jim Brown**, Cleveland Browns, back . . .	19.00	12.00	17.13
☐	30 **John Unitas**, Baltimore Colts, quarterback	6.60	4.80	5.70
☐	41 **Don Meredith**, Dallas Cowboys, quarterback	7.50	5.00	6.25
☐	69 **Kyle Rote**, New York Giants, end	2.20	1.60	1.90

		Current Price Range		Prior Year Average
☐	**88 Bart Starr**, Green Bay Packers, quarterback	5.50	5.00	4.40
☐	**90 Paul Horning**, Green Bay Packers, back	4.50	3.00	3.08
☐	**117 Bobby Layne**, Pittsburg Steelers, quarterback	4.00	2.50	4.25
☐	**155 John Kemp**, San Diego Chargers (AFL), quarterback	8.00	5.00	6.23
☐	**166 George Blanda**, Houston Oilers (AFL), quarterback/kicker	5.50	4.40	4.95

TOPPS — 1956
(2⅝″ x 3⅝″, Numbered 1-120, Color)

☐	Complete Set	175.00	100.00	135.00
☐	**6 Norm Van Brocklin**, Los Angeles Rams, quarterback	5.25	3.00	4.25
☐	**28 Chuch Bednarik**, Philadelphia Eagles, center	2.50	1.50	2.83
☐	**29 Kyle Rote**, New York Giants, end	4.00	2.50	3.08
☐	**36 Art Donvan**, Baltimore Colts, tackle	1.50	.90	1.90
☐	**53 Frank Gifford**, New York Giants, back	14.00	8.00	7.30
☐	**60 Lenny Moore**, Baltimore Colts, back	2.75	1.75	2.83
☐	**78 Elroy Hirsch**, Los Angeles Rams, end/back	3.50	2.00	2.83
☐	**87 Ernie Stautner**, Pittsburgh Steelers, tackle	2.75	1.75	1.63
☐	**101 Roosevelt Grier**, New York Giants, tackle	1.75	1.00	1.90
☐	**110 Joe Perry**, San Francisco 49ers, back	1.75	1.00	2.83

TOPPS — 1957
(2½″ x 3½″, Numbered 1-154, Color)

☐	Complete Set	215.00	125.00	155.00
☐	**11 Roosevelt Brown**, New York Giants, tackle	1.50	.90	1.50
☐	**22 Norman Van Brocklin**, Los Angeles Rams, quarterback	6.50	3.50	4.20
☐	**28 Lou Groza**, Cleveland Browns, tackle/kicker	3.50	2.00	2.70
☐	**30 Y.A. Tittle**, San Francisco 49ers, quarterback	6.00	3.25	5.00
☐	**31 George Blanda**, Chicago Bears, quarterback/kicker	8.50	4.50	7.20
☐	**32 Bobby Layne**, Detroit Lions, quarterback	7.00	4.00	7.45

		Current Price Range		Prior Year Average
☐ 88	**Frank Gifford**, New York Giants, back .	12.00	7.00	7.98
☐ 119	**Bart Starr**, Green Bay Packers, quarterback	23.00	14.00	11.75
☐ 151	**Paul Horning**, Green Bay Packers, back	17.00	10.00	11.80

FRANKOMA POTTERY

DESCRIPTION: Founded in 1933 by John Frank, the Frankoma Pottery continues to produce earthenwares made from Oklahoma clays to the present day. Located in Sapula, Oklahoma, the wares of this company are known for their color and durablility.

Frankoma Bottle Vase Series, Left to Right: 1974, item #V-6, **$38.00-$46.00;** and 1975, item #V-7, **$33.00-$39.00**

TYPES: Many types of objects have been produced by Frankoma including jewelry, limited edition plates, miniatures, trivets, Christmas cards, sculpture, novelties and of course, dinnerware.

RECOMMENDED READING: For more in-depth information you may refer to *The Official Price Guide to Pottery and Porcelain* and *The Official Identification Guide to Pottery and Porcelain,* published by The House of Collectibles.

	Current Price Range		Prior Year Average
☐ **Bowl,** 14 ounces	3.50	5.00	4.25
☐ **Bowl,** divided, 11", item #49d, peach glow, .	6.00	8.00	7.00
☐ **Butter Dish,** item #4k, peach glow, lidded . . .	7.00	10.00	8.50
☐ **Creamer And Sugar,** 8 ounces, item #4a, peach glow.	8.00	10.00	9.00
☐ **Creamer And Sugar,** items #7a, 7b, woodland mossand, C-shape handles, the sugar bowl's lid with a plug-type handle, the creamer featuring a vaulted pouring spout. .	13.00	16.00	14.50
☐ **Cup,** item #4c, clay blue	4.00	5.50	4.75
☐ **Cup,** item #7c, woodland moss, sculptured handle.	4.00	5.00	4.50
☐ **Dinner Plate,** 9", item #7f, woodland moss . .	4.00	5.50	4.75
☐ **Dinner Plate,** 10", item #4f, peach glow	5.00	6.00	5.50
☐ **Fruit Dish,** 8 ounces, item #7xo, woodland moss	4.00	5.50	4.75
☐ **Juice,** 6 ounces	3.00	4.00	3.50
☐ **Lazy Suzette,** 5 sections, on ball bearing base, made from 1957-1982	22.00	24.00	23.00
☐ **Mug,** item #7cl, woodland moss, modified loop handle.	3.00	4.00	3.50
☐ **Pitcher,** item #4d, two quart, clay blue	9.00	12.00	10.50
☐ **Pitcher,** item #7d, woodland moss, pot form with tall loop handle.	10.00	14.00	12.00
☐ **Plate,** 7"	3.00	4.00	3.50
☐ **Plate,** 10"	6.00	8.00	7.00
☐ **Plate,** 15"	16.00	18.00	17.00
☐ **Platter,** 11"	5.00	6.00	5.50
☐ **Platter,** 13", shallow	7.00	10.00	8.50
☐ **Platter,** serving, 12⅞", item #4p, clay blue . .	11.00	14.00	12.50
☐ **Pot,** 3 quart, lid, lidded	16.00	18.00	17.00
☐ **Salad Bowl,** 20 ounces, item #7x1, woodland moss	6.00	8.00	7.00
☐ **Sauce Dish,** 10 ounces, item #7s, desert gold, lidded	2.50	3.25	2.75
☐ **Saucer,** 5", item #7e, woodland moss	2.75	3.75	3.25
☐ **Saucer,** 5¼", item #4e, clay blue	1.75	2.00	1.85

	Current Price Range		Prior Year Average
☐ **Shakers,** salt and pepper	5.00	6.00	5.50
☐ **Soup Cup,** 11 ounces, ...	4.00	6.00	5.00
☐ **Spoon Holder,** 6″	3.00	5.00	4.00
☐ **Sugar Bowl,** item #7b, prairie green, unlidded	9.00	12.00	10.50
☐ **Teapot,** 2 cup	7.00	9.00	8.00
☐ **Teapot,** 6 cup, tall, short lip spout	10.00	12.00	11.00
☐ **Tray,** 9″	5.00	7.00	6.00
☐ **Tumbler,** 12 ounces	4.00	6.00	5.00
☐ **Vegetable,** 24 ounces	5.00	7.00	6.00
☐ **Vegetable Bowl,** one quart, item #7n, woodland moss	7.00	9.00	8.00

FRUIT CRATE ART

DESCRIPTION: The decorative labels that adorned the sides of wooden fruit crates have become popular collectibles.

PERIOD: The oldest and most rare versions of fruit crate art date to the 1880s.

ORIGIN: Fruit crate labels were originally designed to attract potential fruit buyers. In the 1950s collecting such art work began when the use of decorated wooden crates declined.

COMMENTS: Rarity and desogn are the important variables with fruit crate art. California labels are usually worth more than Florida labels, and orange labels usually have more ornate designs. Label designs changed over the years, and some collectors focus on labels that have undergone design changes.

ADDITIONAL TIPS: The listings are alphabetical according to fruit company name. Following names are descriptions of the label art, type of fruit and price range. Size of label and states are listed when available.

☐ **All American,** patriotic design, apples, 9″ x 10″	.90	1.25	1.00
☐ **American Maid,** maid in bonnet, pear, 7½″ x 11″	.40	.90	.50
☐ **Arboleda,** coastal orchard scene, lemons, 9″ x 12½″	1.25	1.75	1.40
☐ **Bee-N-Sweet Pears,** bee, 7½″ x 11″	.75	1.50	1.00
☐ **Big City,** city skyline, pears, 7½″ x 11″	.75	1.25	.95
☐ **Bird Valley,** dark bird, apples, 9″ x 10″	2.00	3.00	2.30
☐ **Black Joe,** old man with white hair, grapes .	.75	1.50	1.00
☐ **Blazing Star,** yellow flower, pears	.35	.60	.40

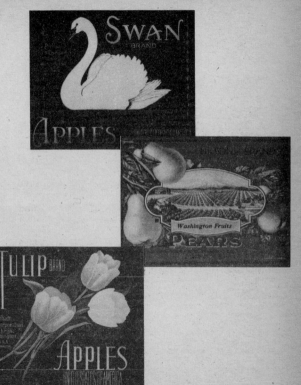

Top to Bottom: **Swan Apples**, *black background, white swan,* **$7.00-$10.00; Hi-Tone Pears**, *red background, yellow pears, colorful orchard in center,* **$3.00-$5.00; Tulip Apples**, *black background, blue, orange and yellow tulips,* **$4.00-$6.00**

	Current Price Range		Prior Year Average
☐ **Blue Anchor,** large anchor, pears, 7½″ x 11″	.75	1.15	.85
☐ **Blue Circle,** pears, 7½″ x 11″	.35	.60	.40
☐ **Blue Circle,** oranges	3.75	4.50	4.00
☐ **Blue Goose,** large blue goose, pears, 7½″ x 11″	.35	.60	.40
☐ **Blue Tip,** large feather, oranges, Florida, 9″ x 9″	.65	.90	.75
☐ **Buy The Best,** black with pears, 7½″ x 11″	.35	.60	.40
☐ **Cambria,** eagle and flame, oranges, California, 10″ x 11″	.60	1.00	1.25
☐ **Camel,** desert with camel, pears, 7½″ x 11″	.75	1.20	.85
☐ **Canadian,** three apples, apples, 9″ x 10″	1.75	2.50	2.00
☐ **Capitol Pak,** state capitol of California, pear, 7½″ x 11″	.60	.80	.65
☐ **Channel,** Islands with sailboat and seagulls, lemons, 9″ x 12½″	1.25	1.75	1.40
☐ **Coast King,** crown, brussel sprouts, 9½″ x 10½″	.25	.75	.50
☐ **Columbia Belle,** Miss Columbia with sword, apples, 9″ x 10″	1.30	2.00	1.50
☐ **Corona Lily,** oranges	3.75	4.50	4.00
☐ **Dixie,** Indiana apples, 9″ x 10″	.25	.75	.50
☐ **Dixie Boy,** black boy, grapefruit, Florida, 9″ x 9″	2.00	2.75	2.15
☐ **Eatum,** yellow and red apples, apples, 9″ x 10″	.75	1.50	1.00
☐ **Elmwood,** blue anchor, pears, 7½″ x 11″	.30	.60	.40
☐ **Embarcadero,** pier, pears, 7½″ x 11″	1.75	2.25	1.80
☐ **Evening Star,** nighttime mission scene, lemons, 9″ x 12½″	2.50	3.50	2.75
☐ **Fall Fruit,** waterfall, apples, 9″ x 10″	.30	1.00	.50
☐ **Festival,** parade carriage, lemons, 9″ x 12½″	4.75	5.50	4.85
☐ **Gladiola,** oranges	3.75	4.50	4.00
☐ **Golden Eagle,** orange	2.75	3.50	3.00
☐ **Goodfruit,** apples, 9″ x 10″	1.80	2.50	2.00
☐ **Green Bluff,** apples, 9″ x 10″	2.50	3.50	2.90
☐ **Guide,** orchard, lemons 9″ x 12½″	.75	1.25	.85
☐ **Have One,** hand holding orange, oranges, California, 10″ x 11″	2.75	3.50	2.90
☐ **High Hand,** arm holding four aces, pears, 7½″ x 11″	.50	1.00	.60
☐ **High Sea,** beach scene with seagulls, apples, 9″ x 10″	1.30	1.75	1.50
☐ **Idylwild,** orchard, oranges, California, 10″ x 11″	1.75	2.50	1.85
☐ **Independent,** Liberty Bell, apples, 9″ x 10″	1.90	2.25	2.00
☐ **Keeper,** gold keys, lemons, 9″ x 12½″	1.25	1.75	1.35

	Current Price Range		Prior Year Average
☐ **Kingfish,** fish with crown, asparagus, 9½″ x 10½″	1.30	1.75	1.50
☐ **King Pelican,** crown, lettuce	.60	1.00	.75
☐ **King Tut,** table scene, lemons, 9″ x 12½″	4.50	5.50	4.75
☐ **Lemonade,** large lemons, 9″ 12½″	.75	1.25	.85
☐ **Lake Ridge,** orchard and lake, pears, 7½″ x 11″	1.75	2.10	1.80
☐ **Lake Wenatchee,** mountain scene with lake and cabin, apples, 9″ x 10″	.60	1.00	.75
☐ **Life,** trout fisherman in mountians, pears, 7½″ x 11″	1.30	1.60	1.35
☐ **Mad River,** river and pears, pears, 7½″ x 11″	.75	1.15	.85
☐ **Maggie,** Indian on mountain, asparagus, 9½″ x 10½″	.75	1.50	1.00
☐ **Magnolia,** valley scene, apples, 9″ x 10″	.30	.60	.40
☐ **Metropolitan,** city market scene, oranges, California, 10″ x 11″	2.00	3.00	2.30
☐ **Mischief,** Indian maid with apple, apples, 9″ x 10″	1.80	2.50	2.00
☐ **Mountain Goat,** apples, 9″ x 10″	1.25	2.00	1.50
☐ **Mt. Lasson,** volcano, pears, 7½″ x 11″	1.75	2.10	1.85
☐ **Mt. Shasta,** mountain scene, pears, 7½″ x 11″	1.30	1.65	1.38
☐ **Orchard,** ranch scene, pears, 7½″ x 11″	1.75	2.10	1.85
☐ **Oriole,** oranges	4.50	5.50	4.75
☐ **Our Pick,** rooster picking fruit, pears, 7½″ x 11″	1.75	2.15	1.85
☐ **Peacock,** bird, pears, 7½″ x 11″	2.75	3.50	2.90
☐ **Perfection,** lemons, 9″ x 12½″	.75	1.25	.85
☐ **Piggy Pears,** cartoon pig with basket, pears, 7½″ x 11″	1.30	1.75	1.45
☐ **Pride of the River,** riverboat, asparagus, 9½″ x 10½″	3.50	4.50	3.75
☐ **Pride of Venice Cove,** rooster, oranges, California, 10″ x 11″	1.75	2.15	1.85
☐ **River Maid,** river with boat and girl, pears, 7½″ x 11″	.50	1.25	.75
☐ **Rose Apples,** two roses, apples, 9″ x 10″	1.30	1.75	1.50
☐ **Safe Hit,** baseball scene, lettuce	.60	1.00	.75
☐ **Sanclair,** pears. 7½″ x 11″	.75	1.10	.80
☐ **Santa,** Santa Claus with toy sack, lemons, 9″ x 12½″	3.00	3.75	3.15
☐ **Snow Owl,** white owl, pear, 7½″ x 11″	1.75	2.15	1.85
☐ **Sky Ranch,** cowboy with head like an apple, apples, 9″ x 10″	.75	1.50	1.00

	Current Price Range		Prior Year Average
☐ **Stafford Blacks,** grapes	1.75	2.50	2.00
☐ **State Seal,** George Washington, apples, 9" x 10"	.75	1.50	1.00
☐ **Statue of Liberty,** pear, 7½" x 11"	.30	.60	.45
☐ **Straight Arrow,** flying arrow, apples. 9" x 10"	.75	1.50	1.00
☐ **Sunflower,** orange	3.50	4.75	3.70
☐ **Tartan,** lemon on plaid background, lemons, 9" x 12½"	.75	1.10	.80
☐ **Up-N-Atom,** rabbit, lettuce	.60	1.00	.75
☐ **Valley,** field and orchard, apples, 9" x 10" . .	.75	1.50	1.00
☐ **Viewmont,** mountain view, pears, 7½" x 11"	.75	1.15	.80
☐ **Waldorf,** bellboy with apples, apples, 9" x 10"	.75	1.50	1.00

FRUIT JARS

DESCRIPTION: Fruit jars are glass containers which were sold empty and were intended for use in the home preservation of food.

TYPES: There were several types of fruit jars produced including those with either the manufactures's name or a decorative motif printed on the jar.

MAKER: One of the most familiar names in fruit jars is the Mason jar produced by John Landis Mason in the early 1800s. One of Mason's innovations was a zinc lid which provided greater air tightness.

COMMENTS: Fruit jars of the 1800s are highly collectible. Before 1810, few glass containers were manufactured.

ADDITIONAL TIPS: For more information, consult *The Official Price Guide to Bottles,* published by The House of Collectibles.

☐ **ANCHOR MASON'S,** Patent in 3 lines, sheared top, Mason seal, qt., clear	35.00	45.00	40.00
☐ **ATLAS EZ SEAL,** In 3 lines all in a circle, sheared top, lightning seal, qt., aqua, lt. blue	13.00	18.00	15.00
☐ **ATLAS E.Z,** Seal all in 3 lines, under bottom Atlas E-Z jar, aqua pt. jar, clear or aqua . . .	1.50	2.50	2.00
☐ **ATLAS IMPROVED MASON** (c. 1890's), Glass lid, metal screw band, aqua or green	8.00	10.00	9.00
☐ **ATLAS MASON'S PATENT** (c. 1900) , Zinc lid, olive green, quart	18.00	20.00	19.00
☐ **ATLAS MASON'S PATENT NOV. 30, 1858,** Zinc lid, olive green, ½ gallon	20.00	28.00	24.00

	Current Price Range		Prior Year Average
☐ **ATLAS MASON'S PATENT NOV. 30th, 1858,** Screw top, olive green, quart	20.00	28.00	24.00
☐ **ATLAS MASON'S PATENT,** Screw top, green, quart	4.00	6.00	5.00
☐ **ATLAS SPECIAL** (c. 1910), Screw top, clear or blue	6.00	8.00	7.00
☐ **B & CO. LD,** Under bottom, stopper finish (neck) per glass stopper, cork jacket (English) 2 Sizes lt. green	8.00	10.00	9.00
☐ **BAKER BROS.** (c. 1865), Wax sealer, groove ring, green or aqua, pint	30.00	35.00	32.50
☐ **BALL,** Vaseline glass, screw top, pint, quart	6.00	8.00	7.00
☐ **BALL** (c. 1890), Screw top, green, three sizes	7.00	10.00	8.50
☐ **THE BALL** (c. 1890), Screw top, green, quart	7.00	10.00	8.50
☐ **BALL** in script, **IDEAL,** Wire top clamp, clear, 3" or 4¾"	6.00	8.00	6.00
☐ **BALL** in script, **IDEAL,** In back, Pat. July 14, 1908, wire top clamp, green or clear, three sizes	5.00	7.00	6.00
☐ **BALL IDEAL PATD JULY 14 1988,** (error in date), blue green, pint	18.00	24.00	21.50
☐ **BOYD MASON** (c. 1910), Zinc lid, olive green, pint, quart	40.00	50.00	45.00
☐ **BOYD PERFECT MASON,** Zinc lid, green ½ pint, pint, quart	5.00	7.00	6.00
☐ **BOYDS GENIUNE,** Mason under bottom inside of diamond IG Co. sheared top, Mason seal, qt., aqua	3.00	5.00	4.00
☐ **BRAUN SAFETEE MASON,** Zinc lid, aqua ..	5.00	7.00	6.00
☐ **MASON'S,** Swirled milk glass, 7¼"	75.00	90.00	82.00
☐ **MASON'S CG, PATENT NOV 30, 1858,** Zinc lid, green, quart	5.00	8.00	6.50
☐ **MASON'S-C-PATENT NOV. 30TH 1858,** Green, 7"	10.00	12.00	11.00
☐ **MASON'S IMPROVED,** Zinc screw band and glass insert, aqua or green, pint	10.00	14.00	12.00
☐ **MASON'S IMPROVED BUTTER JAR,** Sheared top, aqua, ½ gallon	10.00	14.00	12.00
☐ **MASON'S IMPROVED,** Hero F J Co. in cross above, zinc band and glass lid covered with many patent dates, earliest Feb. 12, '56, aqua	10.00	14.00	12.00
☐ **MASON'S KEYSTONE** (c. 1869), Zinc screw band and glass insert, aqua, quart	15.00	20.00	17.50
☐ **MASON'S "M" PATENT NOV. 30TH 1858,** Green, 7"	5.00	8.00	6.50

	Current Price Range		Prior Year Average
☐ MASON'S, under it "M" PATENT NOV. 30TH 1898, Screw top, aqua, quart	11.00	15.00	13.00
☐ MASON'S PATENT 1858, Zinc lid, amber or green, pint	15.00	20.00	17.50
☐ PEERLESS, Wax dipped cork, green, quart	55.00	75.00	65.00
☐ SAFETY VALVE PATD. MAY 21, 1895, With emblem in center on bottom, ground top, aqua, pint	8.00	10.00	9.00
☐ SAFETY VALVE PATD. MAY 21, 1895, Midget jar, ground top, clear, 3¾"	12.00	15.00	13.50
☐ SAFETY WIDE MOUTH MASON, SALEM GLASS WORKS, SALEM, N.J., Zinc lid, aqua or green, quart, ½ gallon	12.00	18.00	15.00
☐ SAMCO in center, GENUINE MASON, Zinc screw band and opal insert, clear, all sizes	1.00	2.00	1.50
☐ SAMCO SUPER MASON (c. 1920), Zinc screw band and opal insert, clear, all sizes	1.00	2.00	1.50
☐ SAMPSON IMPROVED BATTERY (c. 1895), Screw-on lid, aqua, quart	12.00	17.00	15.00
☐ SANETY WIDE MOUTH MASON (c. 1920), Zinc lid, wide mouth, aqua, quart	12.00	15.00	13.50
☐ SANFORD (c. 1900), Metal screw band and glass insert, clear, quart	10.00	12.00	11.00
☐ SANITARY (c. 1900), Glass lid and wire bail, aqua, quart	12.00	15.00	13.50
☐ SAN YUEN CO. (c. 1925), Glass lid and half wire bail, clear, quart	3.00	5.00	4.00
☐ TF, Monogram on base, clear, quart	3.00	4.50	3.75
☐ TIGHT SEAL PAT'D. JULY 14, 1908, Half wire bail and glass lid, green or blue, all sizes	2.50	4.00	3.25
☐ TROPICAL CANNERS, Metal top, clear, quart	2.00	3.00	2.50
☐ TRUE FRUIT (c. 1900), Glass top and metal clamp, clear, quart	10.00	12.00	11.00

FURNITURE

COMMENTS: Interest in antique and collectible furniture is growing, according to auction houses and dealers around the country. Record prices were realized for American Federal and Victorian period pieces this year. European furniture is also very strong. Experts feel that the current design trends featuring "Country" and Victorian styles have had a major impact on this upward movement in the popularity of antique furniture. Also, prices for fine old pieces compare very favorably to the cost of new furniture.

RECOMMENDED READING: For more in-depth information on furniture you may refer to *The Official Identification Guide to Early American Furniture, The Official Identification Guide to Victorian Furniture, The Official Price Guide to Wicker, The Official Price Guide to Oriental Collectibles, The Official Guide to Buying and Selling Antiques and Collectibles* and *The Official Encyclopedia of Antiques and Collectibles,* published by The House of Collectibles.

	Current Price Range		Prior Year Average
☐ **Adams Style,** English, armchairs, pair, walnut, squared back, open lyre splat, arms with beaded molding and bowfront, tapering reeded legs, 32″ high, 1900.	2900.00	3100.00	400.00
☐ **Art Deco,** American, bedroom suite, five pieces, red and black laquer and chrome. . .	800.00	1100.00	950.00
☐ **Art Nouveau,** English, sideboard, mahogany, floral carved top section	600.00	700.00	650.00
☐ **Biedermeier,** credenza, inlaid walnut, rectangular top above three frieze drawers over three cupboard doors, raised on tapering square legs, 39″ high x 54½″ long x 17¾″ deep	800.00	1200.00	1000.00
☐ **Brass,** canopy bed, knob and tube style, twin size, 81″ long x 43″ wide x 84″ high	800.00	1200.00	1000.00
☐ **Duncan Phyfe Style,** dining table, mahogany, reeded edge top, three reeded legs, brass paws and casters, two leaves, English, 28½″ high x 46″ wide x 51″ diameter, early 20th century	2800.00	3200.00	3000.00
☐ **Eastlake,** bureau and matching bedstead, incised mahogany and walnut, bureau has gray marble top over three long drawers, mirror has stylized floral crest, bedstead is 5′2″ high x 4′9½″ wide	400.00	500.00	450.00
☐ **Louis XV Style,** parlor set, settee, armchair and sidechair, giltwood, early 20th century .	1200.00	2300.00	1200.00
☐ **Louis XVI Style,** bedroom suite, eleven pieces, painted off-white, caned head and foot boards, swag decoration	1100.00	1500.00	1300.00
☐ **Louis XVI Style,** settee, square back, beribboned crest bowfront seat, cream gessoed woodwork, brocade upholstery	800.00	1200.00	1000.00
☐ **Oak,** golden, armchair, pressed carving in back splat, upholstered seat, 38″ high x 27″ wide	125.00	200.00	170.00

	Current Price Range		Prior Year Average
☐ **Oak,** golden, china cabinet, curved front, mirrored back, three glass shelves, 87″ high x 44″ wide	600.00	800.00	700.00
☐ **Oak,** golden, dentistry cabinet, 54″ high x 36″ wide x 13″ deep	800.00	1000.00	900.00
☐ **Oak,** golden, dining table, round with center pedestal and four carved feet, 1 leaf, 30″ high x 42″ diameter, 1880	600.00	800.00	700.00
☐ **Oak,** golden, ice box, zinc lined, two doors, some chestnut, 42″ high x 35″ wide x 18″ deep	350.00	450.00	400.00
☐ **Oak,** golden, Morris Chair, 38″ high x 27″ wide x 28″ deep, 1880s	300.00	400.00	350.00
☐ **Oak,** golden, rocker, pressed carving	200.00	400.00	300.00
☐ **Oak,** golden, sideboard, mirrored, elaborate carvings, plain, quarter, and tiger stripe wood, 82″ high x 60″ wide	800.00	3000.00	1400.00
☐ **Queen Anne Style,** English, tea table, walnut, flip top, adjustable, brass pulls, two drawers, 22″ x 15″ x 30″ high	300.00	500.00	400.00
☐ **Sheraton Style,** bed, mahogany, queen size, four posters, carved and fluted columns, swan nock headboard	850.00	950.00	900.00
☐ **Sheraton Style,** dining chairs set of twelve, painted, rounded back, open splat, painted serpentine front, 37½″ high, early 20th century	2200.00	2700.00	1000.00
☐ **Sheraton Style,** fern stand, pair, mahogany, square tops with notched corners, turned standards, raised on tripod bases, 36″ high	325.00	375.00	350.00
☐ **Stickley, Gustav,** bookcase, oak, double doors, 56″ high x 62″ wide x 12¼″ deep, 1907	2600.00	3100.00	2850.00
☐ **Stickley, Gustav,** desk, slant front, oak, opens to fitted interior, 40″ high x 29″ wide x 17″ deep, 1915	425.00	475.00	450.00
☐ **Stickley, Gustav,** table, dropleaf, oak, two hinged flaps, three drawers, 28″ high x 16¼″ deep, top is 43″ long when extended, 1910	600.00	700.00	650.00
☐ **Victorian,** corner cabinet, rosewood, marquetry inlaid, top has beveled glass display cabinet, 79″ high x 32″ wide x 19″ deep, late 19th century	1000.00	1800.00	1400.00

	Current Price Range		Prior Year Average
☐ **Victorian,** hall tree, walnut and burl walnut, arched and thumb molded cornice above a central mirrored panel flanked by pilasters and brass lion head knobs, plinth base with single drawer flanked by wells, 9'8" high x 4'11" wide x 19½" deep, late 19th century ..	750.00	950.00	850.00
☐ **Victorian,** parlor suite, six pieces, mahogany and burl walnut, includes settee, gentleman's armchair, lady's chair and three side chairs, settee is 6'8" long, late 19th century .	1000.00	1900.00	1450.00
☐ **Victorian,** pedestal table, oak round top, pedestal base with carved lion's mask, paw feet, 30" high x 62" diameter	1900.00	2100.00	500.00
☐ **Victorian,** Renaissance Revival, American, bedroom suite, two pieces, dresser and bed, black walnut, dresser has white beveled marble top, ebony finish wood drawer pulls, elaborate mirror, both bed and dresser have carved bust of Columbia at top, raised panels in burl walnut, headboard is 93½" high x 61¼" wide, dresser is 102" high x 51½" wide x 21½" deep, made by Berkey and Gay, Grand Rapids, Michigan, 1870-1876	3500.00	5000.00	4250.00
☐ **Victorian,** stool, walnut, covered in needle-point	450.00	550.00	500.00

GAMES

TOPIC: Games are amusing activities that people participate in. The games that collectors are primarily interested in are board games, which are played on the decorated surface of a board or platform.

PERIOD: The first American board game was produced 1843 by W. and S.B. Ives Company. Monopoly, the most famous of all American games, was invented around 1934.

COMMENTS: From 1850 to 1920, games were made using lithography. Some parts were hand painted. The most collectible board games were made by Ives Company or the McLoughlin Brothers.

ADDITIONAL TIPS: American board games do not have a high survival rate. When selecting a collectible game, look for one in good condition and with all its pieces intact. For further information, please refer to *The Official Price Guide to Collectible Toys,* published by The House of Collectibles.

Radio Game for Little Folks, ©*Alderman Fairchild Co., 12", 1926,*
$15.00-$25.00

		Current Price Range		Prior Year Average
☐	**Age Cards,** Germany, seven cards, 2″ x 2″ . . .	2.00	5.00	2.50
☐	**Air Mail,** Milton Bradley, c. early 1930's, roll marble across board with obstacles	30.00	40.00	32.00
☐	**Alphabet Game,** c. 1950's, "Pinkey Lee's" . . .	7.00	14.00	6.00
☐	**Bear Game,** lithographed paper under glass, put knife and fork in bear's hands by shaking	20.00	30.00	23.00
☐	**Bingo Game,** Germany, c. 1920's, twelve cards, wood numbers	3.00	6.00	3.50
☐	**Blackout,** World War II era, covered with glass, tin sides, shows planes about to bomb town, object: to cover windows with rolling windows	30.00	40.00	33.00
☐	**Chalk and Checkers,** The Ohio Art Company, #523, c. 1960's, metal, slate, plastic, eraser, chalk	7.00	12.00	8.00
☐	**Checker Board,** advertising giveaway for Preferred Accident Insurance Company, c. 1930's	8.00	12.00	9.00

	Current Price Range		Prior Year Average
☐ **Checkers,** The Ohio Art Company, #97, c. 1950's, tin, multicolored, Chinese, and regular checkers, diameter 13"	8.00	12.00	9.00
☐ **Chinese Checkers,** The Ohio Art Company, #535, 1960's, metal, marbles, multicolored	8.00	12.00	9.00
☐ **Chinese Checkers and Checkers,** The Ohio Art Company, #538, c. 1960's, metal board, glass marbles, plastic checkers	12.00	18.00	15.00
☐ **Cinderella Game,** Bavaria, nine cards, 3" x 3"	2.00	5.00	2.50
☐ **Dad's Puzzler,** J. W. Hayward, c. 1926, wood block puzzle game	15.00	20.00	16.00
☐ **Deluxe Chinese Checkers and Checkers,** The Ohio Art Company, #539, c. 1960's, metal board, glass marbles, plastic checkers, storage drawer, diameter 18"	20.00	25.00	21.00
☐ **Eddie Cantor Tell it To The Judge,** Parker Brothers	20.00	25.00	21.00
☐ **Education Board,** Brill Monfort Company, New York, multiply and divide, 12" x13"	6.00	12.00	7.00
☐ **Game of Chance,** c. 1940's, wooden box, disc that spins causes dice to tumble	75.00	95.00	82.00
☐ **Game of Venetian Fortune Telling,** Parker Brothers	5.00	10.00	7.00
☐ **Gee-Whiz Horse Race,** Wolverine, flywheel game, tin with steel wheel, horses race to flag	50.00	60.00	53.00
☐ **Goose Game,** dice, pegs, multicolored pictures, 15" x 11"	10.00	15.00	11.00
☐ **Heads Down,** puzzle game, under glass with tin sides, object: put trucks standing on heads, 3" x 4"	20.00	30.00	23.00
☐ **Hold the Fort,** Parker Brothers, c. 1895, Civil War cover	35.00	45.00	40.00
☐ **Horsehoe Set,** The Ohio Art Company, #531, c. 1950's, metal, vinyl, black, red	7.00	12.00	8.00
☐ **Jolly Darkie Target Game,** McLoughlin, late 19th century, cardboard with colored lithographed covering, game in which the target is a likeness of a black man with wide open mouth, 11½"	140.00	170.00	150.00
☐ **Jolly Old Maid,** Parker Brothers	5.00	10.00	7.00
☐ **Kick Back,** pinball game, spring action, board 15" x 24"	20.00	30.00	23.00
☐ **Koo Koo Choo Choo,** The Ohio Art Company, #647, c. 1960's, metal plastic, exploding train game, mechanical	12.00	22.00	15.00

	Current Price Range		Prior Year Average
☐ **Let 'Em Have It,** World War II era, lithographed cover and game board with battle scenes	30.00	40.00	32.00
☐ **Lightning Express,** Milton Bradley, game board part of box	22.00	28.00	24.00
☐ **Mickey Mouse Club Magic Adder,** battery operated, red light turns on when correct answer is given	18.00	22.00	19.00
☐ **Money Box,** The Ohio Art Company, #121, c. 1950's, tin, multicolored, rectangular, play coins, bills	8.00	12.00	9.00
☐ **Old Maid,** Bavaria, nine cards, 2″ x 2″	2.00	5.00	2.50
☐ **Peter Coddles Visit to New York,** c. early 1900's, word game, lithographed cover, 5″ x 6″	12.00	18.00	14.00
☐ **Picture Puzzle,** McLoughlin Brothers, New York, wood backed	35.00	45.00	38.00
☐ **Pike's Peak or Bust,** Parker Brothers, c. 1895	15.00	20.00	17.00
☐ **Pollyana,** Parker Brothers, c. 1915, game board and cards, lithographed	30.00	40.00	33.00
☐ **Ring Toss,** c. 1940's, wood, rope, post length 6″	7.00	12.00	8.00
☐ **Roulette,** Reliable Toys, England, c. 1930's, roulette wheel, metal ball	35.00	45.00	39.00
☐ **Rubber Ball Shooting Gallery,** Schoenhut, c. 1910-1915, wood and cardboard covered in lithographed paper, bell rung by clown when shooter makes a direct hit, three additional targets, 16″	360.00	420.00	380.00
☐ **Shoot-A-Loop-Marble Game,** Wolverine	18.00	22.00	20.00
☐ **Spinner,** lithographed box, 7″ x 7″	12.00	18.00	14.00
☐ **Spudsie,** The Ohio Art Company, #514, c. 1960's, plastic, hot potato game, length 7″ .	5.00	10.00	6.00
☐ **Steeple Chase,** Bavaria, dice, marker, grand national, 15″ x 15″	12.00	20.00	13.00
☐ **Table Golf,** The Ohio Art Company, #549, c. 1960's, metal, plastic, felt, putting green, hazards, golfers	15.00	25.00	16.00
☐ **The Spider and The Fly,** Waverly Toy Works, c. 1869, wood, glass cover, picture of spider and web, four felts, 4″ x 4″	12.00	18.00	14.00
☐ **Through The Locks To The Golden Gate,** Milton Bradley, comes with spinners and wooden playing pieces, label pictures Panama Canal and 1915 Expo building	8.00	12.00	9.00

	Current Price Range		Prior Year Average
☐ **Tic Tac Toe,** The Ohio Art Company, #528, c. 1960's, plastic, marbles	5.00	10.00	6.00
☐ **Tiddly Winks,** Milton Bradley, box 4″ x 5½″ .	12.00	18.00	14.00
☐ **Touring,** Parker Brothers	8.00	12.00	10.00
☐ **Toy Soldiers And Battle Game,** Parker Brothers, lithographed paper on box, nine standup paper soldiers, five wooden shells, and a wooden cannon	40.00	50.00	43.00
☐ **U.S. Map Puzzle,** Parker Brothers, c. 1907, wood backed, diecut, 12″ x 20″	45.00	55.00	49.00
☐ **What's The Time,** Parker Brothers, c. 1898, lithographed cover, teaches how to tell time	18.00	22.00	19.00
☐ **When My Ship Comes In,** Parker Brothers, c. 1888	12.00	18.00	14.00

GOLF MEMORABILIA

This section features only a sampling of golf items. In order to accurately present the vast amount of information required by serious collectors, a special edition devoted to sports collectibles is published by The House of Collectibles, Inc. This handy, pocket-size guide, *The Official 1985 Price Guide to Sports Collectibles,* features more than 12,000 prices for a host of sporting collectibles. It is available at bookstores for $3.95.

TYPES: All types of golf memorabilia are collectible, from gloves to bags, balls, clubs and autographs.

COMMENTS: Golf memorabilia collectors are not as large a group as collectors of baseball and football memorabilia. Most collectors seek golf clubs, and as with most collectibles age and rarity account for high prices.

ADDITIONAL TIPS: The listings are alphabetical according to item. For further information, contact the Golf Collectors' Society, 638 Wagner Road, Lafayette Hill, PA 19444.

☐ **Driver,** wooden shaft, c. 1910	142.00	180.00	160.00
☐ **George Low Wizard 600 Putter,** flanged	490.00	720.00	610.00
☐ **Golf Bag,** leather, c. 1930	220.00	265.00	240.00
☐ **Golf Glove,** c. 1910	34.00	42.00	38.00
☐ **MacGregor R. Armour Set,** wood and irons, c. 1950	1070.00	1450.00	1200.00
☐ **Marathon Wards Set,** wood and irons, c. 1922	238.00	312.00	275.00
☐ **Power Build Driver,** c. 1950	120.00	150.00	135.00

	Current Price Range		Prior Year Average
☐ **Putter**, two-way blade with wooden shaft, c. 1920	71.00	85.00	78.00
☐ **Reuter Bull's Eye Putter**	100.00	150.00	125.00
☐ **Score Card**, Master's Tournament	59.00	97.00	78.00
☐ **Golfer's Manual** by H.B. Farnie, c. 1857	625.00	725.00	675.00
☐ **Tommy Armour Wedge**, c. 1959	168.00	212.00	190.00
☐ **Wedge**, Walter Hagen, c. 1930	112.00	137.00	125.00
☐ **Wilson**, Sam Snead set, woods and irons, c. 1940	458.00	542.00	500.00
☐ **Wilson**, R-20 wedge, c. 1930	168.00	212.00	190.00

GRANITEWARE

DESCRIPTION: Metal ware with an enamel coating, Graniteware often has a mottled or marbleized appearance. Most Graniteware is made for use in the kitchen.

Left, ¼ Gallon Milk Container with tin lid and strap handle; **Right, ¼ Gallon Milk Container, $30.00-$40.00**

PERIOD: 1870s to the present.

ORIGIN: First featured in 1876 at the Centennial Exposition in Philadelphia, Graniteware became popular immediately.

COMMENTS: Graniteware was made in large quantities and it's still produced today. There is a fairly consistent demand for the ware, and prices are reasonably stable.

ADDITIONAL TIPS: The listings are in alphabetical order according to item. For further information on Graniteware, refer to *The Official Price Guide to Kitchen and Household Collectibles.*

	Current Price Range		Prior Year Average
☐ **Basting Spoon,** true blue enamelware, pointed bowl, threaded handle	7.00	9.00	8.00
☐ **Bathtub,** for baby, mottled, gray	70.00	80.00	75.00
☐ **Batter Bucket,** tin lid, handle	45.00	58.00	49.00
☐ **Berry Bucket,** small, blue and white marbleized swirls	12.00	18.00	15.00
☐ **Biscuit Pan**	12.00	17.00	13.00
☐ **Bowl and Pitcher,** blue and white streaked, matched set	47.00	58.00	49.00
☐ **Bowl,** mixing, blue and white marbelized . . .	11.00	17.00	12.00
☐ **Bowl,** mixing, grey, 8″ diameter	5.50	9.00	6.00
☐ **Bread Box,** white with blue swirls, circular, hinged lid	47.00	55.00	49.00
☐ **Bread Pan**	12.00	17.00	13.00
☐ **Bucket,** curled rim	15.00	29.00	17.00
☐ **Cake Mold,** twelve sided, tube mold	22.00	36.00	24.00
☐ **Candleholder,** saucer, scalloped edge, curled handle	17.00	30.00	19.00
☐ **Canning Kettle,** six quart size, gray	35.00	38.00	45.00
☐ **Casserole,** grey mottled, dome lid, two quart	24.00	34.00	36.00
☐ **Chamber Pot,** blue and white streaked, cover	30.00	55.00	34.00
☐ **Chamberstick,** white, scalloped base	33.00	37.00	34.00
☐ **Cheese Grater,** white	37.00	50.00	40.00
☐ **Coffee Boiler,** blue and white marbelized, enameled steel, dome lid, eleven quart	40.00	52.00	42.00
☐ **Coffee Boiler,** brown and white marbelized, dome lid, six quart	58.00	70.00	62.00
☐ **Coffee Pot,** black and white mottled, eleven quart, dome lid	26.00	37.00	29.00
☐ **Coffee Pot,** black and white, small	12.00	17.00	13.00
☐ **Colander,** white with black rim, side handles, footed	17.00	27.00	19.00
☐ **Cream Can,** dark grey, ribbed effect, flat lid and bail handle, two quart	32.00	41.00	34.00

	Current Price Range		Prior Year Average
☐ **Dipper,** blue and white Windsor, marbelized with long handle, 5″ diameter	22.00	35.00	24.00
☐ **Dipper,** blue and white mottled, white interior, black rim	15.00	27.00	17.00
☐ **Dishpan,** threaded hole for hanging, 18″ diameter	20.00	24.00	21.00
☐ **Draining Basket,** handle, brown swirls	18.00	25.00	20.00
☐ **Egg Plate,** diameter 8″, red with mottled gray	12.00	18.00	15.00
☐ **Fish boiler,** oval, white and cobalt, end handles, handles on cover	22.00	30.00	24.00
☐ **Flask,** grey ribbed	55.00	65.00	58.00
☐ **Flask,** screw cap	37.00	44.00	38.00
☐ **Foot Tub,** blue and white swirls, round	46.00	56.00	49.00
☐ **Frying Pan,** diameter 9″, marbleized green and white	65.00	67.00	75.00
☐ **Funnel,** blue and white swirls	17.00	30.00	19.00
☐ **Grater,** cheese, steel handles	34.00	45.00	36.00
☐ **Ham Boiler,** blue and white, bail handle, oval, white liner, 19″ x 9″	22.00	30.00	24.00
☐ **Heater,** kerosene, blue and white mottled, bail handle, 20″	48.00	58.00	53.00
☐ **Irrigator,** blue and white mottled, dome shaped	16.00	34.00	20.00
☐ **Kettle,** "Berlin Kettle", wooden finial on lid, bail handle, one quart	11.00	17.00	13.00
☐ **Kettle,** preserving and canning, flared pouring lip, blue and white	17.00	30.00	18.00
☐ **Kitchen Tool Set,** wooden hanger with splatter plate, hooks for assortment of utensils .	58.00	70.00	60.00
☐ **Ladle,** half cup size	8.00	11.00	9.00
☐ **Ladle,** cup size	10.00	15.00	12.00
☐ **Lid Racks,** wood, 3″ long	12.00	24.00	14.00
☐ **Lunch Box,** pewter lid, wood knob, leather latch	32.00	55.00	36.00
☐ **Lunch Box,** wooden latch, bail handle	24.00	34.00	26.00
☐ **Lunch Bucket,** grey and white mottled, black rim, miner's style, 24″ diameter	50.00	60.00	52.00
☐ **Lunch Bucket,** White, tin handle and lid	25.00	35.00	27.00
☐ **Measures,** one-half cup	7.00	13.00	8.00
☐ **Measures,** quart	7.00	15.00	10.00
☐ **Milk Can**	30.00	42.00	32.00
☐ **Miniature,** pie plate, grey and white mottled	25.00	35.00	26.00
☐ **Miniature,** platter, blue and white mottled . .	20.00	34.00	22.00
☐ **Miniature,** skillet, granite, grey	44.00	55.00	46.00
☐ **Miniature,** strainer, triangular	22.00	38.00	25.00
☐ **Mold,** strawberry and grapes	32.00	38.00	32.00

	Current Price Range		Prior Year Average
☐ **Mold,** tube	16.00	22.00	15.00
☐ **Muffin Pan,** eight cup, blue and white	15.00	22.00	15.00
☐ **Muffin Pan,** six cup, grey	23.00	32.00	26.00
☐ **Muffin Tin,** twelve section, scalloped cups .	12.00	20.00	13.50
☐ **Muffin Tin,** white and grey marbleized	52.00	65.00	55.00
☐ **Mug,** marbleized yellow and white	18.00	24.00	19.00
☐ **Napkin Holder,** white, black detail	32.00	42.00	34.00
☐ **Pail,** berry, blue and white mottled, with cover 8″	45.00	55.00	47.00
☐ **Pail,** blue and grey mottled, 7″	24.00	34.00	26.00
☐ **Pail,** blue, bail handle, dome lid, 5″ x 7″	45.00	55.00	47.00
☐ **Pan,** jelly roll, blue and white swirl, 12″ diameter	16.00	26.00	18.00
☐ **Pan,** loaf, grey and white	12.00	18.00	14.00
☐ **Pan,** milk, blue and white marbleized, white liner, 12″	23.00	39.00	26.00
☐ **Percolator,** blue and white marbleized, six cup	26.00	35.00	29.00
☐ **Percolator,** yellow, dome lid	18.00	33.00	20.00
☐ **Picnic Set,** coffee flask	36.00	45.00	39.00
☐ **Pie Pan,** grey and white	12.00	20.00	14.00
☐ **Pie Pan,** shallow, scalloped edge	7.00	14.00	8.00
☐ **Pie Pan,** deep, white interior	8.00	17.00	9.00
☐ **Plate,** diameter 10″, marbleized red and white	20.00	30.00	25.00
☐ **Pots and Pans,** double boilers, true blue ...	20.00	28.00	22.00
☐ **Preserving Kettle,** grey, dome lid	14.00	24.00	16.00
☐ **Roaster,** oval, grey, two handles	16.00	30.00	19.00
☐ **Salt Box,** blue and white swirl, hinged lid ...	46.00	55.00	49.00
☐ **Salt Box,** wooden lid, flared	46.00	59.00	49.00
☐ **Saucepan,** blue and white marbleized, two quarts	35.00	55.00	40.00
☐ **Saucepan,** gray	20.00	34.00	25.00
☐ **Saucepan,** one quart size, flared lip	12.00	20.00	14.00
☐ **Saucer,** dark blue and white marbleized, 5″ .	16.00	26.00	19.00
☐ **Scoop,** candy	40.00	46.00	41.00
☐ **Scoop,** druggist's	56.00	62.00	58.00
☐ **Scoop,** grocer's	28.00	35.00	30.00
☐ **Scoop,** grocery, grey and white	58.00	62.00	60.00
☐ **Scoop,** ice, flared end	16.00	26.00	18.00
☐ **Scoop,** snub handle	5.00	8.00	6.00
☐ **Scoop,** utility	30.00	37.00	32.00
☐ **Serving Dish,** blue-green and white	18.00	25.00	19.00
☐ **Sieve,** grey, round	13.00	22.00	15.00
☐ **Skillet,** large, dark blue and white swirl, 12″ .	50.00	60.00	52.00
☐ **Soap Dish,** white, two piece	19.00	38.00	22.00

	Current Price Range		Prior Year Average
☐ **Soup Strainer**, mottled grey	18.00	24.00	20.00
☐ **Steamer**, insert, grey, 12″	52.00	68.00	55.00
☐ **Stew Pot**, blue and white marbleized, bail handle, wood grip, dome lid	34.00	44.00	37.00
☐ **Stoves**, electric burner	42.00	48.00	44.00
☐ **Stoves**, kerosene	195.00	245.00	210.00
☐ **Sugar Bowl**, grey mottled, black trim, dome lid	184.00	235.00	195.00
☐ **Tea Cup**, grey mottled, 4″ diameter, matching saucer	14.00	18.00	15.00
☐ **Tea Kettle**, "S" curved spout, wood handle, ten quart	30.00	40.00	32.00
☐ **Tea Kettle**, whistler	28.00	46.00	32.00
☐ **Teapot**, blue	78.00	135.00	85.00
☐ **Teapot**, blue and black dome, glass knob, bail handle	147.00	165.00	150.00
☐ **Teapot**, wooden knob, "S" curved spout ...	16.00	34.00	18.00
☐ **Tea Set**, child's white with black trim, flowers in relief, twelve piece	93.00	100.00	95.00
☐ **Tea Strainer**, grey	18.50	32.00	20.00
☐ **Tea Strainer**, white, six cup	20.00	30.00	22.00
☐ **Tray**, diameter 17¾″, blue swirls	40.00	50.00	45.00
☐ **Turner**, long handle, hanging hole	9.00	17.00	11.00
☐ **Wash Basin**, black rimmed basin	13.00	23.00	15.00
☐ **Water Pitcher**, lip guard	14.00	25.00	16.00
☐ **Whiskey Flask**, porcelain stopper, blue	65.00	75.00	70.00

GREETING CARDS

TYPES: All types of greeting cards are collectible. Prices may vary. The first greeting card, a Christmas card, was produced in 1843. However, the tradition of greeting cards didn't take hold until 1860 and the introduction of small visiting greeting cards.

MAKERS: Popular publishers of cards include Marcus Ward & Co., DeLaRue & Co., Raphael Tuck & Co. and L. Prang and Co.

COMMENTS: Greeting cards from the 19th century are the most beautiful and the most sought after. Greeting cards are easy to find and most are reasonably priced.

ADDITIONAL TIPS: The listings are alphabetical accodding to type of greeting. Also see the section in this book on Valentines.

Christmas Advertisement for Raphael Tuck & Sons, $12.00-$16.00

	Current Price Range		Prior Year Average
☐ **Christmas,** "A Merry Christmas and Happy New Year," children playing under Christmas tree, c. 1870's	3.75	6.50	4.50
☐ **Christmas,** "A Merry Christmas to you All," family strolling through snow-blanketed woodland, c. 1880	5.00	8.00	6.00

	Current Price Range		Prior Year Average
☐ **Christmas,** child in 19th century, bonnet . . .	3.00	7.00	4.50
☐ **Christmas,** children and farm scene	3.00	6.00	4.50
☐ **Christmas,** flowers and birds, Merry Christmas and Happy New Year, 4 pages	9.00	20.00	13.00
☐ **Christmas,** Fold out Christmas card, Santa Claus	11.00	16.00	13.00
☐ **Christmas,** Fold out Christmas card, Nativity scene, c. 1820	7.00	12.00	8.00
☐ **Christmas,** "Hail, Day of Joy," card by L. Prang and Co., angel kneeling with dove on finger, c. 1870's	14.00	19.00	15.00
☐ **Christmas,** "Here Comes the New Year with Lots of Good Cheer," child with Christmas tree and toys, c. 1870	10.00	16.00	12.00
☐ **Christmas,** "Here, Open the Door," card by Kate Greenaway, young messenger boy knocking on door, c. 1880	40.00	55.00	43.00
☐ **Christmas,** ice pond, boy putting skates on a girl, fringed and embroidered, German	8.00	12.00	10.00
☐ **Christmas,** "Merry Christmas and Happy New Year," children romping in snow, church in background, c. 1860	3.75	6.00	4.50
☐ **Christmas,** "Merry Christmas to You All," card by L. Prang and Co., brown suited Santa in chimney, square, c. 1880's	21.00	30.00	23.00
☐ **Christmas,** "My Lips May Give a Message," card by Kate Greenaway, young girl holding letter, c. 1880	40.00	55.00	43.00
☐ **Christmas,** Pop up Christmas card, ice skating scene, England, c. 1890	22.00	30.00	25.00
☐ **Christmas,** Prang's American Third Prize Christmas Card, designed by C. C. Coleman, oriental scene	17.00	25.00	20.00
☐ **Christmas,** Victorian Christmas card, paper lace border surrounds season's greeting, c. 1800's	9.00	15.00	12.00
☐ **Christmas,** "Wishing You a Happy New Year," card by L. Prang and Co., folded, young girl on front, old man on back, fringed, tied with tasseled cord, c. 1884	24.00	34.00	27.00
☐ **Christmas,** "Wishing You a Merry Christmas," card by L. Prang and Co., fireplace scene, cat and kittens looking up chimney, square, c. 1880's	21.00	29.00	24.00
☐ **Christmas,** "With Best Christmas Wishes," card by Raphael Tuck and Sons, young girl holding spray of flowers, c. late 1800's	12.00	18.00	15.00

	Current Price Range		Prior Year Average
☐ **Christmas,** "With the Season's Greetings," card by W. S. Coleman, girl on swing (back view), c. 1890	7.00	12.00	9.00
☐ **Easter,** angels on front, by Whitney, New York, 19th century	4.00	6.00	5.00
☐ **Easter,** Bible verses, birds, late 19th century	3.00	6.00	4.50
☐ **Easter,** booklet, poem, cross with flowers, German	2.00	5.90	3.00
☐ **Easter,** child coming out of egg, gold fringed	6.00	10.00	8.00
☐ **Easter,** cross on reef in sea, by Carter and Karrick, 19th century	4.00	8.00	6.00
☐ **Easter,** floral cross on front, German, 19th century	4.50	6.50	5.50
☐ **Easter,** girl climbing out of an egg shelf, fringed German, 19th century	8.50	15.00	12.00
☐ **Easter,** religious, floral, Tuck	10.00	18.00	14.00
☐ **Greetings,** cupid with ribbon holding flowers, 19th century	7.00	15.00	10.00
☐ **Greetings,** heads of children in flower pot, 19th century	1.00	4.00	2.00
☐ **Greetings,** Shakespeare, "Heaven Give You Many Merry Days," 19th century	3.00	6.00	4.00
☐ **Happy Birthday,** blue fringed, floral design, c.1880	15.00	25.00	18.00
☐ **Happy Birthday,** booklet, flowers, 19th century	3.00	6.00	4.00
☐ **Happy Birthday,** children, 19th century	2.00	4.00	3.00
☐ **Happy Birthday,** maroon floral, fringed, 19th century	14.00	20.00	16.00
☐ **Happy Birthday,** maroon fringed, flowers	8.00	12.00	10.00
☐ **New Year,** girl holding bird under palm tree, 19th century	3.00	6.00	4.00
☐ **Religious,** blue fringed, 19th century	3.00	6.00	4.00
☐ **Religious,** eggs and feathers, c.1880	7.00	12.00	9.00
☐ **Religious,** embossed card, "I Go to Prepare A Place for You"	1.00	2.00	1.50
☐ **Religious,** Welcome to Happy Morn, 19th century	4.50	6.50	5.50
☐ **Season's Greetings,** card shaped like fan	2.50	5.00	3.50
☐ **Season's Greetings,** mechanical, boy with flowers, 19th century	15.00	25.00	20.00
☐ **Season's Greetings,** river and small boat, 19th century	4.00	8.00	5.50

HALL CHINA

DESCRIPTION: Hall's best known dinnerwares were in white or cream usually with a gilt border and decorated with soft pastel flowers. This was the standard line which found new customers in each succeeding generation. In addition, it manufactured numerous other styles in creative patterns, including solid-color wares with richly painted decoration.

INNOVATIONS: This giant of the dinnerware industry was noteworthy not only for the volume of its sales and variety of its patterns, but because it produced the first leadless glaze in the trade. This resulted in strong hardpaste wares with non-porous surfaces which required only a single trip through the firing kiln. Not only were labor costs reduced, but the sales impact was enormous. Hall could authentically claim it was manufacturing chinaware by the same process used in China centuries earlier. The ancient Oriental potters fired their wares only once.

MARKS: There are numerous marks and variations of them, sometimes accompanied by trade names applying to the different lines. The earlier markings were very simple compared to those of later eras, usually consisting of nothing more than the words *HALL'S CHINA* arranged in a plain circular frame, containing a mold or pattern number at the center. This was sometimes accompanied by *MADE IN U.S.A.* directly beneath the stamp. Later, the name Hall was placed in a rectangular frame with wider border, with a small R in a circle beneath it (signifying registration as a trademark). A more eleborate marking reads *HALL'S SUPERIOR QUALITY KITCHENWARE* in a rectangular frame with bars above and beneath. There are also many retailers' marks to be encountered on the Hall products.

RECOMMENDED READING: For more in-depth information on Hall China you may refer to *The Official Price Guide to Pottery and Porcelain* and *The Official Identification Guide to Pottery and Porcelain,* published by The House of Collectibles.

AUTUMN LEAF (Introduced 1933)

Hall produced this pattern for the Jewel Tea company.

	Current Price Range		Prior Year Averages
☐ Baker, 9½ "	14.00	16.00	15.00
☐ Bowl, 3½ "	4.00	6.00	5.00
☐ Bowl, 5 "	5.00	8.00	6.50
☐ Bowl Set, 6 ", 7½ " 9¼ ", mixing	30.00	34.00	32.00
☐ Bowl, 6½ "	8.00	10.00	9.00

	Current Price Range		Prior Year Average
☐ **Bowl,** 8″	10.00	12.00	11.00
☐ **Casserole,** covered, round	24.00	27.00	25.50
☐ **Casserole Set,** covered, three pieces	55.00	60.00	57.50
☐ **Coffeepot,** covered, metal insert	37.00	40.00	38.50
☐ **Cookie Jar,** covered, c. 1936-39	70.00	75.00	72.50
☐ **Creamer,** ruffled	10.00	12.00	11.00
☐ **Creamer And Sugar,** covered sugar, pair ...	22.00	26.00	24.00
☐ **Cup And Saucer,** pair	6.00	8.00	7.00
☐ **Custard Cups,** set of six	30.00	34.00	32.00
☐ **Dish,** 7½″, swil design	6.00	8.00	7.00
☐ **Dish,** covered	95.00	105.00	100.00
☐ **Dish,** gravy	10.00	12.00	11.00
☐ **Dish,** pickle	12.00	15.00	13.50
☐ **Dish,** with lid	24.00	28.00	26.00
☐ **Jar,** cover and underplate, three piece set ..	50.00	58.00	54.00
☐ **Pitcher,** 6″	15.00	20.00	17.50
☐ **Pitcher,** ice lip	27.00	33.00	30.00
☐ **Plate,** 6″	3.00	6.00	4.50
☐ **Plate,** 7″	5.00	7.00	6.00
☐ **Plate,** 8″	6.00	8.00	7.00
☐ **Plate,** 9″	7.00	9.00	8.00
☐ **Plate,** 9½″	6.00	8.00	7.00
☐ **Plate,** 10″	10.00	12.00	11.00
☐ **Plate,** 13″, oval	13.00	16.00	14.50
☐ **Salad Bowl,** c. 1937	12.00	15.00	13.50
☐ **Saucer**	2.00	4.00	3.00
☐ **Sauce,** 5½″	5.00	6.00	5.50
☐ **Shakers,** salt and pepper, pair, c.1933	32.00	35.00	33.50
☐ **Stove Set,** 4 pieces	28.00	32.00	30.00
☐ **Sugar**	4.00	6.00	5.00
☐ **Teapot,** covered	50.00	58.00	54.00
☐ **Vegetable Dish,** covered	30.00	35.00	32.50
☐ **Vegetable Dish,** 10½″, oval, open	13.00	16.00	14.50

MISCELLANEOUS

☐ **Bowl,** 5½″, red outside, white inside	5.00	8.00	6.50
☐ **Coffeepot,** large, red	18.00	22.00	20.00
☐ **Coffeepot,** red flamingo design	12.00	14.00	13.00
☐ **Coffeepot,** white porcelain, floral decals, lid and basket	15.00	18.00	16.50
☐ **Cookie Jar,** daffodil with gold	25.00	30.00	27.50
☐ **Cookie Jar,** white with gold	28.00	33.00	30.00
☐ **Creamer,** 4″, light green	7.00	10.00	8.50
☐ **Jug,** handled	25.00	30.00	27.50
☐ **Jug,** powder blue	10.00	14.00	12.00

	Current Price Range		Prior Year Average
☐ **Jug**, turquoise	25.00	30.00	27.50
☐ **Pitcher**, 8″, covered, blue, no mark	15.00	18.00	16.50
☐ **Shakers**, round	25.00	30.00	27.50
☐ **Shakers**, 5″, salt and pepper, no mark	5.00	7.00	6.00
☐ **Sugar**, 4″, covered, light green	7.00	10.00	8.50
☐ **Teapot**, red, bulbous body	14.00	16.00	15.00
☐ **Teapot**, with lid, high gloss dark green	6.00	8.00	7.00
☐ **Teapot**, 3¾″, with lid, high gloss yellow	6.00	8.00	7.00
☐ **Tile**, 6″, light green	4.00	6.00	5.00
☐ **Vase**, 6″, blue	5.00	8.00	6.50

HANDGUNS

In order to accurately present the vast amount of information required by serious collectors, a special edition devoted to firearms is published by The House of Collectibles, Inc. This handy, pocket-size guide, *The Official 1985 Price Guide to Collector Guns*, features prices and data on model names, barrel lengths, calibers and sight types. It is available at bookstores for $3.95. For more extensive information refer to *The Official 1985 Price Guide to Antique and Modern Firearms*, or *The Official 1985 Price Guide to Collector Handguns*. Each guide is $10.95.

HARLEQUIN WARE

ORIGIN: Harlequin tableware was introduced by the Homer Laughlin Pottery Company in 1938 and continued to be produced until 1964.

DESCRIPTION: The Harlequin wares are similar to Fiesta, having bright colors and simple shapes. They have an Art Deco flair with the same series of rings, but they are not on the rim. Instead, they appear farther into the center after a thin band with no design.

COLORS: The colors used on Harlequin are tangerine, salmon, forest green, medium green, light green, chartreuse, Harlequin yellow, gray, turquoise, mauve blue, maroon and spruce green.

MARKS: Harlequin was not marked.

RECOMMENDED READING: For more in-depth information on Harlequin tableware you may refer to *The Official Price Guide to Pottery and Porcelain* and *The Official Identification Guide to Pottery and Porcelain*, published by The House of Collectibles.

	Current Price Range		Prior Year Average
☐ **Ashtray,** with three impressions	17.00	22.00	19.50
☐ **Baker,** 9″, oval, with lid and pointed handles	5.00	8.00	6.50
☐ **Bowl,** fruit, 5½″, flared rim	3.00	5.00	4.00
☐ **Bowl,** salad, 7″, shallow, no rings	6.00	8.00	7.00
☐ **Butter Dish,** with cover	27.00	32.00	29.50
☐ **Candleholder,** inkwell shape, with three level base, pair	32.00	37.00	34.50
☐ **Casserole,** with lid	18.00	24.00	21.00
☐ **Creamer,** inverted dome shape, with pointed handles	4.00	6.00	5.00
☐ **Creamer,** inverted dome shape, with high lip, with pointed handles	16.00	22.00	19.00
☐ **Cup,** coffee, with pointed handle	8.00	11.00	9.50
☐ **Cup,** cream soup, with two pointed handles	5.00	8.00	6.50
☐ **Egg Cup,** on pedestal base	11.00	14.00	12.50
☐ **Egg Cup,** double, on round pedestal base ..	5.00	8.00	6.50
☐ **Jug,** 22 ounce, cylindrical, with pointed handle	11.00	14.00	12.50
☐ **Jug,** water, spherical, with handle	11.00	14.00	12.50
☐ **Nappy,** 9″, flared rim	5.00	8.00	6.50
☐ **Pitcher,** syrup, with twist-on lid, and slide back release	52.00	62.00	57.00
☐ **Plate,** 6″, recessed center	1.25	2.50	2.00
☐ **Plate,** 7″, recessed center	1.50	2.75	2.00
☐ **Plate,** 9″, recessed center	3.00	4.00	3.50
☐ **Plate,** 10″, recessed center	4.00	5.00	4.50
☐ **Platter,** 11″, oval, recessed center	4.50	8.00	5.25
☐ **Platter,** 13″, oval, recessed center	4.50	8.00	5.25
☐ **Salt And Pepper Shakers,** inverted dome shape, on small pedestal base	6.00	8.00	7.00
☐ **Sauceboat,** oblong, squared, with handle ..	6.00	8.00	7.00
☐ **Saucer,** with recessed ring for cup	1.25	2.00	1.75
☐ **Sugar Bowl,** inverted dome shape, with lid, with pointed handles	5.00	8.00	6.50
☐ **Tea Cup,** inverted dome shape, with pointed handles	4.00	6.00	5.00
☐ **Teapot,** inverted dome shape, with pointed handles	13.00	17.00	15.00
☐ **Tumbler,** water, cylindrical	11.00	14.00	12.50

HARMONICAS

DESCRIPTION: A harmonica is a rectangular instrument with air slots. Musical tones are produced by blowing air into the slots.

PERIOD: Harmonicas were first produced in the 1800s.

COMMENTS: Material, maker and rarity play important roles in determining the value of a harmonica.

Harmonica, *Germany, 4½", 1800s,* **$35.00-$45.00**
(photo courtesy of ©The Metropolitan Museum of Art, The Crosby Brown Collection of Musical Instruments, 1889)

	Current Price Range		Prior Year Average
☐ **Angel's Clarion,** made by Weiss, 28 holes, brass reed plates, c. 1900	35.00	50.00	42.00
☐ **"Baseball Club Band Mouth Organ,"** 32 bell metal reeds, two sound horns, 1920s	10.00	15.00	12.50
☐ **Bell Harmonica (Richter),** 10 single holes, brass reed plates, German silver covers, extended ends, one bell	30.00	40.00	35.00
☐ **As Above,** with two bells	35.00	45.00	40.00
☐ **Bohm's Professional Harmonica,** 10 single holes, 20 brass reeds, 1890s	25.00	35.00	30.00
☐ **Bohm's Jubilee Harmonica,** 10 single holes, 20 brass reeds, brass reed plates, c. 1900 . . .	20.00	25.00	22.50
☐ **Bohm's Sovereign,** 5½" x 1½", 16 double holes, 32 steel reeds, nickel covers	20.00	25.00	22.50
☐ **The Brass Band Clarion,** by Weiss, 10 single holes, 20 reeds, c. 1900	25.00	35.00	30.00

	Current Price Range		Prior Year Average

☐ **Columbian Exhibition Harmonica,** 10 single holes, nickel reed plates and covers, bronzed wood 60.00 80.00 70.00

☐ **Concert Harmonica,** two bells, 10 double holes with 40 reeds, brass reed plates, engraved German silver covers 45.00 60.00 52.00

☐ **Doerfel's International,** made of celluloid, 10 double holes, 40 reeds, brass reed plates ... 50.00 65.00 57.00

☐ **Doerfel's New Best-Quality Harmonika,** 48 steel and bronze reeds, brass reed plates, in original box -........................ 11.00 15.00 13.00

☐ **Doerfel's Patent Universal Harp,** made of celluloid, 10 single holes, 20 reeds, brass reed plates, one of the earliest celluloid harmonicas, 1890s 40.00 50.00 45.00

☐ **Duss Band Harmonica,** 14 double holes, 28 metal reeds set on brass plates, nickel covers, 4¾", 1920s 15.00 20.00 17.50

☐ **Duss Band Tremelo,** three-in-one harmonica, each tuned to a different key, 32 double holes, 96 reeds, brass reed plates, nickel covers, 8¾", post-World War I 20.00 25.00 22.50

☐ **Duss Full Concert Harmonica,** 10 single holes, 40 reeds on brass plates, nickel covers, 4½" 10.00 15.00 12.50

☐ **Carl Essbach's French Harp #44,** 10 single holes, 20 German silver reeds, brass reed plates, nickel covers 14.00 20.00 17.00

☐ **European Brass Band Harmonica,** 10 double holes, 40 reeds, brass reed plates 40.00 50.00 45.00

☐ **European,** 10 single holes, white metal reed plates with steel reeds, 1890s 20.00 25.00 22.50

☐ **High Art,** 16 double holes, 32 reeds, brass plates, curved mouthpiece, nickel covers, 4" 10.00 15.00 12.50

☐ **Hohner Auto Harmonica,** shaped like auto, 14 double holes, 28 reeds, metal cover 25.00 35.00 30.00

☐ **Hohner Concert Harmonica,** marked "Ulm 1871-Philadelphia 1873," 20 double holes, 80 reeds, brass reed plates, nickel covers, 1890s 20.00 300.00 250.00

☐ **Hohner Double Side Harmonica,** 64 reeds, brass plates, steel covers, nickel-plated, 1920s 25.00 35.00 30.00

☐ **Hohner "Grand Auditorium,"** 16 double holes, 32 reeds, brass reed plates, nickel covers 130.00 200.00 165.00

☐ **M. Hohner Harmonica,** 10 single holes, brass reed plates, c. 1900 .... 20.00 30.00 25.00

	Current Price Range		Prior Year Average
☐ Hohner Harmonica, 20 double holes, 80 reeds, brass reed plates, nickel covers, c. 1900	70.00	90.00	80.00
☐ Hohner, harp shaped, 14 double holes, 28 tremolo reeds, brass plates, nickel-plated covers, 4⅝"	20.00	30.00	25.00
☐ M. Hohner's Newest And Best Full Concert Harmonica, 10 double holes, 40 reeds, brass reed plates, nickel covers	45.00	60.00	52.00
☐ Hohner, 10 double holes, 40 reeds, brass reed plates, nickel covers	70.00	90.00	80.00
☐ "The Improved Emmet," 10 single holes, brass reed plates, nickel-plated covers, 1890s	35.00	45.00	40.00
☐ Ludwig Harmonica, double sided with 10 holes and 20 reeds on each side, 1890s	55.00	75.00	65.00
☐ Ludwig Harmonica, Richter Pattern, 10 single holes, 20 reeds, 1890s	30.00	40.00	35.00
☐ Ludwig Harmonica, 20 double holes, 40 brass reeds, heavy brass reed plates and nickel covers, c. 1900	65.00	85.00	75.00
☐ Gebruder Ludwig's "Professional Concert Mouth Organ," 10 double holes, 40 reeds, brass reed plates, German silver covers	60.00	80.00	70.00
☐ "The New Troubador," 20 single holes, ten on each side, c. 1897	25.00	35.00	30.00
☐ "The Prairie Queen," 10 single holes, steel and bronze reeds, nickel-plated reed plates and covers	40.00	60.00	50.00
☐ "The Quadruple Reed Mouth Organ," 160 reeds, insscribed "House Music, Best Harp for Artists from Ocean to Ocean," 7¼"	15.00	20.00	17.50
☐ "Radio Band" Harmonica, two sets of reeds, pitched in different keys, in the original box, 1920s	10.00	15.00	12.50
☐ "Radio Band Jazz Mouth Organ," novelty harmonica in shape of flashlight with horn at end, sold in U.S. 11", 1929	15.00	20.00	17.50
☐ "Reveille Mouth Organ," nickel-plated covers, c. 1925	6.00	8.00	7.00
☐ Richter "C," 10 single holes, brass reed plates, nickel covers	14.00	20.00	17.00
☐ "The Silver-Tongued Richter," 10 double holes, brass reed plates, nickel covers	42.00	60.00	51.00
☐ Sousa's Band Harmonica, 10 single holes, 20 brass reeds, 4", c. 1900	25.00	35.00	30.00

	Current Price Range		Prior Year Average
☐ **Sousa Band Harmonica,** 20 holes, 40 brass reeds, 4¾", c. 1900	35.00	50.00	42.00
☐ **"World's Fame,"** 10 single holes, 20 reeds, brass plates, nickel covers, 4"	5.00	10.00	7.50

HUMMELS

In order to accurately present the vast amount of information required by serious collectors, a special edition devoted to Hummels is published by The House of Collectibles, Inc. This handy, pocket-size quide, *The Official Price Guide to Hummels,* features more than 2,000 current collector prices for Hummels. It is available at bookstores for $3.95. For more extensive information refer to *The Official Price Guide to Hummel Figurines and Plates.* This guide costs $9.95 and features more than 18,000 prices.

INKWELLS AND INKSTANDS

TOPIC: Inkwells are containers for holding ink. They were used in the days before pens had their own ink supply. An inkstand is composed of two or more inkwells and a tray. Other accessories are often included.

PERIOD: Most of the collectible inkwells and inkstands will date from the 1800s and early 1900s.

ORIGIN: These items have been in use for over 4,500 years.

MATERIAL: Glass is the most common material for collectible inkwells and inkstands. Other popular materials include stone, metal, wood, pottery and porcelain.

COMMENTS: Many collectors focus on glass inkwells and inkstands. The variety and beauty of these pieces make them wonderful collectibles.

ADDITIONAL TIPS: It is rare to find an inkwell with an intact separate glass cover. These pieces are valuable. Inkstands with numerous accessories in good condition are worth the most.

INKWELLS

☐ **Brass,** Art Deco, glass insert	45.00	55.00	50.00
☐ **Brass,** crab, glass insert, hinged lid	85.00	105.00	95.00

	Current Price Range		Prior Year Average
☐ **Brass,** cups on brass, tray, 6" x 9", c. 1900s .	225.00	275.00	250.00
☐ **Brass,** devil, German, c. 1900	80.00	98.00	89.00
☐ **Brass,** horse, two milk glass inserts, 5½" x 9½"	115.00	135.00	125.00
☐ **Brass,** scrollwork, porcelain insert, square .	80.00	98.00	89.00
☐ **Brass,** shape of kettle, Japanese, 2½", 1800s	230.00	260.00	245.00
☐ **Brass,** Victorian, two glass inserts	80.00	100.00	90.00
☐ **Bronze,** Art Deco, glass insert, silver inlay .	80.00	100.00	90.00
☐ **Bronze,** Art Nouveau, ornate sailing vessel .	140.00	160.00	150.00
☐ **Bronze,** Art Nouveau, woman's head with flowing hair for lid	130.00	170.00	150.00
☐ **Bronze,** clay pot of natural flowers	140.00	170.00	155.00
☐ **Cast Iron,** car, two glass inserts, 5½" x 10" .	150.00	180.00	165.00
☐ **Cast Iron,** cat's head, 4", c. 1800s	225.00	275.00	250.00
☐ **Cast Iron,** globe, Columbian Exposition	60.00	80.00	70.00
☐ **Cloisonne,** stone wall and tray, 7", c. 1900s .	110.00	130.00	120.00
☐ **Delft,** lion, Germany, 7½" x 9"	170.00	190.00	180.00
☐ **Delft,** windmill, Germany, 3" x 3½", c. 1800s	100.00	130.00	115.00
☐ **Glass,** cut, eagle finial on brass lid, c. 1800s	160.00	210.00	185.00
☐ **Glass,** cut, hinged crystal lid	100.00	126.00	113.00
☐ **Glass,** cut, sterling silver lid, 2"	100.00	130.00	115.00
☐ **Glass,** pressed, chair with cat on cushion, 4", c. 1800s	150.00	190.00	170.00
☐ **Glass,** blue, hinged brass lid, 2½"	160.00	180.00	170.00
☐ **Glass,** sterling silver overlay	100.00	120.00	110.00
☐ **Glass,** umbrella shape, c. 1800s	225.00	275.00	250.00
☐ **Glass And Bronze,** Tiffany Favrile, mosaic, height 3", c. 1910	1300.00	1500.00	1400.00
☐ **Glass And Bronze,** Tiffany Favrile, mosaic, iridescent cover, height 4", c. 1910	1100.00	1400.00	1250.00
☐ **Marble,** blue and gray, cherubs, French, 4"	150.00	190.00	170.00
☐ **Metal,** enameled, camel, glass insert, c. 1900s	180.00	240.00	210.00
☐ **Metal,** enameled, camel, glass, insert, c. 1900s	180.00	240.00	210.00
☐ **Metal,** enameled, floral motif, Chinese, c. 1800s	120.00	150.00	135.00
☐ **Metal,** enameled, gold and brass trim, glass inset	60.00	80.00	70.00
☐ **Milk Glass,** cat on iron base, 5"	140.00	160.00	150.00
☐ **Milk Glass,** dogs on iron base, 4"	120.00	140.00	130.00
☐ **Papier Mache,** Japanned, gold figures, black lacquer, length 8½", c. 1800s	80.00	100.00	90.00
☐ **Pewter,** blue pottery insert, 9", c. 1820	160.00	180.00	170.00
☐ **Pewter,** dome rolltop, 5"	80.00	110.00	95.00
☐ **Pewter,** pear with bees on tray, Kayserzinn .	225.00	255.00	240.00

	Current Price Range		Prior Year Average
☐ **Pewter,** round, 6½″	100.00	130.00	115.00
☐ **Porcelain,** Limoges, gilded, floral motif, hinged top	70.00	85.00	77.50
☐ **Porcelain,** boy wearing hat, French, 12″, c. 1880s	150.00	170.00	160.00
☐ **Porcelain,** hinged lid, painted flowers	70.00	100.00	85.00
☐ **Porcelain,** Victorian woman, 4″	60.00	78.00	69.00
☐ **Silver-Plated,** figural, dog's head, hat is ink-well cover	55.00	65.00	60.00
☐ **Silver-Plated,** Tiffany Studios, pine needle design on white glass, 5½″	90.00	100.00	95.00
☐ **Soapstone,** carved dog on stand, Italian, 8″, 1700s	120.00	140.00	130.00
☐ **Stoneware,** dark red glaze, roped edge, four pen holes, signed, 5″	135.00	155.00	145.00
☐ **Stoneware,** round, chiseled edge	50.00	68.00	59.00
☐ **Wood,** carved, Black Forest deer	135.00	155.00	145.00
☐ **Wood,** glass insert, four pen holes, 4″	60.00	80.00	70.00
☐ **Wood,** porcelain insert, 3″	50.00	68.00	59.00

INKSTANDS

	Current Price Range		Prior Year Average
☐ **Brass,** with two milk glass ink bottles, hinged lid, height 2½″	85.00	95.00	90.00
☐ **Bronze,** crab and shell, Tiffany Studios, 7″, c. 1910	2000.00	2500.00	2250.00
☐ **Bronze,** French, gilded, shell boat pulled by swan, oval stand, length 11¼″, c. 1800s . . .	400.00	500.00	450.00
☐ **Iron,** horse, brass cap, 5″	45.00	65.00	55.00
☐ **Silver,** Austrian, oval, pierced, panel feet, beaded rim, length 11⅜″, c. 1795	900.00	1100.00	1000.00
☐ **Silver,** engraved, Paul de Lamerie	5250.00	6250.00	5750.00
☐ **Silver,** George III, rectangular, panel feet, cut-glass receptacles, length 11″, c. 1800 . .	1200.00	1500.00	1350.00
☐ **Silver,** George IV, flowers, oblong, paw feet, c. 1822	4500.00	4800.00	4650.00
☐ **Silver,** Georgian	900.00	1300.00	1100.00
☐ **Wood,** J. R. Chappell, 3¾″	60.00	80.00	70.00

INSULATORS

DESCRIPTION: Insulators are the nonconducting glass figures used to attach electrical wires to poles.

ORIGIN: The first insulator was invented in 1844 for a telegraph line.

COMMENTS: Insulators became collectible after World War II. Old electrical lines with insulators were taken down during the early post war stages of urban development.

Color, age and design determine value. Threadless insulators are older, more rare and usually more valuable than threaded ones.

Clear glass is most common. Colors, including green, milk white, amber, amethyst and cobalt blue are more valuable.

ADDITIONAL TIPS: The listings are alphabetical according to manufacturer. Other information including color and size is also included.

	Current Price Range		Prior Year Average
☐ **A.G.M.**, amber, 3¾" x 2¾"	12.00	24.00	18.00
☐ **A.T.& T. Co.**, aqua, single skirt, 2⅛" x 3¾", c. 1900	7.00	12.00	9.00
☐ **A.T.& T. Co.**, aqua, 3⅜"	7.00	12.00	9.00
☐ **A.T.& T. Co.**, aqua, two-piece, 2¾" x 3⅝"	5.00	8.00	6.50
☐ **A.T.& T. Co.**, green, single skirt, 2½" x 3¾"	5.00	12.00	7.50
☐ **Agee**, clear amethyst, 3⅝" x 2¾"	12.00	16.00	14.00
☐ **American Insulator Co.**, aqua, double petticoat, 4⅛" x 3⅛"	10.00	14.00	12.00
☐ **Armstrong**, amber 4" x 3¼"	10.00	14.00	12.00
☐ **Armstrong**, No. 5, clear, double petticoat, 3⅛" x 3¾"	5.00	8.00	6.50
☐ **A.U. Patent**, green, 4⅜" x 2¾"	29.00	39.00	33.00
☐ **B. & O.**, aqua, 3⅞ x 3¼"	29.00	39.00	34.00
☐ **B.F.G. Co.**, aqua, 4" x 3½"	39.00	49.00	44.00
☐ **B.G.M. Co.**, clear amethyst, 3⅜" x 2¼"	17.00	25.00	21.00
☐ **Barclay**, aqua, double petticoat, 3" x 2¼"	17.00	25.00	21.00
☐ **Boston Bottle Works**, aqua, 4⅛" x 3"	44.00	54.00	48.00
☐ **Brookes, Homer**, aqua, 3¾" x 2¾"	21.00	31.00	26.00
☐ **Brookfield**, No. 36, aqua, green, 3⅞" x 3⅛"	12.00	18.00	15.00
☐ **Brookfield**, No. 45, aqua, green, 4⅛" x 3⅛"	7.00	12.00	9.50
☐ **Brookfield**, No. 55, aqua, green, 4" x 2½"	12.00	18.00	14.00
☐ **Brookfield**, No. 83, aqua, green, 4" x 3⅛"	17.00	25.00	21.00
☐ **Brookfield**, dark olive green, double petticoat, 3¾" x 4"	7.00	12.00	8.50
☐ **Brookfield**, green, double petticoat, $3\frac{5}{16}$" x 3⅝", c. 1865	7.00	12.00	8.50
☐ **B.T. Co. of Canada**, clear, amethyst, 3½" x 2⅛"	15.00	25.00	20.00
☐ **B.T. Co. of Canada**, aqua, green, 3¼" x 2⅜"	12.00	16.00	14.00
☐ **C. & P. Tel Col.**, aqua, green, 3½" x 2⅜"	10.00	14.00	12.00
☐ **C.E.L.**, amethyst, 4⅛" x 2¾"	12.00	16.00	14.00
☐ **C.E.N.**, amethyst, 3¼" x 2½"	34.00	44.00	39.00
☐ **C.G.I.**, clear, amethyst, 3½" x 2⅛"	21.00	27.00	24.00
☐ **Cable**, aqua, green, 4½" x 3¼"	23.00	30.00	26.00

	Current Price Range		Prior Year Average
☐ **California,** aqua, green, 3½″ x 2⅛″	23.00	30.00	26.00
☐ **California,** clear, amethyst, 4⅜″ x 3½″	32.00	40.00	37.00
☐ **California,** clear, amethyst, 4⅛″ x 3¼″	5.00	10.00	7.50
☐ **California,** CK-162, purple, double petticoat, 3¾″ x 4″	7.00	12.00	9.50
☐ **Canadian Pacific,** blue, green, aqua, 3⅝″ x 2¾″	44.00	54.00	49.00
☐ **Canadian Pacific,** clear, amethyst, 3½″ x 2¾″	15.00	20.00	17.00
☐ **Castle,** aqua, 3⅞″ x 2½″	44.00	54.00	49.00
☐ **Chester,** aqua, 4″ x 2⅜″	48.00	58.00	53.00
☐ **Columbia,** aqua, green, 3¾″ x 4″	38.00	48.00	33.00
☐ **Derflinger, T.N.I.,** aqua, green, 4″ x 3½″	17.00	25.00	21.00
☐ **Dominion** No. 9, amber, aqua and clear, 3¾″ x 2½″	3.00	6.00	4.50
☐ **Duquesne,** aqua, green, 3⅜″ x 2⅜″	30.00	40.00	35.00
☐ **Dwight,** aqua, 4″ x 3″	30.00	40.00	35.00
☐ **E.C. & M. Co.,** green, 4″ x 2½″	23.00	30.00	26.50
☐ **Electrical Supply Co.,** aqua, green, 3⅝″ x 2⅝″	30.00	40.00	35.00
☐ **Folembray,** No. 221, olive green, 2⅝″ x 3⅜″	38.00	48.00	43.00
☐ **Gayner,** 36-190, aqua, 3¾″ x 3¼″	10.00	14.00	12.00
☐ **Gayner,** green, double petticoat, 3 3/16″ x 3⅞″	23.00	30.00	27.00
☐ **H.G. Co.,** amber, double petticoat, 3¼″ x 3¾″	12.00	16.00	14.00
☐ **H.G. Co. Petticoat,** aqua, green, 3¾″ x 3¾″	5.00	8.00	6.50
☐ **H.G. Co. Petticoat,** clear, 4⅛″ x 3¼″	10.00	14.00	12.00
☐ **Hawley,** aqua, 3¼″ x 2¼″	15.00	20.00	17.50
☐ **Hemingray,** No. 2 Cable, aqua, green, 4″ x 3⅝″	22.00	30.00	26.50
☐ **Hemingray,** No. 7, aqua, green, 3½″ x 2½″	3.00	6.00	4.50
☐ **Hemingray,** No. 8, aqua, green, 3⅜″ x 2⅜″	14.00	18.00	16.00
☐ **Hemingray,** No. 9, aqua, single skirt, 2¼″ x 3½″	17.00	23.00	20.00
☐ **Hemingray,** No. 10, clear, single skirt, 2⅝″ x 3½″	12.00	16.00	14.00
☐ **Hemingray,** No. 16, green, single skirt, 2⅞″ x 4″	3.00	6.00	4.50
☐ **Hemingray,** No. 19, aqua, double petticoat, 3¼″ x 3″	28.00	38.00	33.00
☐ **Hemingray,** No. 25, aqua, green, 4″ x 3¼″	14.00	20.00	17.00
☐ **Hemingray,** No. 95, aqua, green, 3⅝″ x 2⅞″	34.00	40.00	37.00
☐ **Hemingray Beehive,** green, double petticoat, 3⅛″ x 4⅜″	17.00	23.00	20.00
☐ **Hemingray Petticoat,** cobalt blue, 4″ x 3¼″	30.00	40.00	35.00
☐ **Hemingray Transportation,** green, 4½″ x 3¼″	23.00	30.00	26.00

	Current Price Range		Prior Year Average
☐ **Jeffery Mfg. Co.,** aqua, 3⅝" x 2¾"	30.00	40.00	35.00
☐ **Jumbo,** aqua, 7¼" x 5¼"	21.00	27.00	25.00
☐ **Knowles Cable,** aqua, green, 4" x 3⅝"	32.00	40.00	36.00
☐ **Fred M. Locke,** No. 14, aqua, 4⅜" x 3⅛"	21.00	27.00	24.00
☐ **Fred M. Locke,** No. 21, aqua, green, 4" x 4"	5.00	8.00	6.50
☐ **Lynchburg,** No. 10, aqua, green, 3⅜" x 2¼"	7.00	14.00	10.50
☐ **Lynchburg,** No. 31, aqua, green, 3½" x 2⅜"	7.00	12.00	9.50
☐ **Lynchburg,** No. 44, aqua, single skirt, 2¼" x 3⅝"	10.00	14.00	12.00
☐ **Lynchburg,** No. 44, 4" x 3⅝"	5.00	8.00	6.50
☐ **Maydwell** No. 9, clear, aqua, 3⅝" x 2⅛"	5.00	8.00	6.50
☐ **Maydwell,** No. 9, clear, single skirt, 2⅛" x 3½"	5.00	8.00	6.50
☐ **Maydwell,** No. 16, amber, 3⅞" x 2¾"	5.00	8.00	6.50
☐ **Maydwell,** No. 20, white milk glass, 3⅝" x 3⅛"	21.00	27.00	24.00
☐ **McLaughlin,** No. 9, green, single skirt, 2¼" x 3⅝"	12.00	16.00	14.00
☐ **McLaughlin,** No. 16, amber, aqua, green, 3⅝" x 2⅝"	5.00	10.00	7.50
☐ **McLaughlin,** No. 19, aqua, 3¾" x 3¼"	3.00	6.00	4.50
☐ **McLaughlin,** No. 42, aqua, 4" x 3⅝"	5.00	10.00	7.50
☐ **McLaughlin,** No. 62, aqua, 3⅝" x 3⅝"	7.00	11.00	9.00
☐ **Mershon,** aqua, 5" x 5½"	31.00	38.00	34.50
☐ **Monogram H.I. Co.,** aqua, 4½" x 3⅛"	21.00	27.00	24.00
☐ **Mulford & Biddle,** aqua, 3¼" x 2⅝"	34.00	40.00	37.00
☐ **N.E.G.M. Co.,** aqua, green, 3½" x 2⅛"	14.00	18.00	16.00
☐ **N.E.G.M. Co.,** aqua, 3½" x 3¼"	17.00	23.00	20.00
☐ **N.E.T. & T. Co.,** aqua, green, 3⅝" x 2⅜"	5.00	8.00	6.50
☐ **N.E.T. & T. Co.,** blue, 3½" x 3"	12.00	16.00	14.00
☐ **Noleak,** aqua, green, 4" x 4"	31.00	36.00	33.00
☐ **O.V.G. Co.,** aqua, 3½" x 2¼"	7.00	12.00	10.00
☐ **O.V.G. Co.,** aqua, green, 3½" x 2¼"	12.00	16.00	14.00
☐ **Pettingel Anderson Co.,** aqua, 4" x 2¾"	17.00	23.00	20.00
☐ **Pony,** blue, 3⅛" x 2⅜"	21.00	27.00	24.00
☐ **Postal,** aqua, green, 4⅛" x 3½"	15.00	18.00	16.50
☐ **Pyrex,** carnival glass, 3⅛" x 3¾"	17.00	23.00	20.00
☐ **Pyrex,** carnival glass, 3" x 3¾"	12.00	16.00	14.00
☐ **Pyrex,** double threads, carnival glass, 2⅝" x 4¼"	14.00	18.00	16.00
☐ **S.B.T. & T. Co.,** aqua, green, 3½" x 2¼"	14.00	18.00	16.00
☐ **Santa Ana,** aqua, green, 4¼" x 4¾"	28.00	35.00	31.50
☐ **Standard,** clear, amethyst, 3⅝" x 2¾"	12.00	16.00	14.00
☐ **Star,** aqua, single skirt, pony, 2⅜" x 3½"	7.00	10.00	8.50
☐ **Sterling,** aqua, 3¼" x 2¼"	14.00	18.00	16.00
☐ **T.C.R.,** aqua, 4" x 3¾"	12.00	16.00	14.00
☐ **T.H.E. Co.,** aqua, 4" x 3⅛"	29.00	35.00	32.00

	Current Price Range		Prior Year Average
☐ **Thomas,** brown pottery, 2½" x 1⅛"	5.00	10.00	7.50
☐ **Transportation,** No. 2, aqua, 4¼" x 2⅞"	21.00	27.00	24.00
☐ **U.S. Tel. Co.,** aqua, 3¾" x 2⅝"	14.00	18.00	16.00
☐ **V.M.R. Napoli,** aqua, green, 4" x 2¾"	12.00	16.00	14.00
☐ **W.F.G. Co.,** clear, amethyst, 3½" x 2⅛"	14.00	18.00	16.00
☐ **W.G.M. Co.,** clear, amethyst, 3½" x 2¼"	23.00	30.00	26.00
☐ **W.G.M. Co.,** clear, amethyst, 3⅞" x 3⅛"	17.00	23.00	20.00
☐ **W.V.,** No. 5, aqua, 4¼" x 2¾"	17.00	23.00	20.00
☐ **Westinghouse,** aqua, green, 3⅛" x 2⅝"	27.00	33.00	30.00
☐ **Whitall Tatum,** amber, 3⅞" x 3¼"	12.00	16.00	14.00
☐ **Whitall Tatum,** 512-A, amber, red, 3½" x 3⅝"	5.00	10.00	7.50

IRONS

TYPES: Various types of collectible irons include: the charcoal iron; the box iron which featured a heated metal slug placed inside the hollow iron; and the sadiron, a solid iron that was heated on the hearth or stove. In 1871 Mary Potts invented a detachable handle for the sadiron. The Potts iron led to self-heating irons fueled with gasoline or cooking gas. These were dangerous and unsatisfactory. The electric iron was patented in 1882.

ORIGIN: Irons were used in Asia for centuries before their 17th century Western introduction.

COMMENTS: Collectible irons are still reasonably priced. Collectors should seek odd shaped irons.

ADDITIONAL TIPS: The listings are alphabetical according to type of iron.

☐ **Alcohol Iron,** wooden handle, c. 1880	65.00	80.00	70.00
☐ **Box Iron,** heated slug, c. 1890	45.00	65.00	53.00
☐ **Box Iron,** English, heated slugs, c. 1800	82.00	125.00	90.00
☐ **Box Iron,** solid brass, punch decoration on top surface, height 5" x 4½"	105.00	117.00	110.00
☐ **Charcoal Iron,** brass fittings, chimney vent	70.00	90.00	75.00
☐ **Charcoal Iron,** twisted handle, chimney vent	75.00	90.00	78.00
☐ **Charcoal Iron,** wooden handle	42.00	50.00	45.00
☐ **Charcoal Iron,** wooden handle, c. 1890	45.00	60.00	48.00
☐ **Charcoal Iron,** wooden iron, with trivet	65.00	80.00	69.00
☐ **Flat Iron,** all iron	6.00	7.50	6.50
☐ **Flat Iron,** bail handle	8.00	12.00	10.00
☐ **Flat Iron,** charcoal, chimney vent, c. 1860	29.00	40.00	33.00
☐ **Flat Iron,** hollow handle	29.00	40.00	33.00

	Current Price Range		Prior Year Average
□ Flat Iron, no handle, asbestos	4.00	6.00	5.00
□ Flat Iron, no handle, Blass and Drake, Newark, New Jersey, height 6″	4.00	6.00	5.00
□ Flat Iron, red, small, c. 1877	45.00	50.00	47.00
□ Flat Iron, removable handle, c. 1870	29.00	38.00	32.00
□ Flat Iron, rope handle	28.00	35.00	30.00
□ Flat Iron, stone body, metal handle, c. 1850 .	45.00	60.00	50.00
□ Flat Iron, wooden handle, child's, c. 1860 ...	29.00	40.00	33.00
□ Flat Iron, wooden handle, large	34.00	45.00	36.00
□ Fluting Iron, brass rollers, with black enamel and red and gold stripes, two slugs, height 9″	85.00	95.00	89.00
□ Fluting Iron, double, with holder	65.00	80.00	68.00
□ Fluting Iron, Geneva, c. 1870s	50.00	65.00	57.00
□ Gasoline Iron, Coleman	28.00	38.00	30.00
□ Gasoline Iron, wooden handle, c. 1910	55.00	70.00	58.00
□ G.E. Electric Iron, c. 1905	39.00	50.00	42.00
□ G.E. Electric Iron, c. 1920	34.00	45.00	37.00
□ Iron, for a child, glass base, wooden handle	4.75	6.25	5.50
□ Laundry Stove, cast iron, double burner	170.00	220.00	190.00
□ Laundry Stove, cast iron, single burner	120.00	180.00	135.00
□ Laundry Stove, fancy cast iron, c. 1895	500.00	600.00	520.00
□ Nickel Plated Iron	24.00	37.00	27.00
□ Polishing Iron, oval shaped, c. 1845	48.00	58.00	52.00
□ Sadiron, alcohol iron, nickel plated, black wooden handle, Foote Manufacturing Co., Dayton, Ohio	47.00	55.00	50.00
□ Sadiron, for child, removable wooden handle, 2″ x 4″	40.00	52.00	45.00
□ Sadiron, waffle pattern on bottom, "Genoa"	30.00	37.00	33.00
□ Tailor's Iron	34.00	45.00	37.00
□ Travel Iron, asbestos	29.00	40.00	33.00

IRONWARE

DESCRIPTION: Nineteenth century kitchenware and other household items were often made of iron because of its durability.

COMMENTS: Ironware usually can be found for fairly low prices. Marked prices are of greater value and importance. Dates on ironware do not always stand for the year made, some dates stand for the year the patent was issued.

Oiling or polishing old ironware decreases its value.

ADDITIONAL TIPS: The listings are alphabetical according to item.
For further information, refer to *The Official 1984 Guide to Kitchen Collectibles,* published by The House of Collectibles.

	Current Price Range		Prior Year Average
☐ **Apple Parer,** cast, clamp-on type, pares, marked "Simplex"	25.00	40.00	30.00
☐ **Apple Parer,** cores and slices, marked "Vermont Apple Parer"	21.00	29.00	23.00
☐ **Apple Segmenter,** bolt type, cast iron, patented 1809	23.00	35.00	27.00
☐ **Ashtray,** round, "Griswold"	18.00	24.00	20.00
☐ **Basket,** a 20th century, iron grate, 20″ x 10″ x 14″	120.00	180.00	126.00
☐ **Bean Slicer,** German	15.00	25.00	20.00
☐ **Bread Pan,** hinged cover, black, c. 1890	15.00	25.00	20.00
☐ **Broiler,** also called gridiron or hearth broiler, hand wrought, 13″ diameter, 4 legs, revolving	68.00	80.00	72.00
☐ **Butter Tester,** narrow borer for testing butter and cheese, 15″ x 18″	9.00	18.00	12.00
☐ **Can Opener,** bull's head and tail	20.00	30.00	25.00
☐ **Candle Snuffer,** footed	20.00	30.00	24.00
☐ **Charcoal Iron,** a mid 19th century, 7″ high	126.00	190.00	132.00
☐ **Cheese Cutter,** iron on round wood base, counter used	100.00	125.00	105.00
☐ **Cherry Pitter,** c. 1880	18.00	28.00	22.00
☐ **Cherry Pitter,** on wooden board	10.00	16.00	13.00
☐ **Cherry Pitter,** 3 legs, c. 1860	40.00	60.00	50.00
☐ **Cherry Pitter,** enterprise 1870, iron, 4 spider legs with bolts	42.00	55.00	43.00
☐ **Cherry Seeder,** also called cherry stoner, table model type	26.00	55.00	32.00
☐ **Chopper,** Blacksmith made, all iron, oblong shape, hanging loop	20.00	35.00	23.00
☐ **Choppers,** early, all iron, hand wrought, crescent-shaped	19.00	35.00	23.00
☐ **Cigar Mold,** 20-cigar size	18.00	24.00	20.00
☐ **Coal Tongs,** for handling hot coals, hand wrought	19.00	40.00	28.00
☐ **Coffee Mill,** iron, wheel turn, c. 1898	26.00	40.00	33.00
☐ **Coffee Roaster,** iron, wood, crank handle	32.00	42.00	35.00
☐ **Corkscrew,** magic patent, c. 1900	42.00	52.00	46.00
☐ **Corn Dryer,** iron branch-like rod for holding ears of corn to dry, handwrought	19.00	40.00	25.00
☐ **Cornstick Pan,** cast iron, 7 sticks with kernels, marked "Krusty Korn Kobs, Wagner ware, patented July 6, 1920"	19.00	40.00	25.00

	Current Price Range		Prior Year Average
☐ **Cornstick Pan,** 7 ears	15.00	25.00	20.00
☐ **Cracker Stamp,** iron, early 19th century	9.00	13.00	10.00
☐ **Cranberry,** picker, tinned handle, 45 teeth, 4½″ x 14½″ x 10″	79.00	100.00	83.00
☐ **Cuspidor,** mechanical, turtle shape, "patented '91"	125.00	250.00	175.00
☐ **Dipper,** applebutter, iron, wood handle, 9″ diameter, 1700s	115.00	140.00	130.00
☐ **Doughbowl,** fine ironstone, 10″ x 14″ diameter	99.00	120.00	103.00
☐ **Dough Scraper,** hoe shaped, for scraping dough from mixing bowl or dough box, all wrought iron	13.00	27.00	15.00
☐ **Dutch Oven,** three legs, bail handle, deep lid for setting coals on top	53.00	65.00	56.00
☐ **Dutch Oven,** with handle and trivet, "Griswold"	30.00	40.00	35.00
☐ **Eggbeater,** 1876 patent	30.00	40.00	35.00
☐ **Eggbeaters,** crank handle, marked "Dover, patented 1878", 10½″ family size	16.00	33.00	19.00
☐ **Egg Boiling Rack,** on stand, c. 1900	20.00	30.00	25.00
☐ **Fish Broiler,** c. 1700s	236.00	255.00	243.00
☐ **Fish Roaster,** 18th century, wrought iron, wood	26.00	36.00	28.00
☐ **Flat Iron Saw Tooth Blade,** with wooden handle	4.00	7.00	5.00
☐ **Flat Iron,** gas, late 19th century, heated by gas jet	16.00	35.00	18.00
☐ **Flat Iron,** gasoline	16.00	32.00	18.00
☐ **Flat Iron,** hand forged, has door for coals, 1700s	89.00	105.00	93.00
☐ **Fork,** lifting plain, 2 tined, 18″ long with hanging hole, hand forged	13.00	27.00	15.00
☐ **Fork,** toasting 2 or 3 tined long handled fork, long, flat prongs, hand wrought	21.00	35.00	23.00
☐ **Fruit Press,** combination fruit, wine and jelly press, heavy iron, clamp-on type, crank handle	19.00	38.00	22.00
☐ **Gophering Iron,** iron poker-like stick with sheath-like holder, footed	110.00	140.00	118.00
☐ **Griddle,** solid oblong piece of wrought or cast iron for grilling food, also called grill, with grease catching trough all around edge and end handles, oblong	21.00	35.00	23.00
☐ **Ice Crusher,** marked "Chandler's Ice Cutting Machine", crank handle, 4 legs	37.00	47.00	40.00

	Current Price Range		Prior Year Average
☐ **Ice Pick**	5.00	12.00	8.00
☐ **Ice Shaver**, rectangular hand shaver, hinged cover with advertising of ice company or iron works	9.00	18.00	11.00
☐ **Ice Tongs**, 22″ long, hand forged	26.00	53.00	28.00
☐ **Kettle**, Gypsy, 3 footed, 1 gallon, bail handle	42.00	53.00	45.00
☐ **Ladle**, hand wrought, 5¼″ bowl, 15″ handle	30.00	40.00	32.00
☐ **Ladle**, soup ladle with twisted shank and hanging loop	30.00	55.00	35.00
☐ **Lemon Squeezer**, hinged cast iron, handle holes for hanging, plain solid cup part, pouring lip	11.00	17.00	13.00
☐ **Letter Holder**, coiled spring	6.00	12.00	8.00
☐ **Mail Box**, "Griswold"	65.00	80.00	72.00
☐ **Matchholder**, mechanical, cast iron, Phoenix Bird picks up matches with beak	95.00	99.00	115.00
☐ **Meat Chopper**, Russwin No.0, patented 1901-02, crank handle, clamp-on type	13.00	17.00	14.00
☐ **Mortar**, urn shaped, 5½″, with pestle	37.00	52.00	40.00
☐ **Muffin Pan**, 8 oval compartments, c. 1855 ..	20.00	30.00	35.00
☐ **Muffins Pans**, plain nine hole muffin mold, hanging hole, no maker	13.00	27.00	15.00
☐ **Nail Tray**, revolving	50.00	62.00	55.00
☐ **Nutcracker**, crank handle, clamps on table, marked "Home Nut Cracker, St. Louis, U.S.A.", patented August 24, 1915	15.00	30.00	17.00
☐ **Nutmeg Grater**, Victorian, with compartment for spare nutmeg in the handle, 7½″ long ..	21.00	33.00	23.00
☐ **Olive Forks**, 8″ long double tines, open ring end marked "Olive & Pickle Fork"	3.00	6.00	4.00
☐ **Pancake Turner**, opener combo, advertising pat. 1914	9.00	13.00	10.00
☐ **Paperweight**, 2½″ x 4½″	70.00	83.00	75.00
☐ **Paring Knife**, marked "C.W. Dunlap", steel blade, wood handle	3.00	6.00	4.00
☐ **Pea Sheller**, clamp on type	17.00	30.00	20.00
☐ **Pie Crimper**, also called pastry jagger, pie edger, pie cutter, revolving cast iron cutter, wood handle, factory made	10.00	16.00	11.00
☐ **Porringer**, about 5″ diameter, marked with maker's name, double or single eared	80.00	98.00	82.00
☐ **Potato Basket**, potato or vegetable boiler, to set in cookpot in fireplace	27.00	53.00	30.00
☐ **Potato Parer**, cast iron, clamp on type, crank handle, marked "Vermon Potato Parer"	19.00	24.00	21.00
☐ **Potato Ricer**, cast iron frame and handles, tin-plate, strainer	11.00	20.00	14.00

	Current Price Range		Prior Year Average
☐ **Pot Hook,** for lifting pots from fireplace or oven, also called pot lifter, hand wrought, wood handle	13.00	26.00	15.00
☐ **Raisin And Grape Seeder,** clamp on type, made by Enterprise	26.00	38.00	28.00
☐ **Range,** cast iron, finished in blue vitreous enamel, each of the five access doors decorated, 40″ wide	525.00	750.00	600.00
☐ **Range,** cast iron, marked L. Blton Perinster, finished in black-leading and ceramic tiles, Belgian, 35½″ x 31″, c. 1910	630.00	850.00	650.00
☐ **Rug Beater,** many different wire patterns with wood handles	13.00	26.00	15.00
☐ **Rushlight,** English, 18th century, on oak base, 10″ high	315.00	420.00	325.00
☐ **Saratoga Potato Chipper,** clamp on type, crank handle	19.00	25.00	21.00
☐ **Sardine Shears,** narrow, pointed spring action shears, marked "C.W. Dunlap"	9.00	18.00	11.00
☐ **Sausage Stuffer**	60.00	70.00	65.00
☐ **Scales,** brass and cast iron salter, spring balance kitchen, 17″ high, c. 1940	156.00	220.00	160.00
☐ **Scissors,** candlewick, hand wrought	30.00	40.00	35.00
☐ **Skewer Set,** wrought skewer holder with various length skewers	105.00	155.00	110.00
☐ **Skillet,** 3 legs, 12″ handle, for fireplace cookery, also called spider	52.00	65.00	55.00
☐ **Stamp Box,** signed "Simpson Iron Works"	50.00	63.00	55.00
☐ **Stove,** Art Grand, #12, coal heating, round, Utica, New York	326.00	360.00	335.00
☐ **Stove,** Charter Oak #580, cook, missing reservoir	1250.00	1650.00	1350.00
☐ **String Holder,** looks like ball of twine, c. 1860	90.00	110.00	95.00
☐ **Sugar Devil,** iron, to loosen hardened chunks of sugar, brown	84.00	100.00	90.00
☐ **Tea Kettle,** gooseneck spout	40.00	50.00	43.00
☐ **Toaster,** wrought iron, jointed head which flipped to allow toast to be browned on both sides, footed for hearth use	136.00	170.00	145.00
☐ **Tongs,** pair of late 18th century, goffering, 10½″ long	21.00	35.00	24.00
☐ **Trivet,** Mrs. Potts Co. Philadelphia, PA, ftd, for sadiron	15.00	20.00	17.00
☐ **Trivet,** musical lyre, brass and iron, handles and feet	37.00	80.00	40.00
☐ **Turner-Fork,** hand-wrought, fork on one end, flat turner on other, 16″ long	26.00	55.00	28.00

	Current Price Range		Prior Year Average
☐ **Twine Holder,** also called string holder, hanging or sitting holder for ball of twine or string, lacey design	37.00	70.00	39.00
☐ **Wafer Iron,** oval or round, 6″ diameter heads, 3′ long handle	79.00	100.00	83.00
☐ **Waffle Iron,** cast iron for coal stove, ball bearing joint, pie shaped design on grid, marked "Fanner Mfg. Co., Cleveland, O., Crescent Waffles No.7"	28.00	53.00	29.00
☐ **Windmill Weight,** model of bull, Boss	325.00	380.00	350.00
☐ **Windmill Weight,** model of cow, 19th century	400.00	475.00	440.00
☐ **Windmill Weight,** model of horse, "Demster"	80.00	140.00	95.00

KITCHEN COLLECTIBLES

PERIOD: Most collectible kitchen items were made in the 19th century and 20th century. Those from the 17th and 18th centuries, though highly sought after, are much more rare.

MATERIAL: Most kitchen items are made of brass, copper, iron, wood and pewter.

COMMENTS: Hearth cooking utensils, such as Dutch ovens, kettles, ladles and chimney cleaners are quite sought after items. Also popular are items made specifically for wood and coal burning stoves. Other utensils are also collectible. Prices vary greatly from item to item due to age, material and rarity. Most kitchen items from the late 19th century and early 20th century are reasonably priced.

ADDITIONAL TIPS: The listings fall under headings according to type of material. Under those headings, items are listed alphabetically. There is also a special section of miscellaneous kitchen items.

RECOMMENDED READING: For more complete information, see *The Official Price Guide to Kitchen and Household Collectibles.*

☐ **Apple Corer,** carved bone, early 1800's	38.00	45.00	41.00
☐ **Apple Peeler,** geared, crank, clamp on type, c. 1860, 10″ long	40.00	40.00	41.00
☐ **Apple Peeler,** cherry, table model, walnut, clamp, footed, c. 1650	260.00	285.00	273.00
☐ **Apple Peeler,** table mounted, hand crank, c. 1880	28.00	40.00	32.00
☐ **Apple Peeler,** iron, c. 1880	28.00	40.00	32.00
☐ **Baller,** nickel plated, wooden handle	5.00	8.00	7.50
☐ **Bee Smoker,** cylindrical can, wood handles, leather bellows, base	20.00	37.00	23.00

Butter Churn,
glass, cast iron,
tin and wood,
$27.00-$33.00

	Current Price Range		Prior Year Average
☐ Berry Press, ...	45.00	60.00	47.00
☐ Biscuit Cutter, aluminum	1.00	5.00	2.50
☐ Biscuit Cutter, c. 1915	1.00	5.00	2.50
☐ Biscuit Cutter, c. 1925	1.00	5.00	2.50
☐ Biscuit Cutter, c. 1890	10.00	18.00	11.00
☐ Bottle Opener, wood handle, c. 1920	1.50	5.00	2.50
☐ Bottle Opener, all tin, c. 1940	2.00	6.00	3.50
☐ Candelabra, gilded over copper, cut glass droppings, c. 1800	700.00	800.00	758.00
☐ Cherry Pitter, on legs	30.00	38.00	33.00
☐ Cherry Pitter, says "Reading Hardware Company"	25.00	37.00	30.00
☐ Cherry Pitter, Rollman Company	25.00	35.00	28.00
☐ Corn Popper, c. 1910-1940, steel wire, wood ..	10.00	15.00	10.50
☐ Corn Stick Pan, ...	14.00	20.00	15.00
☐ Cream Can, c. 1920	65.00	80.00	74.00

	Current Price Range		Prior Year Average
☐ **Custard Cup**, ovenware, c. 1910	48.00	58.00	52.00
☐ **Dillworth Coffee Ad**, cooking in a pot or cauldron suspended from crane, c. 1880's . . .	4.00	8.00	4.50
☐ **Dipper**, handle and bowl, c. 1850, 14″ long . . .	22.00	30.00	24.00
☐ **Dish Cross**, wrought iron, footed plate for use at the dining table, sometimes used in connection with a spirit lamp, intricately ornamented, hinged c. 1750, 10″ diameter	330.00	375.00	349.00
☐ **Dish Drainer**, c. 1890's to 1920, wire and mesh	10.00	15.00	10.50
☐ **Dish Drainer**, c. 1890, wood, pegged with separate partition for utensils	18.00	25.00	19.00
☐ **Egg Basket**, folding type, wire	14.00	18.00	16.00
☐ **Egg Beaters**, three gears, crank, c. 1920 . . .	8.00	10.00	9.50
☐ **Egg Whips and Whisks**, 1880's to 1940's, wire, wood	8.00	15.00	8.50
☐ **Feather Fluffer**, series of loops, 19″ long . . .	58.00	62.00	60.00
☐ **Fire Back**, enameled decoration of flowers and foliage, 25″ high	110.00	225.00	121.00
☐ **Fireback**, figural man with medieval motif, enamel on hammered tin	50.00	100.00	58.00
☐ **Fireback**, hunting scene with marsh, fowl, and labradors, 27″ long	180.00	240.00	200.00
☐ **Fire Dogs**, brass	60.00	80.00	68.00
☐ **Fire Kindler**, 1890-1900, wire, 8″ long	10.00	15.00	10.50
☐ **Fireplace**, marble, c. 1790, 70″ long	490.00	625.00	525.00
☐ **Flax Breaker**, c. 1840	170.00	185.00	179.00
☐ **Fruit Jar Holder**, c. 1881	3.00	6.00	3.50
☐ **Fruit or Vegetable Peeler**, patented 1904	3.00	6.00	3.50
☐ **Food Chopper**, c. 1860, 16″ high	270.00	310.00	289.00
☐ **Food Grinder**, Universal Company, c. 1895 . .	10.00	25.00	13.00
☐ **Frame**, relief decoration of nymphs and unicorns, wood and glass	130.00	175.00	142.00
☐ **Frame**, ornate, circular with door	120.00	168.00	132.00
☐ **Fruit Jar Sealer**, nickel plate, dome shape with three legs	10.00	12.00	10.50
☐ **Fruit Press**, Enterprise, table top model	16.00	25.00	19.00
☐ **Fry Basket**, fine mesh, 1912	8.00	15.00	8.50
☐ **Grabber**, long wood handle with grasper ends	22.00	35.00	26.00
☐ **Graters**, clamps to surface, wood frame with steel blades	8.00	16.00	10.50
☐ **Grater**, handled, handmade, 1800's, 12″ x 8″ .	45.00	60.00	52.00
☐ **Grater**, nutmeg, c. 1870	8.00	16.00	10.50
☐ **Grater**, revolving type, clamp, blade, c. 1870 .	20.00	32.00	25.00
☐ **Griddle**, 17″ long	12.00	21.00	15.00
☐ **Hammered Bowl**, 20″ diameter	60.00	75.00	68.00
☐ **Heat Vent Cover**, intricate embossment, c. 1890	33.00	55.00	37.00

	Current Price Range		Prior Year Average
☐ Ice Card, ...	7.00	12.00	8.00
☐ Ice Cream Freezer, ...	33.00	43.00	37.00
☐ Ice Cream Freezer, single action, cedar pail, c. 1900's	42.00	52.00	47.00
☐ Ice Cream Freezer, c. 1910, six quart capacity	38.00	48.00	42.00
☐ Ice Cream Freezer, American made	42.00	50.00	47.00
☐ Ice Cream Freezer, White Mountain Freezer Company, tin pail, grind and gears	38.00	48.00	42.00
☐ Ice Pick, American made	14.00	25.00	16.00
☐ Ice Pick, c. 1900	5.00	8.00	6.50
☐ Ice Pick, chrome and wood	6.00	10.00	7.50
☐ Ice Pick, White Mountain Company	5.00	8.00	6.50
☐ Ice Picks, says "Coca-Cola"	7.00	12.00	8.50
☐ Ice Shaver, Logan and Strobridge Company .	8.00	12.00	9.50
☐ Ice Shaver, wood grip handle, steel blade, 12" long	30.00	40.00	32.00
☐ Jaggers, ivory scrimshaw, 19th century, fine workmanship, rare	175.00	275.00	185.00
☐ Jar Lid Remover, mechanical action, grip, c. 1860, 4" diameter	70.00	85.00	74.00
☐ Jelly Strainer, c. 1891, wood, string, cloth ...	5.00	6.00	5.50
☐ Julien Soup Cutter, and cutting disks, c. 1870's	35.00	50.00	37.00
☐ Kettle, chrome and enamel, 11" high	23.00	30.00	26.00
☐ Kettle, black enamel over chrome, 12" high ..	12.00	18.00	15.00
☐ Kettle Scraper, patented 1894, metal	10.00	20.00	10.50
☐ Kitchen Cabinet, c. 1895, shelves, drawers, smooth surface for counter space	68.00	92.00	74.00
☐ Kraut Cutter, American made, c. 1900	42.00	55.00	47.00
☐ Ladles, vegetable, c. 1890, wire, wood handled	7.00	14.00	8.00
☐ Lemon Squeezer, late 1800's	58.00	75.00	63.00
☐ Marshmallow Toaster, long handle	5.00	12.00	6.50
☐ Matchholder, wall hangar, says "Adriance Farm Machinery"	68.00	90.00	74.00
☐ Matchholder, ...	35.00	42.00	39.00
☐ Matchholder, figural of little girl, bisque construction, table model	88.00	100.00	95.00
☐ Oyster Broiler, wire, c. 1890	12.00	22.00	13.00
☐ Palette Knives, c. 1900, steel, wood	11.00	18.00	11.50
☐ Pan, handled, round bottom, tri-legged, c. 1790, 7½" diameter	90.00	105.00	99.00
☐ Pan, round bottom, tri-legged, 15" diameter .	78.00	90.00	84.00
☐ Pastry Cutter, 12" long	28.00	35.00	32.00
☐ Peanut Grinder, 3" high	78.00	90.00	84.00
☐ Pencil Sharpener, home, c. 1920	25.00	35.00	26.00

	Current Price Range		Prior Year Average
☐ Piecup, glaze cracked, 3" diameter	8.00	15.00	10.50
☐ Pie Lifter, wire, wood handle	14.00	25.00	17.00
☐ Pie Lifter, wire, old	23.00	30.00	26.00
☐ Pie Stacker, three layer, c. 1920's	14.00	20.00	16.00
☐ Poacher, for eggs, 3 cup stand	12.00	18.00	13.00
☐ Pot/Pan Scraper, Babbitt's Cleanser	14.00	20.00	15.00
☐ Pot/Pan Scraper, Better Butter, Fairmont Creamery	22.00	31.00	23.00
☐ Pot/Pan Scraper, King Midas Flour	16.00	24.00	17.00
☐ Pot/Pan Scraper, Sunshine Finishes	18.00	26.00	19.00
☐ Potato Peeler, bright metal, Clipper, 6½"	3.00	7.00	3.50
☐ Potlid, revolving, rattail and ornate handle, 1600's	185.00	205.00	194.00
☐ Protectors, skirt, c. 1870's, wire	15.00	22.00	16.00
☐ Push Handle Whipper, galvanized, thumb handle on side	11.00	16.00	12.00
☐ Push Handle Whipper, wooden handle	10.00	16.00	10.50
☐ Rack, for towels, c. 1870	8.00	14.00	8.50
☐ Raisin Seeder, Enterprise, patented 1895	21.00	30.00	22.00
☐ Raisin Seeder, wire with wooden handle, "Everett," patented 1888	21.00	30.00	22.00
☐ Raisin Seeder, c. 1890	16.00	24.00	18.00
☐ Raisin Seeder, table model, c. 1890	18.00	20.00	19.00
☐ Rake, potato, iron and brass, scythed edge, c. 1800-1830	50.00	100.00	52.00
☐ Range, army field, coal burning, 1946	600.00	689.00	630.00
☐ Roach Traps, various patterns, earthenware, c. 1870	6.00	12.00	6.50
☐ Roller,	80.00	90.00	89.00
☐ Rolling Pin, German, decorated	35.00	40.00	40.00
☐ Rubber Plate Scraper, c. 1940, metal, wood	3.00	5.00	3.50
☐ Salad Shaker, Victorian, 10"	10.00	20.00	10.50
☐ Sausage Stuffer, c. 1870's, tin, wood	6.00	10.00	6.50
☐ Scale, professional model, with scoop, c. 1900	125.00	140.00	131.00
☐ Scale, egg, "Jiffy Way", painted sheet metal, c. 1940	13.00	19.00	13.00
☐ Scale, for meat, professional style, Hanson Company	85.00	110.00	94.00
☐ Steamer, pudding, lidded	22.00	30.00	26.00
☐ Strainers, wire, c. 1870	5.00	12.00	5.50
☐ Stringholder, apple, mid 1800's	13.00	20.00	16.00
☐ Stringholder, c. 1790	13.00	25.00	16.00
☐ Stringholder, love bird, china, c. 1800's	13.00	25.00	16.00
☐ Stringholder, Mammy, plaster of paris, wall hangar, c. 1810, 7" high	18.00	30.00	21.00

	Current Price Range		Prior Year Average
☐ **Stringholder,** pear, c. 1810	23.00	35.00	26.00
☐ **Stringholder,** lady figural, porcelain, wall hangar, c. 1810	12.00	25.00	16.00
☐ **Stringholder,** leather, wall hangar, steel hooks	6.00	8.00	6.50
☐ **Sugar Bowl,** porcelain with enamel, American made, c. 1900, 2¾″ diameter	40.00	50.00	47.00
☐ **Sugar Nipper,** spring handle, wide mouth, semicircular pattern, c. 1835	110.00	128.00	121.00
☐ **Sugar Shaker,** enamel and gilt, apple blossom motif	40.00	52.00	44.00
☐ **Sugar Shaker,** white opalescent	85.00	105.00	94.00
☐ **Sugar Shaker,** leaf green	85.00	105.00	94.00
☐ **Sugar Shaker,** enamel and gilt, flowers and leaves in yellow	32.00	45.00	39.00
☐ **Sugar Shaker,** enamel and gilt, orange and purple flowers	30.00	38.00	37.00
☐ **Sugar Shaker,** blue opalescent, honey comb design	120.00	145.00	131.00
☐ **Tabletop Churn**	37.00	48.00	41.00
☐ **Tea Caddy,** wood with enameled bird and tree decoration, lidded, handled	165.00	185.00	173.00
☐ **Tea Caddy,** plaster with inlay on cover, 15″ long	62.00	75.00	68.00
☐ **Tea Caddy,** wooden, oblong rounded corners, intricate scrollwork, tortise shell glaze, c. 1740, 13″ long	235.00	259.00	240.00
☐ **Tea Caddy,** porcelain, scalloped edge, flower decoration of yellow and aqua, over gilt	190.00	250.00	210.00
☐ **Tea Cake Pan,** hanging loops, c. 1760	110.00	128.00	116.00
☐ **Tea Kettle,** 7½″ diameter	38.00	50.00	42.00
☐ **Teapot,** gold luster	80.00	100.00	94.00
☐ **Teapot,** marbleized band, white enameled spout and handle, 3″ diameter	320.00	350.00	331.00
☐ **Teapot,** dark yellow with fernery, lidded, 3″ diameter	690.00	810.00	735.00
☐ **Teapot Stand,** wire, c. 1870's	3.00	6.00	4.50
☐ **Teapot Stand,** intricately decorated silver, pierced or woven, footed, square for use on the dining table, c. 1800, 6″ diameter . .	28.00	40.00	32.00
☐ **Telescopic Candlesticks,** raise and lower to change the light, usually made in silver, sometimes gold, cloth lined, 6″ to 12″ high . .	290.00	315.00	309.00
☐ **Toaster,** wire frame, stove top, handle, 8″ long	25.00	42.00	30.00
☐ **Toaster,** electric, chromium alloy, two slots, c. 1930's	9.00	14.00	10.50

	Current Price Range		Prior Year Average
☐ **Tomato Slicer**	15.00	28.00	19.00
☐ **Toothpick Holders**	13.00	17.00	16.00
☐ **Toothpick Holders,** banded, clear, with gold .	18.00	22.00	21.00
☐ **Toothpick Holders,** red glass, arched, advertising	12.00	35.00	15.00
☐ **Toothpick Holders,** glass with twisted wire handle, dark blue	20.00	28.00	24.00
☐ **Toothpick Holders,** souvenir of Colorado	48.00	55.00	52.00
☐ **Toothpick Holders,** green	11.00	20.00	16.00
☐ **Toothpick Holders,** cut crystal	42.00	50.00	47.00
☐ **Toothpick Holders,** Grecian urn shape, silver fittings, flower motif	50.00	60.00	58.00
☐ **Toothpick Holders,** frog, and cornucopia	35.00	48.00	39.00
☐ **Toothpick Holders,** hat	35.00	48.00	39.00
☐ **Toothpick Holders,** glass and gilt, souvenir from Minnesota	25.00	32.00	29.00
☐ **Toothpick Holders,** monkey	65.00	75.00	68.00
☐ **Turbine Egg Beater,** or cream whip, stamped metal, wire, c. 1930	15.00	18.00	16.00
☐ **Utensil Holder,** metal, c. 1906	4.00	12.00	4.50
☐ **Waffle Iron,** corrugated iron, with base, American made, c. 1900	20.00	34.00	23.00
☐ **Warmer,** for dishes, wire, c. 1881	8.00	12.00	8.50
☐ **Wire Cutter,** c. 1870's	6.00	12.00	6.50

KNIVES

This section features only a sampling of knives. In order to accurately present the vast amount of knife information required by serious collectors, a special edition devoted to knives is published by The House of Collectibles, Inc. This handy, pocket-size guide, *The Official 1985 Price Guide to Pocket Knives,* features thousands of values for all popular collector knives. It is available at bookstores for $3.95. For more in-depth knife information, consult *The 1985 Official Price Guide to Collector Knives* for $10.95.

MAKER: Well known knife manufacturers include Russell, Case, Winchester and Remington.

COMMENTS: Most collectors of American knives are interested in specific types, including seaman's knives, military knives, knives adapted for hand-to-hand combat and bowie knives.

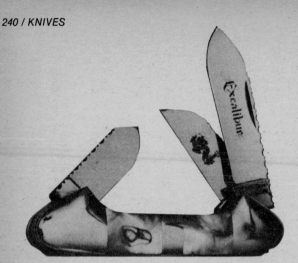

Parker Knives, *Excaliber, 4⅝" long,* **$75.00-$150.00**

ADDITIONAL TIPS: Two prices are given for the knife section. The manufacturers, listed in alphabetical order, make a variety of knives so the prices indicate the range for each manufacturer.

For more complete information, refer to *The Official 1985 Price Guide to Collector Knives,* published by The House of Collectibles.

	Current Price Range		Prior Year Average
☐ A-1 Novelty Cutlery Canton, OH	20.00	130.00	60.00
☐ Ack Cutlery Co. Freemont, OH	40.00	100.00	40.00
☐ Adams & Bros.	55.00	130.00	55.00
☐ Adams & Sons	40.00	100.00	55.00
☐ Adolph Blaich, San Francisco, CA	20.00	175.00	80.00
☐ Adolphuis Cutlery Co. Sheffield, England	10.00	70.00	30.00
☐ Aerial Mfg. Co., Marionette, WI	10.00	115.00	50.00
☐ Akron Cutlery Co., Akron, OH	30.00	70.00	40.00
☐ Alamo, Japan	3.00	7.00	4.00
☐ American Cutlery Co., U.S.A.	17.00	38.00	22.00
☐ American Cutlery Co., Germany	9.00	22.00	13.00
☐ Armstrong Cutlery Co., Germany	7.00	14.00	8.00
☐ Arnex (stainless), Solingen, Germany	5.00	11.00	7.00

	Current Price Range		Prior Year Average
☐ **Bassett**, Derby, CT	10.00	30.00	15.00
☐ **Bastian Bros. Co.**, Rochester, NY	30.00	75.00	40.00
☐ **R. Bunting & Sons** Sheffield	80.00	550.00	280.00
☐ **Burkinshaw Knife Co.** Pepperell, MA	40.00	320.00	100.00
☐ **Frank Buster Cutlery Co.**	12.00	1200.00	460.00
☐ **Butler Bros.** Chicago, IL	18.00	95.00	45.00
☐ **Camden Cutlery Co.**, Germany	30.00	115.00	60.00
☐ **Camillus Cutlery Co.** Camillus, NY	10.00	115.00	50.00
☐ **Camillus**, New York, NY	7.00	30.00	15.00
☐ **Camp Buddy**, USA	10.00	30.00	16.00
☐ **Camp King**	10.00	30.00	16.00
☐ **Continental Cutlery Co.** Kansas City, MO.	30.00	70.00	45.00
☐ **Cook Bros.**	80.00	135.00	100.00
☐ **Copper Bros.**	10.00	20.00	13.00
☐ **Delux**	7.00	18.00	10.00
☐ **Depend-on-me-Cutlery Co.**, New York	8.00	40.00	20.00
☐ **E.A.A.** Solingen, Germany	6.00	12.00	7.00
☐ **E. F. & Co.**	70.00	100.00	75.00
☐ **Eagle**	25.00	40.00	26.00
☐ **Eagle Cutlery Co.**	70.00	340.00	180.00
☐ **Eagle Knife Co.**, U.S.A.	35.00	330.00	160.00
☐ **Eagle Pencil Co.**	6.00	17.00	10.00
☐ **Eagleton Knife Co.**	22.00	130.00	70.00
☐ **Emmon Hawkins Hardware**	17.00	110.00	55.00
☐ **Empire Knife Co.** Winsted, CT	32.00	315.00	160.00
☐ **Empire**, Winsted, CT	32.00	315.00	160.00
☐ **Emrod Co.**, Germany	5.00	17.00	9.00
☐ **Wm. Enders Mfg. Co.**, U.S.A.	17.00	130.00	68.00
☐ **Faulkhiner & Co.** Germany	12.00	25.00	14.00
☐ **Favorite Knife Co.** Germany	5.00	27.00	14.00
☐ **Hibbard, Spencer, & Bartlett** Chicago, IL	14.00	370.00	170.00
☐ **Hickory**	5.00	220.00	100.00
☐ **Highcarbon Steel**, U.S.A.	12.00	170.00	90.00
☐ **Higler & Sons**	17.00	80.00	45.00
☐ **Hike Cutlery Co.** Solingen, Germany	12.00	40.00	22.00
☐ **Hill Bros.**	22.00	65.00	40.00
☐ **Honk Falls** Napanoch, NY	40.00	930.00	450.00
☐ **Imperial Knife Co.** Providence, RI	3.00	80.00	38.00
☐ **Imperial**, Mexico	1.50	3.50	2.00
☐ **Imperial**, Germany	7.00	28.00	15.00
☐ **Joseph Allen & Sons**	12.00	260.00	120.00
☐ **K.I.E.**, Sweden	4.00	17.00	10.00
☐ **Ka-Bar**, U.S.A.	12.00	630.00	300.00
☐ **Kabar**, U.S.A.	12.00	315.00	150.00
☐ **Kamp Cutlery Co.** Germany	6.00	17.00	9.00
☐ **Kamp Huaser** Plumacher, Germany	17.00	64.00	37.00

	Current Price Range		Prior Year Average
☐ R. Murphy, Boston, MD	17.00	27.00	21.00
☐ New Port Cutlery Company Germany	13.00	20.00	15.00
☐ Newton Premier Sheffield	11.00	27.00	16.00
☐ New York Knife Company Walden, NY	30.00	1050.00	500.00
☐ Norsharp	12.00	36.00	24.00
☐ N. American, Wichita, KS	12.00	57.00	32.00
☐ Oicut, Olean, NY	45.00	320.00	145.00
☐ Old Cutlery Olean, NY	17.00	130.00	65.00
☐ Old American Knife, U.S.A.	12.00	38.00	19.00
☐ Old Hickory (Ontario Knife Company)	5.00	14.00	8.00
☐ Parker-Frost	12.00	220.00	100.00
☐ Wm. & J. Parker	110.00	420.00	200.00
☐ Petters Cutlery Company Chicago, IL	30.00	90.00	45.00
☐ Phoenix Knife Co. Phoenix, NY	12.00	140.00	70.00
☐ Pic, Germany	3.50	9.00	6.00
☐ PIC, Japan	2.50	5.75	4.10
☐ Pine Knot, U.S.A.	37.00	320.00	150.00
☐ Pine Knot James W. Price	47.00	440.00	200.00
☐ C. Platts & Sons Andover, NY	43.00	830.00	400.00
☐ Platts Bros. Andover, NY	42.00	850.00	400.00
☐ Platts Bros., Union, NY	77.00	850.00	390.00
☐ Poor Boy	6.00	110.00	50.00
☐ Pop Cutlery Co. Camillus, NY	6.00	22.00	10.00
☐ Quick Point (Winchester stamped on back of tang)	53.00	78.00	63.00
☐ R. J. Richter, Germany	5.00	17.00	8.00
☐ Ring Cutlery, Japan	1.50	5.75	3.50
☐ Rivington Works	17.00	69.00	37.00
☐ Rizzaro Estilato, Milan, Italy	37.00	80.00	57.00
☐ Roberts & Johnson & Rand St. Louis, MO	17.00	77.00	40.00
☐ Robertson Bros. & Co. Louisville, KY	17.00	315.00	150.00
☐ Robeson, Germany	27.00	80.00	40.00
☐ Robeson, Rochester, NY	17.00	420.00	210.00
☐ Robeson, Suredge	12.00	130.00	60.00
☐ Sizeker Manstealed, Germany	12.00	17.00	14.00
☐ Sliberstein Laporte & Co.	38.00	69.00	45.00
☐ Simmons Hardware Co. Germany	22.00	320.00	150.00
☐ Simmons Hardware St. Louis, MO	27.00	315.00	150.00
☐ Simmons Warden White Co. Dayton, OH	17.00	80.00	50.00
☐ Spartts, England	37.00	95.00	60.00
☐ Spear Cutlery Co., Germany	12.00	27.00	16.00
☐ Spring Cutlery Co. Sheffield	17.00	130.00	50.00
☐ Springer, Japan	5.00	16.00	8.00
☐ Standard Cutlery Co. Germany	5.50	26.00	15.00
☐ Thomas Turner & Co. Sheffield, England	17.00	180.00	100.00
☐ United, Germany	4.00	12.00	8.00
☐ Universal Knife Co. New Britain, CT	17.00	38.00	25.00

	Current Price Range		Prior Year Average
☐ Utica Co., Czechoslovakia	13.00	38.00	24.00
☐ Utica Cutlery Co. Utica, NY	12.00	160.00	90.00
☐ Utica Knife Co., U.S.A.	12.00	160.00	90.00
☐ V. K. Cutlery Co., Germany	6.00	16.00	9.00
☐ Valley Falls Cutlery Co.	17.00	79.00	45.00
☐ Valley Forge Cutlery Co.	21.00	100.00	50.00
☐ Valor, Germany	3.50	16.00	8.00
☐ Valor, Japan	3.50	16.00	8.00
☐ Van Camp, U.S.A.	4.00	110.00	51.00
☐ Van Camp H & I Co., U.S.A.	17.00	310.00	150.00
☐ Van Camp Indianapolis, IN	17.00	310.00	150.00
☐ Van Camp, Germany	12.00	35.00	19.00
☐ Vanco, Indianapolis, IN	6.00	37.00	19.00
☐ Vernider, St. Paul, MN	6.00	37.00	19.00
☐ John Watts, Sheffield	16.00	33.00	24.00
☐ Webster, Sycamore Works U.S.A.	12.00	36.00	22.00
☐ Webster Cutlery Co., Germany	6.00	17.00	9.00
☐ Weck, N.Y.	17.00	68.00	35.00
☐ Wedgeway Cutlery Co.	15.00	39.00	27.00
☐ Weed & Co., Buffalo	36.00	77.00	52.00
☐ G. Weiland, New York	6.00	27.00	18.00
☐ Marshall Wells Hardware Co.	39.00	130.00	155.00
☐ H. C. Wentworth & Son Germany	6.00	37.00	20.00
☐ Weske Cutlery Co. Sandusky, OH	16.00	38.00	19.00
☐ Westaco, Boulder, CO	32.00	64.00	45.00
☐ Wester, B. C.	6.00	37.00	25.00
☐ Wester Bros., Germany	36.00	260.00	100.00
☐ Wester Stone, Inc., U.S.A.	16.00	118.00	50.00
☐ Western, Boulder, CO	52.00	520.00	240.00

LAMPS AND LIGHTING FIXTURES

TYPES: There are many different types of lighting fixtures, from grease burning to kerosene to electric. Styles of lamps and other fixtures may be named for the designer who innovated them or a distinctive feature of the lamp itself. For instance, the "Emeralite" light is a green glass shaded office lamp.

PERIOD: Lamps and lighting fixtures have been popular since the early 1700s. Collectors focus on the periods that saw significant developments in the field, such as the Art Nouveau period.

ORIGIN: Clay oil lamps have existed for at least 2000 years.

MAKERS: The most prominent makers of lamps and lighting fixtures are Tiffany, Quezal, Handel and Pairpoint. These companies produced some of the finest and most artistic lamps in existence.

COMMENTS: Although few individuals collect lamps and lighting fixtures as a hobby, these items are eagerly sought as accent pieces. Many lamps, especially the most expensive ones, are works of art as much as functional pieces.

ADDITIONAL TIPS: These listings are arranged according to the type of lighting fixture. Lamps by such distinctive makers such as Tiffany and Handel are grouped together.

LAMPS AND LIGHTING DEVICES	Current Price Range		Prior Year Average
☐ **Angle Lamp,** brass, double lacquered	190.00	280.00	235.00
☐ **Argand Lamp,** American Empire, bronze, cut glass shade	200.00	300.00	250.00
☐ **Art Nouveau Figural Lamp,** white paint, metal	170.00	210.00	190.00
☐ **Astral Lamp,** English, classical column, floral motif frosted shade, square base, 17¾″ H., c. 1838	1100.00	1400.00	1250.00
☐ **Betty Lamp,** tin, with hanger	85.00	105.00	95.00
☐ **Boudoir Lamp,** Art Deco, Austrian porcelain, figural, fabric shade	60.00	90.00	75.00
☐ **Boudoir Lamp,** Blanc de Chine, figural base, 11½″ H. base	35.00	60.00	47.50
☐ **Bradley and Hubbard,** caramel shade, signed base, 24″ H.	550.00	700.00	625.00
☐ **Candleabrum,** Art Nouveau, bronze, figural, two lights, pate de verre shades, 20½″ H. ..	1200.00	1400.00	1300.00
☐ **Carriage Lamps,** brass, clear glass and red reflector lenses	275.00	325.00	300.00
☐ **Ceiling Light Fixture,** Art Deco, bronze and onyx, inverted pyramid, bronze mounts, 35″ H., c. 1933	500.00	650.00	575.00
☐ **Chandelier,** tin circle, fifteen candle sockets, 21″ diameter, 1800s	350.00	450.00	300.00
☐ **Chandelier,** Victorian, kerosene lamp with hurricane shade, 42″ H.	270.00	350.00	310.00
☐ **Chinese Lamp,** bronze, urn form, low-relief dragon, 30″ H..	170.00	250.00	210.00
☐ **Courting Lamp,** pewter, clear and frosted front, 4″ H.	90.00	120.00	105.00
☐ **Desk Lamp,** goose neck, quezel art glass shade in trumpet form, iridescent, 15″ H., late 1800s	150.00	200.00	175.00

	Current Price Range		Prior Year Average
☐ **Emeralite Lamp,** brass, green glass globe, square brass base, 13″ H., c. 1920	110.00	150.00	130.00
☐ **Floor Lamp,** French, bronze, reeded shaft, Dresden flowers	80.00	120.00	100.00
☐ **Floor Lamp,** oak, carved diamond shaft, crossbar base	45.00	75.00	60.00
☐ **Gas Sconces,** pair, handwrought, French . .	300.00	360.00	330.00
☐ **"Gone With the Wind" Lamp,** umbrella shade with cupids and foliage, brass foot, 20″ H	280.00	320.00	300.00
☐ **"Gone With the Wind" Lamp,** grape pattern with green leaves, 22″ H	500.00	600.00	550.00
☐ **"Gone With the Wind" Lamp,** magnolia blossoms handpainted, 24″ H	575.00	675.00	625.00
☐ **"Gone With the Wind" Lamp,** red glass with red bull's eye, 28½″ H	650.00	750.00	700.00
☐ **Handel Desk Lamp,** square trunk base, swing porcelain shade, 15″ H.	320.00	400.00	360.00
☐ **Handel Table Lamp,** glass and metal, reverse painted, 24½″ H.	2100.00	2300.00	2200.00
☐ **Handel Table Lamp,** art glass shade, cylindrical base with handles, 24½″ H.	700.00	800.00	750.00
☐ **Handel Table Lamp,** Persian bordered glass shade, 22″ H.	1450.00	1650.00	1550.00
☐ **Hanging Lamp,** brass with chocolate glass panels, 14″ H.	65.00	85.00	75.00
☐ **Hanging Lamp,** cranberry with prisms	700.00	800.00	750.00
☐ **Hanging Lamp,** striped with canopy, 13″ H. .	175.00	225.00	200.00
☐ **Hanging Lamp,** light fixture, brass and crystal, three lights, crystal bulbs, 19½″ H. .	40.00	80.00	60.00
☐ **Hurricane Lamp,** pair 11″ H.	40.00	50.00	45.00
☐ **Kerosene Lamp,** Bohemian crystal, brass shaft, white marble base, cut flowers, red, 22″ H.	55.00	95.00	75.00
☐ **Kerosene Lamp,** cabbage case pattern	60.00	80.00	70.00
☐ **Kerosene Lamp,** country store fixture, brass front	140.00	160.00	150.00
☐ **Kerosene Lamp,** green pattern, milk glass base	80.00	100.00	90.00
☐ **Kerosene Lamp,** hanging fixture, cranberry glass with brass frame	180.00	220.00	200.00
☐ **Kerosene Lamp,** hobnail pattern	35.00	45.00	40.00
☐ **Kerosene Lamp,** table, Lincoln Drape pattern, amber	110.00	150.00	130.00
☐ **Kerosene Lamp,** table, overlay glass, 13″ H.	675.00	775.00	725.00
☐ **Miner's Safety Lamp,** brass and iron, red lens, #1000	110.00	150.00	130.00

	Current Price Range		Prior Year Average
☐ Oil Lamp, dogtooth	30.00	40.00	35.00
☐ Oil Lamp, Hall & Son, brass, tiered square base, frosted vintage globe, 26″ H.	270.00	370.00	320.00
☐ Oil Lamp, green depression glass	40.00	50.00	45.00
☐ Oil Lamp, Victorian, aqua milk glass square pedestal base, hurricane chimney, 23″ H., late 1800s	30.00	50.00	40.00
☐ Oriental Lamp, elephant, bronze, wood base, 19¾″ H.	400.00	580.00	490.00
☐ Pairpoint, butterflies and roses, signed base and shade, 10″ Dia.	1100.00	1300.00	1200.00
☐ Peg Lamp, brass burner, 6″ H.	70.00	90.00	80.00
☐ Peg Lamp, ribbed glass with brass candlesticks, pair	150.00	200.00	175.00
☐ Railroad Switch Lamp, four lenses, red and green, type 1880	40.00	80.00	60.00
☐ Railroad Switch Lamp, Handlan, St. Louis, four lenses	50.00	80.00	65.00
☐ Student Lamp, double brass, green glass shade with original chimney	500.00	570.00	535.00
☐ Student Lamp, hanging double, burnished, green shade	675.00	775.00	725.00
☐ Student Lamp, single brass front, milk glass shade	320.00	370.00	345.00
☐ Table Lamp, American Empire, brass, glass prisms, cut frosted shade	700.00	800.00	750.00
☐ Table Lamp, "Arrow Root," leaded glass shade with bronze base, 25½″ H.	8500.00	10500.00	9500.00
☐ Tiffany Table Lamp, Kapa shell, bronze base, 12¾″ H.	1100.00	1400.00	1250.00
☐ Venetian Mirror, hand cut and etched, carved backing, 5′ x 3′	2200.00	2600.00	2400.00
☐ Whale Oil Lamp, amethyst paneled front with marble base, 10″ H.	320.00	380.00	350.00
☐ Whale Oil Lamp, giant sawtooth, 9″ H.	120.00	140.00	130.00
☐ Whale Oil Lamp, paneled front, blue with marble base, 10″ H.	300.00	340.00	320.00

LANTERNS

☐ Auto Lantern, brass, oil burning, 14½″ H. ..	100.00	136.00	118.00
☐ Barn Lantern, Peter Gray, Boston	100.00	150.00	125.00
☐ Buggy Dashboard Lantern, kerosene	23.00	31.00	27.00
☐ Candle Lantern, sheet metal painted black, 16¼″ H.	65.00	85.00	75.00
☐ Carriage Lantern, brass trim, pair	340.00	400.00	370.00

	Current Price Range		Prior Year Average
☐ **Chien Lung Period Lantern,** porcelain, gourd form, pierced pedestal base, teak stand, hexagonal, 18″ H., late 1700s	320.00	400.00	360.00
☐ **Chinese Junk Lantern,** brass, oil	50.00	66.00	56.00
☐ **Coach Lantern,** pierced, 17½″ H.	170.00	210.00	190.00
☐ **Continental Lantern,** brass and tin, finials, 9½″ H., c. 1800s	400.00	600.00	500.00
☐ **Dietz Driving Lantern,** red glass in rear, 7½″ H.	125.00	165.00	145.00
☐ **Kerosene Lantern,** brass base and top engraved "Joseph Gavett, Roxbury," 17″ H.	250.00	300.00	275.00
☐ **Kerosene Lantern,** Dietz red reflector	28.00	38.00	33.00
☐ **Miner's Lantern,** tin and brass, 5½″ H., Jan. 10, 1882	25.00	40.00	32.50
☐ **Paul Revere Lantern,** tin with swirled punched holes	160.00	190.00	175.00
☐ **Railroad Lantern,** Nazi, marked with Swastika	20.00	40.00	30.00
☐ **Railroad Lantern,** New York City, red or clear globe	15.00	30.00	22.50
☐ **Railroad Lantern,** San Francisco, clear globe	25.00	55.00	40.00
☐ **Skater's Lantern,** brass with glass globe . . .	75.00	100.00	87.50
☐ **Ship's Lantern,** copper, pair, 16″ H.	270.00	320.00	295.00
☐ **Wagon Lantern,** clamp-on type with rear red reflector	25.00	35.00	30.00
☐ **Wood Lantern,** rare second material	160.00	190.00	175.00

MINIATURE LIGHTING DEVICES

☐ **Acorn Burner,** milk glass, white, embossed with iris, clear glass chimney	180.00	220.00	200.00
☐ **Acorn Burner,** opaline glass base and chimney, house scene	190.00	240.00	115.00
☐ **Acorn Burner,** tin	18.00	28.00	23.00
☐ **Artichoke,** red satin	50.00	70.00	60.00
☐ **Aventurine,** green, glass base	40.00	60.00	50.00
☐ **Banquet Lamp,** blue, glass, jeweled base, 10″ H.	270.00	350.00	310.00
☐ **Bristol,** blue enamel flowers, 6½″ H.	80.00	110.00	95.00
☐ **Cosmos,** clear glass, painted base	20.00	30.00	25.00
☐ **Cosmos,** floral motif, 8″ H.	280.00	440.00	360.00
☐ **Cosmos,** pink band base	40.00	50.00	45.00
☐ **Daisy,** by U.S. Glass	80.00	90.00	85.00
☐ **Fleur de Lis,** milk glass, by Eagle Glass Co. .	280.00	320.00	300.00
☐ **Greek Key,** clear glass	42.00	52.00	47.00
☐ **Kerosene Lamp,** pressed glass, daisy motif .	35.00	45.00	40.00
☐ **Lincoln Drape Lamp**	70.00	80.00	75.00

	Current Price Range		Prior Year Average
☐ **Melon Lamp,** yellow cased glass	60.00	70.00	65.00
☐ **Milk Glass,** chimney top with fluted stem, footed base, 5½″ H.	180.00	230.00	205.00
☐ **Night Lamp,** ribbed base	55.00	75.00	65.00
☐ **Nutmeg Burner,** brass saucer, 2″ H.	70.00	100.00	85.00
☐ **Nutmeg Burner,** clear glass base and chimney	45.00	55.00	50.00
☐ **Oil Lamp,** Greek Key	30.00	40.00	35.00
☐ **Oil Lamp,** swirl base and chimney, metal handle, 6″ H., c. 1940s	12.00	18.00	15.00
☐ **Star Lamp,** painted	40.00	60.00	50.00
☐ **Night Lamp,** swirl, narrow	40.00	50.00	45.00
☐ **Skating Lamp,** brass, link chain, 8″ H.	65.00	85.00	75.00
☐ **Table Lamp,** beehive, Pairpoint, 14½″ H. ...	450.00	600.00	525.00

LICENSE PLATES

MATERIAL: Pre-1910 license plates were made of various materials including leather. Since then, plates have been made of metal.

COMMENTS: License plates are the first auto collectible to attract widespread interest. Some collectors focus on plates from the same state, while others collect plates in chronological order. Older plates show changes in design, size and color. Because of materials used, most plates are not in mint condition.

ADDITIONAL TIPS: The following sampling of license plates is listed alphabetically by state. The year follows.

☐ **Arkansas,** 1932	17.50	26.00	18.50
☐ **California,** 1930	17.50	26.00	18.50
☐ **Connecticut,** 1915	80.00	90.00	85.00
☐ **Iowa,** 1932	22.50	38.00	27.00
☐ **Maine,** 1920	7.50	14.00	9.00
☐ **Kansas,** 1933	13.50	20.00	15.00
☐ **Massachusetts,** 1915	22.50	38.00	27.00
☐ **Rhode Island,** 1926	12.50	18.00	14.00
☐ **Wisconsin,** 1925	12.50	18.00	14.00
☐ **Michigan,** good condition, 1916	50.00	60.00	52.00
☐ **Ohio,** good condition, 1922	60.00	70.00	62.00
☐ **Pennsylvania,** 1908	55.00	65.00	60.00

MAGAZINES

   This section features only a sampling of magazine prices. In order to accurately present the vast amount of information required by serious collectors, a special edition devoted to magazines and paperbacks is published by The House of Collectibles, Inc. This handy, pocket-size guide, *The Official 1985 Guide to Paperbacks and Magazines,* features thousands of prices for magazines from the 1800s to the 1980s. It is available at bookstores for $3.95.

COMMENTS: Hobbyists enjoy magazine collecting because periodicals capture a part of history. Magazines detail world events which make interesting reading decades later.

ADDITIONAL TIPS: Many hobbyists collect the issues of only one magazine such as *Life, National Geographic* or *Playboy.* Others collect magazines topically buying periodicals with photographs and articles about their favorite Hollywood stars, presidents or sports heroes. Another way to collect magazines is by subject.

Life,
August 16, 1939,
feature article on
Astaire and Rogers
$15.00-$20.00

LIFE

	Current Price Range		Prior Year Average
☐ November 23, 1936 (first issue, Ft. Peck Dam on cover, message from publisher introducing the magazine)	85.00	115.00	97.00
☐ December 14, 1936 (Archbishop of Canterbury on cover, photos of surrealist art)	35.00	45.00	39.00
☐ December 21, 1936 (story of King Edward of Britain's abdication of the throne, more Spanish Civil War)	35.00	45.00	39.00
☐ December 28, 1936 (coverage of Fred Astaire and book "Gone With The Wind")	35.00	45.00	39.00
☐ January 4, 1937 (Franklin Roosevelt on cover)	18.00	24.00	21.00
☐ January 11, 1937 (Japanese soldiers on cover, birth control article)	15.00	20.00	17.50
☐ January 18, 1937 (portraits of European diplomats)	15.00	20.00	17.50
☐ January 25, 1937 (coverage of Red Chinese army)	9.00	12.00	10.50
☐ March 1, 1937 (cancer research)	6.00	9.00	7.50
☐ April 12, 1937 (anthropology article, paintings by Paul Cezanne)	9.00	12.00	10.50
☐ April 19, 1937 (British ocean liner Queen Mary on cover)	9.00	12.00	10.50
☐ May 3, 1937 (Jean Harlow on cover, special issue devoted mostly to movies)	18.00	24.00	21.00
☐ May 17, 1937 (Dionne Quintuplets on cover)	18.00	24.00	21.00
☐ May 31, 1937 (Golden Gate Bridge on cover, article on Will Hayes movie censorship)	15.00	20.00	17.50
☐ June 21, 1937 (report on Jean Harlow's death)	9.00	12.00	10.00
☐ July 26, 1937 (article on Edgar Bergen and his puppets)	9.00	12.00	10.50
☐ September 6, 1937 (Harpo Marx on cover, coverage of latest Paris fashions)	15.00	20.00	17.00
☐ September 27, 1937 (Nelson Eddy on cover, coverage of Nazi rally)	15.00	20.00	17.50
☐ November 8, 1937 (Greta Garbo on cover)	18.00	24.00	21.00
☐ November 22, 1937 (first anniversary issue)	6.00	9.00	7.50
☐ December 20, 1937 (article on Kennedy family and "Fire Chief" Ed Wynn)	9.00	12.00	10.50
☐ December 27, 1937 (article on the Frick Museum)	9.00	12.00	10.50
☐ January 3, 1938 (coverage of Marlene Dietrich)	6.00	9.00	7.50
☐ February 7, 1938 (Gary Cooper on cover)	15.00	20.00	17.50
☐ February 21, 1938 (Carl Sandburg on cover)	15.00	20.00	17.50

	Current Price Range		Prior Year Average
☐ April 4, 1938 (Anthony Eden on cover, article on circus)	6.00	9.00	7.50
☐ May 2, 1938 (John Nance Garner on cover)	6.00	9.00	7.50
☐ May 23, 1938 (Errol Flynn on cover, article on Hitler)	18.00	24.00	20.00
☐ June 13, 1938 (Gertrude Lawrence on cover)	9.00	12.00	10.00
☐ June 20, 1938 (Rudolph Valentino on cover)	15.00	20.00	17.50
☐ July 4, 1938 (coverage of Joe Louis/Max Schmeling bout)	6.00	9.00	7.50
☐ July 11, 1938 (Shirley Temple on cover)	9.00	12.00	10.50
☐ August 8, 1938 (articles on Mickey Rooney, Sinclair Lewis)	6.00	9.00	7.50
☐ August 22, 1938 (Fred Astaire and Ginger Rogers on cover)	15.00	20.00	17.50
☐ October 17, 1938 (Carole Lombard on cover)	15.00	20.00	17.00
☐ October 31, 1938 (Raymond Massey on cover, article on New York Governor Thomas E. Dewey)	13.00	17.00	15.00
☐ December 19, 1938 (Mary Martin on cover)	13.00	17.00	14.50
☐ January 16, 1939	6.00	9.00	7.50
☐ March 6, 1939 (Tallulah Bankhead on cover, article on Nazis in U.S.)	15.00	20.00	17.00
☐ March 13, 1939 (World's Fair issue)	10.00	14.00	12.00
☐ April 24, 1939 (British Prime Minister Neville Chamberlain on cover)	6.00	9.00	7.50
☐ May 15, 1939 (Anne Morrow Lindbergh on cover)	4.00	6.00	5.00
☐ May 29, 1939 (Eleanor Roosevelt on cover)	6.00	9.00	7.50
☐ June 5, 1939	9.00	12.00	10.50
☐ June 26, 1939	9.00	12.00	10.50
☐ July 3, 1939	4.00	6.00	5.00
☐ July 10, 1939	6.00	9.00	7.50
☐ July 24, 1939 (Anne Sheridan on cover)	15.00	20.00	17.50
☐ July 31, 1939	4.00	6.00	5.00
☐ August 28, 1939	6.00	9.00	7.50
☐ September 4, 1939 (Rosalind Russell on cover)	15.00	20.00	17.00
☐ September 11, 1939 (Benito Mussolini on cover)	18.00	23.00	20.00
☐ September 18, 1939 (coverage of early stages of World War II)	16.00	21.00	18.50
☐ October 9, 1939	9.00	12.00	10.50
☐ November 27, 1939 (Arturo Toscanini on cover)	4.00	6.00	5.00
☐ December 11, 1939 (Betty Grable on cover)	9.00	12.00	10.00
☐ December 11, 1939 (opening of Gone With The Wind)	16.00	21.00	18.50

☐ January 1, 1940	6.00	9.00	7.50
☐ January 15, 1940	4.00	6.00	5.00
☐ January 22, 1940	4.00	6.00	5.10
☐ January 29, 1940 (Lana Turner on cover)	15.00	20.00	16.00
☐ February 12, 1940 (article on Mickey Rooney)	9.00	12.00	10.00
☐ March 18, 1940	6.00	9.00	7.50
☐ March 25, 1940	5.00	8.00	6.50
☐ April 15, 1940	4.00	6.00	5.00
☐ April 22, 1940	9.00	12.00	10.50
☐ May 27, 1940 (war coverage)	18.00	23.00	20.50
☐ June 3, 1940	16.00	21.00	18.50
☐ June 10, 1940	18.00	23.00	20.50
☐ June 17, 1940	16.00	21.00	18.50
☐ June 24, 1940 (article on Dunkirk)	16.00	21.00	18.50
☐ July 1, 1940 (war coverage)	9.00	12.00	10.50
☐ July 15, 1940 (Rita Hayworth on cover)	16.00	21.00	17.00
☐ August 12, 1940 (war coverage)	9.00	12.00	10.50
☐ August 19, 1940 (biography of Hitler)	12.00	16.00	11.00

PLAYBOY

☐ October, 1955	20.00	27.00	22.00
☐ January, 1956	23.00	30.00	25.00
☐ January, 1957	10.00	15.00	12.00
☐ January, 1958	10.00	15.00	12.00
☐ January, 1959	9.00	13.00	10.00

MARBLES

TYPES: Most common are glass marbles. Antique marbles were made of steel, porcelain, clay, agate, onyx, rose quartz and carnelian. Marble was rarely used. Most marbles measure from ½ " to 1½ " in diameter. Larger ones were used for other types of games.

PERIOD: The most collectible marbles were handmade in Germany before World War I, though some were also made in America during that time. Since World War I most marbles have been machine made and hold little interest for the collector.

COMMENTS: Marble value is not based on age. Material, beauty, design and rarity are the variables. Most common are marbles made of crockery, stone or clay. Limestone marbles are more rare. Agate marbles are valuable, as are one-of-a-kind end of day marbles which were made of leftover glass scraps.

ADDITIONAL TIPS: The listings are alphabetical according to type of marble. For more marble information, refer to *The Official 1984 Price Guide to Collectible Toys,* published by The House of Collectibles.

	Current Price Range		Prior Year Average
☐ **Carpet Bowl,** black on white, diameter 3¼″	48.00	56.00	50.00
☐ **Double Ribbon,** one with red, yellow and white, one blue and white, wide ribbons, yellow and white outer strands, diameter 1¾″	62.00	72.00	64.00
☐ **Granite,** large dark brown and gray paint beauty, diameter 3″	77.00	87.00	78.00
☐ **Ivory,** ivory sphere, diameter 2″	8.50	12.50	10.50
☐ **Latticinio Swirl,** white core with four outer bands, two red and white, two green and yellow, diameter 1⅜″	34.00	44.00	36.00
☐ **Latticinio Swirl,** white core with six very bright outer bands, three green and white, three red and yellow, diameter 1⅜″	62.00	72.00	65.00
☐ **Latticinio Swirl,** yellow core with many outer bands, each having red, white, blue and yellow, diameter 1½″	64.00	72.00	66.00
☐ **Latticinio Swirl,** white core with four multicolored outer bands, diameter 1½″	62.00	72.00	64.00
☐ **Latticinio Swirl,** yellow core, six outer bands, three red and blue, three red and green, diameter 1⅝″	62.00	72.00	64.00
☐ **Latticinio Swirl,** yellow core with four wide outer bands of blue, white and yellow, diameter 1⅝″	47.00	57.00	48.00
☐ **Latticinio Swirl,** white core with six outer bands, three blue and white, three red and white, diameter 1⅝″	57.00	68.00	59.00
☐ **Latticinio Swirl,** yellow core with six wide outer bands, three white, one blue, one green, one red, diameter 1¾″	77.00	87.00	79.00
☐ **Latticinio Swirl,** yellow core with wide red, blue and green outer bands, diameter 1¾″	53.00	65.00	55.00
☐ **Latticinio Swirl,** white core with eight outer bands, four red, two blue and white, two green and white, diameter 1⅞″	86.00	97.00	90.00
☐ **Latticinio Swirl,** white core with four wide outer bands one with yellow and blue, one with red and yellow, diameter 1⅞″	87.00	96.00	89.00
☐ **Latticinio Swirl,** white core with blue bands, narrow yellow alternate bands, diameter 1⅞″	93.00	112.00	96.00

	Current Price Range		Prior Year Average
☐ **Latticinio Swirl,** yellow core with four very large bands, red, white, blue and orange, diameter 1⅞"	87.00	96.00	88.00
☐ **Latticinio Swirl,** yellow core, swirls end before pontil, diameter 2"	92.00	112.00	95.00
☐ **Latticinio Swirl,** white core, six very large multicolored outer bands, diameter 2"	72.00	84.00	74.00
☐ **Latticinio Swirl,** white core, six blue and red outer bands, diameter 2¼"	130.00	180.00	135.00
☐ **Latticinio Swirl,** white core, four different wide outer bands, diameter 2"	105.00	157.00	110.00
☐ **Latticinio Core,** yellow core, four very wide outer bands, diameter 2¼"	122.00	154.00	130.00
☐ **Latticinio Core,** white core with eight outer bands, large core, diameter 2¼"	127.00	180.00	135.00
☐ **Latticinio Core,** large white core, six red, white and blue outer bands, diameter 2⅜"	127.00	179.00	130.00
☐ **Lobed Core,** red and white core with three sets of five yellow strands	57.00	67.00	58.00
☐ **Marbles,** nine, mica-flexed	23.00	29.00	25.00
☐ **Marble,** onionskin, diameter 2"	42.00	52.00	44.00
☐ **Onyx,** banded onyx, diameter 2"	14.00	19.00	15.00
☐ **Open Core,** three very wide multicolored bands, diameter 1¼"	18.00	28.00	20.00
☐ **Open Core,** three bands containing green, white, yellow, blue and red, three sets of three outer strands of yellow, diameter 1¼"	32.00	42.00	35.00
☐ **Open Core,** core of red, yellow, blue, white and green bands, yellow and white outer strands, diameter 1½"	63.00	73.00	65.00
☐ **Open Core,** complex center containing blue, yellow, red and white, four outer bands, two with red, white and blue, two with red, yellow and green, diameter 1½"	72.00	82.00	74.00
☐ **Open Core,** two red and white, one red, white and blue, one red, yellow and green band, many yellow outer strands, diameter 1⅝"	42.00	53.00	44.00
☐ **Open Core,** central bands of red, white and green, red white and blue, four outer sets of three white strands, diameter 1⅝"	62.00	73.00	64.00
☐ **Open Core,** red, yellow, blue, green and white bands, white outer strands, diameter 1⅝"	52.00	64.00	54.00
☐ **Open Core,** four wide center bands, two red, yellow and green, two red, white and blue, four sets of three outer strands, two yellow and two white, diameter 1¾"	62.00	73.00	64.00

	Current Price Range		Prior Year Average
☐ **Open Core**, very wide bands, two red, white and blue, two red, yellow and green, two sets of five yellow and two sets of five white outer strands, diameter 1¾″	64.00	74.00	65.00
☐ **Open Core**, wide bands, two red and white, one blue and white, one green and white, yellow outer strands, diameter 1¾″	80.00	97.00	83.00
☐ **Open Core**, four very wide bands, yellow and red, yellow and green, blue and white, red and white with four sets of three outer strands, two white and two yellow, core fills the marble, diameter 1¾″	88.00	100.00	90.00
☐ **Open Core**, four multicolored center bands, four sets of three yellow outer strands, diameter 1⅞″	88.00	100.00	90.00
☐ **Open Core**, two red and two blue center bands, four sets of three white outer strands, gray glass, diameter 1⅞″	63.00	74.00	64.00
☐ **Open Core**, three wide center bands, three sets of four yellow outer strands, diameter 2″	93.00	114.00	95.00
☐ **Open Core**, four wide multicolored central bands, yellow and white outer strands, diameter 2″	87.00	99.00	89.00
☐ **Pottery**, modern, handpainted, glazed, diameter 1½″	14.00	20.00	15.00
☐ **Pottery**, modern, handpainted, glazed, diameter 2″	20.00	26.00	22.00
☐ **Ribbon Swirl**, single very wide ribbon core with two wide sets of yellow outer strands, diameter 2½″	72.00	82.00	74.00
☐ **Solid Core**, triple layer, center core white with narrow red, blue and green overlay stripes, narrow yellow outer strands, diameter 1½″	53.00	63.00	55.00
☐ **Solid Core**, double twist, diameter 1⅝″	67.00	77.00	69.00
☐ **Solid Core**, double twist with red, white, blue and green core, yellow outer strands, diameter 1¾″	72.00	82.00	74.00

MENUS

DESCRIPTION: Collectible menu types include board menus, printed wall menus, novelty, decorated or autographed menus, White House menus and those that commemorate special events.

COMMENTS: Though fun and fairly easy to collect, the value of menus depends on their age, rarity and decoration. Board menus, written and hung on wooden boards, date to the 18th and 19th century and are quite valuable. White House menus, especially those from inaugural ball dinners, are sought after. Special menus, made to commemorate a special event, were often painted or hand lettered on special material. Menus from famous restaurants of New York, Hollywood, New Orleans and Paris are favorites of collectors.

ADDITIONAL TIPS: Menu prices vary greatly in price. The following price sampling is alphabetized according to type of menu.

	Current Price Range		Prior Year Average
☐ **Board Menu,** California, 1850-1880	1800.00	2800.00	2300.00
☐ **Board Menu,** California, 1880-1910	550.00	850.00	700.00
☐ **Board Menu,** Midwestern U.S., 1860-1890 . . .	800.00	1200.00	1000.00
☐ **Board Menu,** Midwestern U.S., 1890-1910 . . .	270.00	420.00	330.00
☐ **Board Menu,** New England, pre-1800	1000.00	1400.00	1200.00
☐ **Board Menu,** New England, 1800-1859	800.00	1200.00	1000.00
☐ **Board Menu,** New York City, pre-1800	1400.00	1900.00	1600.00
☐ **Board Menu,** New York City, 1800-1850	900.00	1400.00	1100.00
☐ **Board Menu,** Southern states, 1800-1850 . . .	3000.00	4000.00	3200.00
☐ **Board Menu,** Southwestern, U.S., 1890-1910 . .	460.00	710.00	520.00
☐ **Famous Restaurants,** menus from the heyday of noted restaurants in New York, Hollywood, New Orleans, Paris	5.50	15.00	8.00
☐ **Hand-painted Bill Of Fare,** unnamed tavern, believed to be Midwest. Flat-cut wooden board with decorative top (spindles at either side), the board painted cream color, lettering in black ink applied with a thin brush, more than 100 items listed, overall size 22″ x 31″, c. 1875	1800.00	2500.00	2000.00
☐ **Lond Boar's Head Coffee House,** paper wall menu, c. 1820	220.00	260.00	240.00
☐ **Silver Star Cafe,** (location unknown, thought to be southwestern U.S.), hand-lettered bill of fare on wooden board. The board shellacked and painted over in various colors with decorations, artistic lettering, etc. Few dishes listed, along with house rules. 18½″ x 33⅔″, c. 1910	600.00	800.00	700.00
☐ **Steamship Menus,** from major steamship lines	2.00	8.00	5.00

Menus, *color artwork, 1890s,* **$12.00-$35.00**

	Current Price Range		Prior Year Average

☐ **Washington Inn,** (probably New Hampshire or Vermont), hand-lettered bill of fare on thick wooden board. The board is white-washed, with list of dishes and prices lettered in dark brown paint. Corners worn down, some of the painted surface cracked, 13″ x 18½″ x 1½″, c. 1835 ....   550.00   700.00   625.00

MILITARY COLLECTIBLES

In order to accurately present the vast amount of information required by serious collectors, a special edition devoted to Military collectibles is published by The House of Collectibles, Inc. This handy, pocket-size guide, *The Official 1985 Price Guide to Military collectibles,* features prices on objects from the 19th century to World War II. It is available at bookstores for $3.95. For more extensive information, refer to *The Official 1985 Price Guide to Military Collectibles.* It costs $10.95 and is the definitive guide to war memorabilia.

MOLDS

DESCRIPTION: Molds are used to hold certain foods while they harden or gel. The food item retains the mold form or design.

VARIATIONS: There are many kinds of molds including butter, chocolate and sugar. Molds are made of wood, copper, tin, iron and graniteware.

COMMENTS: Popular collectibles, molds are often sought after by kitchen collectors. Prices of molds vary greatly, depending on rarity, condition and material.

ADDITIONAL TIPS: The listings are alphabetized according to type of mold or type of material. Descriptions and price ranges follow.

☐ **Buttermold,** apple, wooden	336.00	350.00	343.00
☐ **Buttermold,** eagle with branch, 3″ diameter, wooden	236.00	250.00	243.00
☐ **Buttermold,** eagle, maple, round, wooden ..	215.00	260.00	230.00
☐ **Buttermold,** eagle, wingtip to wingtip, c. 1800s, wooden	131.00	175.00	145.00
☐ **Buttermold,** plum, wooden	252.00	320.00	265.00
☐ **Buttermold,** potted tree, wooden	89.00	100.00	93.00

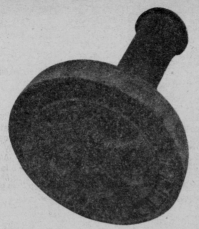

Buttermold, *double strawberry,* **$45.00-$50.00**

	Current Price Range		Prior Year Average
☐ **Buttermold,** primitive, wooden	73.00	90.00	80.00
☐ **Buttermold,** caveman, wooden	105.00	115.00	110.00
☐ **Buttermold,** name, wooden	226.00	255.00	230.00
☐ **Buttermold,** ram and floral design, 4″ diameter, wooden	387.00	400.00	390.00
☐ **Buttermold,** wooden	189.00	200.00	193.00
☐ **Buttermold,** Uncle Remus, wooden	179.00	210.00	181.00
☐ **Buttermold,** rooster, wooden	138.00	150.00	140.00
☐ **Buttermold,** rose and bud, factory made, 3″ diameter, wooden	37.00	50.00	40.00
☐ **Buttermold,** rosebuds, c. 1880s, 2″ diameter, wooden	84.00	110.00	90.00
☐ **Buttermold,** rose, with leaves, factory made, wooden	37.00	50.00	40.00
☐ **Buttermold,** round, four pattern repeat, wooden	37.00	50.00	40.00
☐ **Buttermold,** initials, wooden	188.00	200.00	193.00
☐ **Buttermold,** name, wooden	176.00	200.00	185.00
☐ **Buttermold,** sea shell, wooden	189.00	200.00	193.00

	Current Price Range		Prior Year Average
☐ **Buttermold,** sheaf of wheat, hand carved, 3″ diameter, wooden	47.00	70.00	50.00
☐ **Buttermold,** sheep, with handle, wooden	141.00	160.00	145.00
☐ **Buttermold,** shell, ring border, c. 1800s, 3″ diameter, wooden	121.00	135.00	126.00
☐ **Buttermold,** Tree of Life, 3″ diameter, wooden	126.00	180.00	135.00
☐ **Chocolate,** turkey, tin	20.00	25.00	15.00
☐ **Chocolate,** hen, tin, German	20.00	30.00	25.00
☐ **Buttermold,** eagle, maple, round, wooden	215.00	260.00	230.00
☐ **Copper,** bird	32.00	48.00	35.00
☐ **Copper,** bundt	95.00	115.00	98.00
☐ **Copper,** Easter egg, rabbit	55.00	70.00	60.00
☐ **Copper,** jelly or pudding	53.00	75.00	58.00
☐ **Copper,** quart size	32.00	47.00	35.00
☐ **Copper,** pint size	29.00	42.00	32.00
☐ **Copper,** circular base with fruit or floral motif, quart size	31.00	45.00	33.00
☐ **Copper,** circular base, with fruit or floral motif, pint size	15.00	28.00	17.00
☐ **Copper,** twelve tube, c. 1860	129.00	155.00	135.00
☐ **Copper,** pan	138.00	160.00	142.00
☐ **Copper,** pan, iron, handle, hanging eye	149.00	170.00	153.00
☐ **Copper,** dull finish, copper handles, 6″ x 20″ diameter	149.00	170.00	152.00
☐ **Copper,** iron base, 13″, diameter	68.00	80.00	70.00
☐ **Graniteware,** barley sheaf	27.00	36.00	29.00
☐ **Graniteware,** corn	24.00	32.00	26.00
☐ **Graniteware,** food, grey, 9″, circular	25.00	36.00	28.00
☐ **Graniteware,** gelatin, pineapple	15.00	25.00	18.00
☐ **Graniteware,** pudding, blue and white swirl, ring	37.00	60.00	40.00
☐ **Graniteware,** strawberry and grapes	32.00	40.00	36.00
☐ **Graniteware,** tube	15.00	25.00	18.00
☐ **Ice Cream,** Ace of Clubs, pewter	25.00	35.00	30.00
☐ **Ice Cream,** Ace of Spades, pewter	25.00	35.00	30.00
☐ **Ice Cream,** airplane, pewter	25.00	45.00	38.00
☐ **Ice Cream,** American flag, pewter	30.00	42.00	36.00
☐ **Ice Cream,** apple, pewter	25.00	35.00	30.00
☐ **Ice Cream,** aster, pewter	25.00	38.00	32.00
☐ **Ice Cream,** ball, pewter	15.00	25.00	20.00
☐ **Ice Cream,** banana, pewter	25.00	36.00	31.00
☐ **Ice Cream,** battleship, pewter	42.00	52.00	46.00
☐ **Ice Cream,** bell, pewter	25.00	35.00	30.00
☐ **Ice Cream,** Liberty Bell, pewter	35.00	45.00	30.00
☐ **Ice Cream,** mutton chop, pewter	27.00	37.00	32.00
☐ **Ice Cream,** ocean liner, pewter	35.00	45.00	40.00

	Current Price Range		Prior Year Average
☐ **Ice Cream,** orange, pewter	25.00	35.00	28.00
☐ **Ice Cream,** peach, pewter	25.00	35.00	28.00
☐ **Ice Cream,** pear, pewter	25.00	35.00	28.00
☐ **Ice Cream,** petunia, pewter	25.00	35.00	30.00
☐ **Ice Cream,** potato, pewter	25.00	35.00	30.00
☐ **Ice Cream,** pumpkin, pewter	25.00	35.00	28.00
☐ **Ice Cream,** rose, pewter	25.00	35.00	30.00
☐ **Ice Cream,** rosebud, pewter	30.00	40.00	34.00
☐ **Ice Cream,** Santa Claus, pewter	35.00	45.00	40.00
☐ **Ice Cream,** smoking pipe, pewter	30.00	40.00	34.00
☐ **Iron Mold,** cheese, porcelain and metal	58.00	70.00	60.00
☐ **Iron Mold,** Dariel, cast iron, c. 1870s	26.00	55.00	30.00
☐ **Iron Mold,** for ice cream, heart and cupid pattern	40.00	50.00	42.00
☐ **Iron Mold,** for ice cream, locomotive	68.00	80.00	72.00
☐ **Iron Mold,** for ice cream, pumpkin	38.00	50.00	40.00
☐ **Iron Mold,** for ice cream, rabbit, two part hinged	46.00	60.00	48.00
☐ **Iron Mold,** cast iron, two piece, 11″ long	99.00	120.00	103.00
☐ **Iron Mold,** rabbit, cast iron, two piece, mirror image	37.00	50.00	39.00
☐ **Maple Sugar,** bird	6.00	12.00	8.00
☐ **Maple Sugar,** cookie boy	5.00	9.00	7.00
☐ **Maple Sugar,** cookie girl	6.00	12.00	8.00
☐ **Maple Sugar,** cow	6.00	10.00	8.00
☐ **Maple Sugar,** crouching rabbit	6.00	12.00	8.00
☐ **Maple Sugar,** duck	5.50	10.50	7.50
☐ **Maple Sugar,** elephant	6.00	12.00	8.00
☐ **Maple Sugar,** horse	6.00	12.00	8.00
☐ **Maple Sugar,** horse and bear	12.00	18.00	14.50
☐ **Maple Sugar,** horse and pig	12.00	18.00	14.50
☐ **Maple Sugar,** lion	6.00	12.00	8.00
☐ **Maple Sugar,** pig	5.00	7.50	10.00
☐ **Tin Mold,** jelly, c. 1890	26.00	53.00	29.00
☐ **Tin Mold,** lion, with base, 6″ long	23.00	35.00	28.00
☐ **Tin Mold,** embossed design gives relief on cheese, grape pattern, 6″ long	30.00	50.00	35.00
☐ **Tin Mold,** pierced tin, heart shaped, for cheese, 19th century	16.00	25.00	18.00
☐ **Tin Mold,** tubed, c. 1890	11.00	16.00	12.00

MOVIE POSTERS

TYPES: In 1909, the Motion Picture Patents Company standardized the size and purpose of posters. Today the seven poster types and sizes include lobby card, 11″ x 14″; window card, 14″ x 22″; display card, 22″ x 28″; insert, 14″ x 36″; one sheet poster, 27″ x 41″, two sheet poster, 30″ x 40″ and three sheet poster, 41″ x 81″.

ORIGIN: The Lumiere Brothers of France produced the first movie posters in 1895. The posters featured scenes from the movie as well as pictures of the audience viewing the movie.

COMMENTS: Today, fine poster art is becoming very collectible. Factors that determine a poster's value include the death of a great performer, a new version of an old movie and rarity.

Lobby Card, *San Francisco,* ©*Metro-Goldwyn-Mayer, Clark Gable, Jeanette MacDonald, 1936,* **$300.00-$350.00**
(photo courtesy of ©*Poster City, Orangeburg, NY, 1984)*

ADDITIONAL TIPS: Classic movies like *Phantom of the Opera* or *Gone With the Wind* will always command high prices. Currently, the market is showing an increased interest in western posters, especially those picturing John Wayne, and horror film posters.

For more information, consult *The Official Price Guide to Radio, TV and Movie Memorabilia,* published by The House of Collectibles.

	Current Price Range		Prior Year Average
☐ **Lobby Card,** Abbott and Costello Meet the Invisible Man, 1951, Universal Pictures, Bud Abbott, Lou Costello, scene card	15.00	25.00	20.00
☐ **Lobby Card,** Andy Hardy Comes Home, 1958, Metro-Goldwyn-Mayer, Mickey Rooney, scene card	7.50	13.00	10.50
☐ **Lobby Card,** Bronco Buster, 1952, Universal Pictures, John Lund, Scott Brady, Joyce Holden, Chill Wills, title card	5.00	10.00	7.50
☐ **Lobby Card,** Caine Mutiny, The, 1954, Columbia Pictures, Humphrey Bogart, scene card . .	15.00	25.00	20.00
☐ **Lobby Card,** California Gold Rush, 1946, Republic Pictures, Wild Bill Elliott, scene card	5.00	10.00	7.50
☐ **Lobby Card,** Deadline U.S.A., 1952, Twentieth Century-Fox, Humphrey Bogart, scene card .	12.00	18.00	15.00
☐ **Lobby Card,** Great Gatsby, The, 1949, Paramount Pictures, Alan Ladd, Betty Field, Macdonald Carey, Ruth Hussey, Barry Sullivan, Howard De Silva, scene card	15.00	27.00	19.00
☐ **Lobby Card,** Gun Smoke, 1945, Monogram Pictures, Johnny Mack Brown, scene card . .	12.00	18.00	15.00
☐ **Lobby Card,** Invasion of the Body Snatchers, 1956, Allied Artists, Kevin McCarthy, Dana Wynter, scene card	25.00	40.00	32.00
☐ **Lobby Card,** Julius Caesar, 1953, Metro-Goldwyn-Mayer, Marlon Brando, James Mason, John Gielgud, Louis Calhern, Edmond O'Brien, Deborah Kerr, scene card	4.00	9.00	6.00
☐ **Lobby Card,** One Sunday Afternoon, 1933, Paramount Pictures, Gary Cooper, Fay Wray, scene card	65.00	85.00	75.00
☐ **Lobby Card,** Oregon Trail, 1945, Republic Pictures, Sunset Carson, title card	7.00	15.00	11.00
☐ **Lobby Card,** Outlaw of the Plains, 1946, Producers Releasing Corp., Buster Crabbe, scene card	7.00	15.00	11.00
☐ **Lobby Card,** Singing Cowboy, 1936, Republic Pictures, Gene Autry, Lon Chaney, Jr., scene card	35.00	50.00	42.00

	Current Price Range		Prior Year Average
☐ **Lobby Card,** Sky's the Limit, The, 1943, RKO Radio Pictures, Fred Astaire, Joan Leslie, title card	27.50	43.00	34.00
☐ **Lobby Card,** Young Frankenstein, 1974, Twentieth Century-Fox, Gene Wilder, Madeline Kahn, Peter Boyle, scene card	2.00	3.50	2.75
☐ **Insert,** Hunchback of Notre Dame, The, 1957, Allied Artists, Gina Lollobrigida, Anthony Quinn	10.00	15.00	12.50
☐ **Insert,** Lady From Louisiana, 1942, Republic Pictures, John Wayne, Ona Munson	60.00	68.00	64.00
☐ **Insert,** Legend of the Lost, 1957, United Artists, John Wayne, Sophia Loren	25.00	35.00	30.00
☐ **Insert,** Man Who Knew Too Much, The, 1956, Paramount Pictures, James Stewart, Doris Day	60.00	80.00	70.00
☐ **Insert,** Reveille With Beverly, 1943, Columbia Pictures, Ann Miller, Bob Crosby and His Band, Freddie Slack and His Band, Count Basie and His Band, The Radio Rogues, Frank Sinatra, Mills Brothers	27.50	35.00	30.50
☐ **One-Sheet,** A*P*E, 1976, Worldwide Entertainment Corp., Rod Arrants, Joanna De Varona	3.00	7.50	5.50
☐ **One-Sheet,** Air Patrol, 1962, Twentieth Century-Fox, Willard Parker, Merry Anders, Richard Dix	3.00	8.00	5.00
☐ **One-Sheet,** Back From Eternity, 1956, RKO Radio Pictures, Robert Ryan, Anita Ekberg, Rod Steiger	3.50	7.00	5.50
☐ **One-Sheet,** Barbarella, 1968, Paramount Pictures, Jane Fonda	12.50	16.00	14.50
☐ **One-Sheet,** Blood of Dracula's Castle, 1969, Crown International, John Carradine	5.00	8.00	6.50
☐ **One-Sheet,** Bluebeard, 1972, Cinerama Releasing Corp., Richard Burton, Joey Heatherton, Raquel Welch, Virna Lisi	2.00	6.00	4.00
☐ **One-Sheet,** Carnal Knowledge, 1971, Embassy Pictures, Jack Nicholson, Candice Bergen, Ann-Margret	3.00	6.00	4.50
☐ **One-Sheet,** Dr. Terror's House of Horrors, 1965, Paramount Pictures, Chistopher Lee, Roy Castle, Peter Cushing	5.00	10.00	7.50
☐ **One-Sheet,** Dog of Flanders, 1959, Twentieth Century-Fox, David Ladd, Donald Crisp	2.00	5.00	3.50

	Current Price Range		Prior Year Average
☐ **One-Sheet,** French Connection II, 1975, Twentieth Century-Fox, Gene Hackman, Fernando Rey	1.00	5.00	3.00
☐ **One-Sheet,** Frogs, 1972, American International, Ray Milland, Sam Elliott	2.00	5.00	3.50
☐ **One-Sheet,** Haunted Strangler, The, 1958, Metro-Goldwyn-Mayer, Boris Karloff	20.00	32.00	26.00
☐ **One-Sheet,** If You Knew Suzie, 1947, RKO Radio Pictures, Eddie Cantor, Joan Davis	12.00	20.00	16.00
☐ **One-Sheet,** In Cold Blood, 1967, Columbia Pictures, Robert Blake, black and white	2.00	7.00	5.00
☐ **One-Sheet,** Make Mine Laughs, 1949, RKO Radio Pictures, Ray Bolger, Anne Shirley, Dennis Day, Joan Davis, Jack Haley, Leon Errol, Frances Langford, Frankie Carle and his orchestra, duo-tone	12.00	20.00	10.00
☐ **One-Sheet,** Mexican Spitfire Out West, 1940, RKO Radio Pictures, Lupe Velez, Leon Errol	12.00	20.00	16.00
☐ **One-Sheet,** Omen II, The, 1978, Twentieth Century-Fox, William Holden, Lee Grant, duo-tone	1.00	3.00	2.00
☐ **One-Sheet,** Our Vines Have Tender Grapes, 1945, Metro-Goldwyn-Mayer, Edward G. Robinson, Margaret O'Brien, Agnes Moorehead	22.50	30.00	26.50
☐ **One-Sheet,** Outlaws is Coming, The, 1964, Columbia Pictures, The Three Stooges (Curly, Larry and Moe)	15.00	25.00	20.00
☐ **One-Sheet,** Rose Bowl Story, The, 1952, Monogram Pictures, Marshall Thompson	3.00	8.00	5.00
☐ **One-Sheet,** Roses are Red, 1948, Twentieth Century-Fox, Don Castle, Peggy Knudsen, Jeff Chandler	10.00	20.00	15.00
☐ **One-Sheet,** Solid Gold Cadillac, The, 1956, Columbia Pictures, Judy Holliday, Paul Douglas	15.00	20.00	17.50
☐ **One-Sheet,** Super Sleuth, 1937, RKO Radio Pictures, Jack Oakie, Ann Sothern	25.00	35.00	30.00
☐ **One-Sheet,** Terror in the Wax Museum, 1973, Cinerama Releasing Corp., Ray Milland, Elsa Lancaster, duo-tone	4.00	8.00	6.00
☐ **One-Sheet,** Young Frankenstein, 1974, Twentieth Century-Fox, Gene Wilder, Peter Boyle, Marty Feldman	5.00	10.00	7.50
☐ **One-Sheet,** Youngest Profession, The, 1943, Metro-Goldwyn-Mayer, Virginia Weidler, Edward Arnold	25.00	35.00	30.00

	Current Price Range		Prior Year Average
☐ **Window Card,** Adventures of Huckleberry Finn, The, 1960, Metro-Goldwyn-Mayer, Tony Randall, Patty McCormack, Neville Brand . .	3.00	8.00	5.00
☐ **Window Card,** Alligator People, The, 1959, Twentieth Century-Fox, Beverly Garland, Bruce Bennett, Lon Chaney	15.00	25.00	20.00
☐ **Window Card,** Big Jim McLain, 1952, Warner Brothers, John Wayne	35.00	45.00	40.00
☐ **Window Card,** Creature Walks Among Us, The, 1956, Universal Pictures, Jeff Morrow, Rex Reason, Leigh Snowden	75.00	100.00	87.00
☐ **Window Card,** Cyclops, The, 1957, RKO Radio Pictures, James Craig, Lon Chaney . .	15.00	25.00	20.00
☐ **Window Card,** David and Goliath, 1969, Allied Artists, Orson Wells	8.00	12.00	10.00
☐ **Window Card,** Day the World Ended, 1956, American Releasing Corp., Richard Denning, Lori Nelson, Adele Jergens, Mike Connors . .	25.00	35.00	30.00
☐ **Window Card,** Hot Spell, 1958, Paramount Pictures, Shirley Booth, Shirley MacLaine, Anthony Quinn, Earl Holliman	10.00	20.00	15.00
☐ **Window Card,** Hound of the Baskervilles, The, 1959, United Artists, Peter Cushing, Christopher Lee	65.00	85.00	75.00
☐ **Window Card,** House That Dripped Blood, The, 1971, Cinerama Releasing Corp., Christopher Lee, Peter Cushing	5.00	10.00	7.50

MOVIE SCRIPTS

COMMENTS: Movie scripts are protected by copyright laws and can't be reproduced to increase supply for collectors. All scripts available are the originals that were used when filming a production.

Current low values do not reflect the limited availability of scripts.

ADDITIONAL TIPS: Listings include the title of the production, followed by production date, major performers and number of pages, when available.

For more detailed information refer to *The Official 1984 Price Guide to Radio, TV and Movie Collectibles,* published by The House of Collectibles.

☐ **A-Haunting We Will Go!,** 1942, Laurel and Hardy, 107pp.	95.00	105.00	100.00
☐ **Aaron Loves Angela,** 1974, Kevin Hooks, Irene Cara, 140pp.	25.00	35.00	30.00

	Current Price Range		Prior Year Average
☐ **Abdication, The,** 1973, Peter Finch, Liv Ulmann, 130pp.	40.00	50.00	45.00
☐ **Abilene Trail,** 1950, Whip Wilson, Andy Clyde, 88pp.	20.00	27.00	23.00
☐ **About Mrs. Leslie,** 1953, Shirley Booth, Robert Ryan, 130pp.	30.00	48.00	39.00
☐ **Across 110th Street,** 1972, Anthony Quinn, Anthony Franciosa, 128pp.	25.00	32.00	27.00
☐ **Billy Budd,** 1962, Robert Ryan, Terence Stamp, Peter Ustinov, 178pp.	45.00	55.00	50.00
☐ **Billy Jack,** 1970, Tom Laughlin, 124pp.	35.00	45.00	40.00
☐ **Billy The Kid,** 1941, Robert Taylor, Brian Donlevy, Lon Chaney, Jr., 127pp.	65.00	77.00	72.00
☐ **Billy Two Hats,** 1972, Gregory Peck, 111pp.	40.00	51.00	45.00
☐ **Bing,** 1977, 50th Anniversary gala starring Bing Crosby, Bob Hope, Jack Albertson, Paul Anka, Pearl Bailey, Rosemary Clooney, television, 197pp.	50.00	62.00	56.00
☐ **Bingo Long Traveling All-Stars And Motor Kings,** 1975, Billy Dee Williams, James Earl Jones, Richard Pryor, 129pp.	30.00	41.00	35.00
☐ **Birds And The Bees,** 1955, George Gobel, Mitzi Gaynor, 126pp.	30.00	41.00	35.00
☐ **Birth Of The Blues,** 1941, Bing Crosby, Mary Martin, 127pp.	50.00	62.00	56.00
☐ **Bitter Creek,** 1954, Bill Elliott, 108pp.	25.00	34.00	29.00
☐ **Black Beauty,** 1977, television movie, five parts, 288pp.	40.00	50.00	45.00
☐ **Carousel,** 1955, Gordon MacRae, Shirley Jones, 117pp.	60.00	70.00	65.00
☐ **Caryl Chessman Story,** television movie, 113pp.	20.00	27.00	24.00
☐ **Casablanca,** 1942, Humphrey Bogart, Ingrid Bergman, Claude Rains, 158pp.	40.00	50.00	45.00
☐ **Case Against Brooklyn,** 1957, Darren McGavin, 144pp.	25.00	34.00	29.00
☐ **Case Of Sergeant Grischa,** 1929, Chester Morris, 158pp.	35.00	45.00	40.00
☐ **Cassandra Crossing,** 1975, Burt Lancaster, Sophia Loren, Ava Gardner, 122pp.	45.00	55.00	50.00
☐ **Castle Keep,** 1966, Burt Lancaster, Patrick O'Neal, 153pp.	30.00	39.00	34.00
☐ **Cat And The Fiddle,** 1933, Jeanette Mac-Donald, Ramon Novarro, Frank Morgan, 99pp.	95.00	115.00	105.00
☐ **Catlow,** 1971, Yul Brynner, Leonard Nimoy, 113pp.	35.00	45.00	40.00

	Current Price Range		Prior Year Average
☐ **Dark Purpose,** 1964, Shirley Jones, Rossano Brazzi, 69pp.	20.00	30.00	25.00
☐ **Dark Victory,** 1938, Bette Davis, Humphrey Bogart, Ronald Reagan, 167pp.	100.00	120.00	110.00
☐ **Dark Victory,** 1975, Elizabeth Montgomery, Anthony Hopkins, Michele Lee, three hour Television movie, 156pp.	30.00	40.00	35.00
☐ **David And Bathsheba,** 1950, Gregory Peck, Susan Hayward, Raymond Massey, 133pp.	60.00	70.00	65.00
☐ **Dawn Patrol,** 1938, Errol Flynn, Basil Rathbone, David Niven, 161pp.	40.00	50.00	45.00
☐ **Dawn: Portrait Of A Teenage Runaway,** 1976, Eve Plumb, Leigh McCloskey, Television movie, 107pp.	30.00	40.00	35.00
☐ **Escape From Bogen County,** 1977, Jacklyn Smith, 97pp.	25.00	35.00	30.00
☐ **Escape From The Planet Of The Apes,** 1970, Roddy McDowall, Kim Hunter, 105pp.	55.00	65.00	60.00
☐ **Evel Knievel's Death Defiers,** 1977, Evel Knievel, Television, 109pp.	20.00	29.00	24.00
☐ **Little Miss Broadway,** 1938, Shirley Temple, 141pp.	125.00	140.00	132.00
☐ **Little Miss Nobody,** 1936, Jane Withers, Jane Darwell, 131pp.	40.00	50.00	45.00
☐ **Little Old New York,** 1939, Alice Faye, Fred MacMurray, 163pp.	75.00	90.00	83.00
☐ **Little Princess,** 1938, Shirley Temple, 159pp.	125.00	140.00	133.00
☐ **Little Women,** 1946, June Allyson, Elizabeth Taylor, Margaret O'Brien, 178pp.	95.00	110.00	104.00
☐ **Lost Continent,** 1951, Cesar Romero, 133pp.	27.50	35.00	31.00
☐ **Lost Horizon,** 1972, Peter Finch, Liv Ullmann, Michael York, 120pp.	40.00	50.00	45.00
☐ **Lost In The Stars,** 1973, Brock Peters, final, 90pp.	35.00	45.00	40.00
☐ **Lost Man, The,** 1968, Sidney Poitier, Al Freeman, 142pp.	30.00	40.00	35.00
☐ **Lost World,** 1960, Michael Rennie, Jill St. John, Claude Rains, 125pp.	50.00	60.00	55.00
☐ **Lottery Lover,** 1934, Lew Ayers, Reginald Denny, Sterling Holloway, 125pp.	40.00	50.00	45.00
☐ **Midnight Express,** 1977, Brad Davis, 146pp.	40.00	53.00	44.00
☐ **Midway,** 1975, Charlton Heston, Henry Fonda, James Coburn, Robert Mitchum, Toshiro Mifune, Cliff Robertson, 144pp.	40.00	53.00	46.00
☐ **Mighty Barnum,** 1934, Wallace Beery, Rochelle Hudson, 172pp.	50.00	64.00	57.00

	Current Price Range		Prior Year Average
☐ **Mildred Pierce**, 1944, Joan Crawford, Jack Carson, Zachary Scott, 174pp.	40.00	53.00	46.00
☐ **Monkey Business**, 1952, Marilyn Monroe, Ginger Rogers, Cary Grant, 154pp.	100.00	120.00	110.00
☐ **Monte Walsh**, 1969, Lee Marvin, Jenne Moreau, 109pp.	40.00	53.00	46.00
☐ **Old Barn Dance**, 1937, Gene Autry, Smiley Burnette, 118pp.	45.00	57.00	51.00
☐ **Old-Fashioned Way**, 1934, W. C. Fields, Baby LeRoy, 125pp. Xerox.	40.00	53.00	46.00
☐ **Our Little Girl**, 1935, Shirley Temple, 117pp.	125.00	145.00	135.00
☐ **Our Man Flint**, 1965, James Coburn, 118pp.	60.00	75.00	167.00
☐ **Our Time**, 1973, Pamela Sue Martin, Parker Stevenson, 119pp.	27.50	35.00	31.00
☐ **Outcasts Of Poker Flat**, 1951, Anne Baxter, Miriam Hopkins, Dale Robertson, Cameron Mitchell, 115pp.	45.00	57.00	52.00
☐ **Out-Of-Towners**, 1969, Jack Lemmon, Sandy Dennis, 137pp.	40.00	52.00	46.00
☐ **Pigskin Parade**, 1936, Judy Garland, Jack Haley, Betty Grable, 144pp.	95.00	115.00	105.00
☐ **Pin-Up Girl**, 1943, Betty Grable, Martha Raye, Joe E. Brown, 115pp.	95.00	115.00	105.00
☐ **Pinky**, 1949, Jeanne Crain, Ethel Barrymore, Ethel Waters, 163pp.	60.00	75.00	67.00
☐ **Pinto Bandit**, 1944, Dave (Tex) O'Brien, Jim Newill, Guy Wilkerson, 59pp.	25.00	34.00	30.00
☐ **Pipe Dreams**, 1976, Gladys Knight, 117pp.	22.50	30.00	27.00
☐ **Pirate, The**, 1944, Judy Garland, Gene Kelly, 130pp.	95.00	115.00	105.00
☐ **Romance Of A Horse Thief**, 1968, Yul Brynner, Eli Wallach, 128pp.	35.00	45.00	40.00
☐ **Same Time, Next Year**, 1977, Ellen Burstyn, Alan Alda, 128pp.	40.00	52.00	46.00
☐ **San Francisco**, 1936, Clark Gable, Jeanette MacDonald, Spencer Tracy, ca. 140pp.	30.00	41.00	35.00
☐ **Smilin' Through**, 1932, Leslie Howard, Norma Shearer, 139pp.	75.00	89.00	82.00
☐ **Smoke Lightning**, 1932, George O'Brien, 88pp.	50.00	64.00	57.00
☐ **Smokey And The Bandit**, 1976, Burt Reynolds, Sally Field, 102pp.	45.00	57.00	50.00
☐ **Snake Pit**, 1947, Olivia de Havilland, 159pp.	95.00	115.00	105.00
☐ **Sniper**, 1951, Adolphe Menjou, Marie Windsor, 131pp.	22.50	30.00	27.00
☐ **Spirit Of St. Louis**, 1957, James Stewart, 97pp.	30.00	42.00	36.00

	Current Price Range		Prior Year Average
☐ **Springtime In The Rockies**, 1942, Betty Grable, Carmen Miranda, Cesar Romero, 129pp.	95.00	115.00	105.00
☐ **Spring-Time In Texas**, 1945, Jimmy Wakely, 86pp.	25.00	34.00	29.00
☐ **Spy Chasers**, 1955, The Bowery Boys, 94pp.	35.00	47.00	41.00
☐ **Stage Struck**, 1956, Henry Fonda, Susan Strasberg, Christopher Plummer, 115pp.	40.00	53.00	47.00
☐ **Stage To Blue River**, 1951, Whip Wilson, 76pp.	22.00	30.00	28.00
☐ **Stagecoach**, 1965, Ann-Margret, Mike Connors, Bing Crosby, 121pp.	50.00	64.00	57.00

NAUTICAL MEMORABILIA

DESCRIPTION: Nautical memorabilia refers to such items as figureheads, anchors, windlasses, deadeyes and navigational and weather instruments.

TYPES: Various types of objects encompass the realm of nautical memorabilia including items salvaged from ships, paper items such as ship lists, posters, and ship logs; articles created by sailors; and paintings of ships.

PERIOD: Collectors will usually find items dating from the 1800s. Items before that time are rare and usually housed in museums.

COMMENTS: Nautical memorabilia has become so universally popular that the finer items are very valuable on the collectible market. Ship salvage yards are an excellent place to search for nautical gear.

	Current Price Range		Prior Year Average
☐ **Bill of Lading**, partially printed, Liverpool to Boston, on the ship John and Phiebe, 1799, 5″ x 9½″	13.00	17.00	15.00
☐ **Book**, *Sailing Craft* by Edwin Schpettle, published in New York in 1928, cloth bound, 786 pages	90.00	115.00	100.00
☐ **Deadeye**, wood braced with iron, c. 1860	70.00	90.00	80.00
☐ **Diver's Helmet**, brass with glass viewing shield, some iron and nickel components, complete with partial shoulder plate, late 1800s	300.00	375.00	335.00
☐ **Document**, British Brig Geffrared enters the Port of San Francisco, large document headed Inward Foreign Entry, 1854	35.00	45.00	40.00

	Current Price Range		Prior Year Average
☐ **Document,** Entry of Merchandise from Valpariso to San Francisco on the ship Bark Orient, partially printed, 1853, 14″ x 17″	35.00	45.00	40.00
☐ **Lithograph,** Coleman's Line Clipper Ship, in the form of a huge card, undated, 9″ x 12″ . . .	450.00	550.00	500.00
☐ **Oil Painting,** Clipper Ship by Antonio Jacobsen, oil on board, dated 1915, 16″ x 12″	1600.00	2000.00	1800.00
☐ **Oil Painting,** Sailing in Philadelphia Harbor by James E. Buttersworth, oil on panel, 5¾″ x 9¼″	4000.00	5500.00	4600.00
☐ **Print,** two ships at sea, marked Seamen's Bank for Savings, New York, 1962, 15½″ x 22″	20.00	25.00	22.00
☐ **Sailor's Foot Locker,** made of rough pine joined with copper braces at the sides and back, decorated with simple incised carving of port scenes and several crude representations of sailing ships, 39″ wide x 19″ deep x 18″ high, undated, c. 1875	350.00	450.00	400.00
☐ **Ship's Compass,** in cherrywood box with lid, brass fittings, made in England, undated, c. 1820	400.00	500.00	450.00
☐ **Ship's Log,** Nantucket whaler, 168 pages, some sketches of whales and harpooning in margins, binding loose, stained, dated 1884 .	500.00	650.00	570.00
☐ **Ship's Wheel,** mahogany, well preserved condition, mid to late 1800s, overall diameter including grips 39″	550.00	675.00	610.00
☐ **Ship's Wheel,** rosewood and brass, mid 1800s, overall diameter including grips 44½″	700.00	900.00	800.00
☐ **Trade Sign Figure,** The Little Navigator, carved and painted wood, figure of a man in stovepipe hat holding navigational instrument, c. 1860, 27½″	600.00	750.00	660.00

NEEDLEWORKING TOOLS

DESCRIPTION: The often exquisite sewing utensils used by past generations are sought after collectibles today.

COMMENTS: While most needleworking tools are collectible, and fairly easy to find, thimbles are the most popular. They vary in prices and were made in silver, porcelain and plastic with advertising slogans, but cut glass thimbles are the most valuable and the most rare. Scissors are also sought after, as are workboxes and small cases.

	Current Price Range		Prior Year Average
☐ **Basket**, wicker, 12″ H.	22.50	29.00	23.00
☐ **Darner**, glass, red	31.00	40.00	32.00
☐ **Darner**, glove, sterling silver	44.00	54.00	46.00
☐ **Darner**, sock, brown	31.50	39.00	33.00
☐ **Needlebook**, embossed lithograph decoration on cover	10.00	16.00	12.00
☐ **Needle Case**, brass	16.00	22.00	18.00
☐ **Needle Case**, carved ivory	36.00	44.00	38.00
☐ **Needle Case**, sterling silver	27.00	34.00	28.00
☐ **Needle Case**, tortoise shell	85.00	110.00	92.00
☐ **Pincushion**, ivory, pedestal base	48.00	60.00	52.00
☐ **Pincushion**, sterling silver	120.00	160.00	130.00
☐ **Pincushion**, patchwork, 8″	16.50	22.00	18.00
☐ **Scissors**, embroidery, stork, silver plate, 3″ L.	31.50	39.00	33.00
☐ **Sewing Bird**, brass	49.00	60.00	52.00
☐ **Sewing Bird**, brass, clamp-on, large with cushion	165.00	215.00	275.00
☐ **Sewing Bird**, iron, 6″ L.	35.00	45.00	37.00

NEWSPAPERS

The most valuable newspapers are those which carry major news stories. Some of the most valuable twentieth century newspapers carry premature "Dewey defeats Truman" headlines.

ADDITIONAL TIPS: Prices are for whole issues, not just front pages. Front pages alone are worth less than the prices shown. For more information, consult *The Official Price Guide to Paper Collectibles*, published by The House of Collectibles.

ASSASSINATIONS

☐ **Archduke Francis Ferdinand**	7.75	11.50	9.67
☐ **James Garfield Shot** (still alive)	11.50	16.50	13.50
☐ **James Garfield dies of wound**	5.75	6.75	6.25
☐ **Mahatma Gandhi**	4.00	5.75	4.87
☐ **John F. Kennedy**	11.50	13.50	12.50
☐ **Robert Kennedy Shot** (still alive)	5.75	6.75	6.25
☐ **Robert Kennedy dies of wound**	4.00	5.75	4.87
☐ **Martin Luther King, Jr.**	4.00	5.75	4.87
☐ **Abraham Lincoln**	115.00	170.00	142.00
☐ **Huey Long**	6.75	7.75	7.25
☐ **Huey Long — New Orleans paper**	10.00	13.50	11.75
☐ **William McKinley Shot** (still alive)	11.50	16.50	13.50
☐ **William McKinley dies of wound**	6.75	7.75	7.25
☐ **Anwar Sadat**	.75	1.00	.87

Charleston Daily Courier.

Boston Sunday Post

$100 in Prizes
For your Three for the
Unnamed Picture
See Page 36 Letter

PRICE FIVE CENTS   BOSTON, SUNDAY MORNING, APRIL 21, 1912   PRICE FIVE CENTS

The Story of the Titanic by Mrs. Jacques Futrelle on Page 11

SAYS LOOKOUT THREE TIMES
SENT WARNING OF ICEBERGS

One of Titanic's Crew Declares He Was Told Officer on Bridge Was
Duly Notified—Titanic's Wireless Man Claims Nearest Vessel, German
Steamer Frankfurt, Did Not Respond to Signal of Distress

WEST VIRGINIA
FOR ROOSEVELT

Sweeping Victory of 273 Delegates
to 75—Nebraska and Oregon for
Him by Margin

NEBRASKA FOR COLONEL

SEVERAL IDENTIFY
DORR PHOTOGRAPH

Admits He Ignored Questions
From Her—Felt Carpathia
Would Arrive in Time

SAYS LINER
WARNED BY
LOOKOUTS

Reported Icebergs 3
Tenth to Officer

Newspapers, *American, 1864-1912, each,* **$25.00-$60.00**

ATTEMPTED ASSASSINATIONS	Current Price Range		Prior Year Average
☐ Charles DeGaule	1.35	2.00	1.67
☐ Gerald Ford	.65	.95	.80
☐ Franklin D. Roosevelt	4.00	5.50	4.75
☐ Harry S. Truman	2.75	4.00	3.38
☐ Gov. George Wallace	2.00	3.25	2.62
☐ Pope John-Paul II	.75	1.00	.87

RESULTS OF PRESIDENTIAL ELECTIONS

	Current Price Range		Prior Year Average
☐ 1860, Lincoln/Douglas	33.75	47.25	40.50
☐ 1864, Lincoln/McClellan	27.50	40.00	33.75
☐ 1868, Grant/Seymour	8.00	13.50	10.50
☐ 1872, Grant/Greeley	8.00	13.50	10.50
☐ 1876, Hayes/Tilden	6.75	10.75	8.75
☐ 1880, Garfield/Hancock	6.75	10.75	8.75
☐ 1884, Cleveland/Blaine	6.75	10.75	8.75
☐ 1888, Harrison/Cleveland	6.75	10.75	8.75
☐ 1892, Cleveland/Harrison	6.75	10.75	8.75
☐ 1896, McKinley/Bryan	8.00	12.25	10.00
☐ 1900, McKinley/Bryan	8.00	12.25	10.00
☐ 1904, Roosevelt/Parker	6.75	10.75	8.75
☐ 1908, Taft/Bryan	5.50	9.50	7.50
☐ 1912, Wilson/Rosevelt/Taft	8.00	12.25	10.00
☐ 1916, Wilson/Hughes	5.50	9.50	7.50
☐ 1920, Harding/Cox	4.00	6.75	5.37
☐ 1924, Coolidge/Davis	2.75	4.75	3.75
☐ 1928, Hoover/Smith	2.75	4.75	3.75
☐ 1932, Roosevelt/Hoover	5.50	9.50	7.50
☐ 1936, Roosevelt/Landon	4.00	6.75	5.37
☐ 1940, Roosevelt/Wilkie	4.00	6.75	5.37
☐ 1944, Roosevelt/Dewey	4.00	6.75	5.37
☐ 1948, Truman/Dewey	4.00	6.75	5.37
Note: Papers carrying premature "Dewey Defeats Truman" headlines are worth as much as $200. The New York Times was not one of them.			
☐ 1952, Eisenhower/Stevenson	2.75	4.75	3.75
☐ 1956, Eisenhower/Stevenson	2.00	3.50	2.75
☐ 1960, Kennedy/Nixon	8.00	12.25	10.00
☐ 1964, Johnson/Goldwater	2.00	3.50	2.75
☐ 1968, Nixon/Humphrey	2.00	3.50	2.75
☐ 1972, Nixon/McGovern	2.00	3.50	2.75
☐ 1976, Carter/Ford	1.35	2.75	2.05
☐ 1980, Reagan/Carter	1.00	1.50	1.25

DEATHS OF CELEBRATED PERSONS (WHOLE PAPER)

	Current Price Range		Prior Year Average
☐ Jack Benny	1.35	2.75	2.05
☐ Charlie Chaplin	2.75	4.75	3.75
☐ Winston Churchill	4.00	6.75	5.37
☐ Calvin Coolidge	2.75	4.50	3.62
☐ Charles DeGalle	2.00	3.00	2.50
☐ Edward VII	2.75	4.50	3.62
☐ Adolph Eichmann (Executed)	5.50	9.50	7.50
☐ Dwight D. Eisenhower	2.00	3.50	2.75
☐ Judy Garland	13.50	20.00	16.50
☐ Warren Harding	2.75	4.75	3.75
☐ Adolph Hitler (unconfirmed)	20.00	27.00	24.00
☐ Herbert Hoover	2.00	3.50	2.75
☐ Lyndon Johnson	1.35	2.75	2.05
☐ Nikita Khrushchev	2.00	3.50	2.75
☐ John Lennon	1.00	1.50	1.25
☐ Marilyn Monroe	16.00	23.50	20.00

NIPPON

DESCRIPTION: Nippon porcelain ware is the result of an American tarriff act in the late 19th century which required imports to be marked with the country of their origin. Nippon ware is something of an enigma to all but experienced collectors as it also represents Satsuma, Noritake, Imari and other Japanese wares of a certain period. Nippon ware really is quite beautiful combining a relatively contemporary look with old style crafts-manship, and exquisite taste.

COMMENTS: Nippon was not a popular collectible until the mid 1950s. It is still possible to find Nippon porcelain in flea markets, thrift shops, yard sales, attics, or Grandma's china closet. Really choice pieces are difficult to locate, however, as the owners withhold them from the market to increase their value, or because of sentimental attachment.

MARKS: Nippon marks most frequently depict an M within a green wreath, and the word "Nippon" printed in curved letters underneath. There are many, many variations, however. By the early 20th century, the Nippon emblem was replaced with "Japan," thus ending an era.

ADDITIONAL TIPS: Typical of any lucrative collectible field, Nippon ware has been faked and reproduced on the antiques market. Items are arranged according to function, material and colors.

Egg Warmer, *green M in wreath mark, 5½", $95.00-$130.00*

	Current Price Range		Prior Year Average
☐ **Basket,** *1900's, blown out, molded, acorns, brown, handle extends over the top of the basket*	150.00	200.00	175.00
☐ **Bowl,** *6" in diameter, 1900's, bisque finish, small bowl, tiny brown beading on the outside, scalloped trim, hand painted acorns, leaves, twigs inside the bowl, yellow, brown, maroon and green*	65.00	75.00	70.00
☐ **Bowl,** *9" in diameter, c. 1900's, bisque, walnut motif, green M mark*	50.00	100.00	75.00
☐ **Bowl,** *7" in diameter, c. 1900's, blue, white background, pink, red floral medallions, handles, green M mark*	10.00	20.00	15.00
☐ **Bowl,** *9" in diameter, c. 1900's, mustard color, hand painted, M wreath, blue mark, gold, jewels, rose motif*	35.00	75.00	55.00
☐ **Bowl,** *9" in diameter, c. 1900's, red, black, figural, scenic, floral motif, green, red border, unmarked*	40.00	80.00	60.00

	Current Price Range		Prior Year Average

☐ **Bowl,** *c. 1900's, strawberries, leaves and flowers, leaf shaped handled* 270.00 290.00 280.00

☐ **Box,** *2" high, c. 1900's, blue, gold-raised motif, green M mark* 80.00 120.00 100.00

☐ **Candy Bowl,** *c. 1900's, hand painted scene of palm trees, lake with sailboat, mountains in pastel colors, beaded gold trim around outer rim, two pierced, upturned handles* . . . 55.00 65.00 60.00

☐ **Candy Bowl,** *6" square, c. 1900's, square, beaded, gold rim, blown out sides, two gold handles, floral design, purple, green, yellow and brown, pastel background* 77.00 85.00 82.50

☐ **Ewer,** *10" high, c. 1900's, bulbous body, band of violets, greens and violets, cabinet item, unmarked* 175.00 190.00 182.50

☐ **Ewer,** *12" high, 1900's, bulbous body, long 5½" neck, handle extends from body to neck, folial center piece, red and violet* 200.00 300.00 250.00

☐ **Humidore,** *11" x 7", c. 1900's, bisque finish, tray, match holder, small tray, open cigar cup, seven pieces in all, scene of Arab astride a camel, beside a desert tent, fire and palm trees, sunset colors, flat lid gold round finial (set)* 750.00 800.00 775.00

☐ **Humidore,** *5" high, c. 1900's, bisque finish, winter scene, purple, enamel tracings of leaves* 45.00 55.00 50.00

☐ **Humidore,** *c. 1900's, metal top, glass, painted, roses, base flares out* 55.00 65.00 60.00

☐ **Humidore,** *9" in diameter, c. 1900's, satin finish, round tray, match, ashtray, five pieces, scene of swamp, tree extends onto to the lid* 450.00 500.00 475.00

☐ **Nut Bowl,** *5" in diameter, c. 1900's, black, gold background, green floral motif, floral medallion, three blue leaf mask* 40.00 80.00 60.00

☐ **Nut Bowl,** *6" wide, c. 1900's, brown, raised enamel, bisque finish, walnut motif, three legs, green M mark* 95.00 110.00 100.00

☐ **Stamp Box,** *c. 1900's, slanting top, compartment* 25.00 50.00 37.50

☐ **Vase,** *9" high, c. 1900's, amphore shaped body, no handles, small neck, scenic panel, sunset colors, thatched farm cottage, trees, pond, two swans in the water, top of the vase covered with heavy brown putty in fancy designs, green* 350.00 400.00 375.00

OCCUPIED JAPAN

DESCRIPTION: Collectibles from this category represent Japanese exported items made after World War II, when Japan was "occupied" by a foreign country for the first time in history. The term "occupied" was essential to Japanese economic recovery. Hostile feelings towards the Eastern nation still ran high for many years after the war; people absolutely refused to buy anything with "Made in Japan" as it's trademark, believing that American dollars could not go to a more unworthy cause than to support a country responsible for such economic, personal, and political worldwide upheaval. Since Japanese exports still retained such superior craftsmanship, beauty and aesthetic symmetry despite the scarcity of materials and manpower, the trademark "Occupied Japan," assured consumers, that they were in no way contributing their hard earned dollars to the menacing powers of the prewar era.

COMMENTS: Like Nippon, Occupied Japanese items are steadily growing in value as collectibles, and more and more dealers are scrambling to supply these items to their Orientalia buyers. Identification is fairly simple of course; the trademark is self explanatory. Do not be put off by Westernized motifs and design; the Japanese were, after all, in a state of national transition marking the beginning of their conversion to Westernized ideals and modes of living.

Items are arranged according to category. In large sections, these are further broken down according to type of object. Within the listings, articles are alphabetically arranged by dimension, smallest to largest.

RECOMMENDED READING: For more in-depth information on Occupied Japan, you may refer to *The Official Price Guide to Oriental Collectibles*, published by The House of Collectibles.

	Current Price Range		Prior Year Average
☐ **Ashtray,** 3″ x 2½″, cigarette and match holder, pickanny between pants hanging to dry, "Who left this behind?"	20.00	30.00	25.00
☐ **Ashtray,** 3″ octagonal, iris in relief, gold trim .	5.00	10.00	7.50
☐ **Ashtray,** 3½″ high, boot, cigarette rest, brown flowers and trim	8.00	12.00	10.00
☐ **Bookend,** 4″ high, lady in green bonnet, yellow bodice, blue shawl, lavender layered skirt carries closed parasol, on two books	8.00	10.00	9.00
☐ **Boot,** 2½″ x 1½″, silver plate, etched floral design	15.00	18.00	17.50
☐ **Pin Cushion,** tin, red velvet top, mirror inside lid, marked	20.00	22.00	21.00

	Current Price Range		Prior Year Average
☐ **Plaque,** 4″ x 5″, landscape, gold filigree border	13.00	15.00	14.00
☐ **Plaque,** 5″ x 4″, "It's Later Than You Think" in Japanese and English	9.00	11.00	10.00
☐ **Plaques,** 7¼″ high, in orange, yellow and green, Dutch children hold flower, pair	15.00	17.00	16.00
☐ **Powder Bowl,** 10″ diameter, pale blue, dome lid	13.00	15.00	14.00
☐ **Sweater Clips,** 1¼″ high, porcelain buttons with pansies joined by pearl chain	18.00	22.00	20.00
☐ **Toy Bear,** wind-up, string of fish in mouth ...	31.00	33.00	32.00
☐ **Toy Car,** red, remote control	26.00	28.00	27.00
☐ **Vase,** 4½″ high, Hummel boy next to 2¼″ vase, holds basket of apples	14.00	16.00	15.00
☐ **Vase,** 4½″ high, lakeside scene, side shoulders	9.50	11.00	10.25
☐ **Vase,** 4¾″ high, bud vase, concertina player in brick hat, green and brown jacket, blue pants in front of vase	10.00	12.00	11.00
☐ **Vase,** 4¾″ high, Hummel girl next to 3¼″ vase	14.00	16.00	15.00
☐ **Vase,** 5″ high, bud vase, sax player in red hat, green jacket, yellow pants in front of vase ...	10.00	12.00	11.00

CHILDREN

☐ **Alpine Girl,** 4½″ high, black hat, green dress, lavender apron	7.00	9.00	8.00
☐ **Boy,** 4″ high, blue turban, green jacket, gold and white pants, red shoes, carrying two bottles and a basket of fruit	11.00	13.00	12.00
☐ **Boy,** 4″ high, green hat, red feather, white shirt, brown shorts, seated on bench playing violin	9.00	12.00	10.50
☐ **Boy,** 4″ high, holding basket of apples, duck at feet	8.50	10.00	9.25
☐ **Boy,** 4½″ high, blue hat, brown knickers, toy boat in hands	7.00	9.00	8.00
☐ **Boy,** 4½″ high, green and yellow jacket, dog at side	9.50	11.00	10.25
☐ **Boy,** 4½″ high, orange hat, red jacket, green breeches, plays bass violin	9.50	12.00	10.25
☐ **Boy,** 4½″ high, red kerchief, green jacket, holding picnic basket and bouquet, leaning against fence	11.00	14.00	12.50
☐ **Boy Skier,** 4½″ x 4″, red hat, green pants, brown jacket and skis, fallen, sitting on skis .	21.00	24.00	22.50

	Current Price Range		Prior Year Average
☐ **Colonial Boy,** 5″ high, cape, holding flowers and musical instrument	9.00	10.00	9.50
☐ **Colonial Girl,** 5½″ high, long white dress, blue garden hat, holding umbrella	11.00	13.00	12.00
☐ **Cowboy,** 5″ high, blue, green and yellow costume, rope at side	12.50	14.00	13.25
☐ **Dutch Boy,** 3″ high, yellow and blue costume, one hand in pocket	6.50	8.00	7.25
☐ **Dutch Boy,** 4″ high, blue and white, yoke on shoulders	8.50	10.00	9.25
☐ **Dutch Girl,** 4″ high, seated, open book in hands	5.50	7.00	6.25
☐ **Dutch Girl,** 4¼″ high, yellow and red costume	9.00	11.00	10.00
☐ **Dutch Girl,** 5″ high, yellow hat and apron, basket on arm	8.50	10.00	9.25
☐ **Girl,** 2½″ high, red dress, holding flowers . . .	5.50	7.00	6.25
☐ **Girl,** 3″ high, yellow apron, blue skirt, red shoes, finger to chin, dog at feet, holding umbrella	7.50	9.00	8.25
☐ **Girl,** 3¼″ high, brown kerchief, green skirt, basket on arm	8.00	10.00	9.00
☐ **Girl,** 3¾″ high, red dotted bandana, blue dotted dress, holding flowers, rabbit at feet	8.00	10.00	9.00
☐ **Girl,** 4″, blue and white blouse, red skirt, pigtails, holds book	9.50	12.00	10.75
☐ **Girl,** 4″ high, red and green long dress, standing at fence, holding picnic basket and bouquet	9.00	11.00	10.00
☐ **Girl,** 4½″ high, blonde hair, red ribbon, white blouse, green skirt, holding red flowers in skirt	9.50	12.00	10.75
☐ **Girl,** 4½″ high, red dress, seated on fence, playing guitar, singing	10.00	12.00	11.00
☐ **Girl,** 5″ high, blue bandana, green blouse, yellow and pink apron, red skirt, goose at side	14.00	16.00	15.00
☐ **Oriental Boy,** 8″ high, black coat, pink trim, pink hat	20.00	22.00	21.00
☐ **Oriental Boy,** 8″ high, black jacket and hat, grey pants	19.00	22.00	20.50
☐ **Oriental Child,** 4½″ high, red shirt, black pantaloons, two open baskets at sides, holding a green parasol	10.00	12.50	11.25
☐ **Oriental Girl,** 4½″ high, green blouse, black slacks, holding a red feather	9.00	11.00	10.00

ORIENTAL JEWELRY

ORIGIN: Jewelry from the Oriental countries has been distributed worldwide since the earliest trade agreement narrowed the gulf between the East and West. Low cost labor and an abundance of natural resources have created a vast manufacturing network in Peking and Eastern China and the products of these countries are highly sought after.

MATERIALS: Coral, opal, and jade are commonly used in manufacturing the characteristics heavy pieces. The bright reds and oranges of coral, the fiery streaking effect in opal, and the glow of the ever popular jade is attractive to women and the men who buy jewelry for them. When 14k gold is used in mounts and chains, the price reflects the inherent value of this precious metal. Silver is a popular medium for the intricately forged decorations and often it is washed with gold plating.

DESIGN: The Oriental touch in design is always evident. Whether the motif is geometrical, or an elegant natural pattern there is always precise attention to detail. Even the pieces mass manufactured for western distribution have the Oriental imprint: a stylized look at life.

ADDITIONAL TIPS: Items are arranged alphabetically.

RECOMMENDED READING: For more in-depth information on Oriental jewelry, refer to *The Official Price Guide to Oriental Collectibles,* published by The House of Collectibles.

	Current Price Range		Prior Year Average
☐ **Bracelet,** c. 1900's, Peking, bangle, gold hinges, half light and dark green, half celadon and orange	500.00	600.00	550.00
☐ **Bracelet,** c. 1900's, Peking, bangle, gold hinges, half light green, half light orange	500.00	580.00	540.00
☐ **Bracelet,** c. 1900's, Peking, bangle, gold hinges, white with green spot, half tan	475.00	525.00	500.00
☐ **Bracelet,** c. 1900's, Peking, bangle style, gold-plated hinges, shades of green	125.00	140.00	132.50
☐ **Bracelet,** c. 1900's, Peking, bangle style, gold-plated hinges, white with orange veins	100.00	125.00	112.50
☐ **Bracelet,** c. 1900's, Peking, bangle style, silver hinges, dark celadon color	100.00	125.00	112.50
☐ **Bracelet,** c. 1900's, Peking, Buddhas alternating with heart shapes, green and white, silverplate	75.00	80.00	77.50
☐ **Bracelet,** c. 1900's, Peking, cuff style, carved jade flower button medallion, silver filigree, blue decor	200.00	250.00	225.00

	Current Price Range		Prior Year Average
☐ **Brooch,** c. 1900's, Peking, starburst, 14k gold rays and multicolored jadeite stones	250.00	300.00	275.00
☐ **Brooch,** c. 1900's, Peking, starburst motif, dark green jadeite center, blue enamel	40.00	50.00	45.00
☐ **Brooch,** c. 1900's, Peking, starburst motif, silver filagree and beadwork, jadeite inset . . .	35.00	40.00	37.50
☐ **Brooch,** c. 1900's, Peking, starburst shape, center is ten fire opals, gold rays	275.00	300.00	287.50
☐ **Brooch,** c. 1900's, Peking, teapot shape, with four coral and three turquoise stones	25.00	30.00	27.50
☐ **Brooch,** c. 1900's, Peking, teapot shape with seven amethyst stones, blue enamel	25.00	30.00	27.50
☐ **Brooch,** c. 1900's, Peking, tear drop shape, jadeite leaf, silver filigree border	60.00	70.00	65.00
☐ **Brooch,** c. 1900's, Peking, teardrop shape, jadeite leaf with beadwork and floral motif border	75.00	80.00	77.50
☐ **Earrings,** c. 1900's, Peking, clipback, carved red coral, temple motif	110.00	125.00	117.50
☐ **Earrings,** c. 1900's, Peking, clipback, oval cinnabar inset, character motif, surrounded by gold filigree border	20.00	25.00	22.50
☐ **Earrings,** c. 1900's, Peking, clipback, oval, enameled flowers and leaves, gold background	25.00	30.00	22.50
☐ **Medallion,** c. 1900's, Peking, round, carved malachite, silver background	400.00	425.00	412.50
☐ **Medallion,** c. 1900's, Peking, urn shape, carved ruby, floral motif, with silver frame work	450.00	500.00	475.00
☐ **Necklace,** c. 1900's, Peking, green jade beads with bird and flower pendant	1000.00	1100.00	1050.00
☐ **Necklace,** 16″ long, c. 1900's, Peking, opal beads, green fire	750.00	900.00	825.00
☐ **Necklace,** 23″ long, c. 1900's, Peking, opal beads, red and green fire	1200.00	1400.00	1300.00
☐ **Necklace,** 13″ long, c. 1900's, Peking, opal beads, red fire	850.00	950.00	900.00
☐ **Pendant,** 1¾″ tall, c. 1900's, Peking, bats, butterflies and coins, green and white	75.00	85.00	80.00
☐ **Pendant,** 2″ tall, c. 1900's, Peking, birds and clouds, light green	165.00	175.00	170.00
☐ **Pendant,** 2″ tall, c. 1900's, Peking, blossoms and leaves, light brown	145.00	160.00	152.50

	Current Price Range		Prior Year Average
☐ **Ring**, c. 1900's, Peking, adjustable, carved jadeite, marquise style	125.00	130.00	127.50
☐ **Ring**, c. 1900's, Peking, adjustable, carved jadeite, oval shape, floral motif	125.00	135.00	127.50
☐ **Ring**, c. 1900's, Peking, adjustable, carved jadeite, rose motif	125.00	130.00	127.50
☐ **Ring**, c. 1900's, Peking, adjustable, carved jadeite square	125.00	130.00	127.50
☐ **Ring**, c. 1900's, Peking, adjustable, carved jadeite, teardrop shape	125.00	130.00	127.50

OWLS

ORIGIN: The owl was first used as a decoration on coins in ancient Greece.

COMMENTS: A popular collectible, owls have been used on emblems, shields and beginning in the 19th century, on decorative items.

ADDITIONAL TIPS: The listings are alphabetical according to item. Following the items is a description, followed by maker, date and other information as available.

	Current Price Range		Prior Year Average
☐ **Bookends**, rookwood, tan glaze, pair	120.00	160.00	130.00
☐ **Book Rack**, expanding, cast brass, two owls .	36.00	46.00	40.00
☐ **Chatelaine**, wire plaque, link chains, silver plated	140.00	170.00	150.00
☐ **Cookie Jar**, tan and white, one eye closed, Shawnee Pottery Company	10.00	15.00	12.00
☐ **Doorstop**, carved wood with glass eyes, c. 1920s	21.50	30.00	24.00
☐ **Fairy Lamp**, bisque, owl face, glass eyes, 4½" high	165.00	240.00	185.00
☐ **Figurine**, carved wooden owl	55.00	75.00	65.00
☐ **Figurine**, character owl in checked shawl with ermine collar, Royal Doulton	775.00	875.00	825.00
☐ **Figurine**, Great Horned Owl, ceramic	40.00	60.00	50.00
☐ **Figurine**, Great Horned Owl, porcelain, Royal Copenhagen	450.00	550.00	500.00
☐ **Figurine**, veined owl, Rouge Flambe, Royal Doulton, No. 2249	310.00	360.00	340.00
☐ **Figurine**, wise old owl in red cloak with ermine collar	425.00	525.00	475.00
☐ **Inkwell**, alabaster, owl on pile of books, 19th century	125.00	175.00	150.00

	Current Price Range		Prior Year Average
☐ **Jar,** Atterbury, opal glass, inserted red eyes, 7" high	125.00	165.00	135.00
☐ **Jar,** owl on a pedestal, pastel bisque, head is the jar lid, Royal Doulton-Lambeth	390.00	440.00	400.00
☐ **Painting,** primitive, two owls, late 19th century	107.00	140.00	117.00
☐ **Paperweight,** crystal, round, frosted horned owl, copper engraving	425.00	525.00	475.00
☐ **Pitcher,** owl design, etched, clear green glass	30.00	45.00	35.00
☐ **Plate,** "1981 First Light - Great Horned Owl, The Prowlers of the Clouds Series," by Larry Toschik	60.00	70.00	65.00
☐ **Plate,** "1981 His Golden Throne - Screech Owl, The Prowlers of the Clouds Series," by Larry Toschik	60.00	70.00	65.00
☐ **Print,** Baby Saw-Whet Owls, released 1981, by Guy Coheleach	30.00	60.00	45.00
☐ **Print,** Barn Owl, released, 1980, by Owen J. Gromme	100.00	120.00	105.00
☐ **Print,** Barred Owl, released 1982, by Guy Coheleach	120.00	140.00	130.00
☐ **Print,** Burrowing Owl, released 1975, by Arthur Singer	30.00	60.00	45.00
☐ **Print,** "Eyes of the Night," Great Horned Owl, released 1979, by Owen J. Gromme	100.00	115.00	105.00
☐ **Print,** Great Horned Owl, released 1974, by Roger Tory Peterson	150.00	200.00	175.00
☐ **Print,** Great Horned Owl, released 1979, by Jill Fogelsong	50.00	75.00	60.00
☐ **Print,** Long-Eared Owl, released 1976, by James A. Carson	85.00	100.00	90.00
☐ **Print,** Oval Owl, released 1978, by Stan Brod	45.00	60.00	50.00
☐ **Print,** Pigmy Owl, released 1972, by Peter Parnall	30.00	180.00	80.00
☐ **Print,** Richardson's Owl, released 1972, by Peter Parnall	30.00	215.00	150.00
☐ **Print,** Screech Owls, by E. Gordon West	30.00	45.00	37.00
☐ **Print,** Screech Owl, released 1972, by Gene Gray	25.00	50.00	35.00
☐ **Print,** Snowy Owls, released 1979, by Charles Frace	65.00	95.00	75.00
☐ **Print,** Snowy Owl, released 1972, by Roger Tory Peterson	175.00	575.00	250.00
☐ **Print,** Spectacled Owl, released 1979, by Jill Fogelsong	100.00	150.00	125.00
☐ **Purse,** mesh, diamonds, rubies, gold, owl motif frame, Art Nouveau, c. 1890	23000.00	25000.00	24000.00

	Current Price Range		Prior Year Average
☐ **Salt and Pepper Shakers,** tan and white, one eye closed, Shawnee Pottery Company	8.00	14.00	11.00
☐ **Sculpture,** Snowy Owl, female, by Robert Jefferson, Royal Doulton, 1974	2150.00	2400.00	2250.00
☐ **Sculpture,** Snowy Owl, male, by Robert Jefferson, Royal Doulton, 1974	1750.00	2000.00	1850.00
☐ **Stick Pin,** 14K gold, c. 1895	70.00	80.00	75.00
☐ **Stick Pin,** gold, two diamond chip eyes, 14K gold	140.00	175.00	155.00
☐ **Stick Pin,** gold filled, c. 1895	30.00	40.00	35.00
☐ **Vase,** hand painted owl profile, tan and brown, Weller Hudson	1050.00	1200.00	1100.00
☐ **Vase,** primitive owl design, pottery, Avon Pottery	800.00	950.00	850.00

PAPER COLLECTIBLES

TOPIC: This section covers business correspondence, celebrity items, checks and documents. For listings of other paper items such as books, please refer directly to those individual sections.

TYPES: There is a huge variety of paper items that people collect. If the item is of historical importance it probably has a value to collectors.

COMMENTS: Collectors of paper goods specialize as to the type of item they collect, since the field is too vast for general collecting.

ADDITIONAL TIPS: For further information and listings, please refer to *The Official Price Guide to Paper Collectibles,* published by The House of Collectibles.

BUSINESS CORRESPONDENCE

☐ **California Aeronautics Firm,** 651 letters covering the period January to June 1938, a few of later date, some stained or damaged, in three plywood flip-top cartons with lettered labels (one carton broken).	150.00	170.00	160.00
☐ **Chicago Ice-House,** 421 letters covering the period December 1890 to July 1896, some invoices, etc. included.	90.00	120.00	105.00
☐ **Connecticut Clock Manufacturer,** 68 letters covering the period September 1851 to January 1852, bound in a half morocco case.	180.00	220.00	200.00

	Current Price Range		Prior Year Average
☐ **Massachusetts Leather Goods Manufacturer,** 81 letters covering the period July to October 1870, loose, some letters have a page or more missing.	65.00	85.00	75.00
☐ **New York Cigar Wholesaler,** 223 letters covering the period April 1889 to October 1889.	48.00	68.00	58.00
☐ **New York Optical Goods Company,** 17 letters, 1862.	85.00	105.00	95.00
☐ **Parisian Hat Manufacturer,** 367 letters (plus miscellaneous bills, a few photos and design sketches) covering the period August 1906 to March 1907, enclosed in a buckram folder.	55.00	65.00	60.00
☐ **Tiffany & Co., New York Fancy Goods Retailer,** 891 letters (plus promotional items, notes, memos, etc.) of 1911-1915, enclosed in six cardboard felt-lined cases.	850.00	1050.00	950.00

Parker Fountain Pens, *magazine advertisement, 1920s,* **$1.50-$2.00**

CELEBRITY ITEMS

	Current Price Range		Prior Year Average
☐ **Amos and Andy Map of Weber City,** Pepsodent radio premium, 1935.	38.00	48.00	43.00
☐ **Amos and Andy,** 8″ x 10″ photo, n.d., c. 1935.	13.00	17.00	15.00
☐ **Amos and Andy,** four page brochure about the program, c. 1935.	13.00	17.00	15.00
☐ **Astaire, Fred,** brochure of Fred Astaire Dance School, c. 1954.	2.00	3.00	2.50
☐ **Hopalong Cassidy Western Magazine,** Vol. 1, No. 2, colored cover, published by Best Books, 162 pages, Winter, 1951.	60.00	70.00	65.00
☐ **Hopalong Cassidy with Cole Bros. Circus,** souvenir program, color cover, 32 pages, 1950.	25.00	35.00	30.00
☐ **Hopalong Cassidy Coloring Book,** Abbott Publishing Co., 10″ x 15″, unused, 1950.	18.00	22.00	20.00
☐ **Hopalong Cassidy Returns,** by Clarence E. Mulford, colored cover, "Pocket Book", 250 pages, published 1946.	10.00	12.00	11.00
☐ **Doomed Caravan Featuring William Boyd,** lobby card for motion picture, 1942.	25.00	30.00	27.50
☐ **Hopalong Canasta,** boxed game, includes deck of Hoppy cards, score sheet, rules and plastic card holder designed as a saddle, 1950.	35.00	45.00	40.00
☐ **Judy Garland,** "Wizard of Oz" scrapbook belonging to her, containing numerous press cuttings and other memorabilia.	1000.00	1200.00	1100.00
☐ **Judy Garland,** "Over the Rainbow," musical arrangement prepared for her, for motion picture "Wizard of Oz".	2700.00	3100.00	2900.00
☐ **Judy Garland,** "A Star is Born," first-draft copy of the Moss Hart script for motion picture in which she starred.	1400.00	1600.00	1500.00
☐ **Judy Garland,** telegram sent by her to Louis B. Mayer, 1945.	300.00	340.00	320.00
☐ **"Shirley Temple — in Warner Bros. Pictures,"** 5″ x 7″ photo sold originally as a picture frame insert, probably about 1940.	10.00	14.00	12.00
☐ **"Love, Shirley Temple,"** printed card sent in reply to fan request for photo, listing prices of various photos.	10.00	14.00	12.00
☐ **"Shirley Temple Grows Up,"** cover story from Life magazine, 1942.	11.00	15.00	13.00
☐ **Shirley Temple Edition of the Littlest Rebel,** Random House, 214 pages with photo illustrations taken from movie stills, 1939.	8.00	12.00	10.00

CHECKS, NON-CELEBRITY	Current Price Range		Prior Year Average
☐ Pre-1800.	20.00	26.00	23.00
☐ 1800-1830.	13.00	17.00	15.00
☐ 1831-1859.	9.00	13.00	11.00
☐ 1860-1889.	6.00	10.00	8.00
☐ 1890-1910.	3.00	5.00	4.00

PATTERN GLASS

This section features only a sampling of pattern glass. In order to accurately present the vast amount of information required by serious collectors, a special edition devoted to glassware has been published by The House of Collectibles, Inc. This handy, pocket-size guide, *The Official 1985 Price Guide to Glassware*, contains a variety of glassware information and prices. It is available at bookstores for $3.95. For more in-depth information, consult *The Official 1985 Price Guide to Glassware* for $10.95.

ORIGIN: Glass historians are still undecided as to whether the Americans or the British invented pressed glass. Small objects and feet for footed bowls were first hand pressed in England in the early 1800s, but this method was crude compared to the mechanical process which later evolved. Pressing glass with machinery to produce a wide range of glass objects appears to have originated in America. Glass companies began producing pressed glass in matching tableware sets during the 1840s.

COMMENTS: Although identification of pieces is mainly by pattern name, the novice collector will have some confusion in this area. This is due to the fact that most of the original names have been discarded by advanced collectors who have renamed the pattern in descriptive terms. For the most part these collectors have found it impossible to attribute most patterns to a particular maker.

ADDITIONAL TIPS: Although pattern glass was originally made to imitate cut glass, you will have no problem differentiating one from the other. Despite the similarities pattern glass lacks the deep faceted appearance of cut — the edges of the patterns look rounded, the earlier pieces contain many imperfections — bubbles, lumps, impurities, and sometimes cloudiness.

MARKS: Manufacturers' marks are exceedingly rare and there are few catalogs available from the period before 1850. By studying the old catalogs that do exist, along with shards found at old factory sites, some sketchy information has been provided. But because patterns were so quickly copied by the competition, absolute verification of the manufacturer is impossible.

REPRODUCTIONS: Reproductions can pose a definite problem to the beginning pattern glass collector. Two very popular patterns, Bellflower and Daisy and Button, have been reproduced extensively. With careful, informed scrutiny, you will be able to detect the dullness and lack of sparkle characteristic of remakes. If the reproduction was made from a new mold (formed from an original object), the details will not possess the clarity and preciseness of the original article.

RECOMMENDED READING: For more in-depth information on pattern glass you may refer to *The Official Price Guide to Glassware* and *The Official Identification Guide to Glassware,* published by The House of Collectibles.

BAKEWELL BLOCK

	Current Price Range		Prior Year Average
☐ Butter Dish, covered	185.00	195.00	180.00
☐ Celery	100.00	107.00	96.00
☐ Champagne	100.00	108.00	95.00
☐ Creamer	165.00	175.00	160.00
☐ Decanter	135.00	145.00	131.00
☐ Spooner	65.00	75.00	60.00
☐ Sugar Bowl, covered	85.00	95.00	80.00
☐ Tumbler, bar	85.00	95.00	81.00
☐ Tumbler, whiskey	85.00	95.00	80.00
☐ Whiskey Tumbler, handle	105.00	115.00	100.00
☐ Wine	70.00	80.00	64.00

CANADIAN

	Current Price Range		Prior Year Average
☐ Butter, with cover	60.00	70.00	62.50
☐ Celery	45.00	55.00	4750
☐ Compote, high, with cover	65.00	75.00	67.50
☐ Compote, low	45.00	65.00	55.00
☐ Cordial	40.00	50.00	42.50
☐ Creamer	40.00	50.00	42.50
☐ Goblet	55.00	65.00	57.50
☐ Jam Jar	50.00	60.00	55.00
☐ Milk Pitcher, large	85.00	95.00	87.50
☐ Milk Pitcher, small	70.00	80.00	72.50
☐ Plate, diameter 6½″	45.00	55.00	47.50
☐ Plate, diameter 7½″	60.00	70.00	65.50
☐ Sauce, flat	16.00	18.00	16.50
☐ Sauce, footed	22.00	32.00	22.50
☐ Spooner	40.00	50.00	42.50
☐ Sugar, with cover	65.00	75.00	67.50
☐ Water Pitcher, large	90.00	100.00	95.00
☐ Water Pitcher, small	70.00	80.00	72.50
☐ Wine Glass	50.00	60.00	52.50

DIAMOND THUMBPRINT

	Current Price Range		Prior Year Average
☐ Butter Dish, covered	147.00	157.00	145.00
☐ Cake Stand	220.00	250.00	222.00
☐ Celery	180.00	190.00	175.00
☐ Champagne Glass, rare	230.00	250.00	220.00
☐ Creamer	125.00	140.00	120.00
☐ Compote, footed, scalloped edge	40.00	50.00	42.00
☐ Decanter, no stopper, pint size	75.00	80.00	75.00
☐ Decanter, original stopper, quart size	150.00	165.00	150.00
☐ Goblet, rare	350.00	365.00	345.00
☐ Honey Dish	15.00	20.00	15.00
☐ Sauce Dish	10.00	15.00	11.00
☐ Spooner	80.00	90.00	75.00
☐ Sugar Bowl, covered	150.00	170.00	155.00
☐ Tumbler	100.00	110.00	95.00
☐ Waste Bowl	85.00	95.00	80.00
☐ Water Pitcher, rare	350.00	370.00	352.00
☐ Whiskey Tumbler, handled	275.00	300.00	280.00
☐ Wine Glass, rare	220.00	240.00	205.00
☐ Wine Jug, places for holding glasses	750.00	950.00	600.00

FLUTE

	Current Price Range		Prior Year Average
☐ Ale Glass	30.00	40.00	28.00
☐ Bottle, bitters	30.00	37.00	28.00
☐ Bowl, scalloped edge	30.00	38.00	27.00
☐ Candlesticks, pair	40.00	50.00	37.00
☐ Champagne	30.00	35.00	27.00
☐ Compote, open, diameter 8"	32.00	38.00	30.00
☐ Decanter, quart	50.00	56.00	47.00
☐ Egg Cup, single	15.00	19.00	13.00
☐ Egg Cup, double	30.00	35.00	28.00
☐ Goblet	30.00	40.00	25.00
☐ Honey Dish	15.00	19.00	13.00
☐ Lamp	70.00	77.00	67.00
☐ Mug	50.00	60.00	48.00
☐ Pitcher, water	60.00	70.00	55.00
☐ Salt, footed	20.00	25.00	17.00
☐ Sauce, flat	14.00	18.00	12.00
☐ Sugar Bowl, open	27.00	35.00	25.00
☐ Tumbler	28.00	34.00	27.00
☐ Whiskey, handled	25.00	33.00	23.00
☐ Wine	25.00	30.00	23.00

LEE

	Current Price Range		Prior Year Average
☐ Celery Dish	110.00	120.00	105.00
☐ Champagne Glass	140.00	148.00	135.00
☐ Creamer	130.00	140.00	125.00

	Current Price Range		Prior Year Average
☐ **Decanter**	75.00	90.00	75.00
☐ **Goblet**	135.00	145.00	130.00
☐ **Sugar Bowl**, covered	130.00	140.00	125.00
☐ **Tumbler**	100.00	110.00	96.00

MINERVA

☐ **Butter**, with cover	110.00	115.00	112.50
☐ **Cake Plate**, diameter 12″	115.00	125.00	117.50
☐ **Compote**, high	85.00	110.00	95.00
☐ **Compote**, low	75.00	100.00	78.00
☐ **Compote**, with lid	70.00	75.00	72.50
☐ **Creamer**	65.00	85.00	67.50
☐ **Goblet**, small	75.00	85.00	75.50
☐ **Goblet**, large	90.00	100.00	95.00
☐ **Jam Jar**, with cover	85.00	95.00	87.50
☐ **Plate**, tab handled	65.00	75.00	67.50
☐ **Platter**, oval	50.00	60.00	52.50
☐ **Pickle Dish**, oval, says "Love's Request is Pickles"	40.00	50.00	42.50
☐ **Relish Dish**, three compartment	35.00	45.00	37.50
☐ **Sauce**, flat	25.00	35.00	27.50
☐ **Sauce**, footed	30.00	35.00	32.50
☐ **Spooner**	40.00	50.00	42.50
☐ **Sugar**	75.00	85.00	77.50
☐ **Sugar**, with cover	90.00	100.00	92.50
☐ **Water Pitcher**	125.00	135.00	130.00

PICKET

☐ **Butter**, with cover	70.00	80.00	75.00
☐ **Celery**	45.00	55.00	47.50
☐ **Compote**, high, with cover	60.00	70.00	65.00
☐ **Compote**, low	45.00	55.00	47.50
☐ **Creamer**	45.00	55.00	47.50
☐ **Goblet**	55.00	60.00	57.50
☐ **Jam Jar**	44.00	50.00	46.00
☐ **Pickle Dish**, with cover	45.00	55.00	47.50
☐ **Salt**	20.00	30.00	25.00
☐ **Spooner**	25.00	35.00	27.50
☐ **Sugar**, with cover	52.00	55.00	53.00
☐ **Toothpick**	35.00	40.00	37.50
☐ **Tumbler**	40.00	50.00	42.50
☐ **Water Pitcher**	65.00	75.00	67.50
☐ **Wine Glass**	30.00	40.00	32.50

SCROLL

	Current Price Range		Prior Year Average
☐ Butter	30.00	40.00	32.50
☐ Celery	30.00	40.00	35.00
☐ Compote, high	25.00	30.00	32.50
☐ Compote, low	20.00	30.00	22.50
☐ Creamer	25.00	30.00	27.50
☐ Egg Cup	30.00	40.00	32.50
☐ Goblet	15.00	20.00	17.50
☐ Relish Bowl	20.00	30.00	22.50
☐ Salt	15.00	20.00	17.50
☐ Sauce, flat	10.00	12.00	11.00
☐ Sauce, footed	20.00	30.00	25.00
☐ Spooner	22.00	30.00	24.00
☐ Sugar, with cover	30.00	40.00	32.50
☐ Water Pitcher	40.00	60.00	45.00
☐ Wine Glass	20.00	30.00	22.50

PENS AND PENCILS

TYPES: Pens can be either dip pens, the earliest type, fountain pens or ball-point pens. Dip pens are the style of modern calligraphy pens: a pointed nib is dipped in ink and used quickly. Fountain pens carry their own ink supply, as do ball-points. Pencils are either traditional or mechanical.

PERIOD: The fountain pen, which is the most collectible type, experienced its heyday in the 1920s and 1930s.

ORIGIN: The fountain pen was invented in the 1880s by Lewis Waterman.

MAKERS: The big names in pen and pencil production are Waterman, Parker, Conklin, Sheaffer and Wahl. All of these companies produced fine pens that are currently in great demand by collectors.

COMMENTS: As mentioned before, few ball-point or dip pens are collected by modern enthusiasts. Additional, collectors focus on post-1880 specimens.

ADDITIONAL TIPS: Rarity and condition are very important; the second more so than the first. Historical importance may also play a part, though only in isolated instances.

☐ **Autopoint**, gold filled, 1930s	12.00	18.00	15.00
☐ **Blaisdell**, green, gold plated trim, pencil, 1920s	10.00	20.00	15.00
☐ **Century**, Durapoint, red woodgrain, marbled, 1928	125.00	175.00	150.00

	Current Price Range		Prior Year Average
☐ **Chilton,** cream and gold, marbled, gold plated trim, golf pencil, 1930	20.00	30.00	25.00
☐ **Conklin,** 2P black chased hard rubber, crescent filler, 1918	25.00	40.00	32.50
☐ **Conklin,** Endura, orange, lever filler, gold plated trim, 1920s	30.00	40.00	35.00
☐ **Conklin,** Nozak, gray and red pearl, gold plated trim, 1931	25.00	45.00	35.00
☐ **Cross,** 1888	60.00	70.00	65.00
☐ **Doric,** pearly lined nickle plated trim, pencil, 1935	20.00	40.00	35.00
☐ **Dunn,** sterling silver, fine point, 1922	110.00	150.00	130.00
☐ **Eversharp,** green, chrome gold banded cap, 1951	25.00	35.00	30.00
☐ **Eversharp,** Skyline, black, 1945	15.00	20.00	17.50
☐ **Lincoln,** red, marbled, 1926	25.00	40.00	32.50
☐ **Majestic,** black and cream, 1930s	25.00	35.00	30.00
☐ **Parker,** # 51, Blue Diamond, black, gold plated trim, Lustraloy cap, 1945	32.00	52.00	42.00
☐ **Parker,** Deluxe Challenger, gold plated trim, 1930s	30.00	40.00	35.00
☐ **Parker,** Duofold, gold pearl and black, gold plated trim, 1939	50.00	60.00	55.00
☐ **Parker,** Duofold Sr., Big Red, gold plated trim, 1924	100.00	150.00	125.00
☐ **Parker,** Duofold Jr., black, gold plated trim, 1927	35.00	40.00	37.50
☐ **Parker,** gold filled metal, button filler, 1926 ..	50.00	70.00	60.00
☐ **Parker,** Lady Duofold, red, gold plated trim ..	30.00	50.00	40.00
☐ **Parker,** Pastel, blue, gold plated trim, 1926 ..	35.00	45.00	40.00
☐ **Parker,** silver plate, pencil, 1921	60.00	70.00	65.00
☐ **Parker,** Vacumatic, black, 1947	25.00	35.00	30.00
☐ **Peerless,** black and cream, gold plated trim, lever filler, 1930	20.00	30.00	25.00
☐ **Peerless,** lever filler, gold plated trim, black veined cream, 1920s	18.00	28.00	23.00
☐ **Pilot,** black lacquer and hand painted design, gold fittings, Japanese	50.00	70.00	60.00
☐ **Rider,** black, eye dropper filler, # 6 nib Mabie Todd	50.00	100.00	75.00
☐ **Royal,** Parker Duofold imitation, yellow, gold plated trim, 1928	35.00	45.00	40.00
☐ **Sanford and Bennett,** black, eye dropper filler, 1904	30.00	50.00	40.00
☐ **Sheaffer,** 5-30, black, lever filler, gold plated trim, ladies', 1930s	15.00	25.00	20.00

	Current Price Range		Prior Year Average
☐ **Sheaffer,** Balance, pearl and black marbled, pencil, 1931	40.00	60.00	50.00
☐ **Sheaffer,** black, gold plated trim, pencil, 1925	30.00	45.00	37.50
☐ **Sheaffer,** Lifetime, black and pearl, lever filler, gold plated trim, 1925	50.00	60.00	55.00
☐ **Sheaffer,** Lifetime, black and pearl, lever filler, gold plated trim, 1932	90.00	110.00	100.00
☐ **Sheaffer,** sterling silver, early feed, ladies, lever filler, 1916	40.00	50.00	45.00
☐ **Sheaffer,** Triumph, striped, plunger filled, 1946	30.00	45.00	37.50
☐ **Swann,** solid gold 14K, fine point, 1920s	60.00	80.00	70.00
☐ **Wahl,** # 4, gold filled metal, 1924	80.00	100.00	90.00
☐ **Wahl,** lever filler, gold filled, 1926	35.00	45.00	40.00
☐ **Wahl-Eversharp,** gold filled metal, pen and pencil set, 1924	100.00	130.00	115.00
☐ **Waterman,** # 52, black chased hard rubber nickle plated trim, 1923	20.00	30.00	25.00

PHOTOGRAPHS

TYPES: Photographs are usually one of four varieties: dageurreotypes, ambrotypes, tintypes or modern paper prints. Ambrotypes and tintypes are less valuable but are often collected. Three varieties of pictures made from negatives are original prints, later prints or reproductions. Original prints are those made by the photographer, or someone in his employ, shortly after taking the negative. Later prints are made from the original negative at a later date, sometimes fifty or more years later. Reproductions are made by making a new negative from the photo print. In most instances, original prints are most desired by collectors.

PERIOD: Photographs taken during the 1800s are most in demand by collectors. Early 1900s scenes, especially of the outdoor environment, are becoming more popular.

ORIGIN: The dageurroetype was invented in 1839 by Louis Dageurre.

MAKERS: Works by famous photographers such as Edward Curtis, Mathew Brady, Ansel Adams, Alfred Stieglitz or Carleton Watkins all command high prices in the collector market.

COMMENTS: Value is determined by age and subject matter. Of course the quality of the print in important; it must be in good condition to merit its full value.

Engagement Picture, *sepia tones, Fox Studios, Chicago, January, 1915,* **$5.00-$10.00**

TIPS: For further information, please refer to *The Official Price Guide to Paper Collectibles,* published by The House of Collectibles.

	Current Price Range		Prior Year Average
☐ **Abbott, Berenice,** "Flatiron Building," silver print, mounted, 19¼" x 14¾", 1930s, printed later, date unknown	1200.00	1300.00	1250.00
☐ **Abbott, Berenice,** "New York Fifth Avenue at Eighth Street," plate from Berenice Abbott's New York, silver print, mounted, signed, 18¼" x 23¼", 1930s, printed c. 1979	950.00	1000.00	975.00
☐ **Adams, Ansel,** "Aspens, Northern New Mexico," silver print, mounted, signed, 15⅞" x 19½", 1958, printed c. 1963	4800.00	4900.00	4850.00
☐ **Adams, Ansel,** "Frozen Lake and Cliffs, Sierra Nevada, California," silver print, mounted, signed, 10" x 13", c. 1927, printed in 1973	2100.00	2200.00	2150.00

	Current Price Range		Prior Year Average
☐ **Edgarton, Harold,** "Bullet in Apple," dye-transfer print, signed, matted and framed, 9¾" x 12", c. 1964, printed later, the specific date unknown	400.00	460.00	430.00
☐ **Frank, Robert,** "Florer Seller in Paris," silver print, signed, matted 9" x 13½", c. 1949-50, the specific printing date unknown	700.00	750.00	725.00
☐ **Freaks,** nine carte-de-visites and two cabinet cards, showing sideshow attractions, c. 1860s-1870s	75.00	105.00	90.00
☐ **Gardner, Alexander,** photographic sketch book of the (Civil) war, two volumes, oblong folio, with 100 mounted albumen prints, Washington, D.C. 1866	17000.00	22000.00	19500.00
☐ **Genthe, Arnold,** "Bulletin Board, Old China-town — San Francisco," silver print, mounted, signed, matted, 10⅛" x 13⅛", 1896-1900, the specific printing date unknown	450.00	480.00	465.00
☐ **Genthe, Arnold,** photo, "Elderly Woman with Baby on Her Back," Japan, 7½" x 10"	250.00	350.00	300.00
☐ **Genthe, Arnold,** photo, "Woman Standing in Front of Temple," Japan, 10" x 6½"	250.00	350.00	300.00
☐ **Genthe, Arnold,** photo, "Mountain in Guate-mala," 8" x 9¾"	170.00	230.00	200.00
☐ **Grand Canyon,** group of 14 mounted photos by C. Osborn of Flagstaff, AZ, showing the canyon rim and interior, 4½" x 7½" on 7" x 10" mounts, c. 1870s	125.00	175.00	150.00
☐ **Michals, Duane,** "Magritte," silver print, mat-ted, 4⅞" x 7¼", 1965, printed later in an edi-tion of 100, the specific date unknown	425.00	475.00	450.00
☐ **Monsen, Frederick I.,** "Children of the Desert, Rio Grande, New Mexico," silver print, mounted, title label on the mount, matted, 18⅝" x 13⅛", 1920s, the specific printing date unknown	150.00	180.00	165.00
☐ **Moon, Karl,** "Home from the Hunt," silver print, triple-mounted, 11⅜" x 14⅜", 1920s, the specific printing date unknown	425.00	475.00	450.00
☐ **Morse, Samuel F. B.,** lantern slide reproduc-tion of Bogardus' famous portrait of Morse with his Daguerrotype camera by his side, 3¼" x 4¼", c. 1880	60.00	70.00	65.00

	Current Price Range		Prior Year Average
☐ **Stereograms,** 72 cards by Keystone View Co., mostly of scenes in Africa, India and Sweden, 3½" x 7", c. 1900	55.00	75.00	65.00
☐ **Stieglitz, Alfred,** photo, "Sunlight and Shadow," 8" x 10", (negative made 1889, date of print unknown)	150.00	220.00	185.00
☐ **Stieglitz, Alfred,** photo, "The Steerage," 8" x 10", (negative made 1907, date of print unknown)	150.00	220.00	185.00

PLAYING CARDS

TYPES: Standard playing cards feature a king, a queen and a jack as the court subjects on a face card. The subjects will differ on a nonstandard deck. Tarot cards are also very collectible; they are used in fortune-telling.

ORIGIN: Playing cards are believed to have first appeared in the Far East around the 1100s. Printed playing cards probably were developed in Switzerland around 1430.

COMMENTS: Age usually determines value, although the quality of the artwork will have some influence. Very old playing cards do not often appear on the collectible market.

☐ **Art Nouveaux,** deck depicts turn of the century artists, Grimaud, 1900	4.00	6.00	5.00
☐ **Chicago World's Fair,** deck, c. 1934	15.00	21.00	18.00
☐ **Chinese Art Treasures,** double deck	13.00	18.00	15.50
☐ **Civil War Pack,** Union Playing Cards, American Card Co., NY, 2-color, eagles, stars, flags, shields, 1845	550.00	850.00	700.00
☐ **Coca-Cola,** double deck	5.00	10.00	7.50
☐ **Deck,** 52 cards, Andrew Dougherty, tiny picture of card in two corners, c. 1870	120.00	200.00	160.00
☐ **Deck,** Andrew Dougherty, NY, Owen Jones designs, c. 1880	50.00	130.00	90.00
☐ **Deck,** 36 cards, two information cards, The Game of Kings, Adams, NY, portraits of British monarchs, 1845	220.00	320.00	270.00
☐ **Fleet Wing Gasoline,** advertising deck, c. 1910	16.00	22.00	19.00
☐ **Flinch Cards,** c. 1910	25.00	30.00	27.50
☐ **France Royale,** double deck, by Piatnik	8.00	11.00	9.50
☐ **French Suited Pack,** L.I. Cohen, large size, gold trim, mint	220.00	320.00	270.00
☐ **Grover Cleveland,** campaign deck, reprint of 1888 issue	3.00	7.00	5.00

	Current Price Range		Prior Year Average
☐ **Gypsy Witch,** fortune telling deck	10.00	15.00	12.50
☐ **Hard-A-Port-Cut Plug,** tobacco premium, 52 cards plus joker, c. late 1880s	170.00	350.00	260.00
☐ **Jack Daniels,** 1972 edition	4.00	6.00	5.00
☐ **Mardi Gras,** deck, reprint of 1925 issue	3.00	6.00	4.50
☐ **Nixon,** politicards, 1971 edition	8.00	12.00	10.00
☐ **Panama Souvenir Cards,** 53 plus information cards, USPC, real photos, c. 1908	40.00	80.00	60.00
☐ **Uncle Sam's Cabinet,** 1901	30.00	40.00	35.00
☐ **Vanity Fair Transformation Deck,** United States Playing Card Co., America's first true transformation deck, 1895	450.00	650.00	550.00
☐ **Verkehrvelt Tarock,** reproduction of 1810 edition, "Topsy Turvy Animal Tarot"	50.00	70.00	60.00

POLITICAL BUTTONS

DESCRIPTION: Political buttons usually have a portrait of a politician produced on it with a pin attached to the back.

TYPE: There are several types of buttons produced including celluloids and jugates, which are buttons having both presidential and vice presidential candidates pictured.

MATERIAL: Early pictures used on the pin back buttons from the late 1800s and early 1900s were printed on paper with a metal backing and covered with celluloid. By 1920, pictures were lithographed to the metal with the plastic covering omitted.

ADDITIONAL TIPS: Celluloids and jugates are both sought after collector's items. Rarity plays one of the most important factors in determining the value of political buttons.

	Current Price Range		Prior Year Average
☐ **Bryan/Kern Jugate,** picture of eagle, multicolored	245.00	290.00	265.00
☐ **Coolidge,** lithographed tin, blue and white . . .	13.00	17.00	14.00
☐ **Coolidge/Davis Jugate,** celluloid, black and white, ⅞"	35.00	43.00	38.00
☐ **Eugene Chafin for President,** 1908 Prohibition Party candidate, ⅞"	40.00	55.00	45.00
☐ **Eugene Debs,** celluloid, red, white and black .	70.00	100.00	80.00
☐ **Franklin Roosevelt,** celluloid, "We Are Going to Win This War," red, white and blue, 1½" . .	13.00	17.00	14.00

	Current Price Range		Prior Year Average
☐ **Franklin Roosevelt,** "New Deal, Cowlitz County, Washington," red, white, blue and black	90.00	115.00	100.00
☐ **Governor Franklin D. Roosevelt,** "The People's Choice for President," 1932, brass 1¼"	18.00	23.00	20.00
☐ **Hoover,** black and white, 1¼"	30.00	40.00	33.00
☐ **Hoover/Curtis Jugate,** lithographed tin, red, white and blue, 2½"	110.00	140.00	120.00
☐ **I Like Ike,** lithographed tin, red lettering on white background, no illustration, used in 1952	2.00	3.00	2.50
☐ **Landon for President Club,** red rim	15.00	20.00	17.00
☐ **Lucky Willkie,** red letters on white background, no illustration, used for the 1940 Republican candidacy of Wendell Willkie	7.00	10.00	8.50
☐ **Lyndon Johnson/Hubert Humphrey Jugate,** "Let us Continue," 1964 campaign, ⅞"	38.00	46.00	41.00
☐ **McKinley,** celluloid, red, white and black, "An Honest Dollar Earned and Spent at Home"	65.00	85.00	72.00
☐ **McKinley/Theodore Roosevelt Jugate,** photos in brass shell with flags in red, white and blue, used in 1900 campaign	23.00	29.00	25.00
☐ **Nixon/Lodge Jugate,** lithographed tin, from campaign of 1960 which Richard Nixon lost to John Kennedy	1.00	1.50	1.20
☐ **Ronald Reagan for Governor,** lithographed tin, white border	2.00	3.00	2.30
☐ **Smith/Robinson Jugate,** lithographed tin, from 1928 campaign	20.00	30.00	23.00
☐ **Stevenson,** celluloid, blue and white, shoulder-length portrait, reading 1960 beneath	50.00	65.00	56.00
☐ **Support FDR,** Elect Satini Secretary of State, local button from Massachusetts, blue and white, 1936	13.00	17.00	14.00
☐ **Taft,** oval, celluloid, red, white, blue and green	30.00	35.00	32.00
☐ **Taft/Sherman Jugate,** celluloid, multicolored	35.00	43.00	38.00
☐ **Truman,** lithographed tin, pictures dome of U.S. Capitol, mentions his running mate Barkley	14.00	18.00	15.00
☐ **Willkie,** white and black with shoulder length portrait, wording "For President" at top	16.00	21.00	18.00
☐ **Wilson/Dunne Jugate,** celluloid, blue and white, 1¼"	55.00	70.00	62.00
☐ **Young Republican Hoover League,** blue and white, not illustrated	27.00	34.00	30.00

POSTCARDS

DESCRIPTION: Postcards are cards with a picture on one side and a place to write a message on the other. Postcards are mailed without an envelope.

PERIOD: Postcard collecting began in Europe in 1902 and by 1906 Americans were purchasing them at the rate of 700 million a year. The postcard boom dropped off around 1914 but began again in the 1960s.

TYPES: Hobbyists usually collect postcards by subject with the most popular portraying transportation, political events and advertising.

COMMENTS: The cards from pre-World War I are highly valuable. Artist, signature and category are items that determine value.

	Current Price Range		Prior Year Average
☐ **Bosselman,** Eastern States, color, undivided back	7.00	10.00	8.25
☐ **Clinton & Close,** The Iron Ore Docks of Toledo, color, undivided back	7.00	10.00	8.25
☐ **Detroit Photo Co. #9100,** Indias Amatecas/Mexico, color, undivided back	6.00	8.00	6.85
☐ **Erker #221,** Levee Scene, color, undivided back	5.00	7.00	5.85
☐ **Erker #246,** Soulard Market, color, undivided back	5.00	7.00	5.85
☐ **Erker #250,** Wabash Freight Station, color, undivided back	5.00	7.00	5.85
☐ **Holmes & Warren,** Branding Calves, two-tone, undivided back	5.00	7.00	5.85
☐ **Illinois Postcard Co.,** Indian Encampment on River Bank, color, undivided back	5.00	7.00	5.85
☐ **Leighton,** "Indians," Chief Spotted Tail, color, undivided back	5.00	7.00	5.85
☐ **Louis Levy,** Horse Drawn Double Decker Buses in London's Ludgate Circus, color, divided back	6.00	8.00	6.80
☐ **MacFarlane,** "Wild West" Series, Fur Canoe, color, undivided back	10.00	14.00	11.25
☐ **MacFarlane,** "Wild West" Series, Red River Carts, color, divided back	10.00	14.00	11.25
☐ **Miller,** Two Crow Papooses, black and white, undivided back	5.00	7.00	5.90
☐ **Morris & Kirby,** A Beef Herd on Water, black and white, undivided back	6.00	8.00	6.85

Top: **Postcard,** *birthday,*
1908, **$1.50-$2.50;**
Right: **Postcard,** *1910,*
$1.50-$2.00

	Current Price Range		Prior Year Average
☐ **Ridley**, "Wild West" Series, Antelope Hunting, two-tone, undivided back, artwork by Charles M. Russell	22.00	28.00	24.00
☐ **Samuel Cupples**, "German Tyrolean Alps" Series, Red Roof Tower at Left of Mountains .	15.00	20.00	17.00
☐ **Samuel Cupples**, "German Tyrolean Alps" Series, Residence House at Roof Square	15.00	20.00	17.00
☐ **Samuel Cupples**, "German Tyrolean Alps" Series, The Village Square	15.00	20.00	17.00
☐ **Samuel Cupples**, Oklahoma Building, color, undivided back	7.00	10.00	6.75
☐ **Sunday Post Dispatch (St. Louis)**, Missouri State Building, color, undivided back, c. 1900	7.00	10.00	6.75
☐ **Tammen**, Home Sweet Home, color, undivided back	11.00	15.00	12.50
☐ **Underwood & Underwood**, Austrian Cavalry Patrol Crossing River, color	7.00	10.00	8.20
☐ **Valentine**, The Westmount Club of Montreal, color, divided back	6.00	8.00	6.75

PREMIUMS

DESCRIPTION: Premiums are advertising giveaways used to promote a company's product.

ORIGIN: Premiums proved to be quite successful for radio during the 1930s to 1940s. Giveaways were also used to a smaller extent on television and for some foods like cereal or Cracker Jack.

COMMENTS: Radio premiums, which comprise a large portion of the premium collector market, are more readily available in the Midwest than on the East or West Coast. There were many successful radio shows originating in cities like Detroit, Chicago, Cincinnati and Kansas City, therefore prices are generally lower in these areas than in New York or Los Angeles.

ADDITIONAL TIPS: Paper items are considered more valuable than metal objects simply because paper does not hold up through the years like metal. Character popularity, type of item and rarity are important factors to consider in the premium market.

For additional information, consult *The Official Price Guide to Radio, TV and Movie Memorabilia*, published by The House of Collectibles.

	Current Price Range		Prior Year Average
☐ **Ali Baba And The 40 Thieves,** cardboard album with story and accompanying record, late 1940s, Post Cereal premium	10.00	15.00	12.50
☐ **Amos 'N Andy,** 1930 cardboard figure, Pepsodent premium, large figure of Andy	17.00	25.00	20.50
☐ **Bob Hope,** *They Got Me Covered,* first edition of Hope's book, 1941 Pepsodent premium, illustrated envelope	15.00	25.00	20.00
☐ **Bobby Benson,** card game, 1934 Hecker-H-O premium, 32 card deck with 32 page instruction booklet	15.00	25.00	20.00
☐ **Buck Rogers,** Scout badge, 1935 Cream of Wheat premium	25.00	35.00	20.00
☐ **Captain Hawks,** badge, 1935 newspaper premium, sky patrol member propeller badge	10.00	15.00	12.50
☐ **Donald Duck,** blotter, 1942 Sunoco premium, Donald Duck driving a car	8.00	15.00	12.00
☐ **Ed East,** booklet, *Greetings and Good Morning from Ed East's Breakfast in Bedlan,* 1939, 12 pages	5.00	10.00	7.50
☐ **Eddie Cantor,** *Book of Magic,* 1935 Pebeco toothpaste premium	35.00	45.00	40.00
☐ **Howdy Doody,** Climber, 1951 Welch Grape Juice premium	35.00	45.00	40.00
☐ **Howdy Doody,** History Album, 1950s Wonder Bread premium, 8 page book	15.00	25.00	20.00
☐ **Jack Armstrong,** bowl, 1939 Wheaties premium	30.00	40.00	35.00
☐ **Jack Armstrong,** flashlight, 1939 Wheaties premium	20.00	30.00	25.00
☐ **Jack Armstrong,** gun, 1933 Wheaties premium, daisy shooting propeller plane gun	25.00	35.00	30.00
☐ **Jim Babcock,** book, 1936 Log Cabin Syrup premium, 36 page illustrated book shows rope tricks, explains tracking and trailing of animals, trail blazing, branding, has dictionary of cowboy words	25.00	40.00	32.00
☐ **Jimmie Allen,** identification bracelet, 1935 Richfield Oil premium	45.00	55.00	50.00
☐ **Lone Ranger,** badge, 1949 Cheerios premium	25.00	35.00	30.00
☐ **Lone Ranger,** belt, 1941 Kix premium, rare . . .	80.00	100.00	90.00
☐ **Mickey Mouse,** blotter, 1940 Sunoco premium, shows Mickey Mouse driving a car	10.00	15.00	12.50
☐ **Mickey Mouse,** magic kit, 1955 Mars Candy premium, instructions for 20 tricks	35.00	45.00	40.00

QUILTS

DESCRIPTION: Quilts have been absorbed into the category of Folk Art, though their creators seldom intended them as works of art. Early America, and especially early rural America, thrived on its self-sufficiency: its ability to cultivate foodstuffs and manufacture the necessities of everyday life. Quilts are one example (of many) of our ancestors using their creative skills and their sense of thrift: odd pieces of fabric were cut and sewn into various patterns, to make clothing, bed coverings, etc. Not only was some money saved, but the owner was sure to possess a very unique "original," which made the shopkeeper's merchandise seem pale by comparison.

COMMENTS: Collecting specimens of old quilts was once a very restricted hobby, which seemed destined never to get beyond rural New England, Pennsylvania and some other areas. It has blossomed to full flower today, aided by museum interest and antique shows. On the whole, *Amish* quilts are the leaders in hobbyist appeal and in value, though they are not always the most valuable. The self-contained Amish community (of western Pennsylvania) was intent on "doing for itself," unconcerned about what was fashionable in the world's eyes. These quilts are ample testimony to the Amish artistic spirit.

	Current Price Range		Prior Year Average
☐ **Arkansas Star,** 1930s, cotton, blocks are pieced with various solid colors for star points, prints for center of star, set in blocks of unbleached muslin, lattice strips of yellow, red, white and green print, solid red corner blocks and border, unbleached muslin backing which has been turned up and machine stitched to form binding, leaf and vine quilting design on lattice strips, never washed, excellent condition, 85″ x 67″	150.00	155.00	150.00
☐ **Baseball,** cotton, all-over pattern made of gingham and calico, many colors, good light and dark contrast, border on one end, no set-up blocks or strips, good condition, 70″ x 73″	130.00	155.00	142.00
☐ **Bowtie,** cotton, pieced 5″ red bowties set in white squares alternate diagonally with gold and white blocks, wide inner white border with cable quilting, red outer border with diagonal quilting, white muslin back and binding, good used condition, 65″ x 81″	190.00	215.00	197.00

	Current Price Range		Prior Year Average

☐ **Double T**, Ohio Amish, cotton sateen, blue, turquoise, mauve and green pieced TS are set in diamond block arrangement, deep blue background, blue border with cable stiching, bright green, binding **675.00 725.00 700.00**

☐ **Double Wedding Ring**, 1930s, cotton, pieced rings of various prints and solids, squares where rings meet are solid blue and solid yellow, white background, blue binding, straight rather than scalloped edges, intricate spider web quilting in medium blue thread, good used condition, 70″ x 84″ **130.00 155.00 140.00**

☐ **Double Wedding Ring**, 1930s, cotton, rings and squares where rings meet are all made of various color prints, white background and backing, green binding, good used condition, 86″ x 75″ **195.00 215.00 200.00**

☐ **Dresden Plate**, 1930s, cotton, each 12″ plate is pieced from calico prints and hand appliqued to solid pink blocks, darker pink background, never washed, excellent condition, 65″ x 82″ **90.00 115.00 100.00**

☐ **Dresden Plate**, 1930s, cotton, prints and solids appliqued by hand to white muslin background, centers of plates are yellow and so are lattice strips, borderless, white backing and binding, diagonal quilting, excellent condition, 69″ x 89″ **150.00 175.00 160.00**

☐ **Embroidered Flowers In A Basket**, cotton, 1938, four blocks with embroidered red, gold, blue and purple flowers, green leaves in large brown handled basket, three large embroidered flowers surround each basket, green squares placed diagonally between white triangular pieces form lattice strips which separate the four large embroidered blocks, inner border matches lattice strips, outside border of larger white and green triangular pieces with green pieces forming scalloped edge, green binding, unbleached muslin back, lovely handwork, never washed, very good condition, 86″ x 79″ **225.00 250.00 235.00**

	Current Price Range		Prior Year Average
☐ **LeMoyne Star,** 1930s, cotton, 9″ star blocks are pieced with various prints on solid green background, green binding, whitebacking, fine quilting, never washed, very good condition, 80″ x 71″	150.00	175.00	160.00
☐ **Log Cabin,** cotton, blocks are pieced with old calico prints, navy, red border, red and white print backing, lovely quilting, good used condition, 66″ x 80″	175.00	195.00	182.00
☐ **Lone Star,** 1930s, cotton, pieced large star is made of various percale prints, background and backing are solid green, machine stitched, binding, crossing lines design quilting, good used condition, 82″ x 85″	225.00	250.00	235.00
☐ **Nine Patch,** Ohio Amish, crib, cotton sateen, pieced wine squares form pattern, black blackground and border, wine binding, new	75.00	85.00	80.00
☐ **Nine Patch,** Pennsylvania Amish, wool, pieced with burgundy, plum, brown, navy and teal, loden green background, wine blocks in foot-end corners, wide green border with tulip quilting	600.00	625.00	610.00
☐ **Nine Patch,** Pennsylvania, crib, various old prints, form blocks, background is pieced from mostly pink prints, used condition with some fading and wear	85.00	90.00	87.00
☐ **Oak Leaf Applique,** nine repeats, four yellow-green leaves with four gold flowers, gold eight point star in center of each repeat, vine and bud border, good used condition	300.00	325.00	310.00
☐ **Picture Frame,** Ohio Amish, cotton, solid black with bright blue band in border, bright blue binding, exceptional quilting, very contemporary	250.00	275.00	260.00
☐ **Plain,** Iowa Amish, cotton sateen, one solid piece of celery green sateen, exceptional quilting	350.00	375.00	360.00
☐ **Rainbow Tile,** also called Diamond Field, bright prints and solids are pieced to form pattern, unbleached muslin backing, machine stitched binding, never washed	100.00	125.00	110.00

	Current Price Range		Prior Year Average
☐ **Triple Irish Chain**, 1893, pieced with solid red and white, 1¾″ squares, inside red border, outside white border, white binding and backing, quilted in lines only one half inch apart, embroidered date Dec. 25, 1893, very good condition, 73″ x 68″	325.00	350.00	333.00
☐ **Wild Goose Chase**, cotton, blocks are pieced with triangles of old ginghams, calicoes, chambrays and solids, strips between rows of triangular pieces are solid aqua, unbleached muslin back, aqua binding, nice diagonal quilting, never washed, good condition, 82″ x 72″	150.00	175.00	162.00

RAZORS

MATERIALS: Most commonly, razor handles are made of wood, hard rubber and imitation bone. Finer razors had handles of ivory, bone or sterling silver.

COMMENTS: As with most collectibles, old and rare razors are the most valuable. Along with flea markets and antiques shops, knife shows often feature razors.

ADDITIONAL TIPS: The listings in this section are alphabetical according to manufacturer. When the manufacturer isn't known, the razor is listed by type.

☐ **Antonio Tadros**, straight edge	8.50	12.00	10.00
☐ **Barber**, straight edge in original box	51.50	60.00	53.00
☐ **Cattaraugus Cutlery Co.** with "The Sovereign's Own" imprint	22.50	30.00	26.50
☐ **Chip-A-Way Cutlery Co., England** with "Chip-A-Way" imprint	10.50	13.50	12.00
☐ **Colquhoun and Cadman, Sheffield** with "Little Favorite" imprint	6.50	9.50	8.00
☐ **Curvit**, for women, in flannel pouch	4.00	10.00	6.00
☐ **Electric Cutlery, New York** with "Arlington" imprint	6.50	9.50	8.00
☐ **Elsener, Switzerland** with "Ideal" imprint . .	7.50	10.50	9.00
☐ **Euchler**, straight, with bakelite handle	6.00	10.00	8.00
☐ **G.R.S. Solinger, Germany** with "Extra Superb" imprint	7.50	10.50	9.00

Straight Razor, *Red Injun, ivory celluloid handle, made in Germany, original box,*
$35.00–$40.00

	Current Price Range		Prior Year Average
☐ **Hibbard Spencer Bartlett and Co., Germany** with "May Flower" imprint	16.50	21.50	19.00
☐ **Imperial Razor, Germany** with "Army and Navy" imprint	17.50	22.50	20.00
☐ **Joseph Roger Cutler,** straight edge	13.00	17.00	15.00
☐ **Kewtie,** small plastic safety, pink with pink plastic case	4.00	12.00	5.00
☐ **Kinfolks, Inc.,** with "Real Red Point" imprint	6.50	9.50	8.00
☐ **Petty and Sons, John Manufacturers, Sheffield** with "Magnetic" imprint	7.50	11.50	9.00
☐ **Rector and Wilhelmy Co.** with "XX Clean Clipper" imprint	7.50	11.50	9.00
☐ **Reuter Bros**	5.50	7.50	6.50
☐ **Robeson Shur Edge, New York** with "The Nugget" imprint	6.50	9.50	8.00
☐ **Simmons Hardware Co.** with "Hornet" imprint	6.50	9.50	8.00
☐ **Simmons Hardware Co.** with "Royal Keen Kutter" imprint	16.50	21.50	19.00

	Current Price Range		Prior Year Average
☐ **Sterling Razor Works** with "Rattler" imprint	5.50	7.50	6.50
☐ **Straight,** black scrolled handle	5.00	15.00	8.00
☐ **Straight,** safety, white ivorene handle with blade, "Durham Duplex Razor Co.", NY, USA, c. 1922	12.00	20.00	15.00
☐ **Tally,** straight, celluloid handle, ivory color .	8.00	16.00	12.00
☐ **Traveling,** in velvet lined box, made in Germany	4.00	12.00	6.00
☐ **Victory Hone Co., Iowa** with "Victory Hollow #1" imprint	6.00	8.00	7.00
☐ **Winchester,** straight edge	70.00	90.00	80.00
☐ **Witte Hardware Co., Mo.** with "Witte's Rattler"	5.00	7.00	6.00

RECORDS

This section features only a sampling of collector record prices. In order to accurately present the vast amount of information required by serious collectors, a special edition devoted to collectible records is published by The House of Collectibles, Inc. This handy, pocket-size guide, *The Official 1985 Price Guide to Collectible Records,* features more than 11,500 prices for rock and country recordings. It is available at bookstores for $3.95. At $9.95, *The Official 1985 Price Guide to Records,* features more than 30,000 prices.

TYPES: There are two primary types of records: 45s and LPs. A 45 is a small record that usually features one song on each side. It turns on the turntable at a rate of 45 revolutions per minute; thus, the name. An LP is a long playing album that has several songs on each side. It turns at a rate of 33 revolutions per minute.

PERIOD: Records from the 1950s and 1960s are most popular among collectors.

MATERIALS: Records are almost exclusively made of vinyl. Rare platinum and gold specimens are produced occasionally for superstars, but these almost never make it into the collectible market.

COMMENTS: Rare releases by famous groups and singers are in great demand. Bands like The Beatles and The Rolling Stones command top prices for scarce recordings.

ADDITIONAL TIPS: For further information and listings, please refer to *The Official Price Guide to Records,* published by the House of Collectibles.

	Current Price Range		Prior Year Average
☐ **Johnny Ace**, Flair, #1015, Midnight Hours/Journey/Trouble And Me	20.00	50.00	35.00
☐ **Aladdins**, Frankie, #6, My Charlene/Dot, My Love	50.00	90.00	68.00
☐ **Paul Anka**, RPM, #472, I Confess/Blau-Wile Deveest Fontaine	23.00	32.00	28.00
☐ **Marty Balin**, Challenge, #9146, Nobody But You/You Made Me Fall	8.50	14.00	12.00
☐ **Baritones**, Dore, #501, After School Rock/Sentimental Baby	14.00	24.00	18.00
☐ **Beach Boys**, X, #301, Surfin'/Luau	80.00	130.00	100.00
☐ **Beach Boys**, Candix, #301, Surfin'/Luau	33.00	55.00	40.00
☐ **Beatles**, Decca, #9-31382, My Bonnie/The Saints	375.00	860.00	500.00
☐ **Beatles**, Vee Jay, #581, From Me To You/Please Please Me (promo)	35.00	75.00	50.00
☐ **Beatles**, Swan, #4152, She Loves You/I'll Get You	30.00	65.00	40.00
☐ **Dell-Vikings**, Luniverse, #106, Over The Rainbow/Hey Senorita	17.00	30.00	24.00
☐ **Dell-Vikings**, Fee Bee, #205, Come Go With Me/How Can I Find True Love	40.00	65.00	50.00
☐ **Dominoes**, Federal, #12010, Harbor Lights/No Says My Heart	160.00	275.00	220.00
☐ **Five Satins**, Standard, #105, All Mine/ Rosemarie	55.00	100.00	75.00
☐ **Ronnie Gill**, Rio, #129, Geraldine/Standing On The Mountain	12.00	46.00	28.00
☐ **Buddy Holly**, Loral, #61852, Words Of Love/Mailman Bring Me No More Blues	51.00	96.00	70.00
☐ **Jan Berry**, Rpple, #6101, Tomorrow's Teardrops/ My Midsummer Night's Dream	22.00	40.00	30.00
☐ **Big Bopper**, D, #1008, Chantilly Lace/Purple People Eater Meets The Witch Doctor	38.00	64.00	50.00
☐ **Bluesology**, Fontana, #594, Come Back Baby/Times Are Getting Tougher Everytime I Have The Blues	20.00	34.00	26.00
☐ **Bob And Sheri**, Safari, #101, The Surfer Moon/Humpty Dumpty	260.00	500.00	375.00
☐ **Captain And Tennille**, Butterscotch Castle, #001, The Way I Want To Touch You/Disney Girls	26.00	46.00	34.00
☐ **Ray Charles**, Swing Time, #250, Baby Let Me Hold Your Hand/Lonely boy	20.00	34.00	26.00
☐ **Danny And The Juniors**, Singular, #711, At The Hop/Sometimes	34.00	50.00	42.00

	Current Price Range		Prior Year Average
☐ **Jan And Dean,** Dore, #522, Baby Talk/-Jeanette Get Your Hair Done	50.00	98.00	70.00
☐ **Platters,** Federal, #12153, Give Thanks/Hey Now	55.00	98.00	70.00
☐ **Elvis Presley,** Sun, #209, That's All Right/Blue Moon Of Kentucky	195.00	300.00	240.00
☐ **Elvis Presley,** RCA, #7777, It's Now Or Never/A Mess Of Blues	70.00	125.00	100.00
☐ **Neil Sedaka,** Decca, #30520, Laura Lee/Snowtime	17.00	29.00	23.00
☐ **Shirelles,** Tiara, #6112, I Met Him On A Sunday/I Want You To Be My Boyfriend	54.00	92.00	75.00
☐ **Solitaires,** Old Town, #1000, Wonder Why/Blue Valentine	21.00	35.00	27.00
☐ **Surfaris,** DFS, #11/12, Wipeout/Surfer Joe ..	45.00	78.00	60.00
☐ **Yardbirds,** EPIC, #9709, I Wish You Would/Ain't Got You	12.00	21.00	14.00

SCOUTING

This section features only a sampling of scouting collectibles. In order to accurately present the vast amount of information required by serious collectors, a special edition devoted to scouting is published by The House of Collectibles, Inc. This handy, pocket-size guide, *The Official 1985 Price Guide to Scouting Collectibles,* features thousands of scouting items. It is available at bookstores for $3.95.

DESCRIPTION: Scouting memorabilia includes items for scouting groups including Boy Scouts, Cub Scouts, Camp Fire Girls, Brownies and Girl Scouts.

TYPES: All types of scouting treasures are considered collectible, from cloth badges to metal neckerchief rings and tools, backpacks, uniforms and manuals.

ORIGIN: Englishman Sir Robert S.S. Baden-Powell is the original founder of Boy Scouts and Girls Scouts in England.

The development of scouting in America is due to Daniel Carter Beard, William Boyce and James E. West for Boy Scouts of America, and Juliette Gordon Low for Girl Scouts of America. Both groups are separate and distinct.

COMMENTS: There are more collectors of Boy Scout treasures than of Girl Scout memorabilia. Prices are reasonable and fairly stable.

Handbook,
*blue and green with
Girl Scout symbol,
hardcover,
1954,* **$2.50-$3.50**

For more complete information, refer to *The Official 1984 Price Guide
to Scouting Collectibles,* published by The House of Collectibles.

	Current Price Range		Prior Year Average
☐ **Ash Tray,** Kit Carson House, Philmont, 1950 .	7.00	8.50	7.25
☐ **Bank,** Conn., has another scout behind kettle, 1915	250.00	325.00	275.00
☐ **Bank,** tin lithographed scout, 1912	22.00	28.00	23.50
☐ **Binoculars,** tan leather, 1920's	77.00	88.00	79.00
☐ **Blotter,** BSA/Coca-cola, "Be Prepared, Be Refreshed"	6.00	8.00	7.00
☐ **Belt,** belt and buckle, gun medal, 1930's	7.50	9.50	8.00
☐ **Bookends,** bronze metal, Girl Scout feeding rabbit	20.50	26.00	21.00
☐ **Bookends,** metal, first class Emblem 6″ x 6″ .	24.00	32.00	26.00
☐ **Bookmark,** green and gold, first class emblem, BSA National Council	4.25	5.50	4.75
☐ **Books,** Holy Bible, early BSA seal on cover . .	45.00	57.00	47.00
☐ **Cachet Cover,** Boy Scout stamp club, 1932 . .	9.00	11.00	9.50

	Current Price Range		Prior Year Average
☐ **Camera,** Official 7-Piece flash camera kit ...	12.00	17.00	13.00
☐ **Canteen,** Wearever seamless, felt cover, 1930's	17.00	22.00	18.00
☐ **Cards,** 65 BSA job description cards, 1949-1962	5.00	7.00	5.50
☐ **Collar Monogram,** BSA, brass collar monograms, 1920's	40.00	60.00	46.00
☐ **Comb,** Official BSA comb and clippers in a case	4.00	7.00	5.00
☐ **Compass,** Sylva pathfinder, BSA	2.00	4.00	2.50
☐ **Cut Outs,** Camping with the Scouts, gummed paper in book form, 1930's	22.00	27.00	23.00
☐ **Drum,** "Boy Scout Drum" tin, 6" round 3½" high, 1908	40.00	60.00	44.00
☐ **Figurine,** Head Scout, signaller, arms move, 2"	18.00	24.00	20.00
☐ **Figurine,** Kenner doll, Craig Cub Scout	15.00	21.00	17.00
☐ **Figurine,** Scout with pack and rifle, cardboard, 6" high	4.50	5.50	4.75
☐ **Figurine,** Lead Scout kneeling, frying eggs ..	11.00	14.00	12.00
☐ **Figurine,** Scout plastic figure, tree and flagpole, 3"	8.50	11.00	9.25
☐ **First Aid Kit,** Bauer and Black, gray, oval belt loop kit, rare, 1932	20.00	27.00	22.00
☐ **First Aid Kit,** Johnson and Johnson, swing clasp, 1942	16.00	22.00	17.50
☐ **Gadget Box,** imitation wood, cub, scout, and explorer emblems	4.00	6.00	4.50
☐ **Game,** game of Scouting by Milton Bradley, 1920's	80.00	110.00	87.00
☐ **Game,** target ball game, uses three marbles, like tiddlywinks, Boy Scout target shooting scene	50.00	70.00	55.00
☐ **Handkerchief,** set of 3, Scouts, contained in a Scout box	35.00	45.00	37.00
☐ **Light Bulb,** Boy Scout cheer light, Aerolux Light Corp.	6.00	8.00	6.25
☐ **Membership Card,** Brownie, 1932	6.50	8.50	7.00
☐ **Paperweight,** Cub-Scout-Explorer, glass, 3" dome	20.00	27.00	22.00
☐ **Paperweight,** bronze metal, Girl Scout feeding rabbit	8.10	9.25	8.25
☐ **Paperweight,** "Safety Good Turn 1958," tenderfoot emblem, Lucite	9.00	11.00	9.50
☐ **Pedometer,** Scouts hike-meter, also a compass	9.00	13.00	10.00
☐ **Pin,** Girl Scout logo, stick pin, gold	4.50	6.50	5.00

	Current Price Range		Prior Year Average
☐ **Tie Bars,** Cub Scout, wood	3.00	5.00	3.50
☐ **Tie Rack,** pressed wood, first class emblem and camp scenes, c. 1937	10.00	14.00	11.00
☐ **Tray,** tin, World War II, hinged lid showing Boy Scouts and British military leaders, 4″ x 5″ x 5″	24.00	32.00	25.00
☐ **Utility Book,** Girl Scout, "Don't Forget," book, trefoil on wine red cover, 1930s	8.50	12.75	9.00
☐ **Whistle,** "The Boy Scout," English with small compass, chrome over brass	14.00	19.00	15.00

SEARS-ROEBUCK CATALOGS

COMMENTS: Sears Roebuck catalogs were first collected in the 1960s. They are still popular and prices, especially for rare or mint copies, tend to be high.

Sears Catalog,
*general catalog no. 111,
50¢ cover price,
1902,* **$100.00-$125.00**

CONDITION: Condition standards for such catalogs are fairly liberal, because they were large, soft bound and received much use.

ADDITIONAL TIPS: The listings are in chronological order with a price range.

	Current Price Range		Prior Year Average
☐ **1897**, general catalogue, Chicago, IL	200.00	250.00	220.00
☐ **1899**, general catalogue	175.00	225.00	200.00
☐ **1900-1910**, most editions, food, groceries, tobacco	50.00	65.00	55.00
☐ **1902**, general catalogue #111, 50¢ cover price	120.00	140.00	130.00
☐ **1902**, general catalogue, 1969 reprint (Crown Pub., NY)	10.00	15.00	12.00
☐ **1905**, general catalogue	130.00	155.00	140.00
☐ **1906**, general catalogue	145.00	175.00	155.00
☐ **1907**, general catalogue, 1,240 pages	150.00	185.00	160.00
☐ **1908**, general catalogue, 1,232 pages	175.00	200.00	185.00
☐ **1910**, general catalogue, spring and summer, 1,182 pages	175.00	200.00	185.00
☐ **1911-1920**, most editions, food, groceries, tobacco	40.00	55.00	47.00
☐ **1916**, furniture	60.00	85.00	73.00
☐ **1922**, general catalogue, spring and summer	125.00	145.00	135.00
☐ **1926**, general catalogue, autumn and winter .	110.00	130.00	120.00
☐ **1931**, general catalogue, spring and summer	110.00	140.00	125.00
☐ **1944**, general catalogue, autumn and winter .	80.00	110.00	95.00
☐ **1947**, Christmas catalogue	45.00	60.00	53.00
☐ **1949**, general catalogue, autumn and winter .	40.00	55.00	47.00
☐ **1951**, business equipment	8.00	12.00	10.00
☐ **1951**, Christmas catalogue	35.00	45.00	40.00
☐ **1955**, general catalogue, spring and summer	27.00	40.00	32.00
☐ **1960**, Christmas catalogue	20.00	30.00	25.00
☐ **1963**, general catalogue, autumn and winter .	18.00	28.00	23.00
☐ **1965-1975**, general catalogues, most editions	12.00	18.00	14.00

SHAWNEE POTTERY

DESCRIPTION: The Shawnee Pottery Company was founded in 1937 in Zanesville, Ohio. Its first president was Addis Hull Jr. of the Hull pottery family which owned one of the leading factories in neighboring Crooksville. Discovering an Indian arrow on the grounds when the factory was being readied for opening led to the company being called Shawnee. Shawnee played up the Indian theme at various times in its history, notably with its line of corn-pattern dinnerware. This famous set in yellow and green was textured to resemble an ear of corn. It was officially known as Corn King, then as Corn Queen beginning in the mid 1950s. The final year of the Shawnee operations was 1961.

MARKS: The trademarks used by Shawnee usually carry the letters *U.S.A.*, together with the factory name and a mold number. A low mold number is not necessarily an indication of early production. Most pieces of Shawnee figureware and such novelties as toy banks, ashtrays, etc., can be easily dated (approximately) on the basis of style. The vases are a little more difficult to accurately date, but a collector who makes educated guesses will probably score more hits than misses.

RECOMMENDED READING: For more in-depth information on Shawnee pottery, you may refer to *The Offical Price Guide to Pottery and Porcelain* and *The Official Identification Guide to Pottery and Porcelain,* published by The House of Collectibles.

	Current Price Range		Prior Year Average
☐ **Ashtray,** oak leaf shape, blue, yellow and red blend, detailed vein lines, marked U.S.A. #350	8.00	10.00	9.00
☐ **Ashtray,** orange interior, brown exterior, marked U.S.A. #1014	11.00	13.00	12.00
☐ **Basket,** blue, swirled handled, marked Rum RILL #358	30.00	35.00	32.50
☐ **Book Ends,** pair, two dark green and red flying geese on each bookend, bottom decorated with flowers, marked Shawnee U.S.A. #4000 .	16.00	20.00	18.00
☐ **Bowl,** blue, ruffled edge, marked Shawnee U.S.A. #2500	11.00	14.00	12.00
☐ **Bowl,** green and white, ruffled edge, marked Shawnee U.S.A. #2507	11.00	13.00	12.00
☐ **Bowl,** marbled pattern, set three footed, on stand, ruffled edge	12.00	15.00	14.00
☐ **Candlestick,** pair, marbled design, scalloped edge, marked Shawnee U.S.A.	16.00	20.00	18.00
☐ **Casserole,** lidded, black base, white lid, marked Shawnee U.S.A.	20.00	24.00	22.00
☐ **Coaster,** green with shamrock motif, marked Shawnee U.S.A. #411	12.00	15.00	14.00
☐ **Cookie Jar,** brown and green pig with white face, marked patent Smiley #60	35.00	40.00	37.50
☐ **Corn,** Butter Dish, covered, marked Shawnee U.S.A. #72	25.00	30.00	27.50
☐ **Corn, Bowl,** large, marked Shawnee U.S.A. #6	12.00	16.00	14.00
☐ **Corn, Bowl,** mixing, marked Shawnee U.S.A. #5	10.00	15.00	12.00

	Current Price Range		Prior Year Average
☐ Corn, Casserole, 11", covered, marked Shawnee U.S.A. oven proof #74	20.00	25.00	22.50
☐ Corn, Casserole, covered, marked Shawnee U.S.A. oven proof #73	12.00	15.00	13.00
☐ Corn, Cookie Jar, lidded, marked Shawnee U.S.A. #66	30.00	40.00	35.00
☐ Corn, Mug, marked Shawnee U.S.A. #69	8.00	12.00	10.00
☐ Corn, Pitcher, 8½", marked Shawnee U.S.A. #71	18.00	25.00	22.00
☐ Corn, Pitcher, small, marked Shawnee U.S.A. #70	11.00	15.00	13.00
☐ Corn, Plate, dinner, marked Shawnee U.S.A. #68	10.00	12.00	11.00
☐ Corn, Platter, marked Shawnee U.S.A. oven proof #96	15.00	20.00	17.00
☐ Corn, Relish, oblong, marked Shawnee U.S.A. #79	8.00	12.00	10.00
☐ Corn, Saucer, marked Shawnee U.S.A. #91	5.00	7.00	6.00
☐ Corn, Shakers, 3½", salt and pepper, pair, no mark	12.00	15.00	13.50
☐ Corn, Shakers, 5½", salt and pepper, no mark	13.00	16.00	14.50
☐ Corn, Sugar Bowl, covered, marked Shawnee U.S.A. #78	12.00	15.00	13.50
☐ Corn, Teacup, marked Shawnee U.S.A. #90	6.00	8.00	7.00
☐ Corn, Teapot, covered, marked Shawnee U.S.A. #75	25.00	30.00	27.50
☐ Planter, striking black bull standing on base, marked Shawnee U.S.A.	30.00	35.00	32.50
☐ Planter, two blue birds in front of bird house, marked U.S.A. #830	9.00	12.00	10.50
☐ Pitcher, white and blue chick, marked patent pending	6.00	8.00	7.00
☐ Planter, white and blue elephant, marked U.S.A.	9.00	12.00	10.50
☐ Planter, white and green oriental man pulling cart, marked U.S.A. #539	8.00	10.00	9.00
☐ Planter, white and red dog riding blue, yellow and white tricycle, marked U.S.A. #712	9.00	12.00	10.50
☐ Planter, white and tan butterfly on log, marked Shawnee U.S.A. #524	8.00	10.00	9.00
☐ Planter, white, green and yellow goose, marked U.S.A. #707	9.00	12.00	10.50
☐ Planter, white, pink, dark green fish, marked U.S.A. #717	12.00	14.00	13.00
☐ Planter, white, red and green pig dressed as farmer with yellow wheelbarrow	8.00	10.00	9.00

SHEET MUSIC

COMMENTS: Condition and rarity determine the value of sheet music. Specimens are not always in top condition due to music store stamps, tape marks, staples, binder holes and ownership signatures. Worn copies sell for considerably less than those in good or mint condition.

ADDITIONAL TIPS: Often prices in major hobby marketplaces such as New York and California are higher than prices in more remote areas. Collectors should also beware of high prices placed on sheet music at flea markets.

For more information, consult *The Official Price Guide to Radio, TV and Movie Memorabilia,* or *The Official Price Guide to Music,* both published by The House of Collectibles.

Sheet Music, Revenge,
words by Lewis and Young,
music by Harry Akst,
pub. by Remick Music Corp.,
$3.00-$6.00

	Current Price Range		Prior Year Average
☐ **After I've Called You Sweetheart (How Can I Call You Friend)**, words by Bernie Grossman, music by Little Jack Little, pub. Milton Weil, inset Little Jack Little, c. 1927	3.00	5.00	4.00
☐ **Alexander's Ragtime Band**, by Irving Berlin, pub. Standard Music (reprint)	2.00	3.00	2.50
☐ **All I Want Is You**, lyric and music by Benny Davis, Harry Akst and Sidney Clare, Starmer cover, inset Corinne Arbuckle, c. 1927	3.00	5.00	4.00
☐ **Along The Santa Fe Trail**, words by Al Dubin and Edwina Coolidge, music by Will Grosz, pub. Harms, 1940	3.50	4.50	4.00
☐ **Around The World In 80 Days**, words by Harold Adamson, music by Victor Young, pub. Victor Young, 1956	2.50	3.50	3.00
☐ **Bebe**, lyric by Sam Coslow, music by Abner Silver, pub. W, inset Bebe Daniels, c. 1923 . .	2.00	4.00	3.00
☐ **Breeze (Blow My Baby Back to Me)**, by Ballard MacDonald, Joe Goodwin and James F. Hanley, small inset Owsley and O'Day, black face, c. 1919	3.00	5.00	4.00
☐ **Champagne Waltz, The**, by Con Conrad, Ben Oakland and Milton Drake, inset Fred Mac-Murray and Gladys Swarthout, pub. Famous Music	2.50	5.00	3.75
☐ **Climb Every Mountain**, words by Oscar Hammerstein, II, music by Richard Rodgers, pub. Williamson Music, 1959	2.00	4.00	3.00
☐ **Cryin' For The Carolines**, words by Sam Lewis and Joe Young, music by Harry Warren, 1930	2.50	5.00	3.75
☐ **Desert Song, The**, words by Otto Harbach, Oscar Hammerstein, II and Frank Mandel, music by Sigmund Romberg, 1926	3.00	7.00	5.00
☐ **As above**, different cover issued when picture was released, inset Dennis Morgan and Irene Manning	2.00	4.00	3.00
☐ **Did You Ever See A Dream Walking**, words by Mack Gordon, music by Harry Revel, insets Jack Oakie, Jack Haley and Ginger Rogers, 1933	3.50	7.00	4.20
☐ **Ending With A Kiss**, words by Harlan Thompson, music by Lewis E. Gensler, inset Lanny Ross and Mary Boland, pub. Famous, 1934 .	3.50	7.50	5.50
☐ **Faithful Forever**, words and music by Ralph Grainger	2.50	5.00	3.50

	Current Price Range		Prior Year Average
☐ **From The Top Of Your Head To The Tip Of Your Toes,** words and music by Mack Gordon and Harry Revel, photo Bing Crosby and Joan Bennett, pub. Crawford, 1935	2.50	5.00	3.50
☐ **Good Night Angel,** words by Herb Magidson, music by Allie Wrubel, insets Bob Burns, Jack Oakie, Kenny Baker, Milton Berle, Ann Miller, Helen Broderick, Hal Kemp, Jane Fromna, Victor Moore, Eric Blore	3.00	7.00	5.00
☐ **Happy Days Are Here Again,** words by Jack Yellen, music by Milton Ager, 1929 . . . . . :. .	3.00	7.00	5.00
☐ **I'm An Old Cowhand (From The Rio Grande),** words and music by Johnny Mercer, photo Bing Crosby, pub. Feist, 1936	3.00	6.00	4.50
☐ **In a Shanty in Old Shanty Town,** words and music by Joe Young, John Siras and Little Jack Little, inset Abe Lyman, c. 1932	2.00	3.00	2.50
☐ **Jean,** words and music by Rod McKuen, pub. 20th Century Music	2.00	3.50	2.62
☐ **Just A Little Closer,** words by Howard Johnson, music by Joseph Meyer, colored photo William Haines, 1930	2.75	5.75	4.25
☐ **Lady Of Spain,** words by Erell Reaves, music by Tolchard Evans, photo Eddie Fischer, pub. Fox, c. 1944	2.00	3.00	2.50
☐ **Love Walked In,** words by Ira Gershwin, music by Geo. Gershwin, stars on cover, pub. C, 1938	3.00	5.00	4.00
☐ **Moon Is Low, The,** words by Arthur Freed, music by Nacio Herb Brown, inset Joan Crawford, pub. RO, 1930	3.00	7.00	5.00
☐ **My Blue Heaven,** words by George Whiting, music by Walter Donaldson, pub. Feist, c. 1927, reprint	2.00	3.00	2.50
☐ **My Blue Ridge Mountain Home,** words and music by Carson Robison featured by Vernon Dahlhart, both photos on cover, pub. Triangle Music, c. 1927	2.00	3.00	2.50
☐ **Never a Day Goes By,** words and music by Walter Donaldson, Peter De Rose and Mitchell Parish, inset Guy Lombardo, pub. Miller, c. 1943	2.00	3.00	2.50
☐ **Night and Day,** words and music by Cole Porter, inset Frank Sinatra, pub. Harms, c. 1932	3.00	5.00	4.00
☐ **Old Pal,** lyric by Gus Kahn, music Egbert Van Alsyne, Med. Key of "F"	2.00	3.00	2.50

	Current Price Range		Prior Year Average

☐ **Tell Me Why You Smile,** words by Walter Reisch, American words by Raymond B. Egan, music by Robert Stolz, pub. Feist, c. 1932 .... 2.50 5.50 4.00

☐ **That's My Mammy,** words by Harry Pease, musicy by Abel Baer and Ed Nelson, pub. Feist, inset Harry Richman, c. 1928 ..... 3.00 4.00 3.50

☐ **Trolley Song, The,** by High Martin and Ralph Blane, inset Judy Garland, pub. Feist, 1944 . 5.00 10.00 7.50

☐ **Underneath The Arches,** by Bud Flanagan, inset Sammy Kaye, c. 1932 .... 1.75 2.75 2.25

☐ **Under Western Skies,** by James W. Casey, Harold Weeks and Henry Murtagh, inset Monte Austin, pub. Echo, c. 1920 .... 1.50 2.50 2.00

☐ **Ukelele Lady,** words by Gus Kahn, music by Richard A. Whiting, inset Gendron Orchestra, c. 1925 .... 1.50 2.50 2.00

☐ **Whatever Will Be Will Be, ,** by Jay Livingston and Ray Evans, inset Doris Day and James Stewart, pub. Artists, 1955 .... 2.57 5.50 4.00

☐ **When It's Sunset in Sweden,** lyric by Dave Morrison, music by Earl Burtnett, c. 1919 ... 3.00 4.00 3.50

☐ **When My Ships Come Sailing Home,** words by Reginald Steward, music by Francis Dorel, pub. Boosey, c. 1903 .... 3.00 4.00 3.50

☐ **When The Little Red Roses Get The Blues For You,** words by Al Dubin, music by Joe Burke, insets Joe E. Brown, Winnie Lightner, 1931 .... 2.50 5.00 3.75

☐ **White Christmas,** by Irving Berlin, inset Bing Crosby, Fred Astaire, pub. Berlin, 1942 ..... 3.00 7.00 5.00

SHOTGUNS

In order to accurately present the vast amount of information required by serious collectors, a special edition devoted to firearms is published by The House of Collectibles, Inc. This handy, pocket-size guide, *The Official 1985 Price Guide to Collector Guns,* features prices and data on model names, barrel lengths, calibers and sight types. It is available at bookstores for $3.95. For more extensive information refer to *The Official 1985 Price Guide to Antique and Modern Firearms.* It is $10.95.

SILHOUETTE PORTRAITS

TOPIC: Silhouette are profiles cut out of one color paper and attached to a background of contrasting color. They can have detail added in chalk, pen or watercolors.

PERIOD: Silhouettes became popular in the 1700s and did not fall from popular favor until the middle of the 1800s.

MAKERS: Famous silhouettes artists include Martha Anne Honeywell, William Henry Brown, Sanders Nellis and Auguste Edouart. Any silhouette bearing the name of Jean Millette is a fake; this was a name created by forgers.

COMMENTS: The value of a silhouette depends on the age, quality and size of the specimen; the notoriety of the subject is also very important. Any information marked on the silhouette increases its value.

ADDITIONAL TIPS: Modern and semi-modern silhouettes are not valued in the collector market.

	Current Price Range		Prior Year Average
☐ **Aaron Burr,** bust portrait, black watercolor. Signed Jos. Wood, dated 1812, 3″ x 2¾″ ...	390.00	450.00	420.00
☐ **Admiral,** unidentified, English wax, bowled glass, gilt rim, 3½″ diameter	180.00	210.00	195.00
☐ **Charles Carroll Of Carrollton** (last surviving signer of the Declaration of Independence), holding trowel and cane, dated 1828, 13″ x 10″	260.00	390.00	325.00
☐ **Civil War Officer,** unidentified, violet paper against light pink background, matted and framed, believed to be of Virginia origin, 5½″ x 4″, c. 1865	195.00	260.00	220.00
☐ **Hon. Henry Clay,** bust portrait, inscribed J. W. Jarvis, dated 1810, 8″ x 6¼″	95.00	160.00	140.00
☐ **Couple,** in double frame, 19th-century	285.00	315.00	300.00
☐ **Double Portrait,** of gentleman and lady, full length figures. Signed Aug. Edouart, dated 1844, 9″ x 7⅛″, Edouart was the Stradivari of silhouettists	225.00	325.00	275.00
☐ **Elderly Man,** unidentified, half-length profile. c. 1880	95.00	130.00	115.00
☐ **Miss Elizabeth Frobiser,** clad in bonnet, dress and white pantalettes. Signed Frith, dated 1821	325.00	390.00	360.00

	Current Price Range		Prior Year Average
☐ **Gentleman,** wearing top hat, landscape setting. Signed Aug. Edouart, dated 1829, 8⅞" x 6⅝"	285.00	360.00	320.00
☐ **Alexander Hamilton,** bust portrait wearing frilled smock. Signed J. W. Jarvis, dated 1804, 4½" x 3½"	520.00	650.00	575.00
☐ **Gentleman,** unidentified, English wax, 18th century style, 1¼" high	290.00	320.00	305.00

STAMPS

In order to accurately present the vast amount of information required by serious collectors, a special edition devoted to stamps is published by The House of Collectibles, Inc. This handy, pocket-size guide, *The Official 1985 Blackbook Price Guide to U.S. Postage Stamps,* features listings, prices, photographs and expert advice. It is available at bookstores for $3.95.

STAR TREK COLLECTIBLES

This section features only a sampling of Star Trek items. In order to accurately present the vast amount of information required by serious collectors, a special edition devoted to Star Trek is published by The House of Collectibles, Inc. This handy, pocket-size guide, *The Official 1985 Price Guide to Star Trek/Star Wars Collectibles,* features more than 6,500 prices for a wide variety of items. It is available at bookstores for $3.95.

DESCRIPTION: Star Trek Collectibles include all items dealing with or made for the Television series, cartoon series or its movies.

ORIGIN: Star Trek, a science fiction space thriller, began as a series which ran from 1966 to 1969. After its cancellation, the series was syndicated and by 1978 was shown 300 times per day worldwide. A cartoon series was produced which ran from 1972 to 1974. *Star Trek: The Motion Picture* and *The Wrath of Khan* were two Star Trek movies.

TYPES: There are all kinds of Star Trek memorabilia including animated cels, toys, costumes, books and household ware.

COMMENTS: After the television series, Star Trek Fan Clubs, magazines and conventions sprang up worldwide. With more fans interested in these collectibles, the prices are rising into the double digits.

Star Trek Adventure Set,
*made by Colorforms
under license from
Paramount Pictures Corp.,
punch-out cardboard figures
of characters, 1975,*
$5.00-$7.00

ADDITIONAL TIPS: For more information, consult *the Official Price Guide to Star Trek and Star Wars Collectibles,* published by The House of Collectibles.

	Current Price Range		Prior Year Average
☐ **Animated Cel Of McCoy,** reproduction of drawings by studio animators, clear acetate, 4″ x 8″	3.00	5.00	4.00
☐ **Badge,** card stock with plastic pinback holder, says "Boarding pass, U.S.S. Enterprise" with the picture of the starship	.75	1.00	.87
☐ **Billfold,** TV show, vinyl with zipper, shows Enterprise, 1977	5.00	8.00	6.50
☐ **Blueprints, Enterprise,** Franz Joseph, rolled edition, few produced prior to professional production by Ballantine Books, desirable collectible	150.00	175.00	162.00
☐ **Blueprints Star Trek The Motion Picture,** by David Kimble, shows exterior detail only of the Enterprise bridge, Klingon ship and			

	Current Price Range		Prior Year Average

bridge, Vulcan shuttle, travel pod and more, blue pack, out of print **10.00** **30.00** **20.00**

☐ **Blueprints,** Shuttlecraft plans of the Galileo, set of two, 18" x 24", Starcraft Productions . **4.00** **6.00** **5.00**

☐ **Book, Best Of Trek, The,** W. Irwin and G. Love, volume #1, interviews, convention close ups, close up on special effects, compiled from Trek, the magazine for Star Trek fans, 1974 .... **2.00** **3.00** **2.50**

☐ **Book, Making Of Star Trek, The,** G. Roddenberry, a complete and authorized history of television series, how it was conceived, written, produced and sold, paperback, Ballantine Books, 1968.

☐ **First edition** **15.00** **30.00** **22.50**

☐ **Later edition** **6.00** **12.00** **9.00**

☐ **Book, Official Star Trek Cooking Manual,** Ann Riccard, Bantam, 1978 .... **15.00** **25.00** **20.00**

☐ **Book, Official Star Trek Trivia Book,** hardcover, 205 pp **10.00** **15.00** **12.50**

☐ **Bumper Sticker,** says "Dr. McCoy Doesn't Make House Calls", Aviva Enterprises, blue and white printed on orange **1.00** **2.00** **1.50**

☐ **Bumper Sticker,** says "Spock For President" . **1.00** **2.00** **1.50**

☐ **Button With Dr. McCoy,** Langley Associates, looking puzzled, diameter 2¼" **1.00** **2.00** **1.50**

☐ **Button With Spock,** Star Trek Galore, with harp **1.00** **2.00** **1.50**

☐ **Calendar,** Pocket Books, photos from the first movie, star dates, 1982 .... **10.00** **12.00** **11.00**

☐ **Patch, Enterprise,** black background with white silhouette captioned "Star Trek", 2" x 3" **3.00** **4.00** **3.50**

☐ **Figure,** Mego Corporation, Mr. Spock, dressed in science officer uniform with phaser, 1980, 12½" **25.00** **35.00** **30.00**

☐ **Helmet,** Enco Industries, a similar version of the same thing by Remco, flashing light and sound, 1976 .... **25.00** **27.00** **26.00**

☐ **Memo Pads,** Lincoln Enterprises, miniature versions of the offical stationary used in the Star Trek offices .... **.50** **.75** **.62**

☐ **Postcard Of Sulu,** Lincoln Enterprises, full color, played by George Takei, 5" x 7" ..... **.20** **.60** **.40**

☐ **Puzzle,** H.G. Toys Inc., 150 pieces, series II, cartoons, "The Alien", 14" x 10" **4.00** **8.00** **6.00**

	Current Price Range		Prior Year Average
☐ **Ship Recognition Manual,** The Federation F.A.S.A., all ships of The Federation in color, magazine format, 1983	7.00	8.00	7.50
☐ **Spock Ears,** Don Post Studios, custom hand-made, soft plastic	5.00	7.00	6.00
☐ **Still Khan,** sitting at table turning to side talking	1.00	3.00	2.00
☐ **Still Kirk,** looking to side with bridge in background looking determined	1.00	3.00	2.00
☐ **Still Spock,** in brown coveralls talking in corridor, wall in background	1.00	3.00	2.00
☐ **Still Sulu,** at post listening to Kirk speaking by control panel	1.00	3.00	2.00
☐ **View Master,** series of three reels from "The Omega Glory", in three dimension, 1968	5.00	10.00	8.00

STAR WARS COLLECTIBLES

This section features only a sampling of Star Wars items. In order to accurately present the vast amount of information required by serious collectors, a special edition devoted to Star Wars is published by The House of Collectibles, Inc. This handy, pocket-size guide, *The Official 1985 Price Guide to Star Trek/Star Wars Collectibles,* features more than 6,500 prices for a wide variety of items. It is available at bookstores for $3.95.

DESCRIPTION: Star Wars collectibles include all items made for or about the three Star Wars movies.

ORIGIN: *Star Wars,* a space fantasy, is the name of a movie released in the 1980s. Because of its popularity, two other movies were produced including *The Empire Strikes Back* and *Return of the Jedi.*

TYPES: All types of movie articles and promotional items were produced including posters, toys, patches, household ware and action figures.

COMMENTS: The three Star Wars movies were big hits with movie audiences worldwide. Thousands of Star Wars fans keep the collectible market booming.

ADDITIONAL TIPS: For more information, consult *The Official Price Guide to Star Trek and Star Wars Collectibles,* published by The House of Collectibles.

	Current Price Range		Prior Year Average
☐ **Alarm Clock,** Star Wars Talking Alarm, three dimensional R2-D2 and C-3PO, the Robot's voices are alarm, clock is 30 hour manual wind, 4″ x 6¾″ x 7¾″	10.00	15.00	12.50
☐ **Belt,** Lee, stretch, metal buckle says "Return Of The Jedi", belt is red and black with "Star Wars/Return Of The Jedi" repeated around it, 1982	2.50	3.50	3.00
☐ **Book, Empire Strikes Back, The,** Archie Goodwin and Al Williamson, illustrators, from screenplay by L. Brackett and L. Kasdan, Marvel Comics Group, 1980, paperback, 224 pages	5.00	7.00	6.00
☐ **Book, Han Solo At Star's End,** B. Daley, Chewbacca is kidnapped and Han can only save himself or his friends, hardcover, Del Rey, 1979	6.00	10.00	8.00
☐ **Candy Heads,** Topps, the Empire Strikes Back, Yoda series, plastic figurine heads of Yoda, Tauntaun, Bounty Hunter Bossk, 2-1B, heads, filled with candy, each	1.00	2.00	1.50
☐ **Costume,** Darth Vader, Halloween type, with mask	5.00	7.00	6.00
☐ **Imperial Cruiser,** Kenner, sliding cargo door, captured royal command ship inside, die cast metal and high impact plastic	25.00	35.00	30.00
☐ **Key Chain,** "Darth Vader Lives"	2.00	4.00	3.00
☐ **Lobby Card,** Empire Strikes Back, 11″ x 14″ .	4.00	6.00	5.00
☐ **Mask,** Chewbacca, by Don Post, soft latex, hand applied hair	50.00	70.00	60.00
☐ **Puppet, Yoda,** Kenner, from the planet Dagobah, finely sculpted, head and hands can be manipulated, height 8½″	8.00	10.00	9.00
☐ **Puzzle,** jigsaw, Kenner, 1000 pieces, same as promotional poster for first movie, Star Wars Adventure, 19⅜″ x 26¾″, 1977	9.00	12.00	10.50
☐ **Sheet Music,** "Princess Leia's Theme" by John Williams, from Star Wars, Fox Fanfare Music, Inc., 1977	2.00	3.00	2.50
☐ **Shoelaces,** Stride-Rite, repeat of Star Wars, light blue, 1983	1.50	2.00	1.75
☐ **Tumblers,** Pepperidge Farm, free with purchase of Star Wars cookies, plastic, four different pictures	6.00	10.00	8.00
☐ **Wrapping Paper,** Empire Strikes Back, pictures Yoda and Obi-Wan Kenobi	2.00	3.00	2.50

SUPERMAN

This section features only a sampling of Superman items. In order to accurately present the vast amount of information required by serious collectors, a special edition devoted to comic books is published by The House of Collectibles, Inc. This handy, pocket-size guide, *The Official 1985 Price Guide to Comic Books,* features a special section on Superman. It is available at bookstores for $3.95. For more in-depth Superman information, refer to *The Official 1985 Price Guide to Comic Books and Collectibles,* for $10.95.

DESCRIPTION: Items pertaining to the comic book character Superman are collectible.

TYPES: Toys, games, comic books, newpaper strips, original comic art, and premiums are some examples of Superman memorabilia.

PERIOD: The comic book Superman first appeared in 1938. It was created by Jerry Siegel and Joe Shuster.

COMMENTS: Besides comic books, Superman was portrayed in a television series, radio series and motion pictures.

	Current Price Range		Prior Year Average
☐ **Badge,** movie promotional, emblem shaped (for Superman I)	3.00	4.00	3.25
☐ **Bank,** dime register bank, lithographed tin, square, picture of Superman facing left, breaking chain by expanding his chest	90.00	115.00	100.00
☐ **Belt Buckle,** tin, blue and red on silvered brass, half-length portrait, name at bottom, 1940	90.00	115.00	102.00
☐ **Birthday Card,** You're Ten Today, Birthday Greetings From Superman, copyright by Superman, Inc., 1940s	13.00	17.00	15.00
☐ **Button,** Kelloggs Pep Cereal premium, lithographed tin, multicolored, 1940s	7.00	10.00	8.50
☐ **Button,** Muscle Building Club, lithographed tin, head and chest portrait, c. 1940.	75.00	100.00	86.00
☐ **Button,** Superman of America, club button given to members of the Supermen of America, shows him breaking chains across his chest, 1939	35.00	45.00	40.00
☐ **Clothing,** Superman the Movie t-shirt, with iron-on, made in four different colors, has full standing portrait	6.00	8.00	7.00

	Current Price Range		Prior Year Average
☐ **Clothing,** t-shirt with iron-on, made in four different colors, has wording "Run, Jump, Fly."	6.00	8.00	7.00
☐ **Clothing,** t-shirt with iron-on, has "S" symbol	6.00	8.00	7.00
☐ **Cookie Jar,** California Originals, ceramic, figural, painted, shows him leaving phone booth after switching from Clark Kent identity, 1970s	22.00	29.00	24.00
☐ **Decoder,** Superman's Secret Code, premium from Action Comics sent to members of the Superman of America club, 1938-1942	45.00	57.00	50.00
☐ **Doll,** made by The Toy Works, stuffed fabric, full length with cape, 25½"	22.00	28.00	24.00
☐ **Figure,** Ideal, composition and wood, painted, with cape, one of the earliest Superman figures, 13"	300.00	400.00	350.00
☐ **Figure,** Syrocco, 1940s, 5¾"	165.00	200.00	175.00
☐ **Figure,** Brass Hanging Ornament, shows him standing on top of world, 4"	2.50	3.50	3.00
☐ **Food Carton,** Superman Candy Coated Peanuts, box only, illustrated lid, multicolors, 1966, 5½"	20.00	27.00	23.00
☐ **Mug,** tankard type, made by California Originals, ceramic, high relief, painted, 1978	20.00	25.00	22.00
☐ **Music Box,** made by Price, ceramic, figural, late 1970s, 7"	22.00	29.00	24.85
☐ **Novelty,** Glow-in-the-Dark picture, shows him riding on a bomb with airplanes in background, 9" x 11"	22.00	28.00	25.00
☐ **Pencil Case,** stiff paper, maroon and silver, illustration at top, 8¼"	35.00	45.00	39.00
☐ **Pendant,** lithographed tin, movable arms, 1970s, 2½"	4.00	6.00	5.00
☐ **Pen,** fountain pen, small colored decal of Superman standing with hands on hips, c. 1942	32.00	40.00	35.00
☐ **Phonograph Record,** Superman and the Magic Ring, set of two seven-inch 78 r.p.m. records, Musette label, contains story that was broadcast on the radio with original radio cast, accompanied by a booklet, c. 1947	40.00	50.00	42.00
☐ **Purse,** yellow, 1966	27.00	35.00	30.00

	Current Price Range		Prior Year Average
☐ **Vehicle,** Supermobile, made by Corgi of Great Britain, diecast metal, bearing the number 265	9.00	12.00	10.25
☐ **Wallet,** made by Pioneer, genuine leather, zips on three sides	13.00	17.00	15.00

THIMBLES

TOPIC: Thimbles are small fingertip protectors used during sewing.

MATERIALS: Porcelain and silver are the most popular materials for making thimbles.

COMMENTS: Designs of thimbles are very diverse; the decorations on many thimbles are so exquisite that collectors may devote themselves soley to the porcelain painted or other varieties.

ADDITIONAL TIPS: Since thimbles are very difficult to accurately date, their decoration and design remain paramount to most collectors. Some individuals focus on advertising thimbles, while others prefer the artistic type.

☐ Beer company advertising, porcelain, set of three	2.50	3.00	2.75
☐ **Currier & Ives,** porcelain, blue and white, set of four	1.00	1.50	1.25
☐ **Damron,** Butterfly, cystal	10.00	18.00	14.00
☐ **Delft,** blue, Holland	5.00	10.00	7.50
☐ **Friia,** goldplate, presidents	5.00	10.00	7.50
☐ General store advertising, porcelain, set of four	3.25	3.75	3.50
☐ Goldplate cloisonne, Disney character	5.00	10.00	7.50
☐ **Hummel,** Apple Girl, porcelain	16.00	26.00	21.00
☐ **Hurley,** Calico Cuties, porcelain	12.00	20.00	16.00
☐ **Lefton,** porcelain, floral motif, set of three ..	.75	1.25	1.00
☐ **Limoges,** bird motif, porcelain	10.00	18.00	14.00
☐ **Partridge,** bisque, gold raised lettering, signed Joel	15.00	20.00	17.50
☐ Silver, engraved scenic design	21.00	26.00	24.00
☐ Silver, engraved scenic design on border ...	15.00	18.00	16.50
☐ Silver, hallmarked	25.00	35.00	30.00
☐ Silver, size 9	7.00	13.00	10.00
☐ Silver, size 6, star trade mark	20.00	26.00	23.00
☐ **Spode,** Heavenly cherubs, china	25.00	35.00	30.00

	Current Price Range		Prior Year Average
☐ Tobacco company advertising, porcelain, set of three	2.50	3.00	2.75
☐ Whiskey company advertising, porcelain, set of three	2.50	3.00	2.75

TIN

TYPES: Though all types of tin items are sought after collectibles, this section concerns tin kitchen utensils.

COMMENTS: A light, fusible metal, tin was often used to coat other metals. Early pieces were usually soldered together. Prices are fairly reasonable.

ADDITIONAL TIPS: The listings are alphabetical according to item. For further information, refer to *The Official Price Guide to Kitchen and Household Collectibles.*

Tin Dinner Bucket, *with coffee carrier, coffee flask and cup,* **$16.00-$24.00**

	Current Price Range		Prior Year Average
☐ **Apple Corers,** all tin, 19th century	6.00	9.00	7.00
☐ **Apple Roaster,** tin reflecting oven, c. 1850's	90.00	110.00	93.00
☐ **Bee Smoker,** tin, leather bellows	40.00	50.00	43.00
☐ **Biscuit Cutter,** Victorian tin pig-shaped	11.00	23.00	13.00
☐ **Boiler,** fish, pierced tin, two parts, c. 1890 . .	9.00	17.00	11.00
☐ **Bread Cake Boxes,** tin, brown, No.1, 13½ " x 10½ " x 9¾ "	31.00	41.00	33.00
☐ **Bread Mixer,** White House Bread Mixer and Kneader, tin bucket and cover, crank handle, clamp on table type, awarded gold medal, St. Louis Exposition 1904, made by Landers, Frary and Clark, New Britain, Conn	37.00	47.00	39.00
☐ **Bread Pan,** round, two halves fastened together with wire hoop at one end	11.00	22.00	13.00
☐ **Broom Holder,** embossed blue jays, Marcos Blue Jay, 1910	78.00	100.00	83.00
☐ **Cake Maker,** tin, 3 gears, wood handle, Universal, 8", c. 1905	53.00	65.00	55.00
☐ **Cake Pan,** tube, c. 1920	18.00	25.00	21.00
☐ **Cake or Muffin Pan,** 9 sections, heart mold .	120.00	140.00	130.00
☐ **Cheese Strainer,** heart shaped punched tin on three legs	30.00	55.00	33.00
☐ **Churn,** tin, tin handles, wooden dasher	260.00	310.00	275.00
☐ **Coffeepot,** black, orange, red, green decor, 12" high	280.00	295.00	285.00
☐ **Coffeepot,** 8-10 cup size, crook spout	32.00	45.00	35.00
☐ **Colander**	20.00	28.00	22.50
☐ **Cream Ladle,** marked "Cream Top, Pat. Sept. 2nd 1924, Mar. 3rd 1925"	4.00	6.00	5.00
☐ **Crumb Set,** black wooden handle, embossed metal, decorated	9.00	13.00	10.00
☐ **Dish Pan,** heavy tin, side handles	17.00	27.00	19.00
☐ **Dispenser,** handmade, soldered, 5" x 3" dia.	15.00	30.00	18.00
☐ **Doughnut Cutter,** all tin, with handle, c. 1915	4.00	6.00	5.00
☐ **Dustpan,** tin with wooden handle	10.00	16.00	12.00
☐ **Eclair Pan,** makes 12 eclairs	13.00	18.00	14.00
☐ **Eggbeater,** cream whipper combination, also called whip or syllabub churn, two parts, marked "Patented 1868"	37.00	50.00	40.00
☐ **Flour Scoop,** c. 1870	20.00	30.00	25.00
☐ **Flour Sifter,** Blood's 1861 patent, mesh and wood	84.00	110.00	87.00
☐ **Fly Sprayer,** quick loader	8.00	16.00	10.00
☐ **Food Warmer,** stenciled flowers	193.00	205.00	195.00
☐ **Fruit Press,** Henis fruit and vegetable press and strainer, tinned iron	9.00	13.00	11.00

	Current Price Range		Prior Year Average
☐ **Grater,** fruit and vegetable hand pierced, attached to wooden back with handle	13.00	20.00	15.00
☐ **Grater,** hand-punched tin, wooden handle . .	40.00	60.00	50.00
☐ **Grater,** nutmeg marked "The Edgar," patented 1896, sliding type, two wood knobs	19.00	29.00	21.00
☐ **Hot Water Bottle,** with screw cap, oval with oval top lid, 7″ x 10″	16.00	26.00	17.00
☐ **Ice Cream Scoops,** tinned steel, cone shaped cup, turn knob on top of cone releases ice cream from cup, various sizes, numbers on handle of cup indicate number of dips to the quart, 20 dip size	11.00	19.00	13.00
☐ **Lunch Box,** complete with cup and trays . . .	32.00	65.00	35.00
☐ **Matchsafe,** tin, painted, "Matches", c. 1910	9.00	15.00	11.00
☐ **Meal Funnel,** maple, dovetail 4 corners, c. 1860	50.00	60.00	52.00
☐ **Measure,** handle, mug shape, 4¼″ x 5¾″ . .	37.00	47.00	40.00
☐ **Noodle Cutter**	45.00	55.00	50.00
☐ **Nutmeg Grater,** "The Boyer"	35.00	45.00	38.00
☐ **Nutmeg Grater,** tin, turned wood handles, pat, 4″	42.00	55.00	45.00
☐ **Oven,** open on fireplace side, top handle, back legs, one shelf	105.00	145.00	110.00
☐ **Pastry Board,** tin, rolling pin cradle, hanging ring, 22″ x 18½″	142.00	170.00	150.00
☐ **Pastry Board,** with rolling pin cradle, 22″ x 18½″	146.00	156.00	149.00
☐ **Pie Lifter,** all heavy tinned wire, pitch fork shaped	8.50	13.00	11.00
☐ **Pie Pan,** marked "Crisco," patented Jan. 5, 1926	9.00	13.00	11.00
☐ **Plate Warmer,** dome-shaped top, four splayed legs, side handles	90.00	110.00	99.00
☐ **Popcorn Popper,** fancy pierced hinged lid, rectangular, wooden handle, handmade, 18th century	42.00	55.00	45.00
☐ **Pot,** oval with handle with hanging ring, lid with hanging ring	21.00	32.00	23.00
☐ **Press,** meat loaf wood frame, oblong tin press, top turn handle	37.00	47.00	39.00
☐ **Rolling Pin,** tin body, wooden handles, pat .	37.00	47.00	39.00
☐ **Sausage Gun,** tubular tin, snout on one end, hanging ring on other, with wood plunge . . .	26.00	32.00	29.00
☐ **Sifter,** marked "Kewpie," 3½″ high	21.00	32.00	23.00
☐ **Skimmer,** 6″ round with short finger grip handle	7.00	14.00	8.00

	Current Price Range		Prior Year Average
☐ **Spice Boxes,** set of 6 miniature tin spice canisters in matching tray with handle, contents stencilled on lids	52.00	65.00	54.00
☐ **Steam Cooker,** tin handled top, pat. date 1879, 12½ " dia.	29.00	39.00	32.00
☐ **Strainer,** simple tin-sided tea strainer, wooden handle strainer marked "C.D. Denny Co." a find for Kenny collectors	21.00	33.00	23.00
☐ **Sugar Scoop,** tin, small with strap handle, kitchen container type	13.00	18.00	15.00
☐ **Syrup Pitcher,** green, black, red flowers, 5½ " high	192.00	210.00	198.00
☐ **Toaster,** steel toaster for gas, gasoline, or oil stove, no markings	5.50	14.00	7.00
☐ **Tongs,** for lifting hot foods, marked "Ritz's 'Tasty' Bread"	5.00	10.00	7.00
☐ **Wash Boiler,** heavy tin, copper bottom, side handles, handled lid	36.00	46.00	39.00
☐ **Water Cooler,** metal, two gallon capacity, nickel plated faucets	42.00	55.00	44.00

TOOLS

DESCRIPTION: A tool is a device used by hand. Those who use tools include carpenters, farmers, plumbers, cabinetmakers and wheelwrights.

TYPES: There are several different types of tools but woodworking tools which include planes, saws, measuring implements, augers, bits and bladed instruments are the items most sought after by collectors.

COMMENTS: Handmade tools of the 1800s and factory produced tools of the early 1900s are the most desirable among collectors.

ADDITIONAL TIPS: Some hobbyists collect tools by type while others collect by craft. An entire collection could be comprised of tools used only by a shipwright or it could contain every type of bladed instrument from various occupations.

☐ **Auger,** hand-forged stem is Y-shaped at hickory handle, 24" x 1¼ ", 1850s	22.00	32.00	27.00
☐ **Auger,** hand-forged crude hickory handles, unreadable mark, 15" x 1¼ ", 1850s	20.00	29.00	23.50

	Current Price Range		Prior Year Average
☐ **Auger,** stamped #5, no manufacturer's mark, well shaped hickory handle, 15″ x 1½″, c. 1880	14.00	20.00	17.00
☐ **Axe,** felling type, marked "Stohler"	32.00	40.00	35.00
☐ **Axe,** firefighter's type, made by Warren Axe and Tool Co. of Warren, Pennsylvania	30.00	35.00	32.00
☐ **Axe,** post hole type, made by Hagen of Lancaster, Pennsylvania, wrought single center bit	42.00	55.00	45.00
☐ **Brace,** chairmaker's, spoon bit, beechwood, 13″	145.00	190.00	160.00
☐ **Brace,** 4-post cage head, 13″	270.00	345.00	295.00
☐ **Brace,** made in France, marked Peugeout Freres, polished steel, beechwood head and knob	40.00	50.00	44.00
☐ **Brace,** metal and wood, set screw holds bits (handturned handles), 1850s	35.00	50.00	42.00
☐ **Brace,** metal and wood, set screw holds bits, 1880s	20.00	29.00	23.50
☐ **Brace,** Sheffield, beechwood, unplated, "Coca cola" head	90.00	115.00	97.00
☐ **Brace,** walnut with brass trim, English mark, bit spring broken, 1820s	90.00	120.00	105.00
☐ **Brace,** wrought iron, lignum vitae head, 10″ .	27.00	35.00	30.00
☐ **Chisel,** common, hand-forged, from file, 6½″ W. blade, iron ferrule, 1850s	8.00	12.00	10.00
☐ **Chisel,** corner, hand-forged, each side 11″ W. blade 7¼″L., iron collar on handle, 1810s ..	20.00	28.00	24.00
☐ **Chisel,** marked, "Charles Buck—Cast Steel," brass ferrule, blade ⅞″ W., maple with leather, handle striking surface, 1900s	7.00	10.00	8.50
☐ **Clamp,** all wood, two "bolts," 5″ jaw, marked "William J. Hood, maker, Valley Falls, R.I.," 1870s	14.00	19.00	16.50
☐ **Clamp,** screw type, round, "coca bola" nut, 11″	37.00	45.00	40.00
☐ **Draw Knife,** Cooper's tangs bent through handles, brass ferrule, 1840s	12.00	17.00	14.50
☐ **Draw Knife,** leather working "Snell & Atherton," #5, all metal scraper, c. 1870	14.00	19.00	16.50
☐ **Draw Knife,** open scorp, brass ferrule, 1800s	14.00	19.00	16.50
☐ **Draw Knife,** wagon maker's, "Ohio Tool Co." #9, 9″ blade, eggshaped handles, maple, c. 1870	15.00	20.00	17.50
☐ **Hammer,** caulking, slotted head, iron wings, 1880s	12.00	15.00	13.50

	Current Price Range		Prior Year Average
☐ **Plane,** box type, iron core, beechwood handles, 7¼"	70.00	90.00	77.00
☐ **Plane,** cooper's stoup type, dark beechwood, 7"	23.00	30.00	25.00
☐ **Plane,** iron, Evan's Patent, with patent date of 1862	65.00	80.00	70.00
☐ **Plane,** metal and wood, Stanley Rule and Level Co., #33, 28" L., 1910s	22.00	29.00	25.00
☐ **Plane,** molding, "E. T. Burrones & Co., Portland, Me." printed on side of plane, "Use this tool for fitting Burrowes Patent Sliding Screens"	27.00	36.00	30.00
☐ **Plane,** molding, fancy with brass plow planes	52.00	70.00	61.00
☐ **Plane,** molding, standard, generally priced, up to 1½"	11.00	16.00	13.50
☐ **Plane,** panel raising, Greenfield Tool Co., model #688, nickel blade with two adjustable fences, 14"	210.00	260.00	225.00
☐ **Plane,** Sargent, model #3415, 15"	30.00	40.00	34.00
☐ **Plumb Bob,** turnip shape, brass, 4"	40.00	52.00	45.00
☐ **Ruler,** Chapin Stephens Co., brass trim all around, stamped "JRP," 1880s	22.00	29.00	25.00
☐ **Ruler,** ivory, 24" L., 1800s	55.00	70.00	62.50
☐ **Ruler,** Lufkin #651, brass trim, marked "Boxwood — Made in England"	14.00	19.00	16.50
☐ **Ruler,** Lufkin, pat'd. 12/3/18, brass trim, marked "Boxwood," stamped "Maguire," 1920s	13.00	18.00	15.00
☐ **Ruler,** Stanley, #66½, brass at hinges and end, "Warrented Boxwood," 36" L., 1800s	22.00	29.00	23.00
☐ **Ruler,** Stanley, #68, brass trim on hinges and ends, "Boxwood," 1900s	14.00	19.00	16.50
☐ **Sash Filleter,** made by John Moseley and Son, beechwood, brass tips with depth adjustment	90.00	110.00	97.00
☐ **Saw,** backsaw, Wright & Co. on blade, extra heavy back, beech handle, 11" L., 1890s	14.00	19.00	16.50
☐ **Saw,** keyhole, W. B. Sears & Co. on blade, "C.B." stamped on maple handle, brass bolts, 7" L., 1890s	9.00	12.00	10.50
☐ **Saw,** pad type, beechwood handle, marked "Phila."	20.00	25.00	22.00
☐ **Scale,** lumber, J. Chatillon & Son, New York, in yellow paint, "200," black, 1800s	60.00	90.00	75.00
☐ **Scale,** steelyard, reversible, two hooks on "Heavy" measure, hand-forged, 1820s	50.00	70.00	60.00

	Current Price Range		Prior Year Average
☐ **Scraper,** unusual paint or wood scraper, chestnut, turned handle, "W. S. Thompson," 19th century stamped in 3-sided U-shaped blade, handmade, 3½″ L., 1800s	25.00	35.00	30.00
☐ **Screwdriver,** clockmaster's, brass ferrule, beech handle, marked "Sargent, Cast Steel," 1890s	8.00	12.00	10.00
☐ **Screwdriver,** Primitive Yankee model	20.00	30.00	25.00
☐ **Screwdriver,** Winchester, wood handle	9.00	13.00	10.50
☐ **Screw Plate,** contains 16 sizes, 8½″	25.00	32.00	27.00
☐ **Scribe,** beech with brass facing and trim ...	9.00	12.00	10.50
☐ **Scribe,** handmade, all beech, hand-stamped inches and numbers, 8″ L.	7.00	10.00	8.50
☐ **Scribe,** handmade, beech and mahogany, no inches	7.00	10.00	8.50
☐ **Scribe,** rosewood with brass facings and trim	22.00	29.00	25.00
☐ **Shovel,** carved from one piece, maple or chestnut, grain shovel, c. 1840-1880	18.00	25.00	21.50
☐ **Shovel,** snow shovel, handmade, wood with tin trim, c. 20th c.	12.00	17.00	14.50
☐ **Soldering Iron,** copper, wood handle, large head, 19″	9.00	12.00	10.00
☐ **Splitting Froe,** 12″ blade	19.00	24.00	21.00
☐ **Splitting Wedge,** wood top, iron ring	17.00	22.00	20.00
☐ **Spoke Shave,** beechwood, 10″	12.00	16.00	14.00
☐ **String Winder,** carpenter's type, bent wood, red finish, 12″	50.00	65.00	57.00
☐ **T Square,** rosewood handle, brass plate and three-pointed diamond inlay, stamped "OWO," blade, 7½″ x 1¾″, 1890s	14.00	19.00	16.50
☐ **T Square,** rosewood handle, brass plate and four-leaf clover inlay, "JM" carved in handle, blade 12″ x 2⅛″, 1880s	17.00	23.00	20.00
☐ **T Square,** rosewood handle, "Miller's Falls, Made in U.S.A.," #1438, brass plate, 8″ x 1½″, 1920s.............................	9.00	12.00	10.50
☐ **Wrench Brace,** marked "P. Lowentraut, Newark, 1877 Patent"	85.00	100.00	91.00

VALENTINES

ORIGIN: Valentines have been given for centuries. The first Valentines were handwritten, homemade statements of love and affection. Commercial Valentines were produced by the end of the 18th century.

MAKERS: Popular Valentine makers and companies include Whitney, Taft, Strong, Tuck and Mansell.

COMMENTS: Handmade Valentines are quite disirable and quite rare. Period Valentines are also sought after, such as those from the Civil War, Victorian era, or the World Wars.

ADDITIONAL TIPS: The listings are in alphabetical order according to country of origin, type of Valentine or company, depending on available information.

Valentine Postcard,
1911, **$2.00-$3.00**

	Current Price Range		Prior Year Average
☐ **American,** heart shaped, lace, c.1905	9.00	16.00	12.00
☐ **American,** honeycomb, "Cupid's Temple of Love," c. 1928	8.00	16.00	12.00
☐ **American,** Maggie and Jiggs, c. 1940	4.00	12.00	8.00
☐ **American,** Popeye, c. 1940	4.00	10.00	6.50
☐ **Art Nouveau,** heart shaped folder	4.50	6.50	5.50
☐ **Carrington,** folder, lace, c. 1937	1.50	4.50	3.00

	Current Price Range		Prior Year Average
☐ **Comic Valentine,** the "Hat Trimmer," Elton and Co., New York, illustration of glum-looking woman sewing hat, with verse, c. 1860	22.00	30.00	25.00
☐ **"Dainty Dimples"** series, per card	3.00	8.00	4.00
☐ **Easel Valentine,** fold back, free standing, c. early 1900s	34.00	44.00	38.00
☐ **German,** 5 layer, pulldown, religious senti-ment, flowers	45.00	65.00	55.00
☐ **German,** large ship, mechanical pulldown	55.00	85.00	70.00
☐ **German,** pulldown, children, c. 1915	4.50	10.00	6.50
☐ **German,** pulldown, gold	10.00	20.00	15.00
☐ **German,** pullout and stand up cottage, c. 1910	7.00	15.00	12.00
☐ **German,** pullout and stand up steam boiler, c. 1910	12.00	18.00	14.00
☐ **German,** stand up, little girl holding opening parasol	15.00	25.00	20.00
☐ **German,** three layers, pulldown, lavendar, pink, gold, green, c. 1920	6.50	15.00	8.50
☐ **Gibson Art,** paper doll mechanical stand up, little girl holding doll, German	20.00	35.00	27.00
☐ **"Hearts Are Ripe,"** children picking heart shaped apples from tree	3.00	7.00	5.00
☐ **H. Dobbs and Co.,** "Pillar Post," illustration of mailbox, c. 1800	22.00	27.00	23.50
☐ **"It Must Be Fine, To Have a Valentine,"** from "Valentine Wishes" series	7.00	12.00	9.00
☐ **"Lady Killer,"** comic valentine by A.J. Fisher, N.Y., c. 1875	29.00	39.00	33.00
☐ **McLoughlin,** folder, no lace, c. 1905	5.00	12.00	7.00
☐ **McLoughlin,** three layer, silver, white, lace, c. 1880	5.00	12.00	7.50
☐ **McLoughlin,** three layer, white, gold, lace, c. 1880	5.00	12.00	7.50
☐ **Mansell,** lace, handwritten verse, c. 1846	75.00	100.00	85.00
☐ **Mansell,** lace paper, lovers in a park, heavily ornamented, white with silver, c. 1855	44.00	54.00	48.00
☐ **Mansell,** cameo embossing, two lovers walk-ing along woodland path, c. 1845	39.00	49.00	43.00
☐ **Mechanical,** set of fifteen, c. 1920	34.00	44.00	38.00
☐ **Mechanical,** "Such is Married Life," c. 1850	39.00	49.00	43.00
☐ **Mechanical,** various animals, c. 1930	10.00	15.00	12.00
☐ **Mechanical,** Walt Disney character, c. 1930	17.00	24.00	20.00

	Current Price Range		Prior Year Average
☐ **Meek,** layered folder, lace, c. 1870	8.00	15.00	12.00
☐ **"Temple of Love,"** from Raphael Tuck's "Betsy Beauties" series, young girl chasing butterfly	5.00	9.00	7.00
☐ **"To My Valentine,"** from Raphael Tuck's "Innocence Abroad" series, two young children, brief verse	5.00	8.00	6.00
☐ **"To My Wife,"** embossed woman, hearts and flowers, cutout flowers tied with satin ribbon, real lace surrounds cutout heart, c. 1936	11.00	16.00	12.00
☐ **Tuck,** folder, heart shaped, little girl on front	4.00	10.00	6.50
☐ **Victorian Valentine,** fold out, paper lace . . .	20.00	25.00	22.00
☐ **Whitney,** embossed paper in pattern, a child delivering a note to a lady, with original embossed envelope, c. 1870	39.00	49.00	43.00
☐ **Whitney,** folder, lace, c. 1920	3.50	8.00	6.00
☐ **Whitney,** heart shape, World War I soldier valentine	5.00	13.00	8.00
☐ **Whitney,** three layer, Art Nouveau design, lace, gold, pink, rose, hearts, c. 1912	15.00	30.00	23.00
☐ **Whitney,** three layer, lace, Art Deco, children	4.50	6.50	5.50
☐ **Whitney,** three layer, lace, Art Nouveau	10.00	18.00	14.00
☐ **Whitney,** three piece, heart shaped, little girls	1.75	3.50	2.10

WICKER

DESCRIPTION: Wicker is the general term for furniture and decorative accessories made of woven rattan, cane, dried grasses, willow, reed or other pliable material.

PERIOD: The wicker heyday in the U.S. was from about 1860 to 1930.

ORIGIN: Wicker can be dated to about 4000 B.C. when the Egyptians used it. The interest in wicker in the U.S. began in the 1850s.

MAKERS: Cyrus Wakefield and the Heywood Brother were the best known wicker manufacturers. They later joined to become the Heywood-Wakefield Company. Other companies include American Rattan Company and Paine's Manufacturing Company.

COMMENTS: While 19th century wicker is more valuable, pieces from the 1920s and 1930s are also very collectible and easier to find. Natural finish wicker is most desirable and less common pieces are the most sought after.

ADDITIONAL TIPS: For more information on wicker, see *The Official 1984 Price Guide to Wicker.*

	Current Price Range		Prior Year Average
☐ **Basket,** sewing, natural finish, c. 1880	165.00	225.00	180.00
☐ **Basket,** sewing, natural finish, loop design on bottom shelf, crisscross weave on basket, c. 1880	250.00	325.00	275.00
☐ **Basket,** sewing, natural finish, rare curlicue and spool design on basket, large birdcage design at middle of brace, c. 1880	300.00	425.00	330.00
☐ **Basket,** wood, natural finish, loop motif set into circular design, closely woven tray, ball feet, c. 1890	135.00	195.00	150.00
☐ **Bookcase,** whatnot, natural finish, height 7', unique "corner" design, five oak shelves, extensive fancywork, c. 1880	2200.00	3000.00	2500.00
☐ **Bookcase,** whatnot, white, elongated birdcage design, four tiers, c. 1890	650.00	850.00	700.00
☐ **Bookcase,** whatnot, white, pineapple motif in back is symbol of hospitality, four oak shelves, c. 1880	285.00	395.00	300.00
☐ **Carriage,** baby, natural finish, elegantly simple, flowing design, wooden wheels, c. 1880	600.00	750.00	625.00
☐ **Carriage,** baby, natural finish, serpentine edges, velveteen upholstery, c. 1890	500.00	650.00	525.00
☐ **Carriage,** baby, natural finish, unique side handles, umbrella, c. 1890	650.00	775.00	680.00
☐ **Carriage,** baby, white, elaborate use of curlicues, rubber tires, c. 1880	400.00	575.00	430.00
☐ **Chair,** armchair, natural finish, caned shield back panel, serpentine edges, c. 1890	400.00	550.00	440.00
☐ **Chair,** armchair, natural finish, rooled headrest, spider-web caned back, wooden beadwork around seat frame, cabriole legs, c. 1880	700.00	950.00	800.00
☐ **Chair,** armchair, natural finish, rare Edwardian gentleman's chair, spider-web caned circular top panel and curved lower back panel, c. 1880	500.00	650.00	525.00
☐ **Chair,** armchair, natural finish, square-shaped design at the lower back and elaborate beadwork in center panel, c. 1890	450.00	550.00	475.00
☐ **Chair,** armchair, white, closely woven design with ram's horn design under arms, c. 1890 .	675.00	750.00	700.00
☐ **Chair,** armchair, white, flowing leaf-shaped back panel, serpentine arm and closely woven flat arm, c. 1890	400.00	575.00	450.00

	Current Price Range		Prior Year Average
☐ **Crib,** standing, natural finish, drop-side panel, flower motif set into headboard, c. 1870	1200.00	1500.00	1300.00
☐ **Crib,** swinging, natural finish, elaborate fancywork, canopy, c. 1890	1000.00	1400.00	1200.00
☐ **Doll Buggy,** natural finish, wickerwork emphasizes flowing design, silk parasol, wooden wheel has metal rims, c. 1880	350.00	450.00	375.00
☐ **Hanging Music Rack,** natural finish, elaborate scrollwork, c. 1880	225.00	350.00	250.00
☐ **Lounge,** natural finish, rare upholstered design, c. 1890	900.00	1500.00	1100.00
☐ **Rocker,** child's, natural finish, serpentine back and arms, wooden beadwork, c. 1890	200.00	300.00	225.00
☐ **Rocker,** platform, natural finish, curved backrest, serpentine back and arms, c. 1890	525.00	650.00	550.00
☐ **Rocker,** platform, white, serpentine, arms and arched platform, c. 1890	600.00	750.00	625.00
☐ **Rocker,** natural finish, chevron-shaped back panel, serpentine back and arms, turned wooden legs, c. 1890	275.00	375.00	300.00
☐ **Rocker,** natural finish, crisscross beadwork, serpentine back and arms, c. 1890	450.00	625.00	500.00
☐ **Rocker,** natural finish, leaf motif set into back panel, hand-caned seat, c. 1880	475.00	575.00	500.00
☐ **Rocker,** natural finish, spider-web caned back panel, c. 1880	275.00	350.00	300.00
☐ **Rocker,** white, banjo motif set into back panel, loop design on back and arms, c. 1880	400.00	575.00	450.00
☐ **Rocker,** white, circular braidwork, spider-web cane back panel, c. 1880	400.00	550.00	475.00
☐ **Sofa,** divan, natural finish, rolled backs and arms employ wooden beadwork, rosette arm tips, set-in cane seat, c. 1890	800.00	1000.00	875.00
☐ **Sofa,** settee, natural finish, serpentine back and arms, closely woven back panel, turned-wood legs, c. 1890	750.00	900.00	800.00
☐ **Sofa,** settee, white, peacock design dominates back panel, birdcage legs, c. 1880	950.00	1300.00	1000.00
☐ **Stand,** music stand, natural finish, oak shelves, beveled mirror, c. 1890	1500.00	2000.00	1700.00
☐ **Stand,** music, white, angled sides, two reed shelves, ball feet, c. 1890	250.00	350.00	280.00

	Current Price Range		Prior Year Average
☐ **Stool,** piano, white, circular woven reed seat, c. 1890	200.00	285.00	225.00
☐ **Stool,** ottoman, white, closely woven top, round rosette design on both ends, c. 1890	175.00	245.00	180.00
☐ **Table,** end table, white, large center bird-cage design, c. 1890	225.00	325.00	260.00
☐ **Table,** oblong table, white, wooden bead-work, c. 1890	285.00	350.00	300.00
☐ **Table,** round, white, cabriole legs, wooden beadwork frames top and bottom shelf, c. 1890	500.00	750.00	575.00
☐ **Table,** square, white, closely woven top, beadwork set into skirting, c. 1880	300.00	385.00	330.00

WOOD

TYPES: While many types of wood items are highly sought after collectibles, this section lists wooden kitchen utensils.

COMMENTS: Wooden utensils are most commonly made of maple. Other woods used include cedar, pine, hickory, ash and oak. Prices vary depending on item and type of wood.

ADDITIONAL TIPS: The listings are alphabetized according to item. For further information, refer to *The Official 1984 Price Guide to Kitchen Collectibles.*

☐ **Biscuit Roller,** wood board with grooved roller, side handturn, c. 1860s	95.00	120.00	98.00
☐ **Bootjack,** primitive wood forked bootjack	11.00	17.00	13.00
☐ **Bottle Corker,** all wood two part gadget for inserting corks into bottles	17.00	25.00	19.00
☐ **Bowl,** burl, 5″ x 13″, c. 1800s	520.00	660.00	530.00
☐ **Box,** quartered oak, inset hinges, 29″ x 15½″ x 7½″ deep	368.00	380.00	373.00
☐ **Bread Boards,** maple, "Bread" carved on border, 9½″	42.00	55.00	45.00
☐ **Bread Board,** pine, hanging eye cut in 1 piece wood, 12″ x 10″	79.00	90.00	82.00
☐ **Bread Board,** round, c. 1918	6.00	12.00	7.00
☐ **Butter Churn,** strap hinges, old red paint	368.00	380.00	370.00
☐ **Butter Churns,** 25½″, wood with bandings, with lid and dasher	205.00	230.00	210.00
☐ **Butter Molds,** box with flower and leaf, hoop type, machine made	32.00	60.00	35.00

	Current Price Range		Prior Year Average
☐ **Butter Paddles,** flat	11.00	16.00	12.00
☐ **Butter Roller,** hand carved birch, in wooden pinned yoke	150.00	170.00	160.00
☐ **Cabbage Cutting Board,** three blades and sliding hoper box, 7¼″ x 20″	47.00	60.00	49.00
☐ **Candle Box,** pine, sliding top, 16″ long	84.00	95.00	87.00
☐ **Candle Dipping Rack,** wooden, mid 1700s	336.00	360.00	345.00
☐ **Cheese Ladder,** wild cherry	84.00	90.00	86.00
☐ **Chopping Knife,** factory made, maple handle, c. 1880-1900	37.00	50.00	40.00
☐ **Chopping Bowl,** turned wood, old mustard paint, early 19th century	90.00	100.00	92.00
☐ **Coffee Grinder,** 19th century, wooden Peugeot	63.00	85.00	67.00
☐ **Cookie Board,** carved daisy pattern, walnut, 6″ x 8″	61.00	75.00	63.00
☐ **Cookie Mold,** musketeer on a saddle strapped to a chicken, large	98.00	115.00	103.00
☐ **Cookie Roller,** handcut from one piece birdseye maple	31.99	40.00	33.00
☐ **Cracker Pricker and Biscuit Stamp,** oval with turned handle, 1½″ x 2½″	146.00	175.00	150.00
☐ **Cranberry Picker,** a toothed rack-like tool for removing cranberries from the bushes, 14″ across	63.00	80.00	65.00
☐ **Cream Skimmer,** pine, handled	63.00	80.00	65.00
☐ **Crock,** pine, stop shelf, deep lower shelf, base bar, 27″ x 37″ x 12″	290.00	310.00	295.00
☐ **Cupboard,** softwood, c. 1800s	605.00	650.00	620.00
☐ **Cutting Board,** walnut	34.00	45.00	37.00
☐ **Dipper,** turned bowl attached by wooden pin, 7″	37.00	50.00	40.00
☐ **Dipper,** honey, maple, wide ridges on one end, 13″ long, 8″	41.00	48.00	42.00
☐ **Dough Bowl,** maple, hand-carved	126.00	160.00	130.00
☐ **Doughnut Box,** cherry, 4 leg frame, one piece lid, self handles, 30″ x 14″, c. 1860	263.00	280.00	270.00
☐ **Doughnut Cutter,** all wood with handle	13.00	20.00	15.00
☐ **Dough Trough,** cherry, no lid, slanted sides, 26″ x 12½″, c. 1830	236.00	310.00	255.00
☐ **Drying Rack,** maple	45.00	65.00	55.00
☐ **Funnel,** small, factory made in 1880s	13.00	20.00	15.00
☐ **Grain Storage Bin,** pine, with roll top, five section	1470.00	1650.00	1500.00
☐ **Ice Tongs,** wood handles, large icehouse size, latter 1800s	63.00	78.00	65.00

	Current Price Range		Prior Year Average
☐ **Lemon Squeezer,** maple early factory period, c. 1850-75	58.00	75.00	63.00
☐ **Mash Agitator,** handfashioned wood, 8″ handle	80.00	90.00	83.00
☐ **Mortar and Pestle,** maple, mid 19th century	95.00	120.00	105.00
☐ **Noodle Roller,** maple, corrugations good condition, 20″ long, c. 1850	61.00	70.00	63.00
☐ **Oak Keg,** staved and hooped with hickory bands	94.00	120.00	100.00
☐ **Paddles,** butter, handcut variations in maple and hickory, 10″	37.00	50.00	40.00
☐ **Paper Roll Holder,** wood and iron, double	30.00	40.00	32.00
☐ **Peel,** all wood peel for removing baked goods from fireplace oven	58.00	68.00	61.00
☐ **Pie Crimper,** wood handle, The Dandy, Gold Medal, April 28, 1925	6.00	9.00	7.00
☐ **Potato Masher,** simple lathe turned, 2 pieces, all wood	9.00	13.00	10.00
☐ **Recipe File Box**	8.00	16.00	11.00
☐ **Rolling Pin,** maple	60.00	70.00	63.00
☐ **Rolling Pin,** birdseye maple, 1 piece carved wood, c. 1800s	37.00	53.00	40.00
☐ **Rolling Pins,** handleless, same diameter throughout	7.00	13.00	8.00
☐ **Rolling Pin,** shaped handles, all one solid piece	8.00	16.00	11.00
☐ **Salt Box,** wooden wall hanging salt box, rectangualar box, sloping lid	58.00	80.00	65.00
☐ **Scouring Box,** rectangular wood frame, approximately one foot long, complete with scouring brick for polishing steel bladed knives	31.00	40.00	33.00
☐ **Scrubbing Stick,** c. 1830, 24″long	105.00	125.00	110.00
☐ **Sugar Bucket,** button hole or eyelet hoops, bail handle, c. 1850-70	194.00	225.00	200.00
☐ **Sweater Stretcher,** large, pegged, folding sweater stretcher	26.00	36.00	29.00
☐ **Tea Caddy,** wooden, apple form body, with cover, late 18th century	495.00	530.00	510.00
☐ **Tobacco Cutters,** counter type, smithy made, wood handled	52.00	62.00	55.00
☐ **Trencher,** hard carved, small	58.00	68.00	62.00
☐ **Vegetable Cutter,** maple board, corrugated tin, c. 1880s	21.00	39.00	24.00
☐ **Vegetable Slicer,** wood, dated 1890, 20″	32.00	42.00	35.00